BROOKLANDS BOOKS

D1811068

ARMSTRONG SIDDELEY
Gold Portfolio
1945~1960

Compiled by
R.M. Clarke

ISBN 1 85520 0694

Distributed by
Brooklands Book Distribution Ltd.
'Holmerise', Seven Hills Road,
Cobham, Surrey, England

Printed in Hong Kong

BROOKLANDS BOOKS

BROOKLANDS ROAD TEST SERIES
AC Ace & Aceca 1953-1983
Alfa Romeo Alfasud 1972-1984
Alfa Romeo Alfetta Coupes GT. GTV. GTV6 1974-1987
Alfa Romeo Giulia Berlinas 1962-1976
Alfa Romeo Giulia Coupes 1963-1976
Alfa Romeo Giulietta Gold Portfolio 1954-1965
Alfa Romeo Spider 1966-1990
Allard Gold Portfolio 1937-1958
Alvis Gold Portfolio 1919-1967
American Motors Muscle Cars 1966-1970
Armstrong Siddeley Gold Portfolio 1945-1960
Aston Martin Gold Portfolio 1972-1985
Austin Seven 1922-1982
Austin A30 & A35 1951-1962
Austin Healey 100 & 100/6 Gold Portfolio 1952-1959
Austin Healey 3000 Gold Portfolio 1959-1967
Austin Healey 'Frogeye' Sprite Col No.1 1958-1961
Austin Healey Sprite 1958-1971
Avanti 1962-1983
BMW Six Cylinder Coupes 1969-1975
BMW 1600 Col. 1 1966-1981
BMW 2002 1968-1976
Bristol Cars Gold Portfolio 1946-1985
Buick Automobiles 1947-1960
Buick Muscle Cars 1965-1970
Buick Riviera 1963-1978
Cadillac Automobiles 1949-1959
Cadillac Automobiles 1960-1969
Cadillac Eldorado 1967-1978
High Performance Capris Gold Portfolio 1969-1987
Chevrolet Camaro SS & Z28 1966-1973
Chevrolet Camaro & Z-28 1973-1981
High Performance Camaros 1982-1988
Camaro Muscle Cars 1966-1972
Chevrolet 1955-1957
Chevrolet Corvair 1959-1969
Chevrolet Impala & SS 1958-1971
Chevrolet Muscle Cars 1966-1971
Chevelle and SS 1964-1972
Chevy Blazer 1969-1981
Chevy EL Camino & SS 1959-1987
Chevy II Nova & SS 1962-1973
Chrysler 300 1955-1970
Citroen Traction Avant Gold Portfolio 1934-1957
Citroen DS & ID 1955-1975
Citroen SM 1970-1975
Citroen 2CV 1949-1988
Shelby Cobra Gold Portfolio 1962-1969
Cobras & Replicas 1962-1983
Chevrolet Corvette Gold Portfolio 1953 1962
Corvette Stingray Gold Portfolio 1963-1967
High Performance Corvettes 1983-1989
Daimler SP250 Sport & V-8250 Saloon Gold Portfolio 1959-1969
Datsun 240Z 1970-1973
Datsun 280Z & ZX 1975-1983
De Tomaso Collection No.1 1962-1981
Dodge Charger 1966-1974
Dodge Muscle Cars 1967-1970
Excalibur Collection No.1 1952-1981
Facel Vega 1954-1964
Ferrari Cars 1946-1956
Ferrari Cars 1973-1977
Ferrari Dino 1965-1974
Ferrari Dino 308 1974-1979
Ferrari 308 & Mondial 1980-1984
Ferrari Collection No.1 1960-1970
Fiat-Bertone X1/9 1973-1988
Fiat Pininfarina 124 + 2000 Spider 1968-1985
Ford Automobiles 1949-1959
Ford Bronco 1966-1977
Ford Bronco 1978-1988
Ford Consul. Zephyr Zodiac MkI & II 1950-1962
Ford Cortina 1600E & GT 1967-1970
Ford Fairlane 1955-1970
Ford Falcon 1960-1970
Ford GT40 Gold Portfolio 1964-1987
Ford RS Escorts 1968-1980
Ford Zephyr Zodiac Executive MkIII & MkIV 1962-1971
High Performance Escorts Mk 1 1968-1974
High Performance Escorts Mk II 1975-1980
High Performance Mustangs 1982-1988
Holden 1948-1962
Honda CRX 1983-1987
Hudson & Railton 1936-1940
Jaguar and SS Gold Portfolio 1931-1951
Jaguar Cars 1957-1961
Jaguar Cars 1961-1964
Jaguar Mk2 1959-1969
Jaguar E-Type Gold Portfolio 1961-1971
Jaguar E-Type 1966-1971
Jaguar E-Type V-12 1971-1975
Jaguar XKE Collection No.1 1961-1974
Jaguar XJ6 1968-1972
Jaguar XJ6 Series II 1973-1979
Jaguar XJ6 & XJ12 Series III 1979-1985
Jaguar XJ12 1972-1980
Jaguar XJS Gold Portfolio 1975-1988
Jaguar XK120.XK140.XK150 Gold Portfolio 1948-1960
Jeep CJ5 & CJ6 1960-1976
Jeep CJ5 & CJ7 1976-1986
Jensen Cars 1946-1967
Jensen Cars 1967-1979
Jensen Interceptor Gold Portfolio 1966-1986
Jensen Healey 1972-1976
Lamborghini Cars 1964-1970
Lamborghini Cars 1970-1975
Lamborghini Countach Col No.1 1971-1982
Lamborghini Countach & Urraco 1974-1980
Lamborghini Countach & Jalpa 1980-1985
Lancia Stratos 1972-1985
Land Rover 1948-1973 - A Collection
Land Rover Series II & IIa 1958-1971
Land Rover Series III 1971-1985
Land Rover 90 & 110 1983-1989
Lincoln Gold Portfolio 1949-1960
Lincoln Continental 1961-1969
Lotus and Caterham Seven Gold Portfolio 1957-1989
Lotus Cortina Gold Portfolio 1963-1970
Lotus Elan Gold Portfolio 1962-1974
Lotus Elan Collection No.2 1963-1972
Lotus Elite 1957-1964
Lotus Elite & Eclat 1974-1982
Lotus Turbo Esprit 1980-1986
Lotus Europa 1966-1975
Lotus Europa Collection No.1 1966-1974

Lotus Seven Collection No.1 1957-1982
Marcos Cars 1960-1988
Maserati 1965-1970
Maserati 1970-1975
Mazda RX-7 Collection No.1 1978-1981
Mercedes 190 & 300SL 1954-1963
Mercedes 230/250/280SL 1963-1971
Mercedes Benz SLs & SLCs Gold Portfolio 1971-1989
Mercedes Bens Cars 1949-1954
Mercedes Bens Cars 1954-1957
Mercedes Bens Cars 1957-1961
Mercedes Benz Competion Cars 1950-1957
Mercury Muscle Cars 1966-1971
Metropolitan 1954-1962
MG TC 1945-1949
MG TD 1949-1953
MG TF 1953-1955
MG Cars 1959-1962
MGA Roadsters 1955-1962
MGA Collection No.1 1955-1982
MGB Roadsters 1962-1980
MGB GT 1965-1980
MG Midget 1961-1980
Mini Cooper Gold Portfolio 1961-1971
Mini Moke 1964-1989
Mini Muscle Cars 1961-1979
Mopar Muscle Cars 1964-1967
Mopar Muscle Cars 1968-1971
Morgan Three-Wheeler Gold Portfolio 1910-1952
Morgan Cars 1960-1970
Morgan Cars Gold Portfolio 1968-1989
Morris Minor Collection No.1
Mustang Muscle Cars 1967-1971
Oldsmobile Automobiles 1955-1963
Old's Cutlass & 4-4-2 1964-1972
Oldsmobile Muscle Cars 1964-1971
Oldsmobile Toronado 1966-1978
Opel GT 1968-1973
Packard Gold Portfolio 1946-1958
Pantera Gold Portfolio 1970-1989
Plymouth Barracuda 1964-1974
Plymouth Muscle Cars 1966-1971
Pontiac Tempest & GTO 1961-1965
Pontiac GTO 1964-1970
Pontiac Firebird 1967-1973
Pontiac Firebird and Trans-Am 1973-1981
High Performance Firebirds 1982-1988
Pontiac Fiero 1984-1988
Pontiac Muscle Cars 1966-1972
Porsche 356 1952-1965
Porsche Cars in the 60's
Porsche Cars 1960-1964
Porsche Cars 1964-1968
Porsche Cars 1968-1972
Porsche Cars 1972-1975
Porsche Turbo Collection No.1 1975-1980
Porsche 911 1965-1969
Porsche 911 1970-1972
Porsche 911 1973-1977
Porsche 911 Carrera 1973-1977
Porsche 911 Turbo 1975-1984
Porsche 911 SC 1978-1983
Porsche 914 Gold Portfolio 1969-1976
Porsche 914 Collection No.1 1969-1983
Porsche 924 Gold Portfolio 1975-1988
Porsche 928 1977-1989
Porsche 944 1981-1985
Range Rover Gold Portfolio 1970-1988
Reliant Scimitar 1964-1986
Riley 11/2 & 21/2 Litre Gold Portfolio 1945-1955
Rolls Royce Silver Cloud 1955-1965
Rolls Royce Silver Shadow 1965-1981
Rover P4 1949-1959
Rover P4 1955-1964
Rover 2000 + 2200 1963-1977
Rover 3 & 3.5 Litre 1958-1973
Rover 3500 1968-1977
Rover 3500 & Vitesse 1976-1986
Saab Sonett Collection No.1 1966-1974
Saab Turbo 1976-1983
Shelby Mustang Muscle Cars 1965-1970
Stubebaker Gold Portfolio 1947-1966
Stubebaker Hawks & Larks 1956-1963
Sunbeam Tiger & Alpine Gold Portfolio 1959-1967
Thunderbird 1955-1957
Thunderbird 1958-1963
Thunderbird 1964-1976
Toyota Land Cruiser 1956-1984
Toyota MR2 1984-1988
Triumph 2000. 2.5. 2500 1963-1977
Triumph GT6 1966-1974
Triumph Spitfire 1962-1980
Triumph Spitfire Col No.1 1962-1982
Triumph Stag 1970-1980
Triumph Stag Collection No.1 1970-1984
Triumph TR2 & TR3 1952-60
Triumph TR4-TR5-TR250 1961-1968
Triumph TR6 1969-1976
Triumph TR6 Collection No.1 1969-1983
Triumph TR7 & TR8 1975-1982
Triumph Herald 1959-1971
Triumph Vitesse 1962-1971
TVR Gold Portfolio 1959-1988
Volkswagen Cars 1936-1956
VW Beetle Collection No.1 1970-1982
VW Golf GTi 1976-1986
VW Karmann Ghia 1955-1982
VW Kubelwagen 1940-1975
VW Scirocco 1974-1981
VW Bus. Camper. Van 1954-1967
VW Bus. Camper. Van 1968-1979
VW Bus. Camper. Van 1979-1989
Volvo 120 1956-1970
Volvo 1800 1960-1973

BROOKLANDS ROAD & TRACK SERIES
Road & Track on Alfa Romeo 1949-1963
Road & Track on Alfa Romeo 1964-1970
Road & Track on Alfa Romeo 1971-1976
Road & Track on Alfa Romeo 1977-1989
Road & Track on Aston Martin 1962-1990
Road & Track on Auburn Cord and Duesenburg 1952-1984
Road & Track on Audi & Auto Union 1952-1980
Road & Track on Audi 1980-1986
Road & Track on Austin Healey 1953-1970

Road & Track on BMW Cars 1966-1974
Road & Track on BMW Cars 1975-1978
Road & Track on BMW Cars 1979-1983
Road & Track on Cobra, Shelby & GT40 1962-1983
Road & Track on Corvette 1953-1967
Road & Track on Corvette 1968-1982
Road & Track on Corvette 1982-1986
Road & Track on Datsun Z 1970-1983
Road & Track on Ferrari 1950-1968
Road & Track on Ferrari 1968-1974
Road & Track on Ferrari 1975-1981
Road & Track on Ferrari 1981-1984
Road & Track on Fiat Sports Cars 1968-1987
Road & Track on Jaguar 1950-1960
Road & Track on Jaguar 1961-1968
Road & Track on Jaguar 1968-1974
Road & Track on Jaguar 1974-1982
Road & Track on Jaguar 1983-1989
Road & Track on Lamborghini 1964-1985
Road & Track on Lotus 1972-1981
Road & Track on Maserati 1952-1974
Road & Track on Maserati 1975-1983
Road & Track on Mazda RX7 1978-1986
Road & Track on Mercedes 1952-1962
Road & Track on Mercedes 1963-1970
Road & Track on Mercedes 1971-1979
Road & Track on Mercedes 1980-1987
Road & Track on MG Sports Cars 1949-1961
Road & Track on MG Sprots Cars 1962-1980
Road & Track on Mustang 1964-1977
Road & Track on Nissan 300-ZX & Turbo 1984-1989
Road & Track on Peugeot 1955-1986
Road & Track on Pontiac 1960-1983
Road & Track on Porsche 1961-1967
Road & Track on Porsche 1968-1971
Road & Track on Porsche 1972-1975
Road & Track on Porsche 1975-1978
Road & Track on Porsche 1979-1982
Road & Track on Porsche 1982-1985
Road & Track on Porsche 1985-1988
Road & Track on Rolls Royce & B'ley 1950-1965
Road & Track on Rolls Royce & B'ley 1966-1984
Road & Track on Saab 1955-1985
Road & Track on Toyota Sports & GT Cars 1966-1984
Road & Track on Triumph Sports Cars 1953-1967
Road & Track on Triumph Sports Cars 1967-1974
Road & Track on Triumph Sports Cars 1974-1982
Road & Track on Volkswagen 1951-1968
Road & Track on Volkswagen 1968-1978
Road & Track on Volkswagen 1978-1985
Road & Track on Volvo 1957-1974
Road & Track on Volvo 1975-1985
Road & Track - Henry Manney at Large and Abroad

BROOKLANDS CAR AND DRIVER SERIES
Car and Driver on BMW 1955-1977
Car and Driver on BMW 1977-1985
Car and Driver on Cobra, Shelby & Ford GT 40 1963-1984
Car and Driver on Corvette 1956-1967
Car and Driver on Corvette 1968-1977
Car and Driver on Corvette 1978-1982
Car and Driver on Corvette 1983-1988
Car and Driver on Datsun Z 1600 & 2000 1966-1984
Car and Driver on Ferrari 1955-1962
Car and Driver on Ferrari 1963-1975
Car and Driver on Ferrari 1976-1983
Car and Driver on Mopar 1956-1967
Car and Driver on Mopar 1968-1975
Car and Driver on Mustang 1964-1972
Car and Driver on Pontiac 1961-1975
Car and Driver on Porsche 1955-1962
Car and Driver on Porsche 1963-1970
Car and Driver on Porsche 1970-1976
Car and Driver on Porsche 1977-1981
Car and Driver on Porsche 1982-1986
Car and Driver on Saab 1956-1985
Car and Driver on Volvo 1955-1986

BROOKLANDS PRACTICAL CLASSICS SERIES
PC on Austin A40 Restoration
PC on Land Rover Restoration
PC on Metalworking in Restoration
PC on Midget/Sprite Restoration
PC on Mini Cooper Restoration
PC on MGB Restoration
PC on Morris Minor Restoration
PC on Sunbeam Rapier Restoration
PC on Triumph Herald/Vitesse
PC on Triumph Spitfire Restoration
PC on VW Beetle Restoration
PC on 1930s Car Restoration

BROOKLANDS MOTOR & THOROGHBRED & CLASSIC CAR SERIES
Motor & T & CC on Ferrari 1966-1976
Motor & T & CC on Ferrari 1976-1984
Motor & T & CC on Lotus 1979-1983

BROOKLANDS MILITARY VEHICLES SERIES
Allied Mil. Vehicles No.1 1942-1945
Allied Mil. Vehicles No.2 1941-1946
Dodge Mil. Vehicles Col. 1 1940-1945
Military Jeeps 1941-1945
Off Road Jeeps 1944-1971
Hail to the Jeep
US Military Vehicles 1941-1945
US Army Military Vehicles WW2-TM9-2800

BROOKLANDS HOT ROD RESTORATION SERIES
Auto Restoration Tips & Techniques
Basic Bodywork Tips & Techniques
Basic Painting Tips & Techniques
Camaro Restoration Tips & Techniques
Custom Painting Tips & Techniques
Engine Swapping Tips & Techniques
How to Build a Street Rod
Mustang Restoration Tips & Techniques
Performance Tuning - Chevrolets of the '60s
Performance Tuning - Ford of the '60s
Performance Tuning - Mopars of the '60s
Performance Tuning - Pontiacs of the '60s

BROOKLANDS
BOOKS

CONTENTS

BROOKLANDS BOOKS

ACKNOWLEDGEMENTS

When Sammy Cahn the great lyric writer was asked what came first the words or the music, he replied — the phone call — and so it was with this book. A few weeks ago an unknown Australian 'phoned to ask if we could supply him with a long out of print book on post war Armstrong-Siddeleys. Regretfully we could not help.

This started the ball rolling. We contacted Peter Sheppard of the Armstrong Siddeley owners Club and outlined what we could do providing we had club support. This was soon forthcoming in the shape of Bill Smith the club historian who kindly opened his files and generously loaned us hard to find copies of articles and period advertisements.

Further support came from Paul Marshall the club photographer based near Lockerbie in Scotland who promptly dispatched a selection of slides, three of which we have used as our cover illustrations.

We have worked with many clubs before but never has it been so enjoyable and nor was the help so unstintingly given.

Our thanks also go to the publishers of the worlds leading motor journals who for over 30 years have supported our reference series by allowing us to include their copyright road tests and other stories in these anthologies. Our special thanks go in this instance to the management of Auto Age, Autocar, Autosport, Classic & Sportscar, Modern Motor, Motor, Motor Manual, Motor Trader, Practical Classics, Practical Motorist, Road & Track, Thoroughbred & Classic Cars and Wheels whos articles can be found within.

R.M. Clarke

All cover illustrations were photographed by Paul Marshall and kindly loaned by arrangement with the Armstrong-Siddeley Owners Club Ltd.

Front Cover   1960 Armstrong-Siddeley MkII Star Sapphire owner by Colin Hood

Back Cover (Top)   1948 Armstrong-Siddeley 16hp Hurricane owned by Derek Aspinal

Back Cover (Bottom) 1956 Armstrong-Siddeley Sapphire owned by Joe McCoy

New Two-litre Armstrong Siddeley

Interesting Mechanical Design of Lancaster Saloon and Hurricane Drop-head Coupé

DURING May of this year a preliminary announcement was made (*The Autocar*, May 11) concerning the style and the coachwork of a new 16 h.p. two-litre six-cylinder Armstrong Siddeley which was to be put into manufacture. Examples of this new model are now coming off the production line, and it is possible to give a more complete description, which includes the features of the mechanical design.

Before continuing it may be remarked that Armstrong Siddeley Motors, Ltd. is one company of a great group controlled by the Hawker Siddeley Aircraft Co., Ltd., and including A. V. Roe and Co., Ltd., Sir W. G. Armstrong Whitworth Aircraft, Ltd., Gloster Aircraft, Ltd., A. W. Hawksley, Ltd., and Air Service Training, Ltd. During the war period this vast combine, in round numbers, employed 100,000 hands, and produced 40,000 aircraft, 38,000 aircraft engines, 7,000 tank gear boxes and 12,000 torpedo engines. It restored to service 11,000 aircraft and 10,000 aircraft engines. These resources are behind the evolution of the new car, and the design bears evidence of a truly progressive spirit.

Modern Features

In the past Armstrong Siddeley's built up a fine reputation for reliable, roomy, comfortable, practical, and well-finished cars. They pioneered, too, the now famous preselective self-changing gear, which inaugurated a new era in ease of driving. The post-war design aims to continue the high quality and the good points, but to embody them in an up-to-date form of essentially stable, roadworthy, fast, and refined automobile, capable of meeting in safety the difficult road conditions of modern times.

From such a parentage it might be expected that the new Two-litre is likely to be an exceedingly attractive car. From the direct evidence of having tried more than one sample on the road *The Autocar* can say definitely that it is a remarkably attractive car. The promise shown in the design, which is outlined later, is amply fulfilled in practice. These are the confirmed impressions: First the driver finds himself seated comfortably in a body which offers plenty of room in all respects, and yet is not high above the ground. He sits *in* the body rather than *on* it, but the height of the scuttle, the slope of the fairly long bonnet and the width of the nose are so well proportioned that forward visibility is good. A steering wheel that comes nicely into place, and a gear lever convenient to the hand—on the synchromesh gear box—add to the primary feeling of well-being. Second gear is engaged and off the car goes.

It is not long before one realises that here is a car of exceptional quality. The engine is smooth and quiet, but it is also very responsive and briskly up to its job. It does not ask the driver to do much gear changing, unless he has a preference for quick acceleration on third, or for using third on corners.

The driving position is decidedly comfortable, the clutch is light and smooth in engagement, and the synchromesh gear box is one of the best of its kind. Next to no judgment is necessary to make an entirely quiet and smooth gear engagement; one merely depresses the clutch pedal and gently moves the gear lever to the next position.

The outstanding quality to come to notice is the suspension. If the driver happens to have come for the appointment on his own war-worn car, and has noticed bad road surfaces on the way, he passes over them again in the Armstrong Siddeley wondering, first, what has become of the bumps, and, secondly, registering the fact that the suspension is remarkably comfortable. The driver begins to realise that he is taking familiar curves rather faster than usual. From that point he commences to try "curving" a little faster still, just to see how the car will behave. Soon he discovers that he can take curves and corners, with or without cambers and bad surfaces, just as fast as his ideas dictate. And so emerges an understanding that he is handling something quite out of the ordinary in the matter of road holding and general safety, and that the hopes and beliefs of the designers of the car are both realised and justified.

When cars such as the new Armstrong Siddeley are born, independent suspension shows that it is really worth while, not merely as a better insulator over really bad surfaces, but also in the matter of accurate steering and improved stability. From the first glance the chassis of this new car inspires interest. There is so much evidence that stability has been given priority in laying out the design.

Wide, Low Frame

This frame is unusually large in section, and the side members are carried out as wide as possible between the wheels so as to give maximum support to the coachwork. Again, the frame is built low, and at the back passes below the rear axle tubes. The half-elliptic rear springs are underslung, and a hypoid bevel final drive gives a low propeller-shaft. Hence the weight of the whole rear structure is as close to the ground as possible. Then the cruciform centre of the frame may be noted. It affords a direct tie between the front end and the rear spring mountings, and is rigid in its centre, where cruciforms are sometimes not so rigid as they might be. This cruciform joins the side members and is welded to form box

(Right) Front view of the independent suspension system showing the upper wishbone with its fulcrum combined with the Luvax-Girling hydraulic damper, and the lower link, which pivots in large rubber bushings, visible below the engine foot.

sections of great stiffness exactly where they are needed.

From this point the eye passes to the front end, where it finds an independent front wheel suspension of considerable interest. Joining the front of the side members is a stout cross-member which is swept down in the middle to clear the underside of the engine. Above each end of this cross-member is a bracket which carries the fulcrum bearings of a "wishbone" or triangular link member. To the point of the triangle a ball joint attaches the upper end of a yoke piece which forms the stub axle and swivel. The lower end of the yoke is attached by a second ball joint to the outer end of a longer articulated link. The inner end of this link is splined on to a sleeve carried in rubber bushings contained in a bracket formed in the lower part of the cross-member. Rearward from the sleeve a stout torsion bar spring on each side runs back to an adjustable anchorage in a second cross-member carried by the forward arms of the cruciform

Simple, Neat Suspension System

In this way a torsion bar independent front wheel suspension is obtained. The wishbones are shorter than the lower links, and the different lengths are so proportioned that the "parallel linkage" is not truly parallel, but so arranged that the point of contact of the front wheel does not "scrub" sideways with the rise and fall of the car on the suspension. The fulcrum bearings of the wishbones are neatly formed in the body of a special type of Luvax-Girling hydraulic damper. It will be appreciated that this suspension is simple, neat, and has a minimum of unsprung weight.

For the steering a Burman-Douglas worm and nut gear is employed; the twin-spoked steering wheel is adjustable for reach, and the column for angle. From the drop arm of the steering gear a drag link runs forward to a steering arm on the off-side stub axle swivel. A rearward arm from the same

swivel is attached to a track rod which is coupled to a joint on the head of a subsidiary lever, carried on the centre of the front cross-member. From a second joint on this head another track rod runs across to the near-side stub axle swivel. It will be recognised that this form of steering linkage follows the original true Ackerman principle.

Before leaving the actual chassis of the car it may be noted that the half-elliptic rear springs are carried on rubber bushings, that the rear axle case is of the cast centre type with tubular arms, and that the latest Luvax - Girling hydraulic dampers are fitted at the rear.

One of the particular features of the car which is at once noticeable on the road is the excellence of the brakes. The pedal pressure required is light, and the brakes are exceptionally responsive and progressive in action. They take hold with a smooth sureness that is most satisfying. Whether they are used lightly for checking at moderate speeds, for stopping in traffic, or

This cutaway drawing of the Two-litre Lancaster saloon shows the 16 h.p. engine to advantage. It has overhead valves, hydraulic tappets, counterbalanced crankshaft, and a cooling system whereby the water is directed towards the valve seats. The pleasing, well-lit body interior has many points of appeal, both major and minor.

This photograph gives an excellent impression of the depth and rigidity of the frame. It also shows the neat design of the torsion bar front suspension, the clean appearance of the six-cylinder engine, and the low position of the propeller-shaft running to a hypoid bevel final drive. The rear end of the frame is underslung.

(Continued)

(Right)   Decidedly an elegant car, the new Two=litre Armstrong Siddeley six=light Lancaster saloon. Note the built=in head lamps, the valance to the bumper bar, and the gene= ral clean run of the lines.

R.E. POULTON

of the new Girling brake will be given on another occasion.

Road experience of this car soon shows that the performance is de- cidedly satisfying. Obviously it can put up a high average speed from place to place without appearing to be travelling fast. The engine is a very willing performer, besides being smooth, quiet and quite happy even on the indifferent fuel of the moment; in other words, pinking is not noticeable. The complete coupé weighs about 27 cwt., and the engine, which is rated at 15.72 h.p., is able to develop a maximum of 70 b.h.p. at 4,600 r.p.m. The gear ratios are nicely chosen, with the result that the car has a good turn of speed on top gear without being fussy, and also good flexibility. For instance, a hill of 1 in 9 approached from a right-angle corner can be climbed just comfortably on top gear. On third a fast climb can be made. All ordinary grades with straight approaches are easy on top gear. Flexibility on top gear at low speeds is also good, so the car is both quiet and pleasant to handle in built-up areas and traffic. More detailed road impressions of this latest Armstrong Siddeley, gained as a result of driving an example of the saloon, appear else- where in this issue.

The six-cylinder engine is of mono- bloc construction, well ribbed for rigidity, and has a large counter- weighted crankshaft carried in four steel-backed main bearings and pro- vided with a torsional vibration damper. Steel connecting rods, also with steel-backed bearings, are coupled to split-skirted aluminium alloy pistons having four rings, of which the lowest is a scraper. Overhead valves are situated in lozenge-shaped combustion chambers in a detachable cylinder head, and are operated by push rods from hydraulic self-adjusting tappets. This is a special feature of the engine. The tappets are supplied with oil from the main oil system; in this, a gear

for emergency at high speed, the re- sults are always the same — a smooth, definite arresting of momentum and no tendency to pull off course. Enquiry into what brakes these may be elucidates something else new, the latest Girling Hydro- mechanical brake being fitted in front, and mechanical operation on the usual Girling principle being em- ployed at the rear. A full description

pump draws oil through a floating intake and delivers it under pressure through a filter to the main bearings, big-ends, distribution, and overhead valve rockers. Mixture is provided by a downdraught Stromberg carburettor with an automatic choke, which draws its air through an AC air cleaner and silencer. It is fed with fuel by an AC mechanical pump from a 12-gallon rear tank, of which one gallon is held in reserve and controlled from the instrument panel by a solenoid switch. The filler cap is large and designed for quick filling.

Cooling is by centrifugal water pump which feeds into the cylinder head and around the valves, the jacket circulation being by thermosyphon. At the front of the engine a triangulated belt drives the water pump, fan, and the dynamo of the Lucas 12-volt ignition and lighting system. The engine is mounted flexibly on rubber at four points.

An interesting feature about this new Armstrong Siddeley is that it will be obtainable with either a preselective self-changing gear or a four-speed synchromesh box. The preselective self-changing gear box with centrifugal clutch and finger-tip control is so well known as to need no description. It has many enthusiastic partisans and is excellent to handle. The synchromesh gear box employs a centrally placed lever, and a dry single-plate clutch operated by pedal. Synchromesh is provided on second, third and top. A great deal of care has been given to this new box and it is a particularly good one to handle.

There are several further special features to be mentioned. The jacking system consists of a pair of permanently fitted mechanical jacks, one on each side close to the centre of the car. By opening a small trap door in

(Right) The horizontally spoked steering wheel allows visibility of the grouped instruments.

(Below) Wide rear seats of the four-door saloon, showing the attractive upholstery and folding centre arm rest.

the floor of the driving compartment the head of a jack is exposed, and a small handle from the wheel changing kit in the lid of the spare wheel compartment can be easily applied. Mention of tools is a reminder of one speciality on this car which will have a great appeal to experienced motorists. On a shelf under the instrument panel is a shapely tool case, almost diplomatic in its portfolio appearance, which houses in recesses an excellent set of tools.

Another point is that air conditioning is provided. An electric fan delivers warm or cool air as required, and ducts below the windscreen glass provide for de-icing and de-misting.

Radio equipment can be installed as an extra; provision is made to accommodate a receiver under the dashboard and the control head on the instrument panel.

Saloon and Drop-head Coupé

Two body styles will be available, the four-door six-light Lancaster saloon, and the Hurricane drop-head coupé. Both are very attractive in style. Not the least interesting point about this entirely new car is the way in which it presents a distinctly modern appearance and yet contrives to suggest the continuity of the Armstrong Siddeley *marque*. The bodies are graceful, and finished very nicely indeed, with walnut woodwork and soft leather trimming pleated laterally. Not only is all necessary equipment found, but also it bears evidence of considerable thought in regard to installation and convenience of use. For instance, the dual screenwipers come into instant use by pressing one small switch; the hands of the clock are visible on the surface of the interior driving mirror and so can be seen by every occupant of the car; the left side of the facia board is formed into a wide cupboard, the lid of which folds down flat and forms a useful shelf. These are a few of the minor points, and the various illustrations complete the story of a fascinating new British production.

TWO-LITRE ARMSTRONG SIDDELEY SPECIFICATION.

Engine : 15.72 h.p., six cylinders. 65 x 100 mm. (1,991 c.c.). Overhead valves, hydraulic tappets, counterbalanced crankshaft, pressure lubrication. Stromberg downdraught carburettor. Lucas 12-volt coil ignition. Pump water cooling.

Transmission : Centrifugal clutch and four-speed preselective self-changing gear box. Ratios : Top, 5.1 : third, 7.24 ; second, 10.67 ; first, 18.4 to 1.
or
Dry single-plate clutch and four-speed gear box with synchromesh on second, third and top. Ratios : Top, 5.1 : third, 7.24 : second, 10.87 : first, 17.6 to 1. Open propeller-shaft to hypoid bevel final drive.

Suspension : Independent front wheel suspension with torsion bar springs. Half-elliptic underslung rear springs. Luvax-Girling hydraulic dampers.

Brakes : Girling Hydromechanical front, and Girling mechanically operated rear, brakes.

Steering : Burman-Douglas worm and nut.

Tyres : Dunlop 5.50 x 17.

Dimensions : Wheelbase, 9ft. 7in. Track (front), 4ft. 6in. : (rear) 4ft. 6¼in. Turning circle, 37ft. Weight of complete car, empty, 27 cwt. (approx.).

The Hurricane, the new Two-litre Armstrong Siddeley drop-head coupé.

The Post-War Armstrong Siddeley

Post-war Armstrong Sidde

The saloon, a six-light four-door design to be known as the Lancaster. Boldness of the frontal treatment is the most immediately striking feature. A one-piece bonnet and built-in head lamps are part of the modern styling adopted.

IT is likely that the excellent reputation built up in the past by one of the pioneer firms of the British motor industry, Armstrong Siddeley Motors, Ltd., will be greatly enhanced by their post-war activities. An entirely new design is going through the final prototype stages for an exceptionally attractive 16 h.p. six-cylinder car.

It is the kind of car which will at once attract the attention of the discriminating owner who appreciates individuality and refinement of looks, and of performance. The first impressions produced by this new Armstrong Siddeley are that it is essentially modern but not extravagant; that it is long, low and broad, yet with ample headroom, and that æsthetically good judgment has put the final touches upon sound and practical appointments. In short, the car looks so good that one feels an immediate desire to try out its performance on the road

Family Characteristics

One of the most noticeable features of this post-war design is the treatment of the front end. The parentage of the car is unmistakable, yet the styling is quite different from anything which has gone before. Behind a modern boldness of outline there is a suggestion of the familiar Armstrong Siddeley prow. The well-known sphinx is there, but is now a motif and not a model. It blends into the car and lightens the appearance of the bonnet. The front, too, is absolutely clean, with no grouping of chromium-plated lamps and fittings, for the head lamps are built into the front wings and the side lamps are integral. These features perhaps are not so important as the rest, but they are bound to attract the attention of anyone who has known the Armstrong Siddeley cars of history, and who takes an æsthetic interest in the preservation of a long-established marque.

Saloon and Coupé

There will be two body types of this new car, a six-light four-door saloon to be known as the Lancaster, and a two-door drop-head coupé called the Hurricane; both names are famous in the field of aircraft, with which the company is associated, technically and in every other respect, through the Hawker Siddeley Group. Both bodies are characterised by smoothly flowing lines, from the long one-piece bonnet at the front to the inbuilt luggage boot at the back. They are wide, coming out to half the width of the wings, and have no running boards, as the frame is low built, and one can step straight in through the wide doors. The front seats are of the chair type, adjustable and most comfortably upholstered. The rear seats are wide, having central folding arm rests as well as side arm rests. It is noticeable that the squabs of the rear seats are higher than usual, though not so high as to interfere with the headgear of the occupants.

Interior Finish

The interior trim is most inviting. Soft leather of light tone is edged with piping of a different depth of colour, and the cushioning is pleated laterally instead of vertically, the effect being a suggestion of soft spaciousness. The trimming of the doors and the design of the window fillets are matched up with the seats to form one harmonious pattern.

Attention has been devoted to giving a maximum degree of outward visibility for the occupants, and the front pillars of the windscreen are of praiseworthy slenderness. Incidentally, to achieve this feature without jeopardising the rigidity of the structure, the windscreen is fixed and does not open. As the cars will have twin electric screenwipers, and an air conditioning equipment which includes de-misting channels playing on to the inner surface of the glass, an opening screen is not considered necessary.

Arrangement of the facia board, which is carried out in dark walnut, is well thought out, from the practical

ey Cars

The saloon from another angle : Absence of running boards will be noticed, also the fact that at the rear the body is extended out to half the width of the wings.

viewpoint, besides being attractive to the eye. In front of the driver is a simple raised panel, presented at a good angle for easy view, carrying the essential instruments—speedometer, fuel gauge, and so forth. These have round dials, clear markings and needles, and concealed illumination. The face of this panel is held in place by invisible spring clips, so that it can easily be removed and the connections of the instruments reached with minimum trouble. To enable the instruments to be seen without obstruction the steering wheel has two horizontally placed spokes instead of three or four.

Practical Points

On the right of the panel is a shallow recess, very convenient to the driver's right hand, where the secondary controls are arranged in two vertical rows of three items. In the centre of the steering wheel are the horn button, the traffic indicator switch, and the dip switch. The left side of the facia forms a long cubby hole. In the saloon this may have a door arranged to open downwards into a horizontal position, where it may be used as a convenient shelf. In the peak of the roof are folding sun vizors, that in front of the passenger having a small mirror on its reverse side. A clock is mounted between the two vizors. A point which deserves notice is the careful avoidance of bright fittings which might reflect light back into the eyes of the driver or passengers.

As already noted, at the rear of each style of body is a large inbuilt luggage boot, well finished and felted as regards its interior. On the coupé the lid of the boot opens upwards, but on the saloon it opens downwards and backwards so as to add to the space for emergency use. Below the luggage boot is a separate compartment housing the spare wheel, and its cover carries wheel-changing tools in clips. When this cover is opened a red rear light is uncovered so as to avoid danger at night.

One provision in particular on these new cars will enormously please the experienced motorist. Under the scuttle in the front is a compartment which houses a most desirable and remarkable tool kit. The tools are neatly arranged in a streamline leather-covered wood case, rather like a fine-quality brief case. The tools themselves are of the best quality, finished off in gun blue. This tool kit is so very attractive that it may be necessary to provide its compartment with a lid and key !

Light Alloys Used

There are many interesting points about the coupé. The drop head is of graceful shape, but it is not heavily padded to attain its shape, and therefore folds away neatly into minimum space. The framework is constructed largely of light alloys. The head can be undone completely from inside the car. Coupés of the past were apt to have a place where draught and wet could easily enter—the joint between the roof fabric and the top frame of the forward windows. On the Hurricane model of the Armstrong Siddeley these two important joints are sealed with zip fasteners.

Cleaning Simplified

The bonnet of the new 16 h.p. Armstrong Siddeley is made in one piece with shallow sides, and the catch is concealed in the grille in front of the radiator. Incidentally the space between the front bumper bar and the front of the car is filled in with a valance, and the car as a whole presents a smooth surface for cleaning purposes, with no projections to catch the leather. In the coachwork construction of these two cars as wide a use as possible has been made of aluminium alloys, especially for such parts as the bonnet, door panelling, boot panel and so forth. One of the objects of the whole design has been to obtain a good power-to-weight ratio.

At the moment it is not desired to disclose overmuch of the mechanical details, but it may be mentioned that

Smoothly flowing lines from front to rear are evident in the new Armstrong Siddeleys, as seen in this side view of the two-door drop-head coupé to be known as the Hurricane. The head is designed to fold down easily and neatly, and its framework is largely of light alloys.

Post-war Armstrong Siddeley Cars

This two-door drop-head coupé will be the alternative coachwork style to be offered on the new 16 h.p. Armstrong Siddeley chassis. It has many practical points of layout and equipment.

the chassis is completely new, though on orthodox lines. The frame is low built and designed for rigidity, and the front suspension is independent. The six-cylinder engine is of 1,991 c.c. capacity. A choice will be offered of the well-known Wilson preselective gear box, or synchromesh.

The post-war Armstrong Siddeleys will be quality cars in every respect, combining the highest features of reliability and easy maintenance with a fine appearance and outstanding performance. The prototype cars which *The Autocar* has examined show every evidence of careful and thoughtful design of a most practical kind. Plans have been laid for production to commence within six months from the cessation of hostilities.

THE FINEST CAR OF ITS CLASS IN THE WORLD

The Hurricane ... the new conception in British Motoring

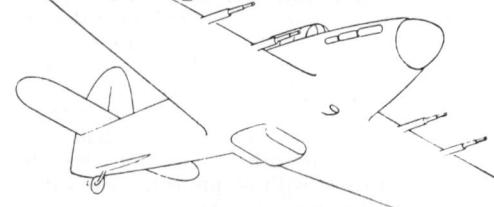

The technicians who designed the famous Hurricane fighter now give you a motor car that is new from front to rear—the practical application of aircraft designing and manufacturing technique towards a lighter and more reliable car. The new 16 h.p. Armstrong Siddeleys translate afresh the words "power," "comfort," "elegance" and "individuality."

The HURRICANE

ARMSTRONG [AS] SIDDELEY

R. P. 1032E

ARMSTRONG SIDDELEY MOTORS LTD., COVENTRY. *Branch of Hawker Siddeley Aircraft Co. Ltd.*

Introducing...

THE technicians who designed, developed and constantly improved the famous 'Lancaster' bomber and 'Hurricane' fighter have turned their activities to motor cars. The post-war Armstrong Siddeley models are entirely new from front to rear ... the wider use of newly developed light alloys ... interior heating and air conditioning ... a new flow line in design. Some of the finest technicians in the aircraft industry have contributed to this new conception in British motoring.

The current programme includes the 'Hurricane' drop-head Coupé and the 'Lancaster' 6-light Saloon ... both 16 h.p., 6-cylinder with 1,991 c.c. high-performance power unit.

THE NEW CONCEPTION IN BRITISH MOTORING

THE "HURRICANE"

ARMSTRONG · SIDDELEY

ARMSTRONG SIDDELEY MOTORS LTD., COVENTRY. *Branch of Hawker Siddeley Aircraft Co. Ltd.*

13

Two-litre ARMSTRONG SIDDELEY

New Era Motoring, on a Higher Plane

By MONTAGUE TOMBS

The Armstrong Siddeley ascending Stoneleigh Hill (1 in 10), once a Midlands test hill for top gear because of the right-angle corner approach. Extensive widening is in progress and much beauty has been lost.

WHEN the new 2-litre 16 h.p. six-cylinder Armstrong Siddeley comes into general public circulation I have no doubt that it is going to cause considerable surprise. Its manners are completely charming.

This car feels so superbly safe. It is a somewhat difficult sensation to describe in words. Perhaps this is close to it: On cars of yesterday, when going round a corner one is aware to a greater or lesser degree of the tendency, induced by centrifugal force, to lean outwards. When coasting at speed on a push bicycle round a curve one automatically heels over and leans inwards. The Armstrong Siddeley feels as if it, too, tended to lean inwards. The answer perhaps is that a low centre of gravity and low seating height combine to produce this sensation, but whatever the explanation this impression is very real.

Corners Unnoticed

As a result the car goes round corners or fast curves as if the road were straight. The steering is very good indeed, and hence the car can be placed to a nicety. Add to this a suspension which is soft enough to absorb most road irregularities completely, but not so soft as to sway or roll or pitch, and one finds a vehicle which is an absolute pleasure not only to the driver but to the passengers as well, in the front or in the rear seats.

Occasions do not as yet offer for long runs to be made on sample cars, and I had to confine myself to a few hours in the Cotswold country close to Coventry. Many motorists know the road which runs from Stratford-on-Avon to Broadway. It is a succession of S-bends. The Armstrong Siddeley revelled in straightening them out. It would put up a very high average indeed over that road if one essayed to try. That perhaps is one of the great charms of the car; it seems so independent of surfaces and bends, and it never gives the impression of hurrying. In fact the ease of the performance makes one doubt the accuracy of a speedometer known to be reasonably accurate, but this is a doubt dispelled by the short time taken between place and place on a journey.

As soon as the driver has settled into the seat and appreciated the luxury of the car's interior appointments, he quickly becomes aware of the fact that an extremely good driving position has been achieved. It might be thought that one driving position is very like another; none the less this one definitely is different, and excellent. The wheel tucks nicely into place, it is low and well out of the vision line, and yet there is plenty of room for your knees. Vision

forward, and in every direction, is really excellent, because the screen is wide and the pillars are thin. This is a car that one sits well into, and yet one does not lack room in any direction. Couple a good driving position with extra good visibility, fine road holding, and accurate steering, and there you have a combination of a most fascinating kind.

For the engine I can find nothing but praise. It starts easily from cold, and pulls well within a short distance. It is smooth and quiet, and pleasantly flexible at low speeds. Like the whole car, it is effortless. To quote maximum speeds and acceleration figures is a waste of time unless there has been opportunity to test and check them on measured distances and with a stop-watch, so all I can say is that the car is obviously a really good performer, and that the maximum speed is quite as fast as any reasonable being can want. It is the average speed that matters, and without any doubt this car has the ability to make effortless high averages.

These remarks are based upon runs made on more than one example of the new model; the others had the synchromesh gear box, which is a particularly good example of its type in the matter of easy changing without conscious timing of movements and judgment of speeds, but the Broadway journey was made on a car with the famous preselector gear and centrifugal clutch. If anyone asked me which I personally prefer I should choose the preselector. It suits this very charming car so well.

You can select a desirable gear in advance on a hill, and negotiate the fast corner with both hands on the wheel. The preselector makes it supremely easy to change down at exactly the right moment without any skilful manipulation, and fast climbs thus become an easy matter. Moreover, quick and faultless changing up when a grade momentarily lessens is made easy. The gear ratios are nicely suited to the power-to-weight ratio, and the result imbues the driver with a sense of superiority over hills.

Brakes Match the Performance

When a car is a star performer, and apt to mislead the driver as to the speed of the moment, it needs good brakes. The brakes on the A.S. are indeed good, and can be applied in emergency with confidence that a true course will be maintained; the stopping effect is in exact accordance with the pressure put on the pedal.

In these few words I have attempted to portray the character of a new car which is superb to handle. There is a common saying that a specialised car must really be special in order to sell. This car is genuinely special, and I fancy that any knowledgeable driver who tries it will find the reasons for a display of enthusiasm.

The Lancaster saloon

The New
Armstrong Siddeley 16

Medium-powered car of modern design with saloon ("Lancaster") and drophead coupé ("Hurricane") coachwork

THE connections of the Armstrong Siddeley concern with the motor industry stretch back to the very beginnings of the century, and their products have maintained a uniformly high reputation for reliability and long life, performance having been a relatively second consideration and the styling remaining on conservative lines.

It is common knowledge that in recent years the cars that have been produced in association with a group of companies in the aircraft world, the products of which are second to none in performance, and the new models reflect this connection both in the names that have been chosen for them—"Hurricane" and "Lancaster"—and also in mechanical design and external appearance. The latter in particular is a considerable break away from anything that has been done hitherto, but, at the same time, the unmistakable impress of Armstrong Siddeley tradition has been maintained at the front end of the car.

The Armstrong Siddeley Co. was the first to announce an entirely new post-war car when in "The Motor" of May 9 we published four photographs in the centre double pages of prototypes of the two models, accompanied by a brief specification. Since then production has reached such a stage that cars are now being exported and deliveries made against M.O.W.T. licences to acquire.

Prices have not yet been announced, but may be expected in the course of a few weeks.

The objective that has determined the appearance of these new models has been a practical "clean up," aimed not at reducing the drag coefficient but at making the car quite easy to keep clean, and to provide harmonious and consistent style from front to back. The former problem must not be dismissed as unimportant, for it may be some time before garages have full facilities for washing and polishing, and the suppression of any nooks, crannies and chromium knick-knacks thus has a real value to the owner.

The illustrations of the two new cars show how the headlamps have been blended into the front wings, the area of chromium plating determined at a reasonable level, and items such as door handles, hinges, bonnet opening, bumpers, etc., designed throughout with the practical problems of everyday motoring constantly in mind. Further evidence on this score can be seen in the fuel cap, which has a large diameter, and the location of the small hand tools which are held in a fitted case placed under the facia panel.

The instruments are yet another feature of the simplicity underlying the whole concept. They are grouped high up on the right-hand side of the panel immediately in front of the driver, and are completely unobstructed as a consequence of using a two-spoke steering wheel. Only

ARMSTRONG SIDDELEY DATA

	"16"
Present tax..	£20
Cubic capacity	1,991 c.c.
Cylinders ..	6
Valve position	Overhead
Bore..	65 mm.
Stroke	100 mm.
Comp. ratio	7 to 1
Max. power (A)	70 b.h.p.
at	4,200 r.p.m.
Max. torque (A)	95 lb./ft.
at	3,000 r.p.m.
H.P. : Sq. in. piston area (A) ..	2·26 h.p.
Wt. : Sq. in. piston area (B) ..	97 lb. (Coupé) 104 lb. (Saloon)
Ft./Min. Piston speed at max. h.p...	2,765 ft. per min.
Carburetter	Single Stromberg d.d.
Ignition	Coil
Plugs : Make and type	Lodge H.N.P.
Fuel pump ..	A.C. Mechanical
Oil filter ..	Tecalemit Full Flow
Oil circulation : Galls. per min. ..	4 gals. per min.
Clutch	Borg & Beck 8 in. dia. Spring Centre Borglite

Overall ratios	SYNCHRO	PRE-SELECTOR
1st gear..	17·6	18·4
2nd gear	10·89	10·67
3rd gear	7·24	7·24
Top gear	5·1	5·1
Reverse	15·2	22·4
Prop. shaft	Hardy Spicer	(Open shaft-needle roller)
Final drive	Hypoid bevel	

Brakes	Girling (Hydraulic front, Mechanical rear)
Drums..	12 in. diam.
Friction lining area	135 sq. in. (Total)
Car wt. per sq. in. (B)	22 lb. (Coupé) 23 lb. (Saloon)
Suspension ..	Independent Torsion Bar—Front Semi-Elliptic—Rear
Steering gear	Burman Douglas (Worm, nut and rocker shaft)
Steering wheel	Two-spoked — 17 in. dia.
Wheelbase ..	9 ft. 7 in.
Track, front	4 ft. 6 in.
Track, rear ..	4 ft. 6¼ in.
Overall length	15 ft. 5 in.
Overall width	5 ft. 8 in.
Overall height	5 ft. 3 in.
Ground clearance..	6¼ in. Laden
Turning circle	37 ft.
Weight—dry	26¼ cwt. (Coupé) 28 cwt. (Saloon)
Tyre size ..	5·5 in. x 17 in.
Wheel type..	Dunlop Disc
Fuel capacity	12 gallons
Oil capacity	11 pints
Water capacity	3 gallons
Electrical system	Lucas
Battery capacity ..	12 volt, 51 amp.

Top Gear Facts:	
Engine speed per 10 m.p.h.	620
Piston speed per 10 m.p.h.	408
Road speed at 2,500 ft./min. (piston) ..	61·5 m.p.h.
Litres per ton-mile	2,800 Coupé 2,550 Saloon

(A) With standard road settings of carburetter, etc.   (B) Dry weight.

OPEN CONVERSION.—This picture shows the Hurricane coupé in fully opened position, that is to say in every way equal to an open touring car. The body is notable for use of light alloys, and it is shown on another page in the fully closed position.

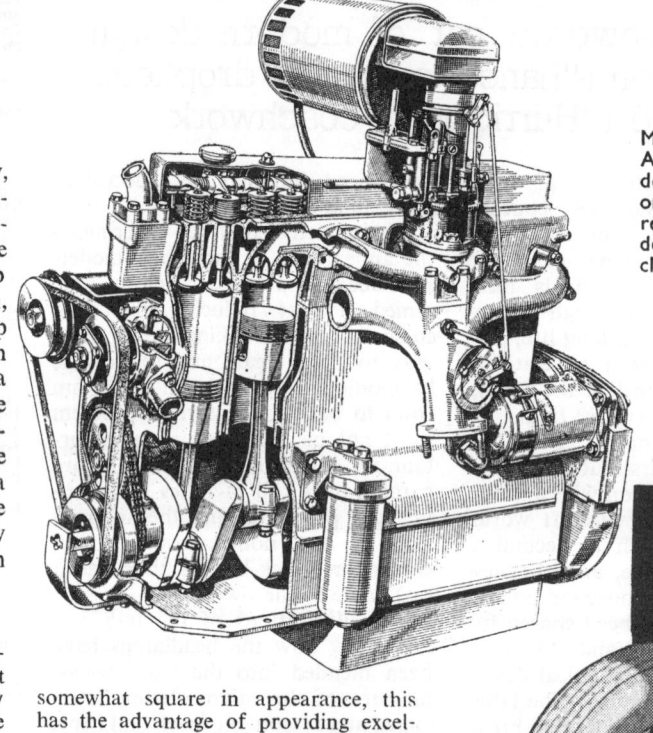

MANIFOLD VIRTUES.—The n Armstrong Siddeley engi develops 108 b.m.e.p. at 4,200 r.p. on 72 octane fuel. This credita result is largely due to the care design of the inlet porting which clearly shown in the draw on left.

essential information, that is to say, road speed, oil pressure and fuel content, is provided, there being, however, a warning light should the parking bulbs in the head-lamp reflectors fail. The starter switch, electrically operated fuel reserve tap and lighting controls are mounted on the extreme right-hand of the facia and are immediately accessible to the driver. By this grouping some two-thirds of the instrument panel can be devoted to a locker beneath which a radio set and heater can be fitted, the controls of these being centrally placed. A clock is incorporated in the rear-view mirror.

Light-alloy Bodywork

In view of Armstrong Siddeley reputation it is hardly necessary to add that the upholstery and fittings generally are of the highest class, but there are some special features on the drop-head coupé which deserve detailed notice.

In the first place, low weight. It is normal for cars of this type to weigh considerably more than corresponding saloon models, but reference to the data panel shows that in this case the " convertible " scales 1½ cwt. less than the saloon. This has been achieved by the widespread use of light-alloy sheet, 100 lb. of which is used all told. The floor is all-steel but the doors and the main part of the rear structure are made on Shore presses using rubber dies—a very economical method for the production of moderate quantities. The rear part of the framework is made of steel but the doors and certain other parts are made of timber, which is first treated against attack by rot or fungi.

Although the rear of the body is

somewhat square in appearance, this has the advantage of providing excellent head room for the rear passengers, and it is possible to have the top open over the front seats only, or fully down at will. Zip fasteners are used to seal the top on to the folding side rails. The floor of both cars is sound-proofed and all floorboards are located by dowels so that there can be no difficulties of alignment when fitting, should they be removed for work on the chassis.

Turning now to the engineering aspects of the car, the frame is of deep U-section steel with an X bracing. There is a box-section formation over the forward and rear parts, and the latter runs underneath the rear axle, which is located by underslung semi-elliptic springs mounted inboard of the frame members. Suspension at the front end is by arms of unequal length and torsion bars. On each side there is a short double wishbone. A drawing shows how this connects to an inbuilt Luvax-Girling shock-absorber on top of the frame and houses a steering pivot at the wheel end. Beneath this, there is a single arm carrying the lower steering pivot (there being no king-pin) which is splined on to an intermediate member, which in turn has external splines engaging internal splines in torsion bars placed parallel to the frame. A pair of track-rods of equal length is used with a central pivot, but the steering is taken direct from a Burman Douglas box to an arm on the off-side stub axle.

High-output Engine

This arrangement of suspension/steering links permits the engine to be placed well forward in the frame, thus increasing the passenger space and improving the weight distribution from the viewpoint of comfort.

The engine itself is generally similar to the pre-war design but output has been increased by nearly 10 per cent., without sacrifice in either fuel consumption or low-end torque. Judged either on the basis of horse-power per square inch of piston area, or the realization of 108 b.m.e.p. at 4,200 r.p.m., the performance of the engine is well above average. This follows from the careful design of the porting, a point of particular interest being the manifold design.

A single down-draught Stromberg carburetter feeds into a short semi-circular external manifold which is bolted on to a longitudinal passage cast into the top near-side of the cylinder head. This passage is closed at each end by a detachable plate and can, therefore, be machined to give accuracy of dimension and good internal finish. From it, steeply inclined individual inlet tracts are taken to vertically disposed push-rod-operated valves. A four-branch exhaust pipe runs beneath the inlet system, there being the conventional central hot-spot arrangement, also an automatic thermostatically operated mixture control for starting. The counter-balanced crankshaft runs in four main bearings and these, together with the big-ends, are of the Vandervell strip type. A full-flow filter is used, clean oil being especially important in view of the use of hydraulic tappets. These are of the now well-known Zero-Lash type which take up all slack in the valve gear, at the same time allowing for expansion effects. By this means the designed valve-timing can be truly maintained, a feature which materially contributes to good idling and fuel consumption.

The valves seat direct in the cast-iron head bolted to a single casting forming crankcase and cylinder block. At the nose of the engine the timing chain is enclosed by a light-alloy casting and a conventional triangulated drive with endless rubber belt is used for the dynamo and water pump. Water flow is from pump to cylinder block and through the head, exit being through a large cast off-take at the front of the head itself.

An A.C. mechanical pump draws fuel from a 12-gallon tank, one gallon being trapped in reserve by a solenoid control. To avoid vapour lock at high air temperatures, fuel line and pump are mounted on the side of the car remote from the exhaust system.

Alternative Transmissions

The engine transmits power to alternative transmission units. In the one case a Borg and Beck clutch is used with a conventional gearbox synchronized on the upper three ratios. In the other, the well-known Wilson epicyclic box, which was first used in this country by Armstrong Siddeley, is employed, the clutch being a Newton centrifugal. Hence on this pre-selector transmission the conventional clutch pedal is used only for engaging the gear train bands, the starting condition being controlled entirely by the centrifugal mechanism in the friction clutch coupled with the flywheel. This scheme gives a very smooth take up and first, second or reverse gears can be fully engaged with the car at rest, so that the slight hum of the rotating gear train, which used to be a feature of the Wilson box, is eliminated.

A large-diameter propeller shaft couples the gearbox to the Spicer type hypoid rear axle, in which the crown wheel is offset by $1\frac{3}{4}$ ins. below the axle centre. Braking is provided by

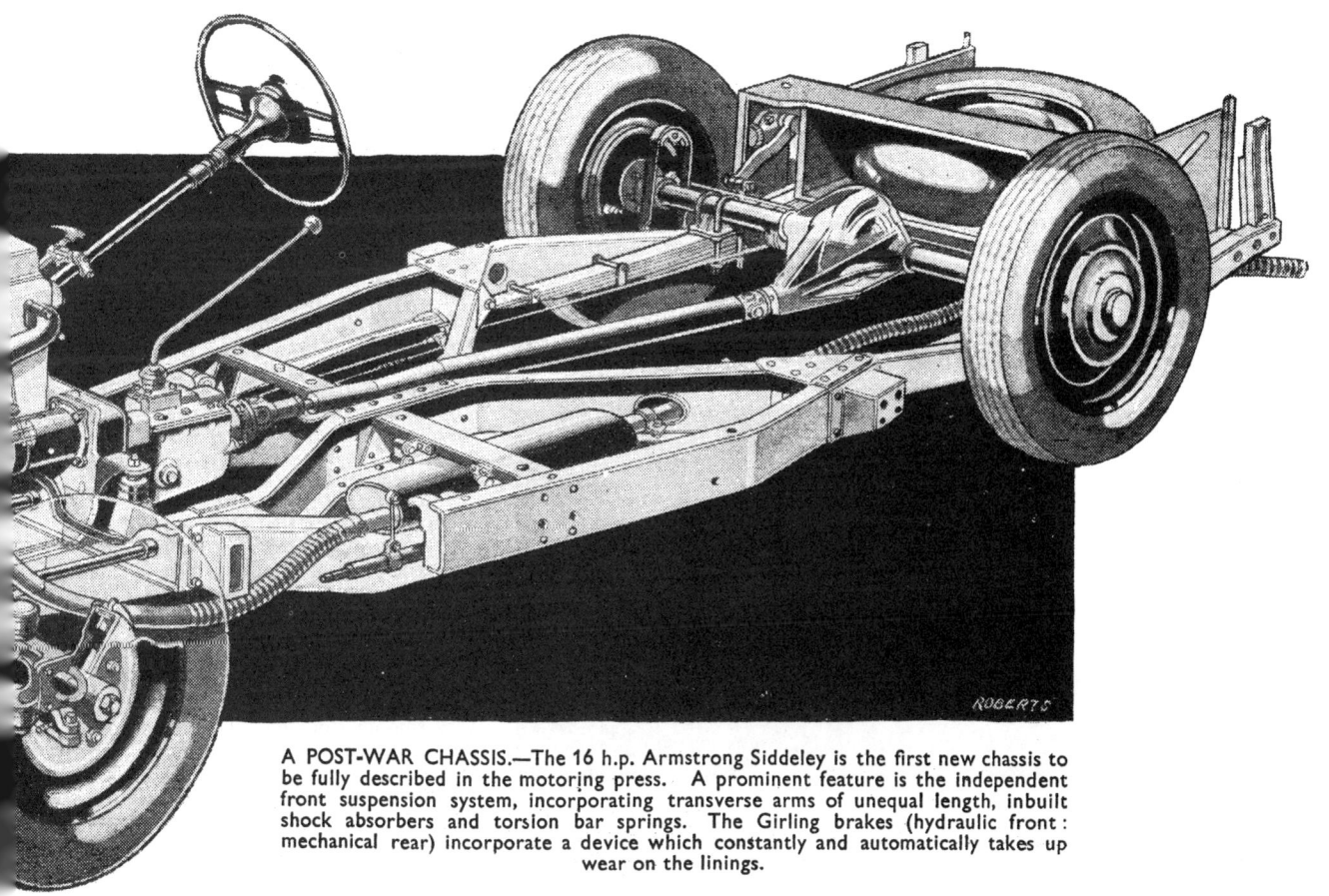

A POST-WAR CHASSIS.—The 16 h.p. Armstrong Siddeley is the first new chassis to be fully described in the motoring press. A prominent feature is the independent front suspension system, incorporating transverse arms of unequal length, inbuilt shock absorbers and torsion bar springs. The Girling brakes (hydraulic front: mechanical rear) incorporate a device which constantly and automatically takes up wear on the linings.

Girling, with hydraulic connections to the front shoes and the well-established Girling system of rods in tension to the rear brakes. The link-up is such that should there be failure in either the hydraulic or the mechanical system, full braking effort is still available on one pair of wheels. This, of course, is additional to the handbrake arrangement which works on the rear wheels only from a pistol grip under the instrument panel.

The wing treatment of the modern car makes it increasingly difficult to jack the car up for wheel changing or adjustment. The use of permanent hydraulic jacks is an obvious answer, but these are not easy to apply to independent front-wheel springing systems and are liable to increase the unsprung

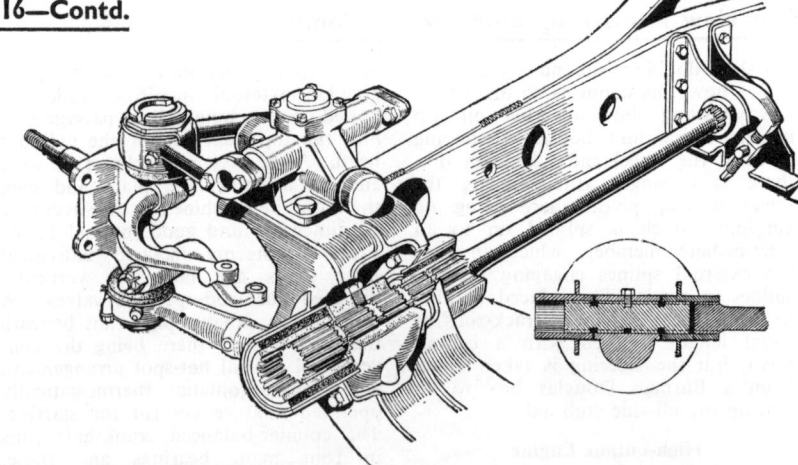

WELL PROVED.—Although embodying the advanced design feature of a torsion-bar spring, the I.F.S. layout on the new Armstrong Siddeley follows well-proved practice. Interesting features are the inbuilt Luvax-Girling shock absorbers and the adjustable reaction point on the remote end of the spring.

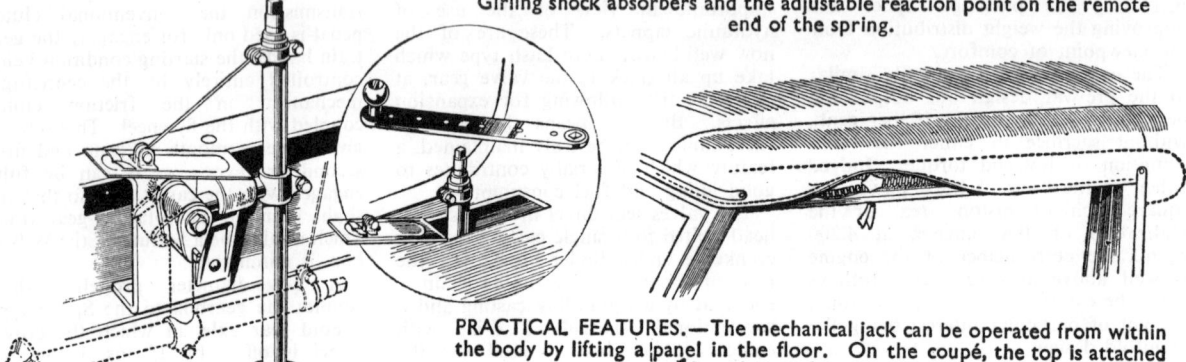

PRACTICAL FEATURES.—The mechanical jack can be operated from within the body by lifting a panel in the floor. On the coupé, the top is attached to the side rails by a Zip fastener.

weight in any event. The bumper form of jack has many good points, but it has to be removed from the tool kit and fitted, and there are obvious advantages of having the jacking system as an integral part of the car.

In the new Armstrong Siddeleys a very ingenious arrangement has been evolved. Two Smith mechanical jacks are used, one attached to the inside of each frame member. Normally, they are disposed horizontally, but by lifting a small cover in the floor boards they can be swivelled through 90 degrees and then rapidly wound down on to the road; this being done, the car can be jacked up with very little effort by means of a ratchet lever. By this

means the whole of one side of the car is lifted with the two wheels clear of the ground. The total weight is low, the unsprung weight nil, and the whole scheme is both efficient and convenient.

Any tools which may be required for wheel changing or other purposes can be extracted without disturbing luggage carried in the rear locker. The wheel brace and jack ratchet lever are carried in a small pivoted panel at the rear of the car, which, when lowered, gives access to the horizontally mounted spare wheel. The rear lamp and number plate are also built into this panel, and for this reason an auxiliary red light is provided to give warning to

oncoming traffic should a tyre change be made at night.

On the Road

A brief run on the road with the saloon car fitted with the pre-selector box showed it to be an eminently suitable vehicle for long-distance travel. The Newton centrifugal clutch took up the drive very smoothly when starting on second gear, and on this ratio the legal limit could be comfortably reached —a useful feature in traffic driving. Third gear also helped in maintaining high average speeds, and 50 m.p.h. could normally be attained thereon. On the direct ratio the car ran exceedingly smoothly and happily between 55 and 60 m.p.h., although well over 70 m.p.h. could be realized on the speedometer and maintained if the driver wished.

The I.F.S. system entirely removes road shock from the steering wheel, and the suspension system and weight distribution are such that although neither over- nor under-steer is prominent, the rear end will break away first if the limit of cornering speed is reached. As one might expect, pitching is entirely absent.

The near-side wing is invisible, but the forward view is well up to modern standards, and the Girling brakes give very smooth stopping. They incorporate a device which compensates for lining wear, thus obviating a service operation which becomes increasingly difficult as the front and rear wheels become more enclosed by modern styling.

CLOSED CONVERSION.—This picture shows the Hurricane coupé in its fully closed position. Full head room for the rear passengers is provided by this design.

Long-Distance Delivery!

by LOUISE BARLOW

Two 1946 Armstrong Siddeleys Driven 3,500 Miles Across America

LOUISE BARLOW is the wife of Roger Barlow, head of International Motors, of Los Angeles, California, and a frequent contributor to "The Autocar". The firm of International Motors has been formed to market high-class British and Continental cars in the United States, and two 2-litre Armstrong Siddeleys were selected by Mr. Barlow as his first representatives from Britain. This new model was fully described in the issues of May 11 and December 14, 1945. Here is the story of their delivery to Los Angeles under their own power.

"WELL, here they are, Mr. Barlow; I hope you like them." Mr. George Kirby, chief tester for Armstrong Siddeley s, indicated the crates that had been unloaded from the ship after the North Atlantic crossing. Workmen soon had one of the crates partly open and my husband looked in, smiled and replied, "She's a little beauty all right." Both cars were covered with a greasy green preparation in order to withstand the salt air, but I felt that I agreed with Roger in spite of that. We were to take them right across the States—two motoring ambassadors from Britain, the 1946 2-litre Armstrong Siddeley Hurricane drop-head coupés. Roger had seized on them as soon as he saw them illustrated in *The Autocar*.

It was dark before wheels were on and radiators and sumps filled in readiness for starting up for the first time in America. Both engines fired instantly, getting another compliment from Roger. Snow was coming down as we rolled out of the huge shed of Pier 54 and found ourselves on the dark, rough, dirty streets of Brooklyn, where the people seem to speak a quite different language from the rest of the Americans. Soon we were crossing Brooklyn Bridge to New York City proper, which, with all its tall buildings and bright lights, looked just like a fairyland. In a few minutes the cars were put away for the night in a warm garage—in America at last! They didn't know how lucky they were—to have a warm garage—for Mr. Kirby couldn't find a hotel room anywhere in New York City.

Looking Them Over

The next morning we really looked the Armstrong Siddeleys over. I liked the colour scheme, upholstery and facia of one, and especially its Newton centrifugal clutch and Wilson gear box. I was very happy when it was decided that this one should be my car on the trip.

The weather was bitterly cold so all of us were very happy to be starting on our way to California the next day. I heard Roger assure Mr. Kirby that in just a couple of days to the south we would find warm spring-like weather, but it hardly seemed possible.

We left New York City by way of the Holland Tunnel under the Hudson River and then for several miles travelled on the elevated roadway that at times rose to 150ft above the surrounding industrial section of Jersey City. However, 150ft was by no means enough elevation to get us above the vile stench of the many chemical plants operating in this area. About fifteen miles from New York we came to the Standard Oil Company's New Jersey refinery and storage plant and here, amidst millions of gallons of petrol, we had our tanks filled to the brim with 83-octane fuel—which was such an improvement over Pool that it was impossible to make the engines pink despite a 7 to 1 compression ratio. Kirby kept advancing the ignition little by little but it took several adjustments before pinking was possible, even on full throttle at low speeds.

Southward Ho!

Soon we came to a tremendous sign with an arrow pointing to the "Fastest Route South" and Roger's Talbot-Darracq took that route and we all followed. But even when we approached Washington, 200 miles farther south, that evening it hadn't got a bit warmer. Both Mr. Kirby and Roger put blankets around their legs to keep warm but my A.S. was fitted with a heater and I was very comfortable. Shortly before we entered the capital city of the United States a police siren burst upon us and a Highway Patrol car signalled Roger, who was then driving A.S. No. 16001, to pull over to the kerb. Two tall, handsome Maryland State troopers got out and quicky assured him that he had broken no law but would he please tell them what in blazes kind of cars these were!

It was completely dark when we reached Washington, D.C., but this was not our final destination for the day—we planned to go on another hundred miles to my home in New Market, Virginia. This certainly sounded like the South, but the temperature was ten degrees lower than in New York City that morning! Fifteen miles beyond Washington the last signs of snow disappeared and we had a fast and enjoyable run over two ridges of the famous Blue Ridge Mountains. Here we had a new experience, for suddenly we were assailed by a strange and pungent odour. Kirby thought that maybe our brakes were burning, but Roger told him that some car passing that way earlier in the evening had run over a skunk, or polecat. Kirby was quite amazed that the odour was really as horrible as he had heard, and I gleefully dubbed the little creatures "Kirby's Kittens."

In New Market was a friend of Roger's, owner of a body repair shop, who stayed up late to let the cavalcade into his warm buildings, where, with 330 miles behind us after our first day's run, we were glad to garage the cars for the night. Mr. Kirby had no hotel troubles here, for my father had secured a room for him at the wonderful Shenvalee Hotel, one of the finest places in the Shenandoah Valley.

The next day the two Armstrong Siddeleys were given a thorough cleaning and waxing, and that awful green stuff was taken off the chromium with quantities of petrol. All day long townspeople came in to see the strange new cars from England, and the features of design were the subject of many long and heated discussions. Much admiration was expressed for No. 16001, which had a maroon stripe along the side to match the red upholstery. Mine had only a thin white line to set off the grey paintwork, so it was decided to give it a band of colour to match the pigskin seats. Harry Ritchie carefully mixed up a special paint just the colour of pigskin, and by that night No. 16002 had a tapering band of colour that made it very difficult to determine just which of the two was the more attractive.

Roger's special Ford V 8-engined Citroen was to be driven out to California by a marine sergeant in a couple of weeks' time, and it was decided the next day to bring it to Washington, where the driver could easily take it over when he was discharged. Kirby took the wheel of the Citroen, as Roger wanted to drive an A.S. really hard over the mountain roads in daylight. Snow had fallen the night before, and the roads were still covered so that he had his work cut out to stay on the road at the speeds around turns, but, although he deliberately forced the car into some slides, he managed all right ! (Afterwards, Roger told people that he might have gone up the mountain a little faster in his 4-litre Talbot-Darracq, but that he doubted whether he could ever come *down* any faster; the braking system and suspension were really good.)

Mishap

Half an hour after leaving the mountains behind we met a huge red van whose driver was so intrigued by the cars' appearance that he stuck his head out of the cab for an additional look as we flashed by. In so doing he let his huge vehicle wander over the centre line and to avoid a head-on collision Kirby pulled the Citroen off the concrete road on to the snow-covered verge. But in regaining the surfaced roadway disaster struck, for, although the front

Near New York's most famous landmark—the Empire State Building, into which an aircraft crashed in 1945.

wheels came back up the sharp four-inch edge of the concrete strip, the rear wheels slid along the edge for some little distance and then came up suddenly, putting the Citroen into a fast spin that took it right across the road and off the opposite side into a 9 ft. ditch, turning it over completely in the process.

Kirby's right arm had a great cut and a large lump which suggested broken bones. After the flow of blood from his wound was staunched, Kirby insisted upon posing for a picture beside the wreck. We left the poor Citroen there in the bushes and went in to Washington where, at the Emergency hospital, four stitches were put in Kirby's arm and X-rays taken, which showed that no bones were actually broken. We remained in New Market for an extra two days to enable Kirby to get some of the stiffness out of his arm and back, and during this time the Citroen came back on tow to be left for Mr. Ritchie to mend.

No. 16001 was running so well with a much advanced spark that it was decided to see just how much its petrol consumption could be improved, so the carburettor jet was changed from .050 to .047.

Our next day's run was to take us to Winston Salem, North Carolina—a distance of about 220 miles. This was accomplished with no difficulty other than being stopped again by inquisitive highway patrolmen. It was a very pleasant

"Kirby's Kittens"—the chief tester of Armstrong Siddeley's gestures appropriately with a dead skunk.

Sunset halt in Delaware—the cavalcade of two Armstrong Siddeleys and a Talbot-Darracq pauses on the fast dual highway to Washington.

Mexican village—one of the Armstrong Siddeleys pauses on the "road" while Mrs. Barlow and Kirby study the sun-baked adobe houses below.

Organ-pipe cactus—a stop to examine the queer growths of the huge plants that people the "petrified forest" area near Phoenix, Arizona.

Snow at 35 degrees North—the white flakes almost blank out the Armstrong Siddeleys as they cross the State line into South Carolina.

(Above, inset): Ice-breakers out—Mrs. Barlow de-ices one of the Armstrong Siddeleys after a night in the open in South Carolina.

drive, first through beautiful Virginia farmland, where by noon we ran beyond the snow. Then through wooded hills until at dusk we arrived in the cigarette manufacturing centre of the tobacco growing section of America, and were fortunate enough to find both hotel rooms and garage space.

Leaden skies threatened snow the next morning and by ten o'clock, just as we reached the cotton belt of the south, the first flakes were hitting our windscreens. Soon Roger pulled up and pointed to some unpicked cotton bolls on the dry, dead plants of last season's crop, and Kirby got out to

a sundown halt by the roadside to watch the long-distance train pass by.

have his picture taken picking cotton in a snowstorm ! After we crossed into South Carolina, snow really began to come down in earnest, and at that moment some dirt got into my car's carburettor, and I lost most of the power. Kirby and Roger cleaned the filters and worked over the engine for some time, but still couldn't get a correct mixture. The entire crew was now soaked to the skin and thoroughly chilled and, as the wet snow was packing on to the road, producing a dangerously slippery surface, it was decided to stop at the first place we found with accommodation.

Fortunately the next small town had a good-looking hotel with available rooms so, even though it was only early afternoon, we gave up for the day—much to my relief, as I dislike driving on icy roads. Unfortunately there was no garage space to be had anywhere, so the cars were parked in the dubious shelter of the rear of the hotel—to the great joy of the highly appreciative negro hotel employees. A couple of hours after we had stopped, the Carolina Highway Police broadcast a request for all motorists to get off the roads as severe and dangerous icing was developing and many serious accidents had already occurred. The temperature was just about at freezing point although the snow had by now definitely turned to rain.

When we went out on an inspection early the next morning the cars looked exactly like three statues—carved in ice ! The rain had frozen the moment it had struck, and they were encased in a sheath of ice ranging from one quarter to two inches thick, and considerable careful work with ice picks was necessary before even a door could be opened. Finally the sheets of ice could be lifted off in great pieces—looking for all the world like pressings of wings, doors and

Mountain climbing in the West—a high-up stop to look down on the artificial lake caused by the immense Coolidge Dam.

Rough going—a Mexican road that looks like beach shingle. The synthetic tyres of the cars gave no trouble during the trip.

Sunset over the Gulf—the cars speed past a beacon on the coastline of the Gulf of Mexico at Biloxi, Mississippi.

bonnets, done in gleaming, translucent plastic !

Needless to say the roads, too, were covered by a sheath of ice, but by noon we heard that the highway workmen had rendered them usable, and we started out, much against my wishes—I protested that I was much happier right in my hotel room than out on the slippery highway dodging skidding 10-ton lorries ! When we left, the side streets of the town were still like glass, but the main road surface was by now a mass of churned snow and slush

Christmas leave, so he was offered the chance of driving the Talbot the next day to enable Roger and me to spend a day together in the same car. The sergeant was an apt pupil, for that evening, after only a few minutes at the wheel of the entirely strange Talbot, he was handling it quite to its critical owner's satisfaction.

Although we were now several hours south of the snow area, the air was colder than ever and by the time we reached Athens as darkness set in the mercury had dropped to twenty-two degrees. Again no garage space was available, so radiators were drained and the cars were left in front of the hotel. As luggage was being unloaded, Kirby was ribbing Roger as to the whereabouts of all that "warm spring-like weather" we were to find only two days south of New York City! This was our fourth day out and it was now even colder than on the morning we left New York!

Bananas! Closing up for the night by a banana plantain at an auto court in New Orleans. Roger Barlow is standing between the cars.

which was messy indeed, but not especially slippery, except in spots and we made fairly good time despite my reluctance to exceed 35-40 m.p.h.

Only a couple of hours further on the carburettor began giving trouble again, and this time we pulled into a petrol station where the operator invited Roger and Kirby to drive in under shelter to work. They took the carburettor off and cleaned it thoroughly, changing the jet to 047 as well. This had the effect of improving the fuel consumption to 19.7 m.p.g. (American gallon) during the rest of the day's run, which was made at a good speed after I was put into the lead, for we soon ran out of the snow area and had good dry roads into Athens, Georgia.

Somehow I was always falling behind the leading car when I was following, but when I was put in the lead I was alleged to go like blazes, leading the rest of our convoy a merry chase—much to the delight of Roger and Kirby. About an hour before reaching our night's destination Roger, in the Talbot, picked up a pleasant young Air Force sergeant who was hitch-hiking to Montgomery, Alabama, our next night's destination (where he was to spend

. . . And oranges! Kirby insists on a photograph showing that they can be picked from a car in the fabulous West.

End in sight—the two British cars reach the orange groves and mountain country of California.

IN last week's instalment, Louise Barlow described how her husband, Roger Barlow, had taken delivery of two 1946 Armstrong Siddeleys in New York with the intention of driving them to Los Angeles. Accompanied by Mr. George Kirby, chief tester of Armstrong Siddeley's, they set out with a cavalcade of the two cars and a Talbot-Darracq, heading south to reach Athens, Georgia, in bitter weather. A U.S. Air Force sergeant, hitch-hiking to Montgomery, Alabama, had joined the crew as temporary Talbot driver.

AN early start was made the following morning and at 5.30 a.m., with the temperature down to fifteen degrees, we refilled radiators. Not fifteen minutes later No. 16002 blew the cap of the radiator and came to a stop with clouds of steam pouring from under the bonnet—the radiator was frozen up! The Sunny South indeed!

However, the blocked radiator was soon thawed out, no damage having been suffered. Later in the afternoon we stopped to visit a negro farm family which had appeared in a documentary film which my husband directed and produced in this part of the country in 1942. When we left the farmer presented us with a large bag of delicious pecan nuts which every one of the party enjoyed immensely.

It was near here at Tuskegee, Alabama, that we narrowly escaped disaster when a school bus loaded with children pulled up without warning, causing everyone to brake heavily, and the Talbot had to take to the ditch to avoid ramming us. Fortunately the ditch was shallow and the Talbot suffered no damage, but some work with a shovel and considerable pushing were required to get it back on the road. It was dark when we reached Montgomery and put up for the night—saying goodbye to the sergeant, who was heart-broken not to be able to accompany us all the way to California, which was actually his home.

Farthest South

It was still below freezing point when we left the next morning but after only an hour or so the sun made it comfortably warm and it began to appear that maybe we would find warm weather in the South after all. By the middle of the afternoon we reached Mobile, on the Gulf of Mexico, having now come as far south as possible. And here was Spring indeed, for trees and grass were green, and flowers in bloom, although there was still a feel of winter in the wind that was blowing down from the North. We continued on westward along the coast to Biloxi, Mississippi, where we stopped for the night at the swank Buena Vista Hotel where everyone had a superb dinner with wonderful fresh Gulf shrimps served in a special sauce. The cars were parked under great semi-tropical trees and for the first time since arriving in America they spent a night in the open without the radiators drained.

The next morning we had only a 75-mile run to New Orleans, but the first part was over twenty-five miles of what must be the roughest paved road in the world. This cut our speed at times to 15-20 m.p.h. and it was almost noon when we were finally settled in a New Orleans auto court—under a banana plantain! It was so warm now that for our sight-seeing trip that afternoon the hoods were rolled back for the first time. We were very disappointed in the appearance of the city, but some of the best food in America is to be had there and the crew made the most of their opportunity—having lunch at Arnaud's and dinner at the world-famous Antoine's. (Roger had

told the A.S. chief tester that, although he couldn't get him into a hotel in New York, he *did* know most of the interesting places in which to eat on the way across the United States and that he would see that some memorable meals were had.

We left New Orleans next morning in a light drizzle which soon turned into a steady downpour as we crossed the Mississippi River and continued persistently, cutting down our day's mileage considerably. Our next day's run took us through many miles of Louisiana swampland where the trees lining the road were covered with the exotic-looking Spanish moss, which is a parasitic growth that eventually kills the trees.

A Virginian farm —an attractive homestead in a southern setting.

Delivery!

ory of a 3,500-mile Journey
Two 1946 Armstrong Siddeleys

George Kirby (seated on bumper) and Roger
Barlow take a rest by the roadside.

At noon we reached Beaumont, Texas, and as our little cavalcade, led by the Talbot, passed through the city we were aware that we were causing more excitement than was usual. When we stopped I recalled that in the previous day's Beaumont paper there had been a picture of a local army officer posing beside Hitler's Mercedes cabriolet and now people were mistaking the Talbot for Hitler's car, which was somewhere in the U.S. on a bond-selling tour. However, no one mistook Roger for Hitler and we safely reached Houston at sundown—on Christmas Eve.

Christmas Day we drove 200 miles to San Antonio, where the

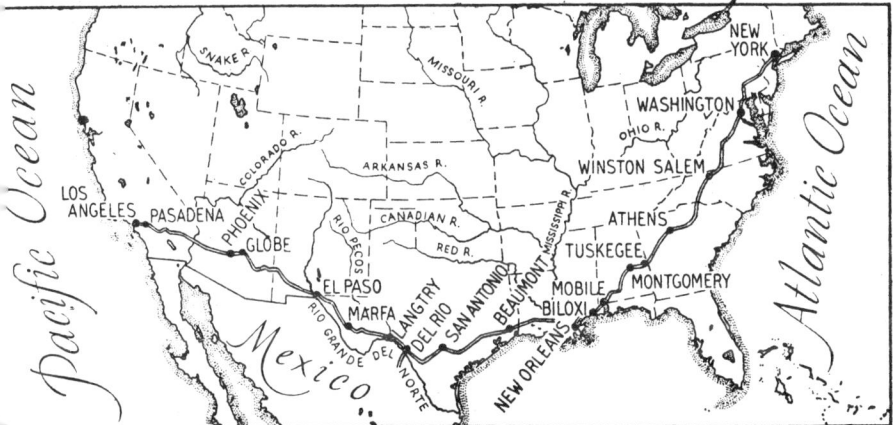

crew had an excellent dinner, Smorgasbord style, and retired early.

We encountered our first really Western scenery next day when we reached the Pecos River canyon. Only a short distance farther we stopped at Langtry for photographs —Langtry was named after Lillie Langtry, the famed Jersey Lily, who once gave a performance in the town, which was then re-named in her honour. Langtry was also the home of self-appointed Judge Roy Bean, dispenser of so-called Texas justice in frontier days. By eleven o'clock we had put 185 miles behind us and reached Del Rio, where we checked in at the hotel and, while No. 16001 was being washed, drove over into Mexico where we took a number of photographs, to the great interest of the Mexicans, who were much intrigued by the cars. It is strange that the

Down Texas way—one of the Armstrong Siddeleys on a rough road.

comparatively uneducated, unsophisticated negro and Mexican workers seem to have an instinctive appreciation of simplicity of line and for good workmanship and materials.

Our next day's run brought us to Marfa, Texas, by 3 p.m., and my husband drove out to the ranch where he stayed when making a documentary film on cowboys in 1942 (which resulted in *The Autocar* story, "Deep in the Heart of Texas", August 20, 1943). He said that the A.S. performed nobly over the trails and ranch roads which he had previously covered in a huge Buick station wagon in which he was always car-sick.

By noon next day we were in El Paso and while parking we were surrounded by a very interested group of motor cycle enthusiasts who got into a lively discussion with Kirby, who used to ride for Triumphs—which machines they seemed to know well. The New Mexico state border was only a short distance out of El Paso, so finally after nearly five days we left Texas, which is actually larger than most European countries. That evening as the cars were being unloaded at an auto court, two soldiers from the airfield near by came over and introduced themselves as enthusiasts who had enjoyed their stay in England because of the opportunity to observe and occasionally to drive thoroughbred cars.

Farewell to the Pecans

We left early in the morning and were soon rolling along at our steady 55 m.p.h. pace, which was broken only for taking an occasional photograph, until we reached the Arizona state line, where there was an agricultural inspection station. Everyone was required to show all fruits and agricultural products and have them inspected in order to prevent the spread of plant diseases. Here it was discovered that some of the pecan nuts, which everyone had been enjoying for days, contained borers—a tiny worm—and they had to be left at the station. We reached Coolidge Dam in the afternoon and stopped for a while to enjoy the immense spectacle.

That night at Globe, Arizona, we stopped at a most

Exotic-looking Spanish moss—a parasitic growth on trees in the humid Louisiana swampland.

attractive ranch-style auto court. I find that the best of these courts is far superior to any hotel accommodation to be obtained in the West. However, it was generally necessary to stop early to find a vacancy at the better ones.

For the first couple of hours the next morning our road wound up and down the steep grades of Devil's Canyon, providing some of the most exciting motoring experienced on the trip. As we neared Phoenix, Arizona, we suddenly left the barren desert-like country behind and entered a rich irrigated agricultural area with fruit trees and vegetables under cultivation as though it were mid-summer rather than mid-winter. We reached the California border just at sunset, but here there was another agricultural inspection station and a line of cars over half a mile long awaiting entry.

140 Miles for a Tyre

Sun-up the next morning saw us out on one of the bleakest stretches of desert road yet encountered and there my husband picked up an Air Force captain who, with his wife, had spent the night beside the road when their spare tyre failed them. We took the officer, who turned out to have been born in England, seventy miles to the nearest town, where we left him trying to purchase a tyre and still faced with a 70-mile return journey to his car and his wife, who must have been, to say the least, anxiously awaiting his return.

Now we left the desert behind and the entire aspect of the country changed. Orchards and farms appeared against a backdrop of snow-capped mountains—our road became a four-lane highway leading from one clean and prosperous-looking town to another. Each town was separated from the next by never-ending rows of orange trees, rich with ripe fruit. Then finally the orchards gave way to a continuous built-up area and we were in Pasadena, and a few

minutes later in Los Angeles itself, halting at the residence of my husband's business associate, right at the top of a hill overlooking a lovely lake, yet in the middle of the city. Thus was ended our 3,500-mile journey made through all kinds of weather, over all kinds of roads, exactly on schedule —on New Year's Eve. The box of spares we carried was unopened and not a bit of trouble was experienced with our synthetic tyres. For hundreds of miles, at a cruising speed of 50-60 m.p.h., No. 16002 had averaged over 19 m.p.g. and No. 16001 over 20 m.p.g., doing as well on the smaller American gallon as the cars had in England on the one quarter larger Imperial gallon.

Having crossed America without difficulty we now encountered in the city of Los Angeles some of the most difficult motoring yet faced. Next to its great size, the most remarkable thing about Los Angeles is its hills—some of the streets have gradients of 1 in 4.3, 1 in 3.6, 1 in 3.3, and I even climbed one with an indicated gradient of 1 in 3.2.

Cars Become Stars

Roger arranged for Mr. Kirby to visit some of the film studios and I then discovered that there is no official city of Hollywood. The world-renowned capital of the cinema is merely a section of Los Angeles and, what is more, most of the film studios are not even located in this non-existent city of Hollywood. The great studios of M.G.M. are eight miles away in Culver City, and Warner Bros. and Universal are over the hills in Burbank! While Kirby was an interested visitor on the shooting stages, I was surrounded by film workers from the sets—actors, directors, technicians of all sorts crowded around me, interested in the newest car from England. Such attention is certainly flattering. That night Roger and I took Kirby on a tour of Hollywood night life, and the Armstrong Siddeleys attracted more attention in the parking lot at Ciro's than did Ginger Rogers and Rita Hayworth inside! Yes, it looks as if Hollywood likes the cars, while I look forward to a trip up the coast—a thousand miles to Seattle, Washington— where a sub-agent for International Motors wants No. 16002 for a demonstration car. I always say travel— particularly in cars like the Armstrong Siddeley—is really *fun*!

At Ciro's, Hollywood, where the Armstrong Siddeleys attracted more attention than the film stars.

LANCASTER

Introducing..

THE NEW CONCEPTION IN BRITISH MOTORING

THE 'LANCASTER'

WHY should the new Armstrong Siddeley motor cars have jumped straight into the lead amongst post war productions? Very largely it is due to the development and application of aircraft designing and manufacturing technique towards a lighter and more reliable motor car, using newly developed alloys and other materials. What more natural than that the technicians responsible for so brilliant an achievement as the 'Lancaster' bomber should, having turned their unique abilities to motor car design, approach the whole problem from an entirely fresh angle, and produce a new conception in British motoring. And so the post-war Armstrong Siddeleys are the most talked-of motor-cars of today . . .

graceful . . . powerful . . . exciting

ARMSTRONG  SIDDELEY

16 h.p., six cylinder 1,991 c.c. high-performance power unit; independent front-wheel suspension, choice of synchromesh or pre-selection gearbox; oil-less and grease-retaining bearings; simple and effective interior

heating and air-conditioning. The current programme includes the 'Hurricane' Drop-head Coupé and the 'Lancaster' 6-light Saloon.

ARMSTRONG SIDDELEY MOTORS LTD., COVENTRY. *Branch of Hawker Siddeley Aircraft Co. Ltd.*

The Armstrong Siddeley

THE Armstrong Siddeley concern was the first to announce an entirely new post-war car, and the distinctive lines of the Lancaster saloon and Hurricane coupé have already become a familiar sight on the road. Now comes the news of an additional model on the same chassis in the shape of the Typhoon sportsman's saloon illustrated on this page. The price is £1,214 12s. 9d. (£950 plus £264 12s. 9d. Purchase Tax)

This new body is of the two-door type and, up to the waist line, it conforms almost exactly to the general shape of the Hurricane coupé. Above, the folding head of the latter gives place to a fixed fabric-covered head of exceptional window area. The result is an ideal combination of elegant line and above-average visibility.

Details which contribute to the latter include unusually thin screen pillars, thin metal-framed windows in the doors and the same treatment for the leading edge of the rear quarter lights, the whole effect being almost akin to a pillarless body. It will be noticed, too, that the rear quarters are carried back level with the top of the rear squab to ensure that this excellent all-round view is not solely the prerogative of the front seat passengers, but is enjoyed also by those in the rear.

For reversing, the driver has the benefit of the large side window area plus a wide rear window which cuts down to a minimum the unavoidable blind spot created by the rear quarters.

Built-in Air Conditioning

So much for visibility. Another " V " feature is ventilation. To achieve results appropriate to their ideas and the weather prevailing at any given moment, the occupants have at their disposal the conventional aids of large winding windows in the doors with hinged glass panels at their leading edges, together with the refinement of a Clayton Dewandre air-conditioning system built in under the scuttle with knob control on the facia board. This system incorporates vents at the base of the windscreen so that, as well as providing warm air at will for actual ventilation, it also acts as a de-mister for the screen.

The roominess of the seating accommodation will be obvious from a glance at the interior illustration[s] and a point to note is the ease of entering or leaving the rear seats. Although the front squabs hinge forward, the wide doors extend back to beyond the leading edge of the rear cushion so that, if a passenger in the rear wishes to leave without disturbing the occupants in front, this is quite feasible.

An interesting point about the doors is the hinging arrangement. A single hinge of massive proportions is employed in each case, the portion attached to the door being, in effect, a stout girder which runs almost the whole depth of the door and is pivoted to the hinge plates on the body sides at two points. Possibilities of misalignment in use are thus ·eliminated and the layout is such that no trace of the hinges is visible when the doors are closed. Other points about the doors include recessed interior handles and map pockets running the full length of the lower portions

The whole interior is an example of good taste applied to produce what can best be described as restrained luxury. Everything is there that could reasonably be required even by exacting owners, but there is a simplicity in the general effect that will please the fastidious.

Walnut is used for the door cappings and facia board and the latter is simply laid out for maximum convenience and attractive effect. The actual dials (for speedometer and petrol and oil gauges) are grouped on an inclined protruding panel just behind the wheel and the latter is of the two-spoke variety to provide an unobstructed view of them; to the right, the various switches are neatly grouped and, to the left, there is a large locker with an ash tray below, together with screen wiper and air-conditioning controls. Switches for the horn, dipper and trafficators (the latter recessed into the body sides just aft of the doors), are located on the steering-wheel boss.

Other interior fittings include visors for driver and front passenger (each fitted with a vanity mirror), a rear-view mirror with clock, a central interior light and ash trays recessed into the backs of the front seats. An additional feature which will make a strong appeal to the driver who believes that the reliability of the modern car does not excuse badly housed tools is a very neat fitted tool case which lives in a recess under the facia board where it remains clean when it is not required and instantly accessible when it is. At the rear, there is a large luggage boot with the spare wheel located beneath.

Interior upholstery is carried out in all-wool carriage cloth and exterior finishes available are fawn, grey, navy blue, maroon or black.

The chassis, as already indicated, is the 16 h.p. model, notable features of which include a six-cylinder o.h.v. engine of 1,991 c.c. with a power output of 70 b.h.p., synchromesh or pre-selector four-speed gearbox to choice (the latter system in conjunction with a centrifugal clutch), Girling brakes (hydraulic at the front and mechanical at the rear), independent front suspension (by torsion bars) and a rear layout embodying semi-elliptic springs and an underslung frame.

It has been the purpose of the designer to produce a car offering first-class reliability together with long life, and offering at the same time an all-round performance of the kind required by the majority of discriminating motorists. For this reason the maximum power has not been exaggerated at the expense of tractability, or good torque at low engine speeds. Similarly, although weight has been carefully studied, stiffness and strength have been considered more important. If particularly rapid acceleration is needed the ease with which the pre-selected gears can be engaged and the rapidity of the change itself results in really good rest-to-50 m.p.h. time.

In the suspension layout, again, the opposing claims of the " boulevard ride " and stability on corners have been excellently balanced so that not only does the car have an appearance representative of modern practice but also a general standard of performance thoroughly in accordance with post-war motoring needs

"Typhoon"

First Details of an Entirely New Body Style on the 16 h.p. Chassis

INTERIOR ARRANGEMENT.—Passenger comfort has been carefully studied in the new model and the deep seats are upholstered in all-wool carriage cloth. Although the front seat squabs hinge forward, the doors are of sufficient width for rear passengers to enter or leave the car without disturbing those in front. The facia is of walnut and the layout convenient and of good appearance.

SWEPT AND ROOMY.—Rear aspect of the car is attractive and houses a capacious luggage compartment to which easy access is obtained as the lid swings well up out of the way.

Two-litre Armstrong

The Typhoon, an Additional Coachwork Model

The Two-litre Armstrong Siddeley has an arresting appearance, and this new Typhoon sports saloon is particularly graceful.

ORIGINALLY the post-war Two-litre Armstrong Siddeley was produced in two styles, the Lancaster four-door six-light saloon, and the Hurricane two-door drop-head coupé. Already this new Armstrong Siddeley has established a considerable reputation as a car of quality and great attractiveness. Now an addition to the coachwork range has been put into production, a two-door four-light sports saloon christened the Typhoon, which is priced at £950 plus £264 12s 9d purchase tax, total £1,214 12s 9d.

As will be seen from the illustrations this is a particularly graceful design, intended primarily for two people and quantities of luggage, yet able to offer adequate accommodation for two more passengers or three children when desired. This rear seat is the same width as in the Lancaster saloon, but the leg room is not so great.

A particular feature of the design is the clear view outwards, which is obtained by the use of wide windows, with narrow pillars for the wide fixed windscreen, and narrow pillars where the division in the glass occurs along the back edges of the doors. The car has a fixed head, which is panelled in perforated sheet metal and covered on the outside with weatherproof material, a system which avoids roof drumming and which also gives an individual appearance. Incidentally the roof is lined with a soft cream-coloured material which can easily be washed to preserve its crisp and bright appearance.

Wide doors give access to the seats, and are hinged along their rear edges, the hinges being concealed but of unusual strength, as the two fitted to each door are part of a single forged bracket to ensure rigidity and prevent sagging. The forward panel of each door window is of triangular shape and swivels outwards to form an extractor flap for ventilation without draught. The larger glass panel can be dropped or raised by means of a winding handle, and moves in a narrow chromium plated framework. A point about the provision of the extractor panel is that it leaves a space in the thickness of the door below it, and in this the interior door handle can be conveniently and neatly recessed. The curved-top glass of the windows in the quarters is fixed, and the rear edges of the door windows overlap the quarter windows to form a weathertight joint.

The front seats are separate and individually adjustable for leg reach. The cushions are deep from back to front, and the backs high and wide. These backs can be tilted forward for ease of entering the back compartment; below the hinged portion there is a recess which gives increased toe room in the back seats. The rear seat is 45 inches wide across the seat and 54½ inches above the comfortably padded elbow rests. A folding centre arm rest is provided.

The interior has a luxurious simplicity. The seat cushions and squabs are trimmed with superfine all-

---

──── SPECIFICATION ────

Engine.—15.72 h.p., six cylinders, 65 × 100 mm, 1,991 c.c. Overhead valves, hydraulic tappets, counter-balanced crankshaft, pressure lubrication. Stromberg downdraught carburettor. Lucas 12-volt coil ignition. Pump water cooling.

Transmission.—Centrifugal clutch and four-speed preselective gear box. Overall ratios: Top, 5.1; third, 7.24; second, 10.67; first, 18.4 to 1; or

Dry single-plate clutch and four-speed gear box with synchromesh on second, third and top. Ratios: Top, 5.1; third, 7.24; second, 10.87; first, 17.6 to 1.

Open propeller-shaft to hypoid bevel final drive.

Suspension.—Independent front-wheel suspension with torsion bar springs. Half-elliptic underslung rear springs. Luvax-Girling hydraulic dampers.

Brakes. — Girling hydromechanical front, and Girling mechanically operated rear

Steering.—Burman - Douglas worm and nut.

Tyres.—Dunlop 5.50 × 17in.

Main Dimensions.—Wheelbase 9ft 7in. Track (front) 4ft 6in; (rear) 4ft 6½in. Turning circle 37ft. Weight, empty, 27 cwt (approx.)

wool carriage cloth. The style of trim is based upon horizontal pleats with a plain panel towards the top of the squabs and towards the front of the seat cushions. Neat piping sets off the effectiveness.

Figured walnut is used for the door cappings and rail, and the door trim is carried out with a piped panel following the contours. There is a wide pocket in the base of each door. Between the top of the rear seat squabs and the wide rear window is a sunk ledge for parcels.

The rectangular instrument board is very neat and of polished walnut. There is a minimum of dials—only three—and these are set in a raised portion immediately in front of the driver and are easily visible through the chocolate-coloured rim of the two-arm spring-spoked steering wheel, in the cream-coloured centre of which are the horn button, the traffic indicators switch, and the head lamp dip-switch. The three dials comprise a central speedometer flanked by a fuel gauge and oil pressure gauge.

Set back on the right side of the instrument panel are controls for the petrol reserve, and the lighting, starter, and ignition switches. To the left of the panel is a single control for the screenwipers, and below that is the

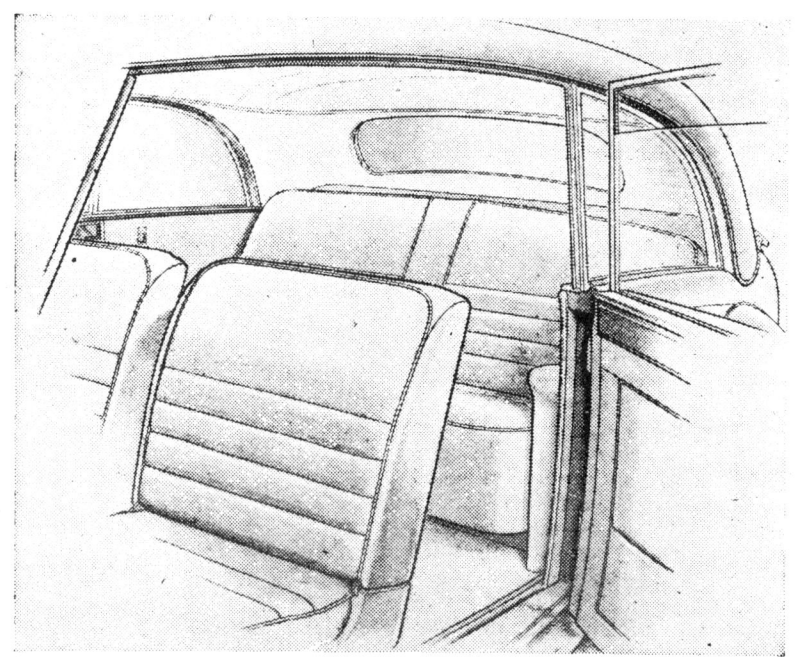

Neatly trimmed in best quality buff cloth with horizontal pleats, and roof lining of a cream coloured washable material, and walnut woodwork, the interior of the Typhoon saloon is most inviting. The backs of the front seats tilt.

control for the fan which provides air temperature control as well as de-frosting and de-misting for the windscreen. On the left is a large lidded locker.

In the peak of the roof are twin sun vizors, and in the centre is a driving mirror, with a small clock. There is a large locker with the spare wheel below

Outward visibility is a feature of the new body, for the windows run almost the full length of the head, and all pillars are made as slender as is consistent with strength.

The First

A typical stretch of the type of surface encountered on some of the unfinished main roads. Right, is the Armstrong-Siddeley "Typhoon" in which the first five thousand miles were covered.

THIS is not the detailed history of a motor trip. On the contrary, the article is built up from odd notes based upon personal experience which may be of value to the intending visitor, tourist or immigrant.

Consult a large-scale map of Cape Province; take a line through Darling due east to Ceres and Prince Albert, thence to Port Elizabeth. The area south of this line has been fairly thoroughly explored during the past three months, covering a total mileage of just over 5,000.

Of the scenery I have no intention of commenting either in detail or superlatives. On a vast panoramic scale, suffice it to say that combined in one place or another one finds the best features of the Lake District, the Scottish Highlands, the northern and western coasts of Ireland, the forests of Sweden, the ruggedness of Norway, the charm of Switzerland and the plains of Lombardy—an international cocktail, both pleasing to the eye and agreeable to the senses. Capetown, point of debarkation, was the main centre in the early stages —a delightful city, wide roads, all in excellent condition, good suburbs, but very hilly and in places awkwardly cambered. Later, Montagu, George Knysna and Port Elizabeth served as focal points.

Road conditions vary enormously. The main and national roads constitute an ideal highway—so far as they have been completed. The uncompleted portion and those roads presumably equivalent to the home "B" class range from fair to deplorable. Of the distance travelled to date, 10 per cent. has been on surfaces coming within the last category.

In dry weather the dust problem is ever present on all roads except in the big towns. In the rainy season there is the possibility of flooding, and on other than the main asphalted roads the use of chains may be necessary. The non-asphalted roads—and occasionally one finds the same conditions on the asphalted roads— nearly always have a corrugated surface; this is best described as indentations traversing the road from 1 to 4 ins. deep, and of varying frequency; add potholes, usually in the most awkward and unexpected places, patches, even stretches of loose soil and stones, particularly on hills, and you have a pretty good picture.

There is only one way to deal with a corrugated surface; take it at a fairly high speed, not less than 35 m.p.h. and up to 50 or over, dependent upon the "frequency" of the corrugation; unfortunately the said frequency varies and speed must be modified accordingly. With practice this becomes second nature, but until acquired may cause alarm and despondency. A satisfactory explanation as to the exact cause of a corrugated surface is not forthcoming; it is generally accepted as due to foundations sinking under traffic in extremes of weather.

A further obstacle not yet encountered to any serious extent is what is known as the middelmannetjie (pronounced middle-monikee), best described as a hump usually in the centre of a narrow road and formed by constant driving over the same tracks; unless care is exercised, especially with a car of low ground clearance, serious damage may result.

Traffic and road regulations are, in the main, the

same as at home. Hand signals are, however, almost essential as few cars are fitted with trafficators, and drivers act accordingly. Parking is a problem in the towns as there are insufficient spaces, and it is only permitted with the car facing the direction of travel— a wise regulation—whilst cutting across or making a U-turn in traffic is an offence. Third-party insurance cover is compulsory. The standard of driving appears no better and no worse than at home and road users, in the main, are courteous and considerate. Despite this view, the incidence of road accidents is high, due partly to carelessness on the part of the pedestrian (both European and non-European) and the inevitable minority of reckless drivers.

Now, still determined to keep off the usual descriptive article, some of the mountain passes and one or two of the high spots are of sufficient interest to warrant comment. The various mountain roads are really remarkable feats of road construction, all impressive and

The Steenbras Reservoir, the main supply to Cape-town, must be seen to be appreciated—an enormous expanse of water amidst mountain and forest, with an approach road from Gordon's Bay of first-gear magnitude.

Montagu radio-active baths and swimming pool, with all the possibilities of a first-class spa—clear, crisp atmosphere and really invigorating—should not be missed.

The Cango Caves at Oudtshoorn, the second largest in the world and a really amazing spectacle, effectively floodlit, should be visited, despite a very bad approach road. Old clothes should be worn as there are one or two strenuous climbs, up narrow chimneys, involved.

The Wilderness, near George, is a scenic memory, the hotel having all recreations literally on the doorstep and gardens of surprising attraction.

The stinkwood forests and coniferous plantations around Knysna and the magnificently wooded gorges on the road to Port Elizabeth are a delight to drive through, despite the continual care which has to be exercised on the narrow, badly surfaced and winding climbs.

ive Thousand

Being Notes and General Comments for Those Interested in Motoring and Other Matters in Cape Province

some—if you are of a nervous disposition or suffer from vertigo—distinctly "wind-upping." The views, however, are just magnificent.

By H. K. Jones

Pass	On road from	Length	Max. altitude	Max. Gradient	Remarks
Bain's Kloof	Wellington to Worcester	18 m.	2000 ft.	1 : 4	Very good surface, sharp bends on northern side.
Michell's Pass	Wellington to Ceres	5 m.	1800 ft.	1 : 4	Good surface, few sharp bends.
Sir Lowry's Pass	Somerset West to Caledon	16 m.	1600 ft.	1 : 6	Very good surface and easy bends.
Chapman's Peak Road	Hout Bay to Kommetje and Fishhoek	5 m.	600 ft.	1 : 6	Fine coastal road, very good surface, sheer drop on one side to sea.
Montagu Pass	George to Oudtshoorn	5 m.	2800 ft.	1 : 3	Extremely bad surface, very narrow, blind corners.
Zwartberg Pass	Oudtshoorn to Prince Albert	25 m.	5000 ft.	1 : 3	Grandfather of all passes; poor surface, narrow, winding and almost a certain "boiler": steep zig-zag on north de.

Sufficient, I trust, to whet the appetite. For the more mundane but none the less essentials:—

Hotels are clean, food good, and refreshment—except Scotch—in abundance. Service is very good and laundry usually on a 48-hour basis. Prices from 12s. to 23s. a day all in, except drinks. The higher price prevails in Capetown only and at some of the seaside resorts during the season. Local gin at 6d. to 9d. per portion is quite good; sherry and light wines at 2s. to 3s. per bottle very good indeed. Local port and brandy is best left alone. Beer is good at 11d. per pint, but even the most argumentative person would not get bellicose on one over the eight. Meals en route can always be obtained without difficulty; lunch from 3s., dinner from 3s. 6d.—and good meals at that. Hotel

The golf course at The Wilderness.
Beyond the railway line, in the
background, is the Indian Ocean.

accommodation can be a problem and booking in advance is advised, especially in towns.

For those with sporting proclivities, all facilities are available, although on occasions the right contact is necessary. The local town hall or equivalent will always assist. Two outstanding golf courses to date outside Cape Town are at George and Port Elizabeth, both really first class.

In general, the shops and stores are extremely well stocked with all classes of goods and commodities (personally I think overstocked, and recent events indicate this) at prices—with the exception of hats and neckties—usually below those prevailing at home and free from restrictions. The fair sex would certainly revel among the array of necessary and luxury articles of equipment available for their particular needs.

The view above is that looking southwards from the top of the Montagu Pass, near George. Left are The Heads, near Knysna, which form the entrance to a large lagoon.

Garage service, not always of a high standard, is readily available. There is no need to carry spare petrol, oil or water as there are stations in abundance, but on the Sabbath opening is on a rota basis and it is as well to fill up beforehand. Strip roads have not yet been encountered; it is gathered that further north they constitute a pleasure and a menace.

To suggest a journey of 300 miles as a casual undertaking appears a little startling at first, but here it is regarded as no hardship and, in actual fact, can be accomplished with ease, as outside the towns little traffic is encountered and a fairly high average can be maintained on the finished roads.

The motoring fraternity will be more interested, however, in the actual vehicle. The market in Cape Province is 85 per cent.—perhaps more—in American hands; understandably so because the American home product is almost ideal for use under conditions which approximate so closely to those prevailing in U.S.A.; is cheap—and there is a lot of " motor car " for your money. General Motors and Ford both have assembly plants at Port Elizabeth, and sufficiently successful to warrant the acquisition of additional land—in each case between 35 and 50 acres—for extensions. Studebaker and Chrysler are also entering the market.

The average resident has, I believe, every sympathy and desire to support British goods, but to take a typical example—a Chevrolet or Ford Mercury at £550 simply cannot be ignored. The equivalent British product as regards seating capacity and general suitability is more than double in price; true, it is better finished, especially if leather upholstered, and has a certain " snob " value.

The present tariff favours the American product. Cars landed at £400 pay a duty of 25 per cent; at £600 and over a duty of 30 per cent. At under £400 the duty is 23s. per 100 lb. weight—and a number of American products come within this category, either by design, fortuitous circumstances, or both. It is believed that the anomaly in the duties will be modified in the near future, but even so there will still be a large price difference in favour of the American product. The smaller British cars are giving splendid service in the town areas and as such are deservedly popular, but in all frankness they cannot be expected to meet the exacting requirements for all-round use.

I am using an Armstrong Siddeley " Typhoon "—the first in the Union. In order to forestall any suggestion of bias, shall I say that it is typical of British products of this class? I have had the opportunity of driving a number of American cars, some of which have yet to make their appearance at home. Let me say immediately that for suspension, road-holding qualities and cornering there is little doubt that the Typhoon is better; but the American car seats six in comfort, has 50 per cent. greater luggage capacity, more power and is half the price. The Typhoon is universally admired and many envious comments engendered, but the price. " Staggering " as one farmer commented,

The First Five Thousand—Contd.

" And I thought England was a poor country." I hope the succinct answer I gave conveyed a satisfactory explanation. Petrol consumption works out at a shade over 21 m.p.g. and oil just under a quart per 1,000 miles. Incidentally, some of the latest American types have experienced odd teething troubles.

May I offer a few suggestions to those intending to visit or settle in this part of the world.

Motorists: If you bring a car out with you, the R.A.C. or A.A. will provide guidance and help, and their offices in Capetown will render all assistance on arrival. Handling, both at Southampton and Cape-town, is inclined to be rough, so be prepared for scratches. Grease all bright parts before dispatch.

Keep the Dust Out

Do all possible to render your vehicles dust-proof. The amount collected in the average boot after a 300-mile journey is unbelievable.

Take particular care to see that all grease used is resistant to tropical conditions, in particular in hubs and steering box.

Unless your sunshine roof is guaranteed dust- and rain-proof—and it really does rain—seal it up. A scuttle ventilator is essential—use if possible the side type opening forward. Heaviest possible tyres, and oversize is an advantage. Do not use synthetic under any circumstances. Check tyre pressures frequently; I run at 28 lb. pressure and find a buildup to 31 after

some of the wide, deep gulleys at entrances to hotels and private houses.

If an American car, you will find service depots everywhere. If British, rely upon the agent (usually very good) and the Lucas and Dunlop depots, which are in all large centres.

Comments perhaps of general interest:—

Travel light. You can buy anything you are likely to require without difficulty. Shortages? Yes, soap and Scotch; bring the former—give up the latter until conditions improve, or drink Irish or Canadian.

Dinner jacket, used infrequently, but necessary on occasions. Overcoat unnecessary to date, but good raincoat essential and, if lined, overcoat could probably be dispensed with. Drought is a serious problem in South Africa, and you may find water supplies cut off for as much as 16 hours per day in some parts. Bathing is not up to home seaside standards—you are warned to beware of rocks, backwash, currents, sharks, or all four. You will find a coloured problem in South Africa; don't try and solve it; it will take you three months to grasp the outline of this and the political situation, and another three to understand.

If you are an intending immigrant, please prepare for some difficulties. The artisan and skilled craftsman, if a real worker, can earn up to £60 per month, or even more, and taxation is on a lower scale. Cost of living is, I think, lower than at home, but there is, if anything, a more serious shortage of accommodation—and living under crowded conditions in hot weather is anything but fun. The posters and pamphlets present an

The Humewood beach at Port Elizabeth; the bathing along this stretch of beach was the safest encountered.

50 miles. If the road is really bad, keep the pressure down; dry skids are fairly frequent on the loose surface roads. It is not necessary to carry other than the standard tool-kit, plus an efficient wrench for wheel nuts and a wooden block or blocks as a jack base. If you can, get an accessory known as the Kool-Kushion —a light but stiff fabric cover with ventilation space for the front seats; this is invaluable in hot weather.

If you can afford to pick and choose your own car, I would humbly but firmly suggest special attention to:—

  (a) Independent front suspension; essential for general touring conditions.
  (b) Not less than 20 h.p. I am not so dogmatic here as the Typhoon has markedly increased my respect for a 16 h.p. car, but on the long mountain passes low gear is continually employed.
  (c) Adequate cooling capacity for the motor. With sun temperatures of over 100, and even up to 115, this is important. If in doubt seek expert advice and modify fan and capacity.
  (d) High ground clearance all round. The Typhoon rear bumper is liable to touch passing over

attractive aspect, but there is invariably another side.

If you are going on the land, you must have some capital and know your job—and as an owner-farmer, thousands are better than hundreds. Farming can be a very lonely and heart-breaking occupation in some parts of the Union, and land is certainly not cheap at the moment. On the other hand, there is a ready market—probably stable for some years—for all your production. Don't come out as a clerical or pro-fessional worker unless you have your job fixed up beforehand; it just isn't worth it unless you have capital resources. There is a shortage of really good female office workers, but salaries of £28 to £35 per month are not uncommon.

The climate is good, despite the Cape South-Easter, and even in Winter the sun shines. The country is ideal for the traveller/tourist and holds a promising future for the energetic skilled worker and agriculturist. I have done little more than lightly touch upon some aspects. If any reader is seriously interested and would like further advice, write to me care of The Editor, indicating the problem, and without making a definite promise, I will do my best to provide guidance.

No. 1349

2-LITRE

ARMSTRONG

SIDDELEY

SALOON

The Autocar ROAD TESTS

DATA FOR THE DRIVER

2-LITRE ARMSTRONG SIDDELEY

PRICE (in Great Britain), with Typhoon two-door sports saloon body, £975, plus £271 11s 8d British purchase tax. Total, £1,246 11s 8d.

RATING : 15.72 h.p., 6 cylinders, overhead valves, 65 × 100 mm, 1,991 c.c.

TAX (in Great Britain) : £10.

BRAKE HORSE-POWER : 70 at 4,200 r.p.m. **COMPRESSION RATIO :** 7 to 1.

WEIGHT, without passengers : 27 cwt. LB. per C.C. : 1.52.

TYRE SIZE : 5.50 × 17in on bolt-on steel disc wheels.

LIGHTING SET : 12-volt. Automatic voltage control.

TANK CAPACITY : 12 gallons : approx. fuel consumption range, 18–21 m.p.g.

TURNING CIRCLE : (R) 37ft ; (L) 39ft. **MIN. GROUND CLEARANCE :** 6½in.

MAIN DIMENSIONS : Wheelbase, 9ft 7in. Track, 4ft 6in (front) ; 4ft 6½in (rear). Overall length, 15ft 2in ; width, 5ft 8in ; height, 5ft 2in.

ACCELERATION

Overall gear ratios	From steady m.p.h. of		
	10 to 30	20 to 40	30 to 50
5.10 to 1	13.1 sec.	13.9 sec.	15.7 sec.
7.24 to 1	9.2 sec.	9.7 sec.	11.8 sec.
10.89 to 1	6.2 sec.	—	—
17.61 to 1	—	—	—

From rest through gears to :—

30 m.p.h.	..	..	..	7.6 sec.
50 m.p.h.	..	..	..	19.5 sec.
60 m.p.h.	..	..	..	29.7 sec.

Steering wheel movement from lock to lock : 4⅜ turns.

Speedometer correction by Electrical Speedometer :

Car Speedometer		Electrical Speedometer
10	=	12
20	=	20
30	=	29
40	=	37
50	=	47
60	=	56
70	=	66

Speeds attainable on indirect gears (by Electrical Speedometer) :

			M.p.h. (normal and max.)
1st	..	..	12–20
2nd	..	..	23–34
3rd	..	..	42–55

WEATHER : Dry, cold ; wind fresh.

Acceleration figures are the means of several runs in opposite directions.

Current model described in " The Autocar " of December 14, 1945, and August 16, 1946.

THIS is one of Britain's new designs introduced since the war, bold and handsome in outward appearance ; comfortable and stable with independent front suspension by means of torsion bars. Already this new postwar type of Armstrong Siddeley is familiar on British roads as well as in many overseas territories. Besides representing an advance in design, it marked a decided departure in appearance for the make in question, resulting in a car that is distinctive yet restrained and still essentially British in the best sense. It is a car for the connoisseur who seeks quality in unseen as well as visible things ; who wants performance but who is also interested in the smoothness and quietness with which the performance is achieved.

The six-cylinder overhead valve engine shows up admirably in these respects, gives the car a good top gear performance, an easy cruising rate as high as 60 m.p.h. if required, and, as a corollary thereto, effortless running of

inherent quality at the more generally used rates up to 50 m.p.h. As soon as one sits at the steering wheel and lets in the clutch that quality is sensed, and never over a period of a week's trial of the car, taking in several hundred miles of varying conditions, was this initial impression retracted. Rather, indeed, can it be said without exaggeration that it was strengthened with experience. All that this car does it achieves well and pleasingly ; and it does much in terms of sheer performance, besides appealing by its air of luxury.

To handle it is a pleasure in itself because of the smooth and easy way in which the controls operate and the efficient responses which they evoke from the various mechanical components. There is a feeling of solidity about the car and it rides exceedingly well, softly yet safely. The comfort of travel in the back seats is particularly commented upon by passengers who possess experience of many different cars under similar conditions.

It is an exceedingly satisfactory car in which to potter around gently, whilst, on a definite journey, very good times can be made without tiring the driver or passengers. Indeed, it is a decidedly fast car from point to point. In this connection it may be mentioned that an average of between 47 and 48 m.p.h. was recorded over a familiar route of approximately 100 miles, and this at night. Certainly conditions on British roads at the moment are favourable to average speed performance, but it has been convincingly demonstrated that the Armstrong Siddeley shows up well on a fast run, holding one speed just as well as another without fuss or protest right up to a genuine 70 m.p.h., a speed which is readily obtained on any suitable stretch of road. The highest speedometer reading seen, with an above-average length of clear road available, was 79, representing a true speed of approximately 75 m.p.h. That figure is above what would be regarded as the normally used speed range of the car, but denotes that it has a useful margin of reserve, and beyond what might be expected at first acquaintance.

Quiet and Easy Travel

Mechanically it is a quiet car, this applying to the gears and rear axle as well as to the engine, but at the higher speeds there is some wind noise. It should be added that particularly strong winds were blowing during part of the test, which, of course, would accentuate any such effect. This car's easy progress is entirely free from any drumming tendency. The driver at once appreciates a thin-rimmed steering wheel, inclined more nearly to the vertical than is general practice, and a separate seat which, whilst its back rest is not shaped to the shoulders, gives firm support where it is needed. The leg position, too, is comfortable, with plenty of room for the left leg clear of the clutch pedal. The outward view is good over a fairly long bonnet, with the off-side wing visible, but not the near-side one.

The car tested had the Typhoon two-door sports saloon body, which is of what used to be commonly called the close-coupled type. Also available, of course, on the same chassis are the Lancaster four-door saloon and the Hurricane drop-head coupé.

Steering, braking—the Girling hydro-mechanical system is used, with hydraulic operation on the front wheels only —gear change and road-holding make up a whole, from

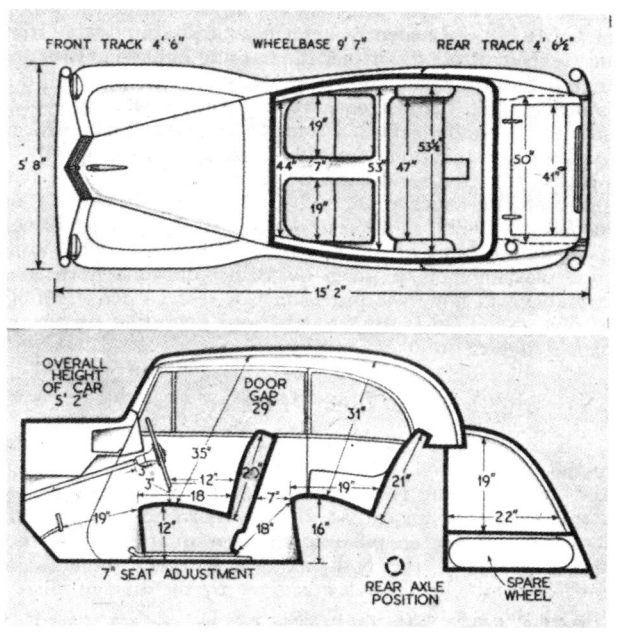

Measurements are taken with the driving seat at the central position of fore and aft adjustment. These body diagrams are to scale.

the handling point of view, which is thoroughly satisfactory, quickly affording confidence that the car is under safe and accurate control. There is a fine feeling of balance on corners, and the car can be swung round bends at speed with only a light hold on the steering wheel and without yawing or rolling. At speed no special concentration is needed to keep on a course. The steering has marked castor action. It is not heavy steering on a sharp corner or when manœuvring, being quite low geared, but for this reason considerable wheel movement is called for at such times. The brakes require fair pedal pressure for maximum results and come on very smoothly with all the power that is wanted for fast driving and emergencies. The hand-brake control is of pull and push type, set conveniently under the instrument panel. Either a synchromesh gear box, as on the car that has been tested, or a pre-selector box, as fitted to Armstrong Siddeley cars before the war, is available. The synchromesh is very effective and the gear change is pleasing.

Hill-climbing Abilities

Although the car is not light in total weight in relation to its engine capacity, the performance range on top gear is good, and even on the present fuel there is only slight pinking when accelerating. In the middle range of speed, from about 35 m.p.h. onwards, the engine really takes hold and sends the speed soaring swiftly into the sixties, carrying the car over gradients in average country with little reduction in speed. Because of the characteristics of the performance no special benefit is obtained from driving this car "on the gears" for acceleration purposes. It would be a particularly severe hill to require lower than second gear. Such is the general performance that there is an impression of the engine being larger than its actual two litres, for it produces a good power output and takes the car quickly up to its fast cruising rate.

An excellent form of telescopic adjustment for the steering wheel by means of a rotating sleeve is appreciated, and the driver can find just the wheel setting that he likes—a position giving a strong feeling of command over the car. The instruments and minor controls are grouped especially compactly, the instruments being simplified to speedometer, oil pressure gauge and petrol gauge, immediately in front of the driver. In addition to the internal illumination of the

The leather upholstery is of excellent quality and attractive in appearance, with horizontal pleats. The adjusting sleeve for the steering wheel will be noticed. The wheel is more nearly vertical than is usual nowadays, giving, in conjunction with a fairly upright back rest to the seat, a most satisfactory driving position. In this two-door Typhoon saloon the front seat back rests tilt forward to allow back passengers to get in and out.

dials, there is a light which shows up the ignition key hole and switches conveniently. It is practically impossible from inside the car to tell whether the parking lights incorporated in the built-in head lamps are on or not, and a tell-tale is provided on the instrument panel which lights up should either of these bulbs fail. From the average speed performance already mentioned in after-dark conditions, it will be realized that the head-lamp beam is good, though it falls short of the superlative. The anti-dazzle control is by means of a switch at the centre of the steering wheel, which has only one bank of spokes. An excellent and at the same time pleasing note is given by twin wind-tone horns. A valuable and now rare provision is a reserve petrol supply of one gallon, instantly brought into operation by means of a switch in front of the driver.

A Light Interior

The interior of the car is light and cheerful by reason of the use of a light-coloured material for the head lining, and also from the fact that the body has no wide pillars at the sides, but instead an almost unbroken area of glass from the windscreen pillar to the rear quarter. The roof and windscreen are both fixed. A good though not entirely comprehensive view is given by the driving mirror, and at the centre of the mirror is a neatly built-in clock. The mirror is of tinted glass which minimizes dazzle from behind at night in the absence, as seems to be becoming increasingly the current practice, of a rear window blind. The rear window itself is of considerable area, helping again towards the effect of lightness within the interior, and also giving good visibility astern. Above the windscreen are anti-sunglare vizors, the one in front of the passenger being provided with a mirror on the inside.

Draughtfree ventilation is something of a problem in two-door bodies with wide doors, and is looked after in the Typhoon by means of pivoting panels at the front, which can be opened while leaving the main window closed. There is a Clayton Dewandre interior heating and de-misting and de-icing installation. This is most efficient in keeping the driver and passengers warm, and also it supplies an ample volume of warm air to the inside of the windscreen through built-in conduits. The rear seat is found to be amply wide for three adult passengers. There are softly upholstered elbow rests, and a single folding arm rest for use by only one or two people using the back seat.

A detail point indicative of the nature of the fittings is the provision in the front compartment of what can only

The under-bonnet layout is neat as well as accessible. The connections for the interior heater are in metal and tidier than is usual. Also well placed is the reservoir for the front hydraulic brakes—the rear brakes are mechanically operated.

be called a tool portfolio, a withdrawable well-finished case with snap fastener, holding the usual small tools, whilst those for wheel changing are carried on the inside of the hinged panel which houses the built-in rear number plate and tail and stop lamps. Jacking is carried out by applying a short flat handle to the permanently attached jacks, the heads of which are reached through trap doors conveniently placed in the front compartment floor; lifting the trap door brings the required jack into the operating position.

Under the bonnet, which opens up from the front and is held by a strut, the engine itself and its auxiliaries are particularly neat and well finished, even the connecting pipes to the interior heater being unusually well done. There is a large oil filler in the top of the valve gear cover. Automatic choking for starting from cold is used, and at all times during the test the engine fired instantly.

This Armstrong Siddeley undoubtedly maintains the traditions which have been built up by the make over the years as well-made cars with an atmosphere about them, which in some respects is indefinable and which belongs only to the better kind of British car.

Below: The luggage boot is of generous size, unencumbered by the spare wheel, which is carried in a separate compartment behind the panel housing the built-in number plate. This can be moved, together with the bumper, after thumb nuts have been undone.

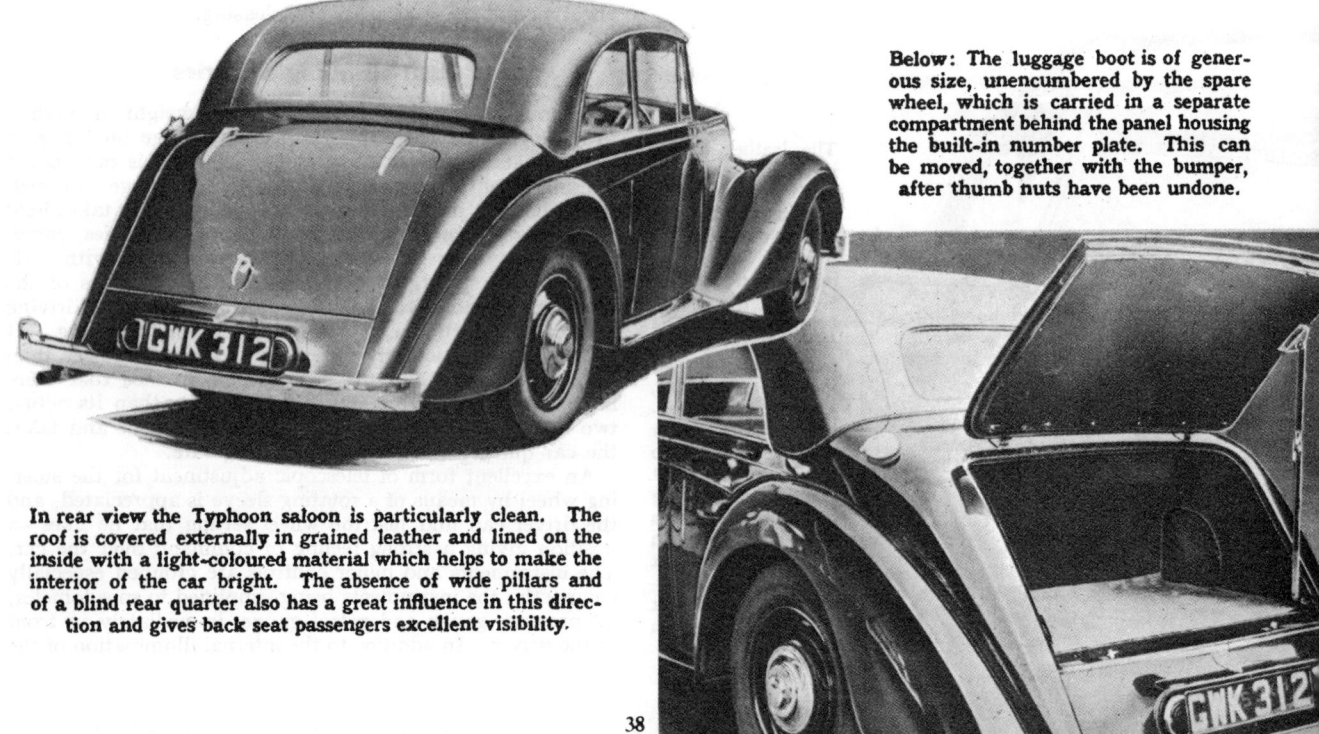

In rear view the Typhoon saloon is particularly clean. The roof is covered externally in grained leather and lined on the inside with a light-coloured material which helps to make the interior of the car bright. The absence of wide pillars and of a blind rear quarter also has a great influence in this direction and gives back seat passengers excellent visibility.

Armstrong Siddeley Sixteen

2-litre, 1946-48

Articles in this series are written by the Technical Staff of " The Motor Trader" and checked by the service managers of the vehicle manufacturers or importers.

Manufacturers : Armstrong Siddeley Motors, Ltd., Parkside, Coventry.

INTRODUCED in 1946, the two-litre model has nothing in common with the pre-war Sixteen except the hypoid rear axle and the basic design of the engine. Even the pre-selector gearbox, when fitted, is of a different pattern. A synchromesh gearbox and normal clutch are available as an alternative. The three body styles—Lancaster saloon, Hurricane drop-head coupé and Typhoon fixed head coupé—are identical as regards service.

Chassis and engine numbers consist of six figures, the first two, 16, indicating the horsepower. The rest are a serial number, which is not necessarily the same for engine and chassis. Engine numbers are prefixed E. The cars are produced in series, each batch of 1,000 being given series letters ZA, ZB, ZC and so on. The post-war series started at ZG. Series letters are used as a prefix for chassis numbers, and are stamped on a plate on the front of the scuttle with the body number. The engine number is stamped on the nearside front mounting bracket boss.

Instruments and controls :

1. Heater rheostat control.
2. Screenwiper control.
3. Mirror clock.
4. Ignition warning light.
5. Petrol gauge.
6. Speedometer.
7. Trafficator switch.
8. Oil pressure gauge.
9. Side lamp warning light.
10. Panel light switch.
11. Starter switch.
12. Petrol reserve switch.
13. Lighting switch.
14. Ignition switch.
15. Handbrake lever.
16. Accelerator.
17. Choke (with preselector gearbox only).
18. Brake pedal.
19. Dipper switch.
20. Clutch pedal.
21. Horn push.
22. Gear control (preselector).
23. Gear lever (synchromesh).

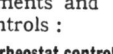

SPECIAL TOOLS		
Extractors for king pin swivel balls ...		GT5374
Extractor for front suspension lower link arm		ST3887
Anvil for riveting timing chain ...		GT5175

Certain important modifications have been carried out and are listed here. Owing to supply difficulties they have been adopted according to circumstances, and it is therefore not possible to quote accurately the chassis numbers at which the changes took place.

ENGINEERING CHANGES

Thermostat, added in cooling system.
Dry cylinder liners standardized.
Two-piece lining adopted for front brake shoes.
Burman F-type steering introduced.
Timing chain tensioner added.
Gearbox (synchro) mainshaft modified for location of third gear.
Lucas RF95 control box replaced RF91.
Twin silencer system introduced.

Special tools are not needed for normal service, except for two operations on the front suspension and for riveting the timing chain. Without these tools it is difficult to avoid damaging the parts. B.S.F. threads and hexagons are standard, except for the rear axle, on which S.A.E. threads are used.

ENGINE DATA			
No. of cylinders			6
Bore and stroke : mm			65 × 100
in			2.559 × 3.937
Capacity : c.c.			1991
cu in ...			121.49
R.A.C. rated h.p.			15.72
Max. b.h.p. at r.p.m. ...			70 at 4200
Max. torque (lb/ft) at r.p.m. ...			95 at 2500
Compression ratio			7.0 : 1
Compression pressure at cranking speed			130 lb/sq in
Firing order			1 5 3 6 2 4

LANCASTER

HURRICANE

DISTINGUISHING FEATURES.—All three models are similar in front view. Hurricane drop-head coupé and Typhoon fixed head coupé are identical except for hood. Lancaster saloon has bottom-hinged locker lid

ENGINE

MOUNTING

Four points. Brackets bolted to front of crankcase and to sides of flywheel housing rest on rubber blocks. Bolts pass right through, with springs between nuts and chassis frame brackets. Tighten nuts until springs have $\frac{1}{16}$in clearance before becoming close-coiled, and split pin.

Packing pieces are used to line up engine-gearbox unit with rear axle to give straight drive with two normal passengers in rear seat.

REMOVAL

Remove bonnet. Drain radiator and engine. Disconnect and remove radiator with support bracket, leaving grille in place. Remove starter, air cleaner, oil filter and starting handle guide bracket. Disconnect all pipes, wires and controls, and take off four mounting bolt nuts. Remove front seats, floorboards and gearbox cowl. Disconnect speedo drive from gearbox, and selector control cable from preselector gearbox. Remove propeller shaft completely, detach gearbox at bell-housing flange and lift out. Sling engine at front and rear, with wooden spreader to prevent slings fouling ignition cable cover, and lift out.

CYLINDER HEAD

Induction manifold cast in head and machined. Ends closed by plugs. Baffle at centre, inserted from side and retained by cover plate, which is dowelled to it and located on manifold stud. Note spring washer between baffle and plate, which is retained by centre manifold clamp. Baffle tapped $\frac{1}{4}$in B.S.F. for extractor.

Induction and exhaust manifolds separate, bolted together at hot spot. If manifolds are separated note on re-assembling that dished plate is present in recess in exhaust manifold, and registering with drain elbow.

CRANKSHAFT

Four main bearings. Thin wall, steel-backed, white metal-lined shells located by tabs. End float controlled by split thrust washers recessed in either side of rear main bearing and located by tabs in cap. No hand fitting permissible.

Main bearing half shells not interchangeable top to bottom. Caps numbered on off side, towards numbers on crankcase. Caps tapped $\frac{1}{4}$in B.S.F.

Thrust washers and bearing shells can be changed with crankshaft in place, but for bearing shells this practice should only be used in emergency.

Flywheel bolted to register on rear flange of shaft with six fitted bolts inserted from front and tab washered. Starter ring gear shrunk on and locked by six screwed pegs. Ball spigot bearing retained in end of crankshaft by plate for synchro gearboxes only.

Split flywheel housing, bolted to rear of crankcase, fits round oil return thread on crankshaft. Halves held together by two long vertical bolts and two setscrews. When assembling tighten these first, and tighten setscrews to crankcase when .004-.006in clearance at oil return thread has been checked. Bottom half only of flywheel housing need be removed for crankshaft removal.

Torsional vibration damper inside timing cover at front end is in four parts. Inner half of hub screwed with cheesehead screws to timing sprocket, which is keyed to shaft with Woodruff key. Friction ring mounted on inner half of hub, followed by pressure plate and six springs. Combined retaining plate and hand starter dog, spigoted on end of shaft and in pressure plate, has oil return thread on outer edge, running in hole in timing cover. Assembly retained on shaft by cap nut inside starter dog, screwed on to stud on end of shaft. Fan pulley spigoted on dog and retained by setscrews.

CONNECTING RODS

Big ends thin wall, steel-backed, white metal-lined shells located by tabs. No hand fitting permissible.

Small ends bronze bushed.

CRANKSHAFT AND CONNECTING ROD DATA				
	Main bearings			Crankpins
	No. 1	Nos. 2 & 3	No. 4	
Diameter Length	2$\frac{1}{4}$in 1.55 in	2$\frac{1}{4}$in 1.65 in	2$\frac{1}{2}$in 2.0 in	1$\frac{13}{16}$in 1.30 in
Running clearance : main bearings ... ... big ends				.0015-.0035in .0015-.003in
End float : main bearings ... big ends ...				.004 -.008in .0055-.008in
Undersizes				.020, .030in
No. of teeth on starter ring gear/pinion				96/10
Con. rod centres				7.0in

Two-litre engine in section

PISTONS

Nelson Bohnalite invar strut. Gudgeon pins located by spring rings.

Big ends will not pass through bores, and pistons will not pass crank throws. Crankshaft must be taken out to remove piston.

PISTON DATA		
Clearance (bottom of skirt)		.0015–.003in
Oversizes		.005, .010, .015, .020, .025, .030in
Weight (with rings and pin)		12oz 7dr
Gudgeon pin :		
diameter ...		⅞in
fit in piston		Tight push cold
fit in con rod		Easy sliding cold
Compression height ...		1.5748in (40 mm)
	Compression	Oil control
No. of rings	2	1 plain 1 slotted
Gap	.006–.010in	.006–.010in
Side clearance in groove...	.001–.003in	.001–.003in
Width of rings ...	⁵⁄₆₄in	⅛in

CAMSHAFT

Duplex roller endless chain drive with soft pins in one link, identified by hand riveting.

Camshaft sprocket keyed with Woodruff key and retained by nut. Latest sprockets incorporate chain tensioner consisting of L-section spring rings located outside sprocket teeth by dished retaining plates riveted through sprocket. Side plates of chain run on spring ring for tension.

Camshaft runs in four white metal-lined thin steel bushes pressed into crankcase. End float controlled by thrust plate trapped between sprocket and shoulder on shaft, and bolted to crankcase with shims (.005in thick) for chain alignment.

CAMSHAFT DATA			
	No. 1	Nos. 2 & 3	No. 4
Bearing journal :			
diameter ...	1⅜in	1⅜in	1½in
length ...	1.25in	1.15in	1.20in
Bearing clearance ...	.001—.00275in		
End float	.003—.007in		
Timing chain :			
make ...	Renold		
type ...	Duplex No. 114036		
pitch ...	⅜		
No. of pitches ...	60		

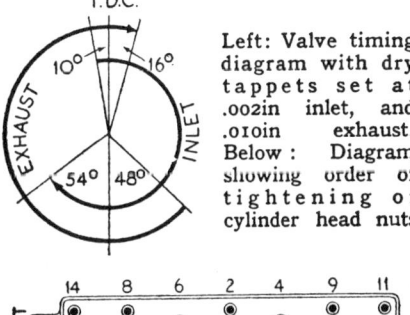

T.D.C.

Left: Valve timing diagram with dry tappets set at .002in inlet, and .010in exhaust. Below : Diagram showing order of tightening of cylinder head nuts

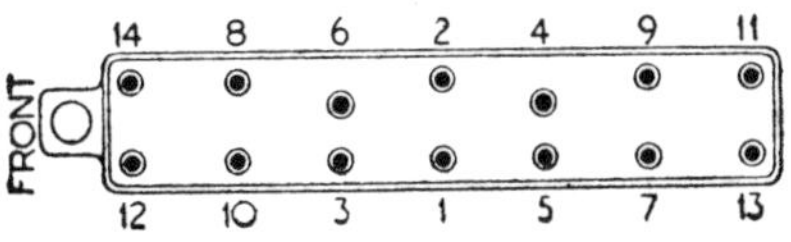

To remove chain take out plug in back of timing case on off side. Turn chain until soft pins are opposite hole, and file until they can be driven out. When refitting chain line up timing marks scribed on sprockets and fit chain so that ends come opposite plug hole. Insert new link through hole, and screw in special anvil, on which pins can be riveted. If special anvil is not available turn chain until flat steel block, such as set-spanner, can be inserted between chain and crankcase.

Camshaft can be removed with engine in place. Remove radiator core and grille, crankshaft pulley, timing cover and chain. Dismantle damper. Remove rocker gear, push rods and tappet blocks, distributor, sump and oil pump. Camshaft can then be drawn out with thrust plate.

To check timing empty hydraulic tappet. To do this extract push rods for No. 1 cylinder and turn engine until oil pressure pushes hydraulic elements out of tappets. Empty oil by opening ball valve with thin rod. Thoroughly dry out tappet. Disconnect oil feed from No. 1 tappet block and put hydraulic elements and push rods back. Set No. 1 inlet valve clearance to .002in, and exhaust to .010in with hydraulic plunger spring fully compressed. Follow timing diagram. Reset valve clearance to .075in with hydraulic plunger spring fully compressed, then re-connect oil feed to tappet block. When engine is run, oil pressure will take up clearance.

VALVES

Overhead, not interchangeable, inlet larger than exhaust (marked on stems). Split cotter fixing, double springs. Spring cups register on valve guide ends. Guides renewable, shouldered. Exhaust guides longer.

VALVE DATA			
		Inlet	Exhaust
Head diameter		1.325in	1.30in
Stem diameter		⁵⁄₁₆in	⁵⁄₁₆in
Face angle		45 deg	45 deg
		Inner	Outer
Spring length :			
free		2.00in	1.95in
fitted		1.55in	1.40in
at load		33lb	62lb

TAPPETS AND ROCKERS

Mushroom tappets in three blocks of four bolted to crankcase with flanged sleeve dowels. Zero Lash hydraulic self-adjusting tappet elements fit inside tappet bodies, and will fall out if tappet is inverted. Oil feed to T-piece on each tappet block from main gallery on near side.

If hydraulic tappets are taken apart, greatest possible care must be

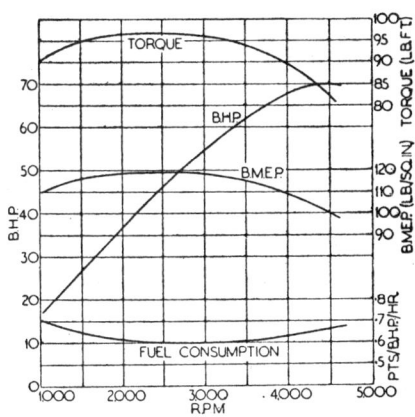

taken to keep dirt out. Pieces must be washed in trichlorethyline and reassembled dry. Plungers must be fitted in original cylinders.

Rocker shaft carried in seven pillars and located by studs. Rockers are bushed and are of two types, inclined left- and right-hand, each pair separated by spring. Pillars Nos. 1, 2, 4, 6 and 7 have stud on near side of shaft, Nos. 3 and 5 have stud on off side. Rear (No. 7) pillar drilled for oil feed, fits on smaller stud.

Push rods numbered for correct assembly cannot be extracted without removal of rocker gear.

LUBRICATION

Gear pump in sump. Integral drive housing spigoted in crankcase and flange-bolted.

To dismantle pump undo nut at lower end of shaft and detach cover. Tip out driven gear and tap out spindle after extracting split pin. Tap end of shaft gently until end of thread is flush with driving gear—no more—then lever gear off and extract Woodruff key. Shaft with integral skew gear can then be drawn out. Driving and driven gears are similar, but can be identified by two oil grooves in driven gear and keyway in driving gear. Shaft runs directly in housing.

Floating gauze suction strainer pivoted on pump body.

Oil delivered by pipe and through drilling in crankcase to Tecalemit full flow filter on near side. Filter bypass valve assembly screwed into top of filter body. From filter oil is delivered to gallery in crankcase from which main and camshaft bearings are fed. Lead to hydraulic tappets taken off gallery near front, through small cylindrical fine mesh filter. Access to filter by removing breather pipe and undoing plug behind. When refitting put blank end in cap, and screw in.

Adjustable spring-loaded ball relief valve assembly screwed into near side of crankcase just in front of starter, and covered by cap nut. Remove assembly complete for cleaning. Oil pressure at normal speed 40 lb/sq in.

IGNITION

Distributor with centrifugal control, and gear pinned on shaft, located by clamp plate in drive housing.

Set points to break three teeth on flywheel before T.D.C.1/6 mark (punch marks on top of ring gear tooth, visible through trap on off side of flywheel housing).

IGNITION DATA	
(All degrees on flywheel rotation)	
Advance range, centrifugal ...	18–22°
Advance starts (crank r.p.m.) ...	650
Max. advance (r.p.m.) ...	3000
Firing point	10° before T.D.C.
Contact breaker gap	.012in
Sparking plugs : make	Champion
type	L10 (offset)
size	14 mm
gap	.018in

COOLING SYSTEM

Pump, fan and non-adjustable thermostat (added to later cars). Pump bolted to front of cylinder block, can be detached with fan.

Adjustable packing gland. To adjust slacken locking setscrew (near bottom of pump body on near side) and tighten gland nut with screwdriver.

To renew packing dismantle pump. Detach fan blades and draw off pulley and centre disc (Woodruff key). Slacken gland nut and tap out shaft, with impeller keyed and pressed on rear end. Extract locking ring and unscrew fan bearing retaining cap nut. Ball bearing in housing can be extracted.

Seal consists of two gland packings separated by gland ring (drilled for grease). Outer gland goes inside gland nut. These parts should be threaded over shaft when it is in place. When gland nut is on, slide on thrower disc (edge turned to rear) and distance-piece, followed by ball bearing in housing. If bearing is renewed see that sealed side is inwards. When fitting locking ring see that free end points towards direction of rotation.

Adjust belt by swinging dynamo until there is $\frac{1}{2}$in movement either way.

FUEL SYSTEM DATA		
Carburettor : make		Stromberg
type : with synchro		DBVA-36
with preselector		DAV-36
Settings : Choke tube		$1\frac{1}{32}$in
Main jet		.049
Bypass jet... ...		.036in
Main dis. jet		EX 943
High speed bleed		68
Idle tube		68–75
Idle discharge		68–54
Needle seat		.1in
Float level... ...		$\frac{11}{16}$ in
Pump jet		70
Pump stroke		S
Vacuum kick		32
Fast idle		67
Thermostat		18
Air cleaner : make		AC
type		1574457
Fuel pump : make		AC
type		1524488
pressure		$1\frac{1}{2}$-2lb

TRANSMISSION

CLUTCH

Synchromesh.—Borg & Beck single dry plate, spring centre. Graphite thrust release bearing. Only adjustment on rear end of pedal pull rod, to give 1in free movement at pedal pad.

Preselector. — Newton centrifugal with no external control. Only normal adjustment is for clearance of centre plate when disengaged, by three large studs with locknuts on backplate (access through inspection hole in top of bell-housing). Clearance between centre plate and pressure plate, with centre plate against flywheel, should be .025-.030in all round.

GEARBOX

Four-speed, with synchromesh on 2nd, 3rd and top gears. Constant mesh 1st gear. Preselector gearbox alternative.

To dismantle synchro gearbox remove top cover with lever, selector

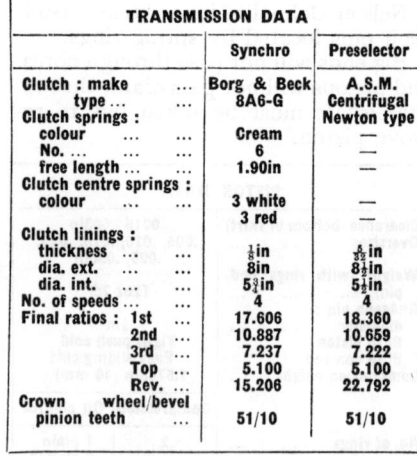

rods and forks, and bell-housing. Undo driving flange nut, holding flange with bar. Draw off flange and remove rear cover. Take out layshaft spindle setscrew (bottom rear) and draw spindle out to rear, when layshaft cluster will drop to bottom of box. Drawhole ($\frac{3}{8}$in B.S.F.) in rear end of spindle. Drive mainshaft forward, making sure that gears are clear of layshaft, but do not remove primary shaft yet. Insert distance-piece $\frac{5}{8}$in thick between 1st gear and back of box (make up horse-shoe plate with

sides bent back to depth of $\frac{5}{8}$in, gap being $1\frac{3}{8}$in wide and $3\frac{1}{4}$in deep), and drive primary shaft back until mainshaft rear ball bearing can be drawn off. Hold mainshaft in place and drive out primary shaft with ball bearing. Mainshaft can then be lifted out through top. Clearance cut in top joint face of box. While driving mainshaft forward and lifting out, take care to hold 1st and reverse gears together to prevent split collar, which locates 1st gear bush, falling out.

Synchromesh gearbox in section

To dismantle mainshaft slide off top and 3rd synchro unit, 1st gear and bush (catching split collar) and 1st and 2nd synchro unit with sliding reverse gear. Extract spring ring and tab-washer locating splined thrust washer inside 3rd gear cone. Third gear, flanged bush, 2nd gear and rear thrust washer can then be slid off.

Before assembling box test layshaft assembly for end float (.006-.010in).

When bolting up bell-housing and rear cover note large washer between rear bearing and driving flange. Fit shims in bearing locations so that when nuts are finger-tight .002in feeler can just be inserted between faces.

TRANSMISSION DATA		Synchro	Preselector
Clutch : make ...		Borg & Beck	A.S.M.
type ...		8A6-G	Centrifugal Newton type
Clutch springs :			
colour		Cream	—
No.		6	—
free length ...		1.90in	—
Clutch centre springs :			
colour		3 white	—
		3 red	—
Clutch linings :			
thickness ...		$\frac{1}{8}$in	$\frac{1}{8}$in
dia. ext. ...		8in	$8\frac{1}{2}$in
dia. int. ...		$5\frac{3}{4}$in	$5\frac{1}{2}$in
No. of speeds		4	4
Final ratios : 1st		17.606	18.360
2nd		10.887	10.659
3rd		7.237	7.222
Top		5.100	5.100
Rev. ...		15.206	22.792
Crown wheel/bevel pinion teeth ...		51/10	51/10

To Adjust Preselector Gearbox.—If gear tends to slip, increase toggle action. Remove top cover and make sure that slipping gear is not engaged. Slacken locknut, screw *in* adjuster stop screw ¼ turn, and lock. Lift eye and loop of automatic adjuster nut spring off pegs, and unscrew adjuster nut ½ turn (use ⅜in B.S.F. bolt and locknut). Refit spring loop and eye. Select gear which has been adjusted, and pump pedal until adjuster nut stops turning.

If pedal becomes heavy or gear engagement is harsh, decrease toggle action. Slacken locknut, screw *out* adjuster stop screw one turn, and lock. Select gear and pump pedal, seeing that adjuster nut turns.

To Dismantle Preselector Gearbox remove top cover and unscrew three spring cap setscrews evenly. Remove cap, shims, spring and guides. Remove side cover with camshaft. Take off five automatic adjuster springs, unscrew nuts (⅜in B.S.F. setscrew and locknut) and lift off rings and tables. Take out thrust pad assemblies and top gear pull rod. Remove seven nuts inside bell-housing, and tap off housing with input shaft and front ball bearing. Draw out outer member, actuating ring, cone and bearing of top gear clutch, guiding strut past casing. Running gear can now be removed piece by piece. Note carefully positions of various bushes and washers. If reverse drum is tight in centre ball bearing, undo rear cover nuts and tap output shaft to rear with flange, oil seal and ball bearing.

If baseplate, with brake band assembly, is removed, note ball valve of oil pump, located in front edge of base. Before detaching base take out screw attaching top gear hooks to box.

To dismantle bell-housing and oil pump assembly detach oil seal housing, undo shaft ring-nut and prise off front cover with outer ball bearing, tapping shaft forward to break joint. Pump eccentric (keyed), plunger and pump body can then be withdrawn. Front bearing held in bell-housing by locking ring with left-hand thread.

To Reassemble Preselector Gearbox assemble input shaft, oil pump and top gear clutch on bell-housing, and place assembly on bench with input shaft vertical. Assemble running gear on input shaft ready to insert into box when baseplate and brake drum assembly have been fitted. Jointing compound should be used on all faces.

PROPELLER SHAFT

Hardy Spicer, needle roller bearing universal joints. Nipples for lubrication of joints. Shafts used with synchro and preselector gear boxes not interchangeable.

REAR AXLE

Salisbury type 2HA (41) hypoid bevel drive, semi-floating shafts.

To remove axle from car jack up in front of rear wheels separately and under middle of axle casing. Remove wheels and disconnect propeller shaft rear end. Support springs with two small jacks. Remove hub grease pipe assemblies (if fitted) and undo spring U-bolts. Draw off brake drums and hubs. Disconnect brake rods from compensator, and detach brake backplates (five nuts outside each), lifting off with shoes, rods and oil seal retainer. Note shims behind each backplate. Detach check straps. Push axle through springs until one end is clear, lower and pull out to side.

Hubs keyed on taper shafts. Taper roller bearings in axle tube ends, retained by backplates with shims

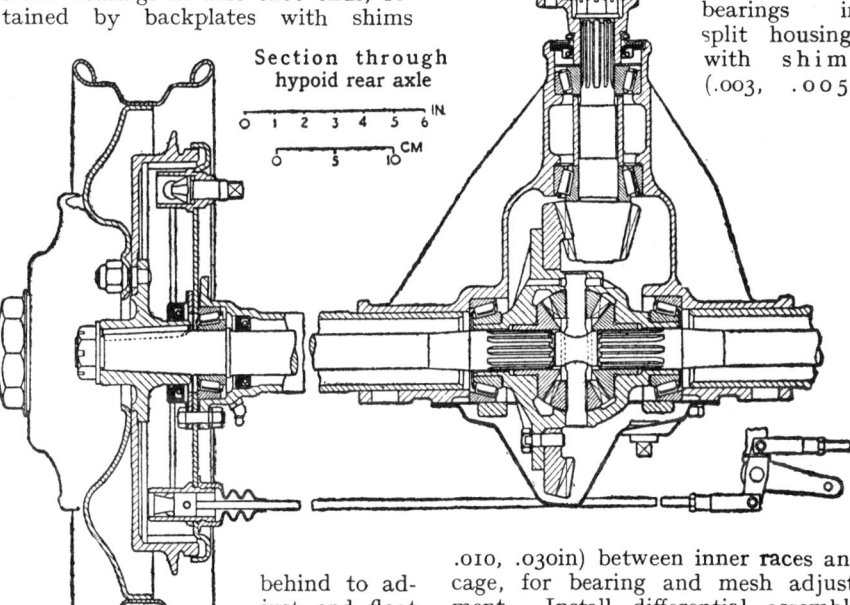

Section through
hypoid rear axle

behind to adjust end float (.001 - .005in). Inner ends of shafts butt on floating thrust block round planet bevel spindle. To remove shaft draw off hub, remove brake shoes and detach backplate with outer oil seal and retainer assembly. Note shims behind. Draw shaft out carefully through inner oil seal (lip inwards) with bearing.

If both shafts are withdrawn see that shims on both sides are of about equal thickness when refitting, so that thrust block remains central. Shims .003, .005, .010 and .030in thick.

Bevel pinion shaft carried in taper roller bearings pressed into final drive housing from front and rear. Distance-piece between inner races. Shims (0.003, 0.005, 0.010, 0.030in) between distance-piece and inner race of front bearing for bearing adjustment. Shims .003, .005, .010in) between outer race of rear bearing and housing for mesh adjustment.

Pinion setting marked on face of pinion may be zero, plus or minus. This indicates amount in .001in above or below nominal distance (2.750in) of face from centreline of crown wheel. Use mesh adjusting shims to obtain setting marked, and assemble pinion in bearings with original bearing shims without oil thrower or oil seal. Tighten driving flange nut and test bearings, which should have slight drag.

Crown wheel spigoted and bolted to flange of one-piece differential cage. Side bevel gears run directly in cage with flat thrust washers behind. Planet bevel pinions have spherical thrust washers and run on spindle retained by pin peened to lock. Axle shaft thrust block round middle of spindle.

Differential assembly carried on taper roller bearings in split housings with shims (.003, .005,

.010, .030in) between inner races and cage, for bearing and mesh adjustment. Install differential assembly *without shims and with bevel pinion removed*, and mount dial gauge on axle casing with button against back face of crown wheel. Move differential assembly to one side of housing with lever, and set gauge to zero. Lever assembly over to other side and note gauge reading (A). This figure indicates play in bearings, and thickness of shims needed to take up play. Add .008in to total to give preload.

After installing bevel pinion reassemble differential, again without shims, lever away from pinion, set indicator to zero, and lever assembly towards pinion. Note reading (B). This figure minus .005in for tooth clearance indicates thickness of shims to go behind crown wheel side bearing. Remainder of shims from total (A + .008in) go behind offside bearing.

When assembly is complete check for backlash (.003in-.006in). Change shims from one side to other of differential bearings if necessary.

CHASSIS

BRAKES

Girling hydro-mechanical. Hydrostatic front brakes have no adjustment. Mechanical rear brakes have normal square-ended adjusters on backplates. Tighten adjuster until shoes are against drum, then back off one or two notches.

No separate adjustment for handbrake unless cable stretches, when slack can be taken up (but no more) by cable adjuster.

BRAKE DATA	
Drum diameter	12in
Lining : length	10½in
width	1.656in
thickness	$\frac{3}{16}$in

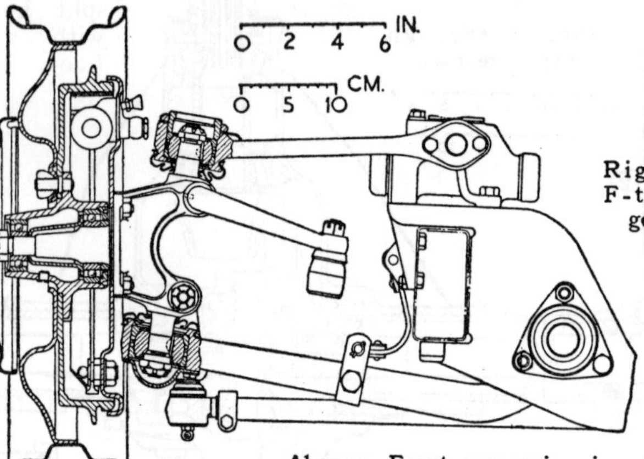

Above : Front suspension in part section

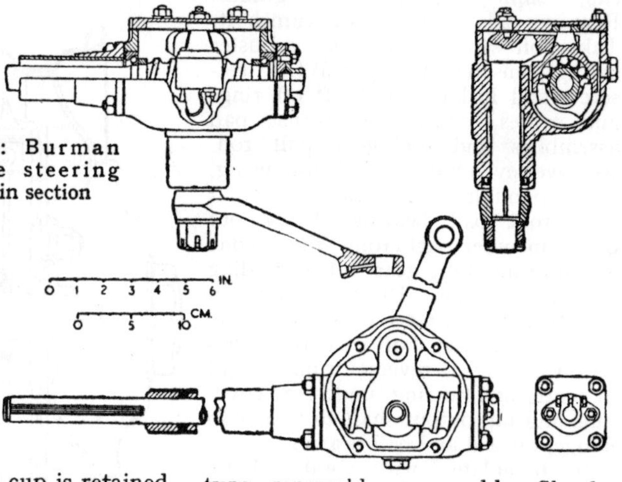

Right: Burman F-type steering gear in section

Inspect front brakes after 15,000-20,000 miles. Renew shoes if linings are worn to within $\frac{1}{32}$in of rivets. Adjustment being automatic, no indication of wear is given until rivets contact drums.

REAR SPRINGS

Semi-elliptic. Silentbloc shackles and anchorages. Tighten nuts fully (spring washers). If spring is removed and refitted, load car before tightening shackle bolts finally.

REAR SPRING DATA	
Length (eye centres, laden)	54in
Width	2in
No. of leaves	8
Free camber	5.7in*
Loaded camber	½in negative*
at load	860lb

* On Lancaster saloon for home use springs have 4.77in free camber and loaded camber at 860lb is nil.

FRONT SUSPENSION

Independent, torsion bars. Upper wishbone links pivoted on shock absorbers. Lower links pivoted in rubber bushes. King pins integral with stub axles, with ball swivel joints to upper and lower links.

To dismantle front suspension, jack up chassis and remove wheel, brake drum, hub and backplate. Disconnect steering ball joints. Unlock and undo large locknut on upper link ball joint, unscrew ring nut and extract upper ball cup and packing washers (keep washers carefully). Undo nut at top of king pin, detach rubber cover under upper link, and draw link with ball and lower ball cup off taper at top of king pin, using extractor GT5374. Note Woodruff key for ball in top of king pin. Remove bosses from inner ends of wishbone link. One is serrated, other plain. Before removing serrated boss, scribe line across boss and shock absorber shaft for correct refitting.

Remove king pin and stub axle assembly from lower link in same way, except that lower ball cup is retained in link by cap and packing washers.

Disconnect check strap and take out setscrew locating inner end of lower link on shaft. Remove front inner rubber bearing and extract serrated link shaft, using extractor ST3887.

When reassembling lower link, insert serrated shaft while holding link in normal laden position, with upper face of cup 5⅛in below horizontal line from shock absorber mounting face.

When fitting torsion bar hold link in "no torsion" position, with upper face of cup 8.8in below level of shock absorber mounting face. Lever at rear end of torsion bar should be in contact with adjusting screw, screwed right back. When car is lowered on to wheels it should take up position giving 5⅛in dimension. Adjust by torsion bar rear adjuster with weight off car.

Torsion bar can be removed without disturbing front suspension. Jack up, remove wheel and disconnect check strap. Slacken adjuster screw at rear of torsion bar and extract split pin or wire locating bar in lever. Dismantle front plate of torsion bar crossmember on frame and draw bar out of front bearing. Before removal mark serrations at both ends for refitting.

STEERING DATA	
Castor	1°
Camber	2½°
King pin inclination	7½°
Toe-pin	$\frac{1}{16}$
No. of turns lock to lock :	
Worm and nut	2¾
F type	3¾

Hubs run on ball bearings, with distance-piece between inner races. Outer bearing press fit in hub. Outer race of inner bearing retained in hub by screwed ring locked by dowel. Tighten stub axle nuts fully.

Steering linkage consists of fore-and-aft drag link, and two-piece track rod, inner ends connected to swinging arm, bushed and pivoted in frame bracket. Pivot bolt shouldered, tighten fully. Ball joints are all sealed side plug type, renewable as assembly. Shanks screwed into link tubes with left-hand thread at one end, right hand at other, and clamped. Drag link and drop arm ball joints not interchangeable. Track adjustment should be made equally on each rod.

STEERING GEAR

Burman F-type worm and nut with recirculating balls. Previously normal worm and nut.

To remove gear from car disconnect column wiring from junction box and remove junction box and bracket from steering box. Take out two grub screws in steering wheel boss and draw out control head and tube. Slacken wheel clamp, push wheel down and extract spring ring at top of column, when wheel can be pulled off. Remove two column fixing brackets and handbrake clamp bracket inside body (with preselector gearbox detach control clamp brackets and choke control).

On older worm and nut type, slacken steering box bracket clamp bolts and take out three bolts holding bracket to frame. Draw off drop arm. Turn column and take off bracket.

Column assembly can then be lifted out to front.

On F-type drop arm cannot be removed first. Remove distributor, petrol pipe and heater duct. Column can then be removed with drop arm and bracket.

When refitting drop arm turn steering wheel to mid position and front wheels straight ahead. Fit drop arm with ball end 7 deg behind vertical centreline. Connect drag link and adjust length if necessary so that on full right lock there is $\frac{1}{2}$in clearance between drag link and tyre.

On worm and nut type column end play is adjusted by thin nut and locknut at top of column tube, adjusting ball thrust bearing.

On F-type column runs in cup and cone ball bearings at lower end, adjusted by shims under lower end plate. End play in rocker shaft adjusted by grub screw and locknut in side cover.

SHOCK ABSORBERS

Luvax Girling piston type. Front pair can be topped up in place, but rear pair must be removed.

BODY MOUNTING

Seven points—five setscrews inside body, one $\frac{3}{8}$in bolt and $\frac{5}{16}$in stud at rear —on each side and eight bolts each side below running boards. To remove body take out also two bolts to front wing stays, six to wing and two to wing stiffener on each side. Steering column can stay in place.

GENERAL DATA		
Wheelbase		9ft 7in
Track : front		4ft 6in
rear		4ft 6$\frac{1}{2}$in
Turning circle		37ft 0in
Ground clearance ...		6$\frac{3}{4}$in
Weight (unladen, full tank) : Lancaster ...		30 cwt
Hurricane		28$\frac{3}{4}$ cwt
Typhoon		29$\frac{1}{4}$ cwt
Tyre size		5.50—17

	Lancaster	Hurricane & Typhoon
Overall length ...	15ft 7$\frac{1}{2}$in	15ft 6 in
Overall width	5ft 8in	5ft 8in
Overall height (laden) ...	5ft 2in	5ft 0in

ARMSTRONG SIDDELEY WIRING DIAGRAM

ELECTRICAL DATA Lucas Equipment		
	Model	Service No.
Dynamo	C45PV	238186
Starter	M418G	255721
Instrument plate assembly	C/C/345	30033A
Switch plate assembly ...	C/C/445	30034A
Lighting switch	S37	31044
Ignition switch	S45	312151
Control box : early	RF91	37032A
later	RF95	37065A
Battery : standard ...	STXW9A	—
Distributor : either ...	DZ6A	40060A
or	DX6A	40110A
Coil	Q12	45020A
Headlamps : nearside	F700P	50165
offside	F700P	50166
Rear No. plate box ...	288	53045
Boot and tail lamp	.-WD-T2A	53019
Trafficators	SF34J	539731
Screenwiper	CR1	75055
Horns : high note ...	WT29	690799
low note ...	WT29	690798
Starter switch	ST900	760205
Stop lamp switch ...	54C	315725
Boot and tail lamp switch	No. 8	359231

BULBS			
	Voltage	Wattage	Lucas No.
Headlamp : nearside	12	36/36	167
offside	12	36	162
Pilot bulbs	12	.6	989
Tail, stop and boot lamps	12	6	207
Ign. and side lamp warning lamps ...	2.5	.5	970
Trafficators and panel lamp (festoon) ...	12	3	256
Panel lamps (screw cap)	12	2.4	987

FUSES		
Accessories	No. FA 25	25 ampere

ARMSTRONG SIDDELEY SIXTEEN MAINTENANCE DIAGRAM

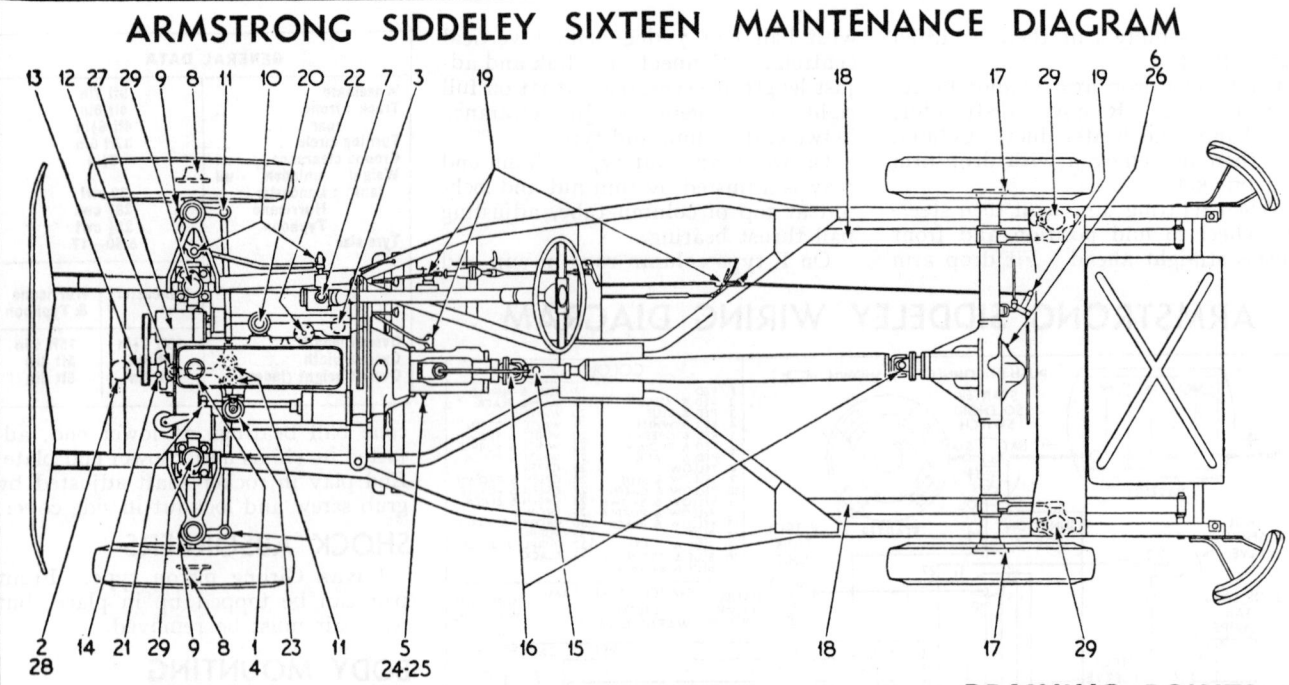

13 12 27 29 9 8 11 10 20 22 7 3 19   18   17 29 19 6 26

2 14 21 29 9 8 1 23 11 5 16 15 18 17 29
28   4   24-25

KEY TO MAINTENANCE DIAGRAM

DAILY
1. **Engine sump** } top up
2. **Radiator**

MONTHLY
3. **Brake fluid reservoir**—top up

EVERY 2,000 MILES
4. **Engine sump**—drain and refill
5. **Gearbox** (both types) }
6. **Rear axle** } top up
7. **Steering box**
8. **Front hubs**—Pack with grease
9. **King pin ball swivels** (4)
10. **Drag link ball joints** (2)
11. **Track rod ball joints** (4)
12. **Track rod centre arm pivot** (1) } grease gun
13. **Fan pulley** (1)
14. **Water pump gland** (1)
15. **Propeller shaft splines** (1)
16. **Propeller shaft joints** (2)
17. **Rear hubs** (2)
18. **Rear springs**—Spray with penetrating oil
19. **Clutch and brake pedals, brake and control linkage**—oil can
20. **Petrol pump filter** } clean
21. **Tappet filter**

EVERY 3,000 MILES
22. **Distributor**—Oil bearings and auto advance (thin oil). Smear engine oil on cam and breaker pivot

EVERY 5,000 MILES
23. **Engine oil filter**—Renew element
24. **Gearbox** (preselector)—Drain, refill and clean filter in base
25. **Gearbox** (synchro) } drain and refill
26. **Rear axle**

EVERY 10,000 MILES
27. **Dynamo**—Pack lubricator with Vaseline
28. **Radiator and cylinder block**—Drain cooling system and re fill

EVERY 25,000 MILES
29. **Shock absorbers**—top up

FILL-UP DATA	
Engine sump	11 pints
plus oil filter	2 pints
Gearbox : synchro ...	3½ pints
preselector ...	4 pints
Rear axle	2½ pints
Cooling system ...	3 gallons
Petrol tank ...	12 gallons (1 gal. res.)
Tyre pressure light load	24 lb front and rear
heavy load	26 lb front and rear

DRAINING POINTS

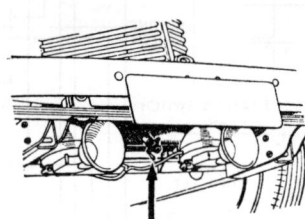

Radiator drain tap below front of car

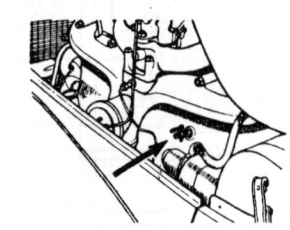

Cylinder block drain tap on near side

RECOMMENDED LUBRICANTS

	Esso	Shell	Filtrate	Vacuum	Price's	Wakefield
Engine Summer Winter	Essolube 40 Essolube 30	Triple Shell S.A.E. 50 Double Shell	A.S. Filtrate Summer A.S. Filtrate Winter	Mobiloil A Mobiloil A	Motorine C Motorine M	Castrol XL Castrol XL
Gearbox (synchro)	Esso gear oil, medium	Triple Shell	Synchro Filtrate	Mobiloil BB	Motorine B de luxe	Castrol XXL
Gearbox (Preselector)	Essolube 40	Double Shell	S.C. Filtrate	Mobiloil A	Motorine M	Castrol XL
Rear axle	Esso Expee Compound 90	Shell Spirax EP90	Hypoid S.A.E. 90 Filtrate gear oil	Mobilube GX	Motorine Hypoid	Castrol Hypoy
Steering box	Esso gear oil heavy	Shell Spirax C (S.A.E. 140)	Filtrate Steering Box Oil	Mobilube C	Motorine Battersea A	Castrol D gear oil
Propeller shaft, hubs, chassis nipples	Esso grease	Shell Retinax RB	Solidified Filtrate oil	Mobil Hub grease	Belmoline C	Castrolease Heavy
Hydraulic brakes		Shell Donax B	Filtrate Hydraulic brake fluid	Mobil brake fluid		Girling brake fluid (Crimson)
Shock absorbers	Esso shock absorber oil	Shell Donax A1	Filtrate shock absorber oil (Piston)	Mobil shock absorber oil light	Motorine SA	Girling Damper oil (thin)

AIR-MINDED TRIO.—Typhoon 2-door saloon, Lancaster 4-door saloon and Hurricane convertible coupé comprise the 1949 range of 2-litre Armstrong Siddeley models.

1949 CARS

THE ARMSTRONG SIDDELEY SIXTEEN

Lower Bonnet Line and Detail Improvements in Range, Otherwise Unchanged

TO Armstrong Siddeley Motors, Ltd., went the credit of making the first announcement of an entirely new post-war car (photographs and a brief specification appearing in "The Motor" as early as May 9, 1945) and as the model concerned, the now familiar Sixteen, embodies many features that have since come to be accepted practice, it is not surprising that the model will appear at the first post-war Motor Show substantially unchanged.

This is not to say, however, that the company has been resting on its laurels and owners who examine the exhibits will notice several detail improvements, some of which have already been incorporated in the course of production.

Most notable amongst them is a slight dropping of the bonnet line, which has effected a subtle change in appearance and an appreciable improvement in driving visibility. Another minor external improvement is the fitting of moulded rubber stoneguards to protect the lower portions of the leading edges of the rear wings.

Export Woodwork

In the interior of the body, all woodwork is now wax polished, as this finish, although initially less brilliant than a high French polish, is much less susceptible to scratches and is considerably more lasting under tropical conditions.

Seating arrangements have also been modified, both the Hurricane drop-head coupé and the Typhoon sportsman's saloon now being fitted with front seats of the close-up type, which, whilst still permitting of individual adjustment, can be aligned to give, in effect, a bench-type seat on which three can be accommodated in comfort. On the Lancaster saloon, on the other hand, a change has been made in the opposite direction, the front seat squabs in this case having been shaped to conform more to the human anatomy. Thus, all requirements in front seating are catered for in the range.

The upholstery of all models, incidentally, is carried out in leather and a pleasing feature (not new to these cars,

but worth mentioning) is the use of a light-coloured washable head lining for the saloons which gives a cheerful effect and is at the same time practical.

Mechanically, the only alteration is an internal improvement in the engine in the shape of a new type of timing wheel embodying a circumferential spring ring which bears against the links of the roller chain and serves as both a tensioner and silencer. Mention of silence also reminds one of the fact that a notable feature of the engine is the use of Zero-Lash hydraulic tappets, which automatically take up clearance, but at the same time allow for expansion of the valve stem.

With the general design it is not proposed to deal in detail here, since the main items of the specification are included in the accompanying panel. It is, however, worth mentioning that buyers of any of the three models (coupé, saloon or sportsman's saloon) are given a choice of either a conventional transmission consisting of a Borg and Beck clutch and four-speed synchromesh gearbox or a Newton automatic clutch and epicyclic preselector gearbox, the latter a feature which was pioneered by Armstrong Siddeley many years ago.

The system of independent front wheel suspension, by torsion bars and transverse wishbones, which was introduced on these models some three years ago, continues without fundamental alteration. The chassis is an X-braced structure well suited to the stylish coachbuilt bodies.

ARMSTRONG SIDDELEY DATA

Engine Dimensions :		
Cylinders	6	
Bore	65 mm.	
Stroke ..	100 mm.	
Cubic capacity ..	1,991 c.c.	
Piston area ..	30.9 sq. ins.	
Valves.. ..	Overhead (pushrod)	
Compression ratio ..	7 to 1	
Engine Performance :		
Max. b.h.p.	70	
at.. ..	4,200 r.p.m.	
Max. b.m.e.p. ..	118 lb./sq. in.	
at.. ..	2,500 r.p.m.	
B.h.p. per sq. in. piston area ..	2.26	
Peak piston speed, ft. per min.	2,780	
Engine Details :		
Carburetter	Stromberg downdraught	
Ignition	12-volt coil	
Plugs : Make and type	Champion L10	
Fuel pump	AC mechanical	
Fuel capacity	12 gallons	
Oil filter (make, by-pass or full flow) ..	Tecalemit by-pass	
Oil capacity	11 pints +2 pints	
Cooling system ..	Pump, fan and thermostat	
Water capacity ..	3 gallons	
Electrical system ..	Lucas 12-volt c.v.c.	
Battery capacity ..	51 amp./hrs.	
Transmission :		
Clutch	Borg and Beck (with synchro box)†	
Gear ratios :		
Top..	5.10†	
3rd	7.24†	
2nd	10.89†	
1st	17.61†	
Rev.	15.21†	

Transmission—cont.		
Prop. shaft		Hardy Spicer
Final drive		Hypoid bevel
Chassis Details :		
Brakes		Girling hydro-mechanical
Brake drum diameter		12 ins.
Friction lining area ..		159 sq. ins.
Suspension :		
Front		Independent (torsion bar)
Rear		Semi-elliptic
Shock absorbers ..		Luvax-Girling
Wheel type		Disc
Tyre size		5.50 × 17 ins.
Steering gear ..		Burman high-efficiency
Steering wheel ..		17 ins.
Dimensions :		
Wheelbase		9 ft. 7 ins.
Track :		
Front		4 ft. 6 ins.
Rear		4 ft. 6¼ ins.
Overall length ..		15 ft. 5 ins.*
Overall width ..		5 ft. 8 ins.
Overall height ..		5 ft. 3 ins.*
Ground clearance ..		6¼ ins.
Turning circle ..		39 ft. (right), 37 ft. (left)
Dry weight		29 cwt.*
Performance Data :*		
Piston area, sq. ins. per ton		21.3
Brake lining area, sq. ins. per ton		110
Top gear m.p.h. per 1,000 r.p.m. ..		16.1
Top gear m.p.h. at 2,500 ft./min. piston speed		61.5
Litres per ton-mile, dry		2,550

Notes.—* The dimensions given refer to the Lancaster saloon model. Other models are both 15 ft. 2 ins. in overall length, 5 ft. 1 in. in overall height, and weigh 28 cwt. † All models are also available with an automatic clutch and Newton preselector gearbox; gear ratios in this case are : 5.1, 7.2, 10.6 and 18.4 ; reverse 22.8.

ARMSTRONG SIDDELEY INNOVATIONS

Existing Body Styles Supplemented by New Whitley Four-door, Four-light Saloon.   All Models Now Fitted With 2.3-litre "Export" Engine

NEWCOMER : Named after a famous bomber built by the same group, the Whitley is a smart new saloon model.

ALL models in the Armstrong Siddeley range are now fitted with a larger (2.3-litre) engine, which, as recently disclosed in "The Motor," has been used in export editions of these cars for some time. Other innovations which apply to all models in the range include a new facia-board design, a modification to the radiator grille by the incorporation of a plated beading at each side, and a very minor change in the hub caps, which now carry the maker's name.

As before, the car is available as a Hurricane drop-head coupé, a Typhoon two-door four-light sports saloon, and a Lancaster four-door six-light saloon, but a new body style has now been added in the shape of a four-door, four-light saloon which is known as the Whitley (and thus, incidentally, carries on the maker's aircraft tradition in the matter of nomenclature).

The price of the new Whitley is the same as that of the Hurricane and Typhoon, which remain unchanged at £975, which with purchase tax of £271 11s. 8d. gives a total of £1,246 11s. 8d.   The price of the Lancaster

saloon also remains unchanged at £995, plus £277 2s. 9d. (£1,272 2s. 9d.).

*   *   *

In considering the 1950 Armstrong Siddeleys in detail, it is interesting to study the influence of the larger engine.   This differs from the previous 1,991 c.c. unit only in an increase in the bore from 65 mm. to 70 mm. and in the use of wet cylinder liners.   The increase in maximum power output resulting from the change is 5 b.h.p., and although this, which is equivalent to a gain of 7.1 per cent., is useful enough, it represents only part (and a slightly misleading part) of the story.

The following comparisons taken from the power curves of the old and the new engines reveal a much more notable tale:—

r.p.m.	1,991 c.c. engine.	2.3-litre engine.	Percentage increase.
1,000	16½ b.h.p.	20 b.h.p.	21.1
2,000	37 b.h.p.	41 b.h.p.	10.8
3,000	54½ b.h.p.	61 b.h.p.	11.9
4,000	68 b.h.p.	74 b.h.p.	8.8
4,200	70 b.h.p.	75 b.h.p.	7.1

From these figures, it is clear that the new engine should offer greatly improved performance in the important low- and middle-speed ranges as well as a worthwhile gain at the top end.   The top-gear ratio, it should be added, has not been changed, so that the full improvement is available in the form of better acceleration and hill-climbing powers.

Looked at another way, and measuring the top-gear potentialities by the yardstick of litres per ton-mile, one finds an improvement in this figure from 2,550 to 3,010.

To turn now to the new body type, the Whitley has been evolved in response to the demand which has been found to exist for a model having the unostentatious elegance of medium-sized four-light coachwork, coupled with the undoubted extra convenience of four doors.   In addition, the designers have carefully schemed the body to give increased passenger accommodation in the rear as compared with the two-door Typhoon.   The gain in this respect can be gathered from the fact that, measured from facia board to rear squab, the Whitley is some 2 ins. bigger than the Typhoon, thus allowing for greater leg-room for the rear passengers.

In seat width at the back, the two cars are similar

DOUBLE DECKER : The spare wheel is housed below the luggage shelf in the Whitley locker, together with wheel-change tools.

FINGERTIP PIONEER.—The optional preselector gear-box which was pioneered by Armstrong Siddeley gives the now-fashionable steering column control.

throughout the range is an attractive style of trim incorporating contrasting piping round the edges of the seats, squabs, and so on. Another attractive quality feature which applies to the whole range is the use of fine-grained walnut for the facia board and all window mouldings and fillets.

In the new facia, which, as already mentioned, is common to all models, the projecting instrument panel on the driver's side has been dropped in favour of more symmetrical treatment, in which the switches are neatly grouped in the centre and flanked by the lid of a cubby hole on the passenger's side and a matching panel in front of the driver carrying the dials. The latter (comprising a speedometer, clock, oil gauge, thermometer and fuel gauge) are clearly visible through the characteristic two-spoked wheel. Beneath the switches is a wide walnut-faced ashtray, which can be removed and fitted beneath the board to make room for a radio control panel if it is desired to equip the car with wireless.

Equipment entirely in keeping with cars of this class is standardized, and includes two items which might well be more common in the shape of a reserve petrol control on the facia and an amber warning light to give notice of lamp bulb failure.

With the chassis details of Armstrong Siddeley models most readers are familiar, and there is no need to add to what is given in the full specification panel on these pages, except to stress that buyers are given the unique choice of either a four-speed preselector gearbox with the usual neat finger-tip control lever on the steering column or a conventional clutch and synchromesh gearbox with central control.

(with a measurement over arm-rests of 54 ins.), but an unexpected gain in the Whitley is an increase in internal width over the front seats of approximately 2 ins., brought about by the fact that the doors, being narrower, have also been made thinner. Head-room in the rear compartment has also been increased compared with the Typhoon.

An interesting design problem arose in this connection, in that, if a similar roof curvature had been adopted to that of the Typhoon, extra rear headroom could only have been obtained at the expense of considerably increased overall height. Instead, the designer adopted the expedient of using slightly angular treatment for the rear of the head and mating this semi-razor-edge treatment with a suggestion of angularity about the windows to give a very harmonious but extremely practical overall effect.

The doors of the Whitley have thin-framed drop windows, with hinged ventilating panels on the leading edges of the front doors. The roof and screen are fixed, but, in common with all Armstrong Siddeley models, a heating and ventilating system is built in, with the motor under the bonnet for silence and the fresh-air intake arranged from a point ahead of the radiator but behind the front grille.

The Whitley front seat is of the bench type, with a central folding armrest, and there are also armrests on the front doors. At the rear, too, there is a central folding armrest, together with the usual rests above the wheel arches. As on all models, the upholstery is carried out in high-grade leather, and a feature which has now been adopted

ARMSTRONG SIDDELEY DATA

	2-3-litre Whitley Saloon			2-3-litre Whitley Saloon
Engine Dimensions :			**Chassis Details :**	
Cylinders	6		Brakes :	
Bore	70 mm.		Front	Girling hydrostatic
Stroke	100 mm.		Rear	Girling mechanical
Cubic capacity ..	2,309 c.c.			
Piston area	35.9 sq. ins.		Brake drum diameter	12 ins.
Valves	o.h. (pushrods and		Friction lining area ..	135 sq. ins.
	hydraulic tappets)		Suspension :	
Compression ratio ..	6.5 to 1		Front	Independent
				(torsion bars)
Engine Performance :			Rear	Semi-elliptic
Max b.h.p.	75		Shock absorbers ..	Luvax Girling
at	4,200 r.p.m.			hydraulic
Max b.m.e.p.	115 lb./sq. in.		Wheel type	Disc
at	1,500–3,000 r.p.m.		Tyre size	5.50 × 17 ins.
B.h.p. per sq. in.			Steering gear ..	Burman reciprocat-
piston area ..	2.09			ing ball
Peak piston speed,			Steering wheel ..	Spring-spoke, 17 ins.
ft. per min. ..	2,760		**Dimensions :**	
			Wheelbase	9 ft. 7 in.
Engine Details :			Track :	
Carburetter.. ..	Stromberg		Front	4 ft. 6 ins.
	downdraught		Rear	4 ft. 6½ ins.
Ignition	Coil		Overall length ..	15 ft. 5 ins.†
Plugs : make and type	Champion N8		Overall width ..	5 ft. 8 ins.
Fuel pump	AC mechanical		Overall height ..	5 ft. 3 ins.†
Fuel capacity ..	12 gallons		Ground clearance ..	7½ ins.
Oil filter (make, by-			Turning circle ..	37 ft.
pass or full flow)..	Tecalemit full flow		Dry weight	28½ cwt.*
Oil capacity ..	11+2 pints		**Performance Data :**	
Cooling system ..	Pump, fan and		Piston area, sq. ins.	
	thermostat		per ton	25.2
Water capacity ..	21 pints (including		Brake lining area,	
	heater)		sq. ins. per ton ..	95.0
Electrical system ..	Lucas 12-volt		Top-gear m.p.h. per	
Battery capacity ..	51 amp./hrs.		1,000 r.p.m. ..	16.1
			Top-gear m.p.h. at	
Transmission :			2,500 ft./min. piston	
	Synchro. box	Pre- selector	speed	61.5
Clutch	Borg and Beck	Auto- matic	Litres per ton-mile,	
			dry	3,010
Gear ratios :				
Top	5.1	5.1	Notes.—* Dry weight of the Whitley is	
3rd	7.28	7.22	estimated. Weights of other models are :	
2nd	10.89	10.66	Hurricane, 27½ cwt.; Typhoon, 28½ cwt.;	
1st	17.61	18.36	Lancaster, 28¾ cwt.	
Rev.	15.21	22.8	† Other models vary as follow : Hurricane	
Prop. shaft	Hardy Spicer		and Typhoon, overall length, 15 ft. 6 ins. ;	
Final drive	Hypoid bevel		overall height, 5 ft. 1 in. Lancaster, overall	
			length, 15 ft. 7½ ins. ; overall height, 5 ft. 3 ins.	

The new Whitley saloon has some of the cleanest of contemporary styling.

NEW CARS DESCRIBED

Armstrong Siddeleys for 1950

BIGGER ENGINE OF 2,309 C.C. : NEW WHITLEY FOUR-DOOR FOUR-LIGHT SALOON

IN the Armstrong Siddeley programme for 1950 the main feature is a change in the size of the excellent six-cylinder overhead-valve engine. In place of the 65 × 100 mm (1,991 c.c.) engine, the new one is 70 × 100 mm (2,309 c.c.). This new engine is similar in detail design, but the increase in size results in an increase of 12 per cent in torque and a maximum power output of 75 b.h.p. at 4,200 r.p.m. with a compression ratio of 6.5 to 1. The b.h.p. per litre figure is 32.5. The higher compression ratio, and other technique, has made it possible to obtain the improved performance without increasing fuel consumption. It will be appreciated that this increase in engine size has a very marked effect upon the liveliness and cruising speed of a most attractive and finely built car of exclusive character. The new engine has been tried by *The Autocar* over a Continental route, as recorded in the August 26 issue.

The New Whitley

Following the practice of distinguishing models by using names from Armstrong Siddeley aircraft successes, the new four-door four-light saloon has been christened the Whitley. It is a graceful design employing a semi-razor-edge styling, and it has, therefore, large window areas and slender pillars, thus ensuring excellent vision for passengers as well as driver, and providing a well-lit interior. Triangular glass flaps in the forward windows provide control of ventilation without draught. The front seat is of the single bench-type and is fitted with a central folding armrest as well as elbow-rests on the doors. The design of the car as a whole brings the wide rear seat ahead of the axle, so obtaining maximum riding comfort. The seats are deeply cushioned, trimmed in real leather which

The semi-razor-edge style of the Whitley blends into a shapely tail with considerable luggage space.

The new facia, common to all models, is of walnut. The central panel below the switches is removable to make way for a radio control panel.

The Lancaster six-light saloon has a single bench-type front seat with central folding armrests and a sunshine roof.

ARMSTRONG SIDDELEYS FOR 1950 . . . . . continued

is pleated and set off by fawn piping.

There is a new design of facia, which has been standardized for all models. Carried out like all the woodwork in the car, in polished grained walnut, this panel has the instruments grouped in front of the driver where they are easily seen through the twin-spoked steering wheel. Minor control knobs are grouped in the centre. On the passenger's side is a large glove box with a lid that opens downward. A small panel below the controls is removable and is for use when a radio set is fitted.

Interior Heating

Air conditioning is part of the equipment and the unit is mounted under the bonnet out of the way. It draws fresh air from the front of the car, which can be circulated warm or cold, and directed on to the windscreen for de-misting. At the back of the body is a shapely luggage locker of large size, with the lid opening upward. The spare wheel is in a separate compartment beneath the luggage space. The fuel filler enters the boot from low down at the side so that it does not obstruct the holding capacity. On all models the bonnet lock is now inside the car; the top panel of the bonnet lifts and the sides remain stationary.

Altogether the Whitley has a fine body, smart but dignified in appearance, inviting, and thoroughly practical in its detail work. Colour schemes are equally tasteful. It will be recollected that the Armstrong Siddeley is obtainable with either a four-speed syncromesh gear box or the preselective epicyclic gear. It is interesting to note that the demand is about 50-50.

There are four models of the 1950

Armstrong Siddeley 2.3-litre series: the Whitley four-door four-light saloon, price £975, plus purchase tax £271 11s 8d; total £1,246 11s 8d; the Lancaster four-door six-light saloon, price £995, plus purchase tax £277 2s 9d;

total £1,272 2s 9d; the Hurricane drop-head coupé, price £975, plus purchase tax £271 11s 8d; total £1,246 11s 8d; and the Typhoon two-door four-light sports saloon, price £975, plus purchase tax £271 11s 8d; total £1,246 11s 8d.

There are three positions for the head of the Hurricane coupé—closed, open and partly furled, giving a coupé de ville effect. This body has separate front seats.

ARMSTRONG SIDDELEY SPECIFICATION

Engine.—6 cyl, 70×100 mm (2,309 c.c.). Wet cast-iron cylinder liners. Overhead valves, push-rods and rockers, self-adjusting tappets. Four-bearing crankshaft. Alloy pistons, four rings. Downdraught Stromberg carburettor, mechanical fuel pump. Pressure lubrication with full-flow filter. Pump water circulation.

Transmission.—Preselector epicylic, centrifugal clutch, four speeds: 5.1, 7.2, 10.65 and 18.3 to 1.

Single-plate clutch. Four speeds, synchromesh: 5.1, 7.23, 10.88 and 17.6 to 1. Open propeller-shaft to hypoid bevel final drive.

Brakes.—Girling Hydrostatic.

Steering.—Burman recirculating ball, worm and nut.

Suspension.—Independent front, wishbones and torsion bar; half-elliptic rear, Girling dampers.

Fuel tank.—12 gallons.

Wheels and tyres.—Dunlop 5.50×17in on bolt-on disc wheels.

Dimensions.—Wheelbase 9ft 7in, track (front) 4ft 6in, (rear) 4ft 6½in. Length, Whitley 15ft 5in, Lancaster 15ft 7½in, Hurricane and Typhoon 15ft 6in. Width (all models) 5ft 8in, height 5ft 3in, ground clearance 7½in. Weight 28¼ cwt.

The Typhoon two-door saloon has independent front seats and looks particularly smart in a contrasting two-colour finish, as shown here.

Re-entering a market where they were well known before the war, Armstrong Siddeley have started production of this coachbuilt limousine with seats for five in the rear and two in front. The body is panelled in aluminium and the structure incorporates several aluminium castings.

Armstrong Siddeley Limousine

WHITLEY AND LANCASTER SALOONS, HURRICANE CONVERTIBLE CONTINUE UNCHANGED

SINCE the war Armstrong Siddeley has produced a range of six-cylinder cars, which have proved popular with a discerning public which appreciates good craftsmanship.

Originally the engines were of 2-litre capacity, but last year the swept volume was raised to 2.3 litres by an increase in the cylinder bore. The change in engine size was accompanied by a useful increase in maximum power and a considerable improvement in low speed torque. No important mechanical modifications have been found necessary for the coming year, but the company is returning to a market where its products were well known in the years before the war, with the production of a limousine on a long wheelbase version of the current chassis.

The body, designed and built in the Armstrong Siddeley works, offers a considerable amount of space to passengers and luggage, but the use of hard-edged styling which harmonizes with the well-known front end treatment of the Armstrong Siddeley has avoided undue heaviness in the appearance. In the rear compartment there is one long seat, 57in wide, with centre armrest, and two wide occasional seats which line up together to form a continuous bench-type seat right across the car, or can be folded away into the division when not required.

Two roof lights, two ashtrays and a clock are among the interior fittings. For the rear compartment cloth upholstery is used, while the driver's compartment is

upholstered in leather. Woodwork throughout the car is in walnut veneer.

The luggage locker is quite capacious for a limousine, and additional baggage can be carried on the lid, which drops down flat for the purpose. For long distance touring, further luggage can be carried at the front of the car. The seat alongside the driver is made quickly detachable, and when this is removed a considerable amount of baggage space is made available. Tools are carried under the driving seat, and the spare wheel is carried vertically inside the luggage locker at the rear.

The car is provided with a well-planned ventilation system, in which cool air is taken in from the front to an electrically driven blower under the bonnet, and from this passes to a heater element on the scuttle. Warm or cool air can then be supplied to the demister slots at the base of the screen, and can be fed through ducts built in the body sills to twin grilles in the division, which ventilate the rear compartment.

As one would expect from a manufacturer of aero engines, the bodywork incorporates aluminium and light alloy wherever possible. All external panelling is of aluminium, with the exception of the luggage locker lid, which may have to bear the weight of a considerable amount of luggage, and the wings. The complete screen pillar and front door post is formed from an aluminium alloy casting and similar castings are used on

several other points on the structure. The scuttle itself, however, is of strongly constructed steel bridge of box section, and steel is also used for the body sills, the inner door panels and for the covering of the centre pillars.

The car division at Armstrong Siddeley's is well equipped with modern painting equipment and drying ovens through which the cars pass on a conveyor system, but a great deal of hand work is still employed, particularly on the limousines, as this is still regarded as the best way to obtain the really high quality finish expected by those who buy the more specialized type of car.

As on the other Armstrong Siddeley models, the limousine is available either with the centrifugal clutch and pre-selector gear box which was pioneered by Armstrong Siddeley 23 years ago, or with a single complete clutch and synchromesh gear box. Buyers' preferences continue to be divided almost equally between the two, although in some markets, particularly Switzerland, there is a marked liking for the pre-selector epicyclic gear box.

The range for 1950 is completed by the Whitley four-door four-light saloon, the Lancaster four-door six-light saloon and the Hurricane convertible. Colour schemes of all these cars can be modified in detail to purchasers' requirements.

SPECIFICATION
ARMSTRONG SIDDELEY

Engine.—6 cylinders, o.h.v. push-rod operated. 70 × 100 mm, 2,309 c.c. 75 b.h.p. at 4,200 r.p.m.

Transmission.—4-speed pre-selector epicyclic gear box with centrifugal clutch. Ratios 5.1, 7.2, 10.66 and 18.36 to 1. Alternative, 4-speed synchromesh gear box with dry single-plate clutch. Ratios 5.1, 7.23, 10.89, and 17.6 to 1. Hypoid axle.

Suspension.—Independent front by wishbones and torsion bars. Half-elliptic rear.

Brakes.—Girling hydrostatic hydraulic.

Wheels and Tyres.—Steel disc wheels with 5.50 × 17in tyres.

Dimensions.—Wheelbase 9ft 7in. Track 4ft 6in (front), 4ft 6½in (rear). Overall length 15ft 6in. Width 5ft 8in. Height 5ft 3in. Weight (Whitley and Lancaster) 3,360 lb. Limousine: Wheelbase 10ft 2in. Track 4ft 6½in (front), 4ft 9in (rear). Length 16ft 3in. Width 5ft 10in. Height 5ft 7½in. Weight 3,920 lb.

Prices.—Whitley and Hurricane £975 plus British purchase tax £271 11s 8d. Total £1,246 11s 8d. Lancaster saloon £995 plus £277 2s 9d. Total £1,272 2s 9d. Limousine, not yet announced.

The cloth-trimmed interior of the roomy new limousine on the long wheelbase Armstrong Siddeley chassis. The two occasional seats fold into the division.

The Armstrong Siddeley Sapphire

Announced Today is an Entirely New 3.4-litre Five/Six-seater High-performance Saloon to Sell at the Notable Basic Price of £1,110.

A NY entirely new model from the Armstrong Siddeley factory would command special attention by reason of the company's reputation for quality and finish—a reputation which, not unnaturally perhaps, seems common to car-manufacturing concerns with aircraft associations. In the case, however, of the new Armstrong Siddeley Sapphire, there are two other notable reasons for this new model having a special claim to attention.

One is that, with its unusual 3.4-litre, six-cylinder "square" engine developing 120 b.h.p. and its relatively light dry weight of 31 cwt., it marks the entry of Armstrong Siddeley Motors Ltd., into the high-performance class, with a potential maximum speed very well in excess of 90 m.p.h.

The other reason is the keenly-competitive price, bearing in mind the appointments, finish and specification, of £1,110. With purchase tax added, the total cost is £1,728 3s. 4d.

As will be seen from the illustrations, the styling represents a modern version of the traditional, in which a characteristic Armstrong Siddeley radiator grille, built-in lamps and full-width body treatment with flowing wings, are blended effectively with a suggestion of knife-edge treatment about the head.

Mechanically, the car is notable for a number of interesting technical details including an engine having hemispherical combustion chambers with inclined valves operated from a single camshaft and for the buyer being given the choice of a conventional clutch and synchro-mesh gearbox or an automatic centrifugal clutch and pre-selector gearbox with an innovation in the shape of electrical operation.

In addition to this new Sapphire, the current 2.3-litre types are continued without change.

* * *

Of entirely new design throughout, the 3.4-litre engine is outstanding as the first British example of a valve layout which enables the benefits of hemispherical combustion chambers and inclined valves to be obtained with a single side camshaft.

In this case, the camshaft (which is carried on four bearings) is located in the right or off side of the cylinder block casting, with its centres approximately $3\frac{5}{8}$ ins. from the top face of the block, the push rods passing diagonally through the block and head castings to operate the valves through the medium of rockers. The push rods are relatively short (8 ins. and $9\frac{3}{4}$ ins. in the case of the inlets and exhausts respectively) and are cupped at each end; at the top, they bear on the usual type of ball-ended adjuster in the rocker and, at the base, are seated on $\frac{1}{2}$-in. steel balls in chill-cast tappets.

The valves (which have double springs located by split

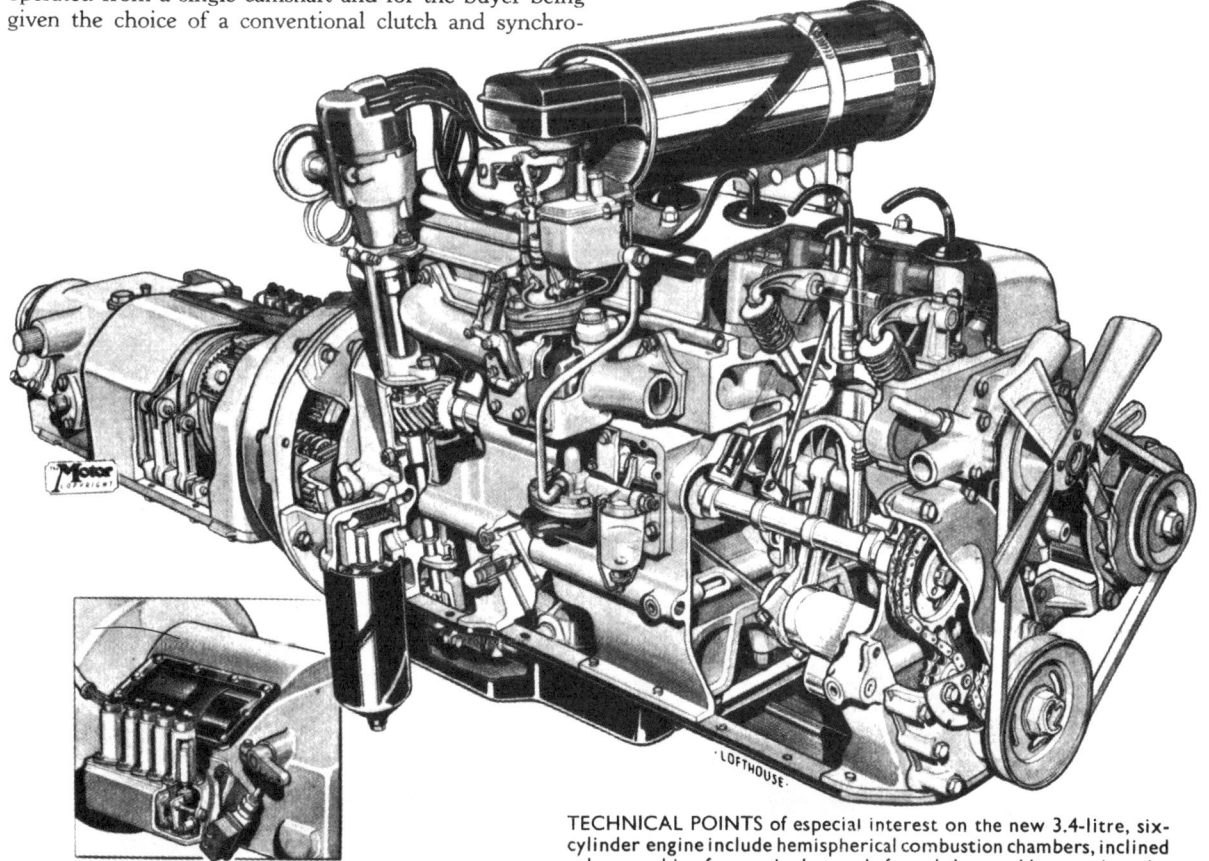

TECHNICAL POINTS of especial interest on the new 3.4-litre, six-cylinder engine include hemispherical combustion chambers, inclined valves working from a single camshaft, and the equal bore and stroke (90 mm. by 90 mm.). Shown, inset on the left, are the solenoids on the pre-selector gearbox casing which provide automatic operation of the epicyclic bands.

cotters) are inclined at an included angle of 70 degrees, with the inlets on the right-hand side of the engine and the exhausts on the left; respective diameters are 1.55 ins. and 1.35 ins.

Between the valves, in the centres of the combustion chambers, are the 14 mm. long-reach sparking plugs, which are situated in tubes; the latter pass through the large single cast-aluminium valve cover which encloses both sets of rockers and the push-on insulated terminals are bell bottomed to contact the tube and guide them on to the plugs. At their tops, the tubes are enclosed by plastic caps through which the leads pass.

Individual exhaust ports, giving a very clear gas flow, lead to a pair of three-branch manifolds, each of which has a separate down pipe leading to a small primary silencer (thus avoiding a "Y" junction which is apt to present flow and noise problems). From the primary silencer, a single pipe leads to the main silencer located alongside one of the members of the "X" frame bracing.

Inlet arrangements are particularly interesting. The single downdraught carburetter is mounted on a four-branch manifold which feeds into a cylindrical cast-in passage running the length of the head, but divided off in the centre by a baffle containing a balance hole. It follows that the front three cylinders and the rear three are treated as separate units; in each case, the two manifold branches concerned are staggered in relation to the three ports they serve, so ensuring equal distribution.

With inlet and exhaust manifolds on opposite sides of the engine, it has been necessary to provide a water-heated induction, but the heating is strictly localized at the point of entry of the mixture into the manifold. Water is taken for the purpose from the cylinder head to the base of a central jacket chamber and is drawn out via a pipe leading to the inlet side of the impeller.

The Stromberg downdraught carburetter is of the 36 mm. size and is of the pump type with a hand strangler; an interesting detail is a weighted float to damp out fluctuations caused by engine movement.

A noteworthy point about the cooling system is that the impeller delivers cool water to a gallery cast in the upper portion of the cylinder block (not head) on the exhaust side; the cool water is, however, insulated from the water in the block by a pipe containing carefully-positioned holes via which it flows upwards into the hottest portions of the head round the exhaust ports. The impeller forms a unit with a two-blade fan and is driven by a triangulated belt drive, which also serves for the dynamo. A thermostat is built into the elbow junction with the header tank and provision is made at the rear of the head for the hot water supply to the heating and demisting system.

The crankshaft is of the four-bearing type with mains $2\frac{3}{4}$ ins. in diameter and big ends of $2\frac{1}{8}$ ins. diameter; the latter are split at an angle of 45 degrees and secured by studs and both the main and big-end bearings are of the Vandervell Micro-babbit strip-metal type.

For lubrication, a gear-type oil pump, with floating

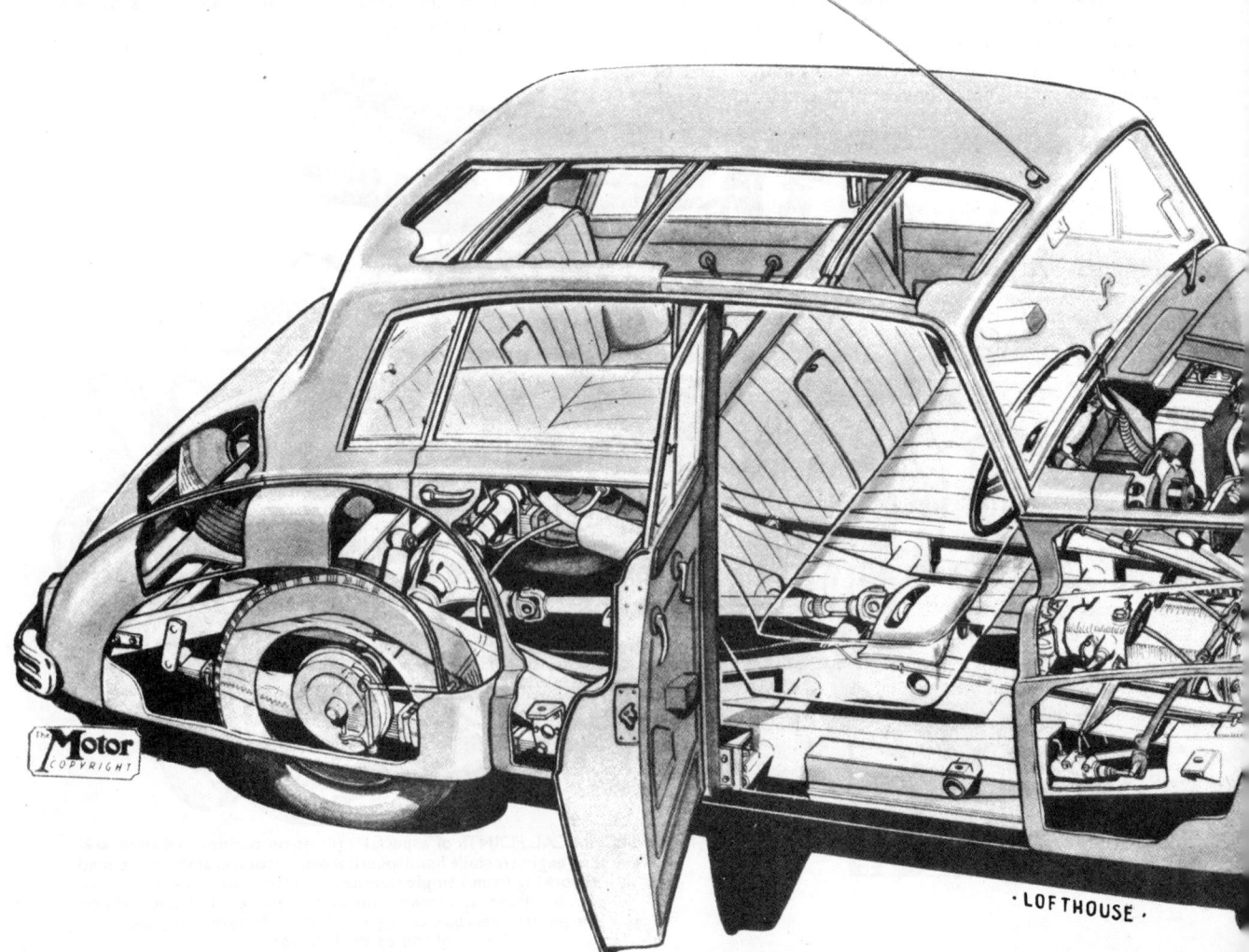

· LOFTHOUSE ·

SWEEPING LINES.—Four- and six-light styles are available on identically-dimensioned bodies. Ample window areas and sweeping wing lines are notable features of the new Sapphire.

intake, is driven by skew gearing from the back end of the camshaft and the supply passes through a full-flow AC or Purolator filter. An extension of the vertical oil-pump shaft drives the very accessible ignition distributor, which has both centrifugal and vacuum control as well as a thumb-screw adjuster. Another maintenance point of interest is that the duplex-roller chain driving the camshaft has an eccentrically-mounted idler sprocket which serves as a tensioner and is adjustable from outside the timing case.

The engine has a narrow three-point flexible mounting. At the front, the unit is carried on bonded-rubber at a single point on a pressed-steel bridge piece and, at the rear, a pair of mountings is set close together at the rear of the gearbox; these are of the Metalastik bonded type, of cone shape, with the rubber partly in compression and partly in shear, whilst a buffer is incorporated to provide an adjustable degree of damping.

In unit with the engine are the clutch and gearbox.

FEATURES EXPOSED here include the deep channel-section frame and cross-bracing, suspension by wishbones and coil-springs at the front, and five/six seating capacity in the all-steel body.

As already mentioned, the buyer is given the option of either a straight-forward Borg and Beck clutch and four-speed synchromesh gearbox with steering-column control or, alternatively, an automatic centrifugal clutch and pre-selector gearbox. This option follows the existing Armstrong Siddeley policy with the current 2.3-litre type.

On the new Sapphire, an important innovation has been made by providing electric operation for the pre-selector bands. This plan makes the control more finger-tip than ever, the steering column carrying a switch in the form of a neat lever working in a miniature gate. This is connected to a series of solenoids mounted on the gearbox casing and arranged to operate the epicyclic bands, movement of the gear-changing pedal serving to complete the electrical circuit to the solenoid operating the gear which has been pre-selected. Thus, so far as the driver is concerned, the method of handling is exactly as before except that the effort required is even less.

From the rear of the gearbox, a short propeller shaft leads to a steady bearing mounted in rubber in the centre of the cruciform chassis-frame bracing, whence a further shaft leads to the final drive which is of the hypoid type in a Salisbury rear axle.

In the design of the chassis frame, special attention has been paid to obtaining adequate strength and torsional rigidity without undue weight. Just how successful these efforts to avoid surplus weight have been can be gathered from the fact that the weight of the complete chassis (including engine and radiator) is only 62 lbs. greater than that of the 2.3-litre Whitley model, despite the bigger engine and greater overall size of the car.

Basis of Strength

The main frame and the cruciform bracing are of deep channel section tapering to the rear, and additional cross-bracing is provided by two $2\frac{1}{2}$-in. tubes amidships and two channel-section cross members at the rear. In addition, there is a massive detachable pressed-steel structure at the front which serves to carry both the forward engine mounting and the front suspension unit.

Coil springs and wishbones of unequal length are used at the front, the wishbones being inclined to the rear to provide a partial trailing effect. The outer bearings of both wishbones take the form of screwed bushes, whilst Metalastik high-duty bonded-rubber bushes are used for the inner fulcrums of the lower wishbones; in the case of the inner bearings of the upper link, one plain and one threaded bush are used.

Control is provided by Girling telescopic dampers contained within the coil springs (but readily detachable without disturbing the latter) whilst an anti-roll bar is fitted. Telescopic dampers of large capacity are also employed for the rear semi-elliptic springs, together with a second anti-roll bar.

Engine Dimensions:	
Cylinders	6
Bore	90 mm.
Stroke	90 mm.
Cubic capacity ...	3,435.3 c.c.
Piston area	59.2 sq. in.
Valves	Overhead (inclined push rods)
Compression ratio ...	6.5 to 1
Engine performance:	
Max. b.h.p.	120
at	4,200 r.p.m.
Max. b.m.e.p. ...	120 lb./sq./in.
at	2,000 r.p.m.
B.H.P. per sq. in. piston area	2.03
Peak piston speed ft. per min.	2,480
Engine Details:	
Carburetter	Stromberg Downdraught (36 mm.)
Ignition	Lucas High-duty Coil
Plugs: make and type	Champion N8B Long Reach
Fuel pump	AC Mechanical.
Fuel capacity ...	16 galls. (including 1$\frac{1}{2}$ reserve)
Oil filter (make, by-pass or full flow) ...	AC or Purolator full flow
Oil capacity	10 pts (+ 1 pt for filter)
Cooling system ...	Pump, fan and thermostat
Water capacity ...	28 pints
Electrical system ...	Lucas 12-volt
Battery capacity ...	64 amp/hr.
Transmission:	**Pre-selector**
Clutch	A.S.M. Centrifugal single dry plate
Gear ratios: Top ...	4.091
3rd ...	5.564
2nd ...	8.153
1st ...	13.909
Rev. ...	19.473

Transmission—(contd.)	**Synchro box**
Clutch	10-in. Borg and Beck
Gear ratios: Top ...	4.091
3rd ...	5.807
2nd ...	8.54
1st ...	12.8
Rev. ...	13.53
Prop. shaft	Divided Hardy Spicer
Final drive	Hypoid bevel
Chassis Details:	
Brakes	Girling hydraulic (2LS on front)
Brake drum diameter	11 in.
Friction lining area ...	184 sq. in.
Suspension: Front ..	Independent (coil)
Rear ...	Semi-elliptic
Shock absorbers ...	Girling telescopic
Wheel type	Dunlop disc
Tyre size	Dunlop 6.50 x 16
Steering gear ...	Burman Recirculatory Ball
Steering wheel ...	18-in.
Dimensions:	
Wheelbase	9 ft. 6 in.
Track: Front ...	4 ft. 8$\frac{5}{8}$ in.
Rear ...	4 ft. 9$\frac{1}{2}$ in.
Overall length ...	16 ft. 1 in.
Overall width ...	6 ft. 0 in.
Overall height ...	5 ft. 3 in.
Ground clearance ...	8 in.
Turning circle ...	42$\frac{1}{2}$ ft.
Dry weight	31 cwt.
Performance Data:	
Piston area, sq. in. per ton	38.2
Brake lining area, sq. in. per ton ..	119
Top gear m.p.h. per 1,000 r.p.m. ..	20.2
Top gear m.p.h. at 2,500 ft./min. piston speed	85.5
Litres per ton-mile, dry	3,300

The Armstrong Siddeley Sapphire - Contd.

Other mechanical points of note include a Burman recirculatory ball steering gear with a ratio of 22 to 1, giving three turns of the wheel from lock to lock; Girling hydraulic brakes with two leading shoes on the front and 11-in. diameter drums; a 16-gallon rear tank carried on flexible mountings and arranged to provide a 1$\frac{1}{2}$-gallon reserve; and provision for a four-point Smith's Bevelift jacking system.

The body is of the all-steel type, and the four-light and six-light versions are identical in all respects except that additional windows (hinged for ventilation) are provided in the rear quarters in the latter case.

Of the five/six-seater type, the body provides generous internal accommodation with measurements of 55$\frac{1}{2}$ ins. across the front seats at elbow level and 54 ins. at the rear, whilst the knee room between the forward edge of the rear seat and the back of the front squab varies from 10$\frac{1}{2}$ ins. with the adjustment in its extreme rear position to 15$\frac{1}{2}$ ins. with the seat right forward. Head room is ample in both compartments and the body provides good visibility, a praiseworthy point being that both front wings are visible from the driving seat through the 14-in. deep curved screen. Wide-opening ventilating panels are fitted to the front doors.

BURR WALNUT is used for trim fillets and the facia panel, a glove locker and radio speaker occupying space in the latter. Fitted on the steering column is an arm carrying the tiny "gate" gear-change now used with the pre-selector box

Folding central arm rests are provided in both the front bench-type seat and in the rear, whilst side arm rests are also arranged in both cases, those at the front being attached to the doors. In the interests of long-legged passengers in the rear, the base of the front squab is cut away.

The upholstery is beautifully trimmed in leather, and that air of refinement which only wood can give is achieved by the use of burr-walnut for both the attractively-designed facia board and the window fillets.

The instrument panel itself is secured to the facia by Dzus clips and can be pulled forward to obtain access to the wiring.

The dials are circular and clear to read, the instruments concerned comprising a speedometer, clock, ammeter, oil gauge, thermometer and fuel gauge, whilst grouped round them are switches for the panel light, two-speed screen wiper, fuel reserve, head and side lamps, starter, heating system motor, ignition and dual built-in fog lamps, which are separately controlled. Below the board on the driver's side is the choke, and in the centre of the board are the controls for the fresh-air heating and demisting system.

Other internal details include visors (with vanity-mirror for the passenger), roof light, map-reading light, foot dipper, three ashtrays, cubby boxes in the rear quarters of the four-light model and deep pockets, with spring flaps, in all doors.

As for luggage, the Sapphire accommodation is outstandingly good. The boot, which has a top-hinged, counter-balanced lid, has a capacity of 17 cu. ft. with a large flat platform for suitcases above the spare wheel; to one side of the latter is a particularly-comprehensive tool kit housed in a fitted drawer with moulded-rubber recesses not only for the tools, but also for spare lamp bulbs, plugs and so on. Wheel-changing equipment is below this drawer, and everything is individually accessible.

The car is available in black or a choice of no fewer than six colours or, alternatively, in any two of these colours combined to produce a two-tone scheme. With its luxurious finish and appointments and its high-performance characteristics, this new Armstrong Siddeley Sapphire would, in any case, be a notable addition to the range of 1953 cars. Its introduction at a figure bringing it within the medium-price class will make it one of the most outstanding cars at the forthcoming Earls Court Show.

2.3-LITRE MODELS

ENGINE.—Dimensions: Cylinders, 6; bore, .0 mm.; stroke, 100 mm.; cubic capacity, 2,309 c.c.; piston area, 35.8 sq. in.; valves, o.h.v. (push-rod); compression ratio, 6.5 : 1. **Performance:** Max. b.h.p. 75 at 4,200 r p.m.; b.h.p. per sq. in. piston area, 2.10. **Details:** Carburetter (with synchro gearbox), Stromberg D.B.A.36; (with preselector gearbox), D.A.A. 36; ignition, coil; plugs, Champion N8; fuel capacity, 12 gallons (including one reserve); oil filter, Tecalemit.

TRANSMISSION —Type of gearbox optional; synchro-mesh; constant-mesh single helical gears; synchro on top, 3rd and 2nd; Clutch, single dry plate, Borg and Beck, 9.A6.G.; overall gear ratios: top, 5.10; 3rd, 7.24; 2nd, 10.89; 1st, 17.61; rev., 15.21; pre-selector: four-speed preselector gearbox with control on steering column; A.S.M. automatic centrifugal type clutch, single dry plate; overall gear ratios: top, 5.10; 3rd, 7.22; 2nd, 10.66; 1st, 18.36; rev., 22.79; propeller shaft, open Hardy Spicer, needle rollers; final drive, hypoid bevel.

CHASSIS DETAILS.—Brakes, front, Girling Hydrastatic; rear, Girling mechanical; friction lining area, 135 sq. in.; suspension, front, independent (torsion bars); rear, semi-elliptic; shock absorbers, Girling; tyre size, 5.50 by 17.

DIMENSIONS.—Wheelbase, 9 ft. 7 in.; track: front, 4 ft. 6 in.; rear, 4 ft. 6$\frac{1}{2}$ in.; overall length, 15 ft. 5 in.; overall width, 5 ft. 8 in.; overall height, 5 ft. 2 in.; ground clearance, 7$\frac{1}{2}$ in.; turning circle, 37 ft ; dry weight (Whitley saloon), 28$\frac{3}{4}$ cwt.

PERFORMANCE DATA.—Top gear m.p.h. per 1,000 r.p.m., 16.2; top gear m.p.h. at 2,500 ft./min. piston speed, 61.6; litres per ton mile dry (Whitley), 2,990.

The Armstrong Siddeley Sapphire has a very pleasing external appearance which combines a modern, functional body style with the elegance and tradition associated with this make.

ARMSTRONG SIDDELEY SAPPHIRE

High-performance 3½-litre with Electric Selection of Epicyclic Gear Bands

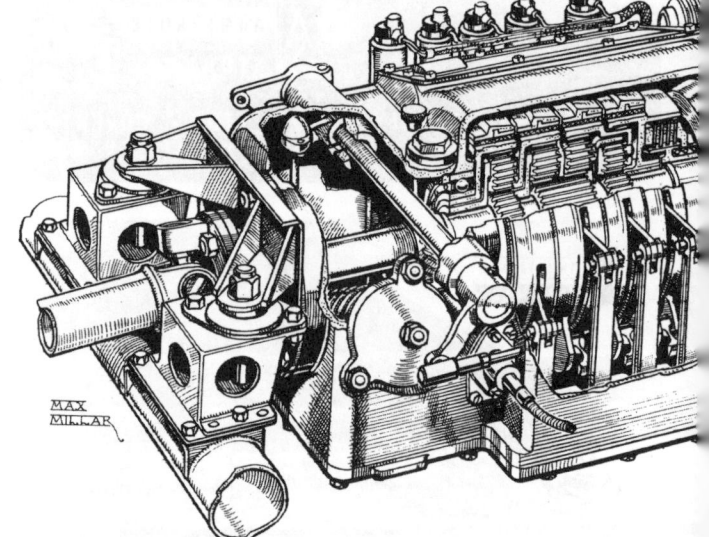

S OME of this country's outstanding producers of cars have a very close connection with the aircraft industry. As a result the extreme limits of accuracy and standards of reliability required of aircraft will also instil into the road vehicle that extra something in these directions. The Armstrong Siddeley company is just such a firm and the latest car produced by them is called the Sapphire, a name already famous in the aircraft world, in which it signifies a very fine engine. The Sapphire saloon is a completely new model powered by a 3.4-litre overhead-valve engine. It is a very smart four-door four-light saloon body and the transmission is by means of an electrically controlled preselector gear box.

In the design of the engine the company has endeavoured to produce a unit of high performance, yet one with the minimum number of working parts, as well as one that is simple to produce. It is well known that the hemispherical combustion chamber is a very popular choice if high power outputs are required, but in order to operate the valve gear with such an arrangement it is often necessary to use either two camshafts or a single camshaft and multiple push rods and levers. The first of these alternatives is often used if cost is a secondary consideration; the second is sometimes found when a high-performance engine has been developed from an o.h.v. unit with an orthodox arrangement of push rods, rockers, and vertical valves. However, on the Armstrong Siddeley engine neither of these methods is adopted, yet the engine has hemispherical combustion

chambers, inclined valves, only one camshaft, and one push rod per valve. In order to produce this layout the single side camshaft is mounted high up in the cylinder block so that the short push rods can operate the valves by means of rockers which are mounted on two rocker shafts (one for the inlet and one for the exhaust valves).

With this arrangement it is necessary to have a difference in length between the inlet and exhaust rods, but this is compensated for by arranging the longer rods to operate the smaller valves. The short push rods operate the large-diameter inlet valves, while the long rods operate the exhaust valves; in this way the difference in weight is reduced to a minimum. The push rods are unusual in that they are cupped at both ends, and not ball-ended at the lower end, as is

usual. A similar effect is produced by placing a steel ball between the push rod and the tappet, which has the advantage of reducing wear, as the ball is free to rotate.

Those who are familiar with the previous post-war Armstrong Siddeley car engines will notice that wet cylinder liners are not used on the Sapphire. Although the wet cylinder liner arrangement is perfectly satisfactory, and enables iron with a high chromium content to be used for the bores only, while the other part of the block may be ordinary good-quality close-grain iron, there are other factors which enter into the adoption or otherwise of this arrangement. For example, on a large engine with a four-bearing crankshaft the rigidity of the crankcase structure is extremely important in order to retain alignment between the bearings.

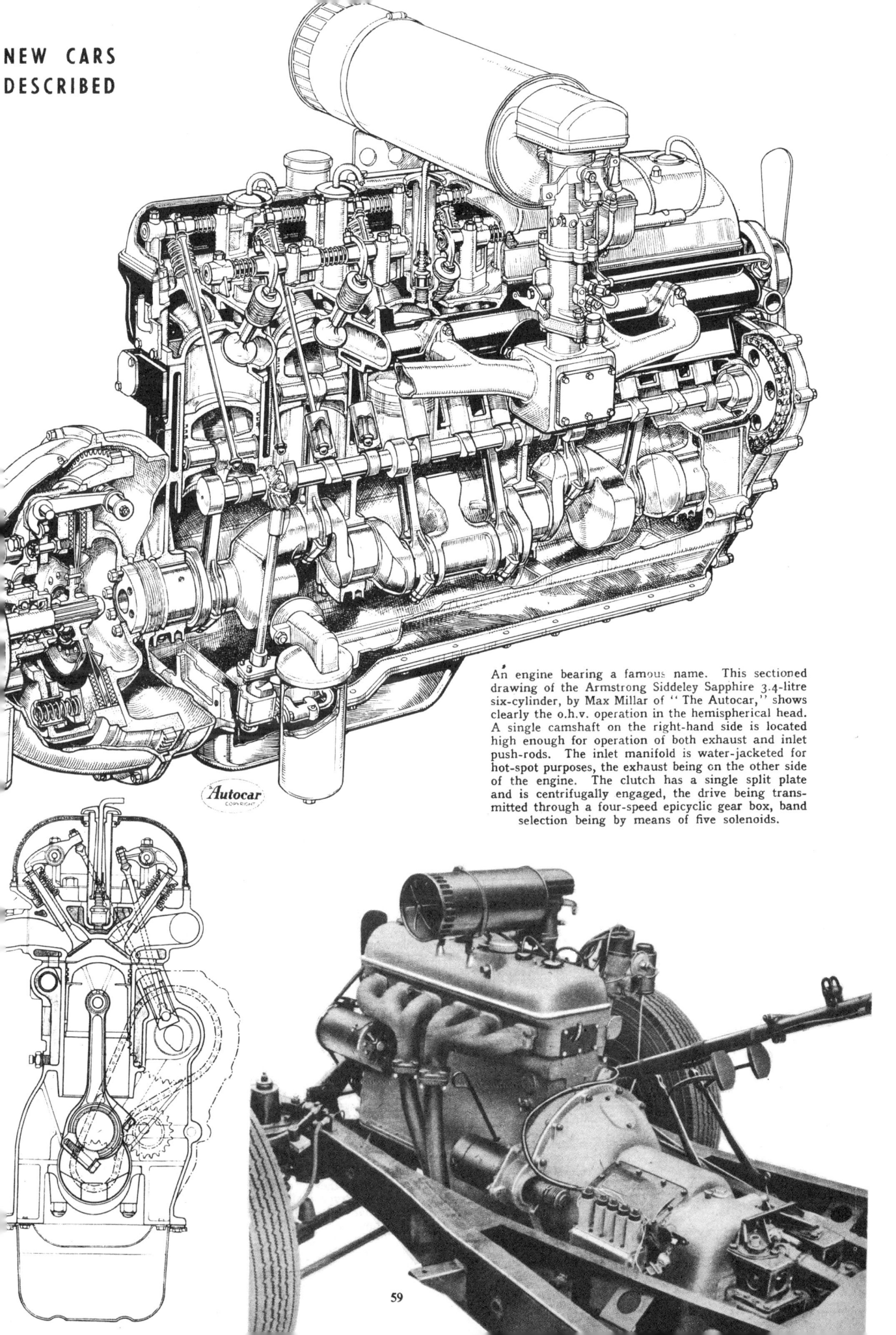

Autocar COPYRIGHT

An engine bearing a famous name. This sectioned drawing of the Armstrong Siddeley Sapphire 3.4-litre six-cylinder, by Max Millar of "The Autocar," shows clearly the o.h.v. operation in the hemispherical head. A single camshaft on the right-hand side is located high enough for operation of both exhaust and inlet push-rods. The inlet manifold is water-jacketed for hot-spot purposes, the exhaust being on the other side of the engine. The clutch has a single split plate and is centrifugally engaged, the drive being transmitted through a four-speed epicyclic gear box, band selection being by means of five solenoids.

The flowing lines of the Sapphire result in a very pleasing shape. The four-door four-light coachwork gives the car a neat, sporting appearance; the luggage locker is of large capacity.

If wet liners are used the cylinder block may require additional ribbing to take the place of the built-in stiffness that is produced if the bores are cast in one with the block. This, of course, is by no means an impossibility, but it tends to make the composite block heavier. On the Sapphire, then, the cylinder bores are cast in one with the block, but to reduce bore wear the top piston rings are chromium plated.

Carbon Steel Crank

The crankshaft is forged from carbon steel. It is of massive construction with balance weights between Nos. 1 and 2, 3 and 4, and 5 and 6 cylinders. The main bearings are 2¾in diameter and 1¼in long for Nos. 1, 2 and 3, while the rear main bearing, which also takes the thrust, is 2¾in diameter and 1½in long. A return thread and oil thrower is machined on the rear end of the shaft, while at the front end a normal type of oil seal is fitted in the timing cover. Both main and big-end bearings are precision steel-backed, while the connecting rods themselves are forged from carbon steel, with big-ends split at an angle. The bearing cap location is by spigot bushes, the two halves being held together by set bolts. Hollow fully floating gudgeon pins located by circlips support the pistons, which carry two compression and one oil control ring.

The crankchamber extends well below the crankshaft centre line, and, apart from increasing the rigidity of the structure, this arrangement also permits a completely flat sump joint base. Two baffle-plates are fitted to the pressed steel sump; there is also a top plate, which is attached to the crankcase before the sump is assembled and prevents oil from splashing on the rotating parts. The Holborn Heaton oil pump is gear driven from the camshaft and is fed through a floating filter. Oil under pressure from the pump passes up to a pressure chamber around the gear pump drive shaft into a full-flow oil filter, and from there to the main oil gallery running along the side of the cylinder block. From here it passes through drillings to the main bearings, and through the crankshaft to the big-end bearings. Further drillings also lubricate the steel-backed bearings which support the case-hardened steel crankshaft. The oil pump drive gear is lubricated by means of a small bleed hole from the oil pressure chamber around the pump drive shaft.

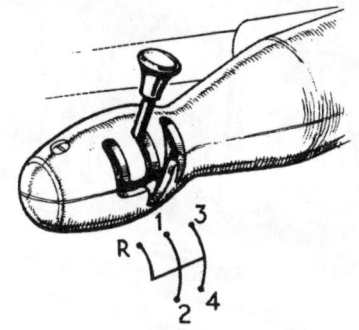

The preselector on the steering column is a five-position switch operated by a short lever moving in a "gate."

A vertical drilling from the front centre main bearing web conveys oil up through the block to the front centre camshaft bearing, past this bearing and up through the cylinder head to the first hollow rocker shaft (the camshaft journal at this point has a small flat on its bearing surface which regulates the oil). Oil to the second rocker shaft is conveyed by means of a short pipe fitted with banjo ends. From the rocker shaft oil is fed to each end of the rockers by means of drillings, which, with the rocker pad, allow oil to travel along the outside of the rocker. To lubricate the ball end which contacts the push rod an internal drilling registers with a groove turned in the threaded portion of the rocker adjusting screw. This in turn is cross-drilled, and centrally drilled, so that oil is fed direct to the ball end of the screw.

The camshaft is driven by a duplex chain fitted with a tensioning device which can be adjusted from the outside of the timing cover, and both the chain itself and the tensioner are fed with oil. A single cover encloses both sets of rockers; it consists of an inner and outer pressed steel skin, between which felt is sandwiched to act as a sound-deadening medium. Because of the one-piece rocker cover arrangement it is necessary to fit tubes around the sparking plug bosses, which extend up through the top of the rocker cover. As is usual when this type of construction is adopted, the high tension leads are fitted with long connectors.

The water pump is belt driven from a crankshaft pulley and supplies coolant to a tube which runs through the length of the cylinder head. This is cross-drilled so that jets of water impinge around the exhaust ports. The coolant then passes out through the radiator and back to the intake side of the pump. The coolant around the bores is semi-stagnant, but there are, of course, water holes between the joint faces of the cylinder head and block. The cooling system is slightly pressurized.

Fuel is metered to the engine by means of a 36mm single downdraught Stromberg carburettor with a manually operated choke device. This method of choking is desirable, as the car is fitted with a centrifugal clutch, and the fairly high tick-over speed during the warming-up operation that is associated with an automatic choke might prove to be a disadvantage. Twin three-branch manifolds convey the exhaust gases to the silencer.

Power from the engine is transmitted by means of an Armstrong Siddeley dry single-plate centrifugal clutch to the preselector gear box. The general operating principles will be briefly described, as it is proposed to deal with this transmission unit in detail at a later date. Briefly, a pedal actuated epicyclic gear box is used, but, whereas with previous models produced by this company the gear selection was made by mechanically operated mechanism, on the Sapphire the gear selection is performed electrically by means of solenoids.

Gear Change Switch

The remote control steering column gear change lever is, in fact, a multi-position switch which selects the solenoid required for the desired gear. Operation of the gear pedal momentarily closes the solenoid circuit and the solenoid thereupon selects the necessary brake band. This is subsequently tightened by the further release of the pedal. By this method the solenoid is energized only briefly and cannot be overloaded by holding the clutch pedal in the fully depressed position. From the gear box the power is transmitted through a two-

A flexible mounting at the frame centre is provided for the middle bearing of the divided propeller-shaft.

Release of the left pedal momentarily closes the circuit to whichever solenoid has been selected, through this master switch on the side of the gear box.

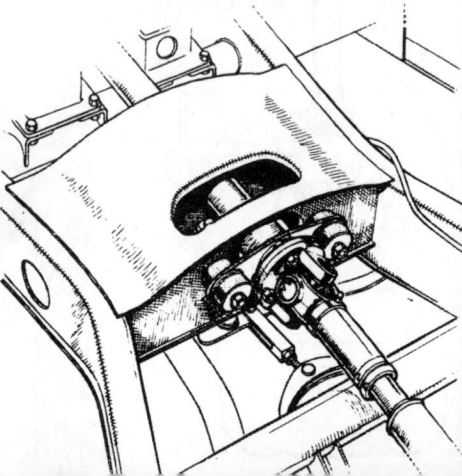

piece propeller-shaft to the Salisbury hypoid final drive.

The chassis frame is of very stiff construction and the deep side members are braced by a modified cruciform centre section; there are also two tubular cross members. The front one is of a very massive construction and is attached to the chassis side members by fourteen $\frac{3}{8}$in diameter high-tensile bolts, four in the horizontal plane and three in the vertical plane on each side. This method of construction enables the front suspension unit to be built up as a complete assembly before it is attached to the main frame. The independent front suspension is by means of semi-trailing wishbones (set at an angle of 25 degrees) and coil springs with telescopic dampers

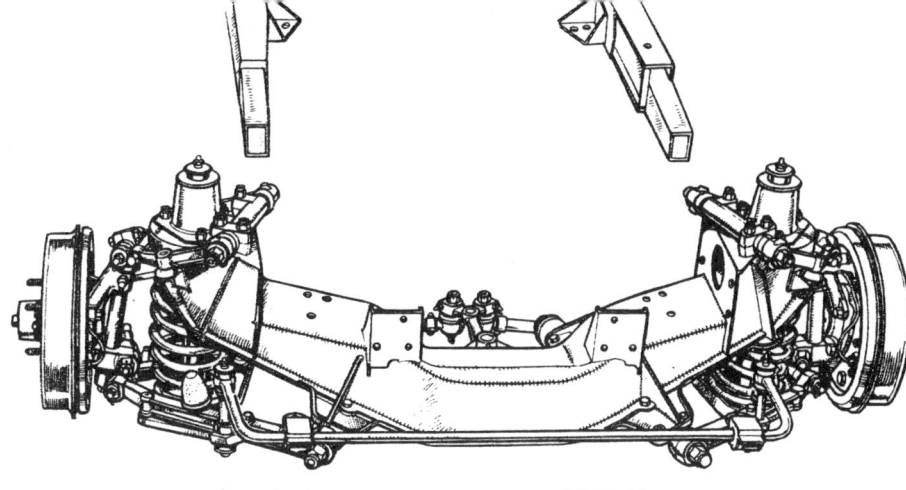

Front suspension is by double wishbones and coil springs which embrace the telescopic dampers. A front anti-roll bar is fitted. The whole suspension assembly, complete with cross-member, can be withdrawn from the chassis as shown.

As is typical with this "classical" type of car, the frame is conventional, having side members and a modified cruciform, supplemented by tubular cross-members. The petrol tank is flexibly mounted.

SPECIFICATION

Engine.—6 cyl, 90×90 mm (3,435.3 c.c.). Compression ratio 6.5 to 1. Four-bearing crankshaft, EN9T55 carbon steel. Hemispherical combustion chambers. Side camshaft, operating inclined overhead valves by push rods and rockers.

Clutch.—Armstrong Siddeley centrifugal $9\frac{1}{4}$in diameter dry single-plate.

Gear Box.—Electrically operated preselector. Overall ratios: Top 4.091 to 1; third 5.564 to 1; second 8.153 to 1; first 13,909 to 1; reverse 19.473 to 1. Alternatively: All-synchromesh; overall ratios 4.091, 5.087, 8.540 and 12.800 to 1. Reverse, 13.530 to 1. Steering column change lever.

Final Drive.—Salisbury hypoid bevel. Ratio 4.09 to 1 (11:45).

Suspension.—Front, independent by coil springs and 25-degree trailing wishbones. Girling telescopic dampers and anti-roll bar. Rear, half-elliptic leaf springs. Girling telescopic dampers and anti-roll bar. Suspension rate (at the wheel), front 90lb per in; rear 109lb per in.

Brakes.—Girling hydraulic two-leading-shoe front, leading and trailing rear. Drums $11 \times 2\frac{1}{4}$in front and rear. Total lining area 184 sq in (93 sq in front).

Steering.—Burman recirculatory ball.

Wheels and Tyres.—Dunlop 6.50-16in on 5-stud steel disc wheels with broad base rims.

Electrical Equipment.—12-volt, 64 ampère-hour battery. Head lamps, single dip, 48-48 watt bulbs.

Fuel System.—16-gallon tank (including 1.5 gallon reserve). Oil capacity 11 pints (total). Full-flow oil filter.

Main Dimensions.—Wheelbase 9ft 6in. Track, front 4ft $8\frac{1}{4}$in; rear 4ft $9\frac{1}{2}$in. Overall length 16ft 1in. Width 6ft. Height (laden) 5ft 3in. Ground clearance (laden) 8in. Frontal area 25 sq ft approx. Turning circle 42ft 6in (3 turns from lock to lock). Weight (in running trim with 16 gallons fuel), $32\frac{1}{2}$ cwt (3,640 lb). Weight distribution 50 per cent front; 50 per cent rear.

Price.—£1,110. Purchase tax in Great Britain £618 3s 4d. Total (in Great Britain), £1,728 3s 4d.

mounted inside them. The upper wishbones pivot on threaded bearings, while the lower ones are provided with Metalastik rubber bushes. The steering unit consists of a Burman recirculatory ball steering box that operates a divided track rod. The rear suspension is a conventional Hotchkiss drive with leaf springs set to give a 5-degree angle of inclination (front end downwards); the rear telescopic dampers are inclined inwards towards the chassis centre line to increase stability, and anti-roll bars are fitted at both front and rear.

The body is produced from 19-gauge steel pressings which are hand fitted as distinct from the full mass production method of multiple jig welding. Both the body framework and the panels are steel. "Snake wire" upholstery with a rubberized hair overlay is used in the front seats, while coil springs are used in the rear seat.

Release of the gear pedal lifts the bus bar and tightens whichever band has been selected by means of the solenoid mechanism.

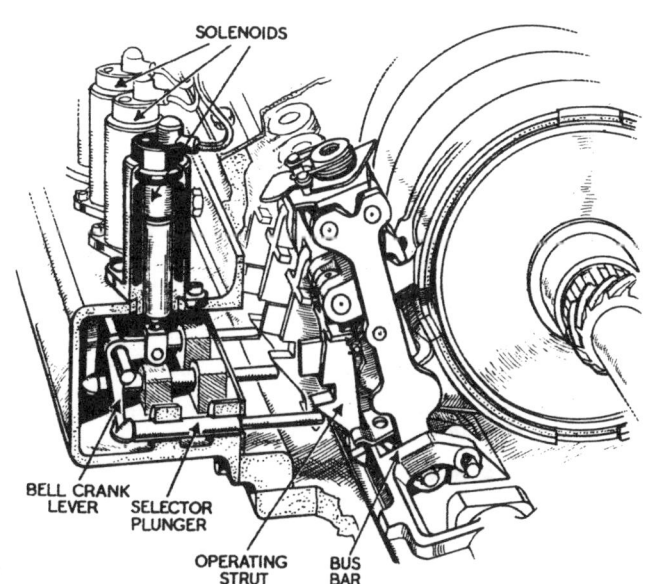

SOLENOIDS

BELL CRANK LEVER

SELECTOR PLUNGER

OPERATING STRUT

BUS BAR

ARMSTRONG SIDDELEY SAPPHIRE

- All-steel bodywork on cross-braced chassis frame.
- Torsion anti-roll bar reinforcing both front and rear suspension.
- Six-cylinder engine with inclined o.h.v. in hemispherical combustion chambers.
- Centrifugal clutch and electrically-controlled, epicyclic, four-speed gearbox.

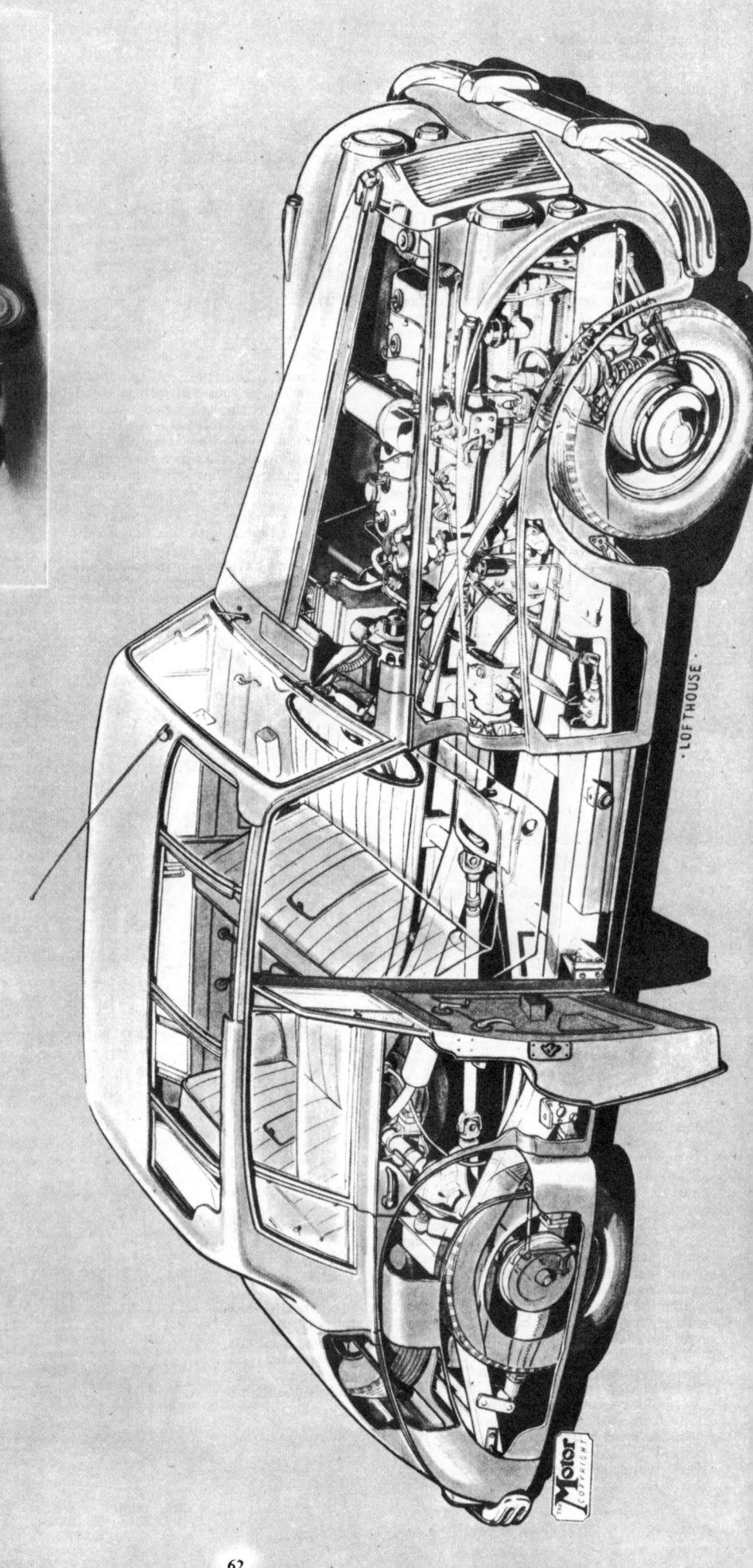

·LOFTHOUSE·

Quality and performance are readily apparent in the Sapphire's appearance and specifications.

New Sapphire

The only completely new British car shown at Earls Court last fall was the Armstrong Siddeley "Sapphire". Not since the prewar high performance "Siddeley Special" has this very conservative firm offered such an interesting automobile. The Sapphire is new from bumper to bumper (of that, more later), and is powered by a "square" six of just under 3.5 litres displacement. Priced at around $4000, it offers 90 mph performance, with traditional Armstrong-Siddeley quality and longevity.

The Sapphire has a conventional channel frame with X member, and the independent front suspension is along more conventional lines than the 2.3 litre model, which incidentally, is to be continued. Whereas the 2.3 has ball joint suspension with torsion bars, the new 3.5 uses coil springs. The upper and lower wishbones are arranged to give more "trailing effect" than is usual, and torsion anti-roll bars are carried on both ends of the chassis. Rear suspension is by semi-elliptic springs, and Girling telescopic shock absorbers are used front and rear.

The new engine sets well forward, and aside from the equal bore and stroke of 90 mm (3.54 in.), its most interesting feature is certainly the use of inclined valves actuated by pushrods and rockers from a single camshaft located high in the cylinder block. A remarkably similar design by the Tech. Ed. appeared in Misc. Ramblings July 1951. This scheme has much to recommend it since the pushrods are only 8 in. and 9.75 in. long.

With a compression ratio of only 6.5 to 1, the maximum output is 120 bhp at 4200 rpm. Since top speed with 120 bhp will not be much over 90 mph (the corresponding rpm is 4450), the need for overhead camshafts does not exist.

The crankshaft is carried in 7 main bearings of 2.75 in. in diameter, and for some reason the connecting rods are split at an angle of 45 degrees, even though the crankpin diameter is only 2.125 in. The usual reason for splitting the rods at an angle is to permit their withdrawal through the cylinder bore, a requirement which is difficult to achieve when the bore is small and the crankpin is large.

Other engine features include a water-jacketed intake manifold, careful attention to secure a free-flowing exhaust, and a very rigid (and heavy) cylinder block and head castings.

Following earlier A.S. policy, the new car is offered with either a conventional clutch and 4-speed transmission, or an improved preselector "box". The preselector transmission uses epicyclic gears controlled by brake bands. A modification is the employment of electric solenoids to energize the bands. In this way, the gear selector level need only be a very small unit similar to the Bendix "electric hand" once used by Hudson and Cord (see page 10). It is well-known that band controlled transmissions do not give smooth starts, and in the A. S. transmission an automatic centrifugal clutch is used to solve this problem. Normal starts can be made by engaging either 1st or 2nd gear, but the car will not move away until the engine has been speeded up to the point that the centrifugal weights cause the clutch to engage. The engagement of the clutch is so smooth that satisfactory starts can be effected in 3rd or even 4th gear, though, of course, such a procedure is not recommended.

The Sapphire designers have, by careful attention to detail, managed to achieve a chassis weight on the new car only 62 pounds greater than on the 2.3 litre model. Nevertheless, the complete car weighs approximately 450 pounds more, due to the more commodious bodies.

For the American market the styling of this interesting car is one of the most unhappy compromises yet seen. It has neither the true classic qualities of, say, the Riley, nor the sleek modern lines of a Mark VII. About all that can be said in favor of the Sapphire's appearance is that the bumpers are exceptionally neat. •

Unusual 3½ litre engine powers this new saloon.

The Sapphire was loaned to "Wheels" by the New South Wales distributors, Buckle Motors (Trading Co.) Pty. Ltd.

Technical Details

ENGINE :

6 cyl., o.h.v., hemispherical head with inclined valves and single side camshaft. 90 mm. bore x 90 mm. stroke. Capacity 3,425 c.c. Comp. ratio 6.5 : 1. Max. b.h.p. 120 at 4,200 r.p.m. Max. torque 165 ft./lb. at 2,000 r.p.m. Road speed 85.5 m.p.h. at 2,500 ft./min. piston speed. 20.2 m.p.h. per 1,000 r.p.m. in top.

Single Stromberg downdraught carburetter. AC mechanical fuel pump. Full-flow oil filter.

SUSPENSION :

I.F.S. by trailing wishbones and coil springs. Semi-elliptics at rear with anti-roll bar. Girling telescopic shock absorbers.

TRANSMISSION :

Fluid flywheel, centrifugal dry-plate clutch, 4-speed electrically-operated preselector gearbox. Miniature gate change on steering column. Ratios 4.091, 5.564, 8.153, 13.909. Reverse 19.473. Semi-floating rear axle with hypoid bevel final drive. Divided propeller shaft.

BRAKES :

Girling hydraulic, two leading shoes in front. Under-facia pull-out handbrake on rear wheels.

WHEELS :

Disc, 6.50 x 16" tyres.

CHASSIS :

Cruciform, boxed in centre section.

BODY :

Pressed steel, 4-light, 4-6 passenger, leather upholstery, walnut cappings.

WEIGHT :

31 cwt.

IGNITION :

12 volt, 64 amp./hour battery.

STEERING :

Burmann recirculating ball, ratio 20.4 : 1; 8 turns from lock-to-lock, turning circle 42 feet.

SPEED :

90 m.p.h.

FUEL CONSUMPTION :

22 m.p.g.

MEASUREMENTS :

Wheelbase 9' 6"; front track 4' 8⅝", rear track 4' 9½"; height 5' 3"; length, 16' 1"; width 6'. Ground clearance 8".

ARMSTRONG SIDDELEY SAPPHIRE

AN unusual new 3½ litre engine, fluid flywheel and electrically-operated pre-selector gearbox are the most interesting features of the Armstrong Siddeley Sapphire, a new high-performance luxury touring saloon which sells competitively at £2,250.

Nothing has been overlooked in designing this four-light saloon, which is a pleasing combination of modernity and tradition. Tastefully finished, it provides luxury travel for four people and ample accommodation for six when required.

The new 120 b.h.p., overhead-valve engine has a top speed in excess of 90 miles per hour, with a comfortable cruising speed of 70 to 75 m.p.h.

Overhead valves in a hemispherical combustion chamber are operated by short push rods, passing through the cylinder block, from a side camshaft —the first time a British production touring car has had this feature.

The all-steel body is in line with the modern trend, displaying clean and pleasing lines. Visibility is excellent throughout; both front wings can be clearly seen from the driver's seat and a low squared window design gives passengers full vision, making the car refreshingly light and airy inside at the same time.

The roomy boot, with a capacity of 17 cubic feet, is well finished; the spare wheel has its own compartment and the tools are nested individually in a moulded rubber tray. The boot lid is counterbalanced by torsion bars and will stay open in any position.

Interior woodwork, including the facia, is of polished burr walnut, and all upholstery is of leather. The divided tail-shaft eliminates the hump in the rear floor. Useful pockets are placed in all doors, and the roof is lined in cream washable plasticised linen.

A heater-and-cooler is standard equipment and full provision has been made for the fitting of a radio. The two-speed, electrically-operated windscreen wipers cover a large area of the screen.

Following a practice adopted by Armstrong Siddeley in 1928, a four-speed pre-selector gearbox is used; a major innovation this year is the addition of electrically-controlled solenoids operating the selector. A touch of a finger on the small switch lever set in a miniature gate beneath the steering wheel selects the gear and foot pressure on the clutch pedal closes the solenoid circuit, changing the ratio.

The Sapphire's performance on the highway is either vivid or gentle, according to the driver's mood.

Acceleration is strong and gear-changing is rapid, particularly downwards. The position of the gearchange pedal could perhaps be changed to give a better leverage for the driver. The gear ratios themselves are well-balanced and third gives an invitation to the driver to use it briskly as it is silent and powerful.

Noise from the new square engine is at a minimum even when it is pressed hard through the gears. The car can be cornered very fast without undue roll or tyre squeal.

Luxury interior has flat floor for comfort, low window line for visibility.

A firm suspension is used, and bumpy surfaces can be felt distinctly at town speeds, although not uncomfortably. Above 40 m.p.h. the ride flattens out and the highest speeds produce no sway, bump-wallowing or dithering, giving both driver and passengers confidence in the car.

The Sapphire responds to being driven—as distinct from the lazy use to which it seems equally suited—and the expert driver will be well satisfied with the results obtainable from free use of the gearbox.

CONTINUED ON PAGE 89

Instruments are neatly grouped in front of driver; a miniature gearshift gate, operating solenoids, replaces the manual control.

Lid of full-width boot is kept open at any angle by torsion bars; spare wheel compartment has rubber-lined tool drawer.

The Sapphire has a smart, distinctive body style with clean lines but an air of individuality. The car is particularly attractive in two-tone exterior treatment.

ARMSTRONG SIDDELEY SAPPHIRE SALOON

THE name Sapphire is well known in the aircraft world as that of a very powerful turbo-jet engine produced by the Armstrong Siddeley company. It is not surprising, then, that this name should be used by the company for their latest car. First shown to the public in the autumn of last year, the Sapphire created very considerable interest, both æsthetically, as the car is striking in appearance and a good-looker, and technically, as the engine and transmission have a number of interesting features such as hemispherical combustion chambers with inclined valves operated by a single side camshaft, and an electrically operated preselector mechanism for the Wilson-type gear box.

With an accent on refinement, the Sapphire has a very definite air of quality together with a very lively performance. It is a car for the specialist motorist who requires a vehicle with a measure of individuality not to be found in a quantity produced car, but who also requires good value for money. Providing a very useful mean maximum speed comfortably over the 90 mark—91.25 m.p.h. under the test conditions, to be exact—the 3½-litre engine is tuned to produce a high torque at low r.p.m., where it is needed for normal purposes, and in consequence the acceleration is very brisk. The time for the standing quarter mile is 20 sec, while half that time is required to accelerate from 30 to 50 m.p.h. on top gear. The Sapphire will cruise comfortably at 75 to 80 on a very accurate speedometer, while at 60 it seems to be taking life very easily indeed. The six-cylinder engine is particularly smooth and silky, although with the ignition set for optimum performance there is a trace of pinking even on first grade fuel. This is a little

surprising in view of the compression ratio and the shape of the combustion chamber.

The transmission includes a four-speed planetary gear box with electrically operated preselection, together with a centrifugal friction clutch. The electrical system does not perform the actual gear change, which is done by the "clutch" pedal, but is used to operate the mechanism which decides which gear is to be selected; the solenoids used for this purpose are energized only momentarily as the clutch pedal is being released. The control switch itself is a finger lever which works in a five-position visible gate on the end of an arm mounted on the steering column. It is well placed and convenient to operate—the only criticism is that it gives a quite loud click when a change of position is made.

The normal system of preselector gear changing is used with this transmission, and the centrifugally operated plate clutch provides a smooth take-up when starting from rest in the forward direction, although on the car tested there was some tendency for it to grab in reverse. This was more particularly noticeable when operating in a confined space, such as parking at the kerb between two other cars or when reversing out of a garage. On the open road the transmission is very pleasant; fast changes can be made without the driver taking his hand off the steering wheel at the time when the actual change is made. The mechanism also proved very convenient for the fast full-throttle gear changes used when taking the performance figures, and under these conditions there was no sign of excessive slip of either the clutch or the gear box band friction linings.

The suspension is an example of modern conventional

There is a folding central arm rest in both seats as well as combined arm rests and pulls attached to the front doors. All the doors have deep pockets with spring-loaded lids. Passenger grab handles are provided in both compartments.

A traditional style of radiator grille blends well with the general lines. Separate built-in fog lamps are mounted below the faired-in head lamps, and an over-rider is fitted to the wide bumper on each side of the front number plate. Right : The clean, sweeping contours can be seen from this angle. The front wing line is carried right through the panel enclosing the rear wheel. Both doors are hinged from the central pillar, and a trap door in the rear wing conceals the fuel filler cap.

design, independent at the front with coil springs and wishbones, and by half-elliptic leaf springs at the rear. It is perhaps a little unusual in that there is an anti-roll bar at both front and rear. The car is very stable on corners and, driven two up, there is a noticeable amount of understeer, but with passengers in the rear compartment and a good quantity of luggage in the locker this is considerably reduced and a condition of neutral steering is obtained. A very slight trace of wander was noticed at speeds above the 90 mark on one particular stretch of Continental road of the *autobahn* type, but that tendency was not noticed in this country and perhaps may have been excited by the expansion joints between the slabs of concrete on the road in question. The springing generally is very good and over all types of road surface the Sapphire provides a smooth ride. The suspension damping also seems just about right for normal operation, although a fast driver might prefer a slightly harder damper setting at the rear.

The steering is geared to give $3\frac{1}{2}$ turns from lock to lock, it is light and positive, and has a good self-centring action; also it does not transmit shocks back through the wheel. The brakes are powerful and progressive and did not show any sign of fade either on the road when the car was driven fast, or during the performance testing. There was no loss of balance or noticeable increase in free pedal travel during a very considerable mileage.

As regards engine noise, the Sapphire is very quiet, but

there is some gear noise in the lower ratios, a slight whine associated with this type of unit used, which is not excessive. No vibrations are transmitted to the car body from the mechanical components. Some tyre noise is noticed, particularly when traversing cat's eye reflector studs. There is comparatively little wind noise even with the windows or ventilator panels open, and draught-free air circulation can be arranged by opening the front quarter lights and the hinged panels which form the rear side windows.

The ultimate test for a car's driving position is to sit in it for a very long journey, when slight discomforts, which may appear to be of only a minor nature on a half-hour trip, become items of major importance. As regards driving comfort the Sapphire earns full marks. The wheel is correctly raked and well placed in relation to both the pedals and the seat, and the pedals themselves are nicely positioned. It would be even better if the throttle pedal were a little larger and perhaps closer to the body side panel to give increased leg support. An unusual feature about the construction of the throttle pedal itself is that the pad is rubber mounted, presumably to insulate the driver from possible vibration. There is plenty of room for the left leg, and the foot-operated dip switch is well placed.

From the driving seat there is good forward visibility and the side lamps on the top of the front wings can be clearly seen. Tell-tale lights are built in to indicate that the side lights are functioning correctly at night, and these also act as useful distance markers. Thin windscreen pillars and a large glass area, together with a carefully placed mirror, produce very good all-round visibility. A two-speed electric motor powers the windscreen wipers, which cover a useful area of the screen. The instruments, together with the minor controls, are grouped in front of the two-spoke steering wheel in a position where they can be readily seen by the driver. The instrument lighting is sufficiently bright to enable the gauges to be seen at night, but it does not cause glare or reflections in the screen.

Although the front doors are quite thick at the bottom, a feature that is inconvenient at times when the car is parked in a relatively narrow garage, under normal conditions when space is not limited the front of the car is very easy to get in and out of. The seats are exceptionally well sprung and upholstered. Both back rest and cushion of the single bench-type front seat are of ample proportions and provide plenty of support. The rear seat, too, is well arranged; there is

The sparking plug leads pass through insulators in the top of the rocker cover. The single carburettor is provided with a large air cleaner placed athwart the engine. All the electrical equipment is conveniently mounted on the bulkhead ; the battery is on the left-hand side, while the coil, regulator box, fuses and windscreen wiper motor are on the left. The ignition distributor is placed high up towards the rear of the engine.

The large luggage locker is lined with insulating material which also prevents damage to the luggage. There is a separate lower compartment for the spare wheel, and the unusually complete range of small tools is carried in a tray above the jack and starting handle.

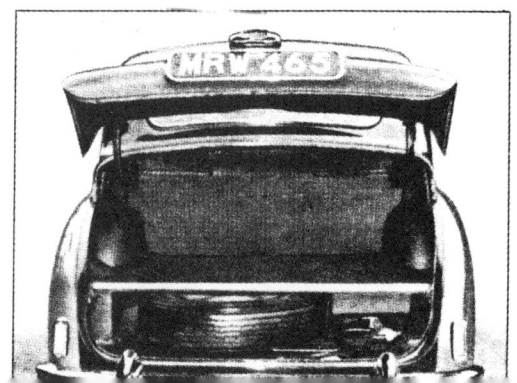

plenty of leg room even with the front seat set well back, and sufficient width to accommodate three people.

The interior generally deserves special comment, as the fittings and trim are all very well finished, without ostentation, a feature that contributes markedly to this car's very definite air of quality and well-being. There is an abundance of genuine leather of fine quality and polished hardwood in specialist bodywork style—materials associated with English quality coachwork. The head lining is a fine-ribbed plastic material which helps to produce a bright and clean interior. In the facia there is a lockable glove box with a sloping floor to prevent the contents from falling out when the lid is opened; there is also a useful tray behind the rear seats. The main luggage compartment is large. The 16-gallon fuel tank can be filled very quickly without risk of blowing back. It is large enough to provide a very useful range, and also incorporates the now rare and sometimes invaluable provi-

sion of a reserve, controlled from the facia. The horns are very effective and have a penetrating yet pleasing note; they are controlled by a button in the centre of the steering wheel. The double dipped head lamps provide a powerful main beam for fast night driving, together with a good spread of light when in the dipped position.

Starting from cold was at all times very good, and little use of the mixture control was required in the fairly high air temperatures prevailing. The front suspension and steering has 17 lubricating points which require attention at intervals of 2,000 miles.

The Armstrong Siddeley Sapphire is a British quality car which sets a high standard of performance and detail finish. It is not excessively thirsty for its engine size, and is very good value for money in its class. More important than all this, perhaps—it is a pleasing car to drive and quite easily the best model yet to issue from a famous factory.

ARMSTRONG SIDDELEY SAPPHIRE SALOON

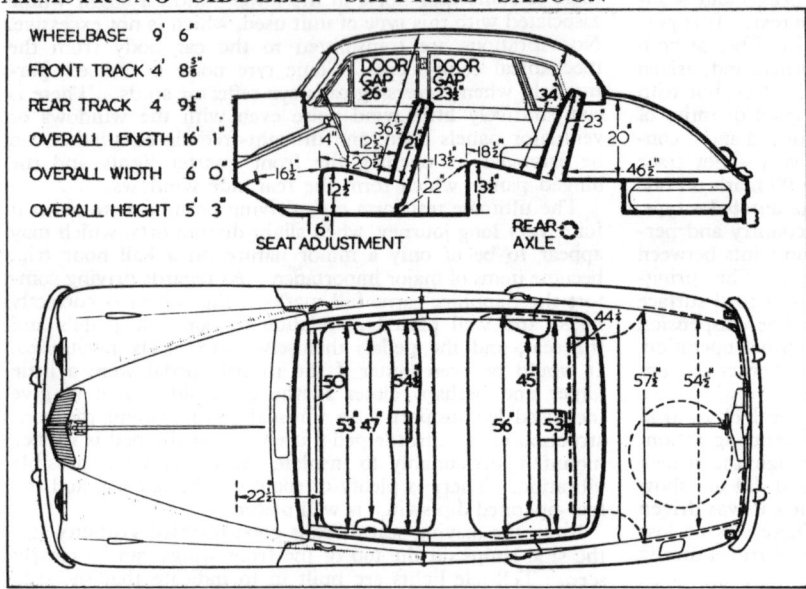

WHEELBASE 9' 6"
FRONT TRACK 4' 8⅝"
REAR TRACK 4' 9½"
OVERALL LENGTH 16' 1"
OVERALL WIDTH 6' 0"
OVERALL HEIGHT 5' 3"

Measurements in these ⅛ in to 1ft scale body diagrams are taken with the driving seat in the central position of fore and aft adjustment and with the seat cushions uncompressed.

── DATA ──

PRICE (basic), with saloon body £1,110.
British purchase tax, £463 12s 6d.
Total (in Great Britain), £1,573 12s 6d.
Extras : Radio £43 18s 4d.
Heater, Fitted as standard.

ENGINE : Capacity : 3435 c.c. (209.64 cu in).
Number of cylinders : 6
Bore and stroke : 90×90 mm (3.543 × 3.543 in).
Valve gear : Overhead, push rods.
Compression ratio : 7 to 1.
B.H.P. 125 at 4,400 r.p.m. (B.H.P. per ton laden 70.2).
Torque 176.5 lb ft at 1,000 r.p.m.
M.P.H. per 1,000 r.p.m. on top gear, 20.2.

WEIGHT (with 5 gals fuel), 32 cwt (3584 lb).
Weight distribution (per cent) 50.8 F ; 49.2 R.
Laden as tested : 35¾ cwt. (3,998 lb).
Lb per c.c. (laden) : 1.16.

BRAKES : Type : F, Two-leading shoe. R, leading and trailing.
Method of operation : F, Hydraulic. R, Hydraulic.
Drum dimensions : F, 11in diameter ; 2¼in wide. R, 11in diameter ; 2¼in wide.
Lining area : F, 93 sq in. R, 91 sq in. (103 sq in per ton laden).

TYRES : 6.70 — 16in.
Pressures (lb per sq in) : 24 F ; 26 R. (normal).

TANK CAPACITY : 16 Imperial gallons (including 1½ gallons reserve).
Oil sump, 10 pints.
Cooling system, 28 pints.

TURNING CIRCLE : 42rt 6in (L and R).
Steering wheel turns (lock to lock) : 3½.

DIMENSIONS : Wheelbase 9ft 6in.
Track : F, 4ft 8⅝in ; R, 4ft 9½in.
Length (overall) : 16ft 1in.
Height : 5ft 3in.
Width 6ft 0in.
Ground clearance : 8in.
Frontal area : 25 sq ft (approx.).

ELECTRICAL SYSTEM : 12-volt, 64 ampère-hour battery.
Head lights : Double dip, 48-48 watt.

SUSPENSION : Front, Independent coil springs and wishbones ; anti-roll bar.
Rear, Half-elliptic leaf springs and anti-roll bar.

── PERFORMANCE ──

ACCELERATION : from constant speeds. Speed, Gear Ratios and time in sec.

M.P.H.	4.091 to 1	5.564 to 1	8.153 to 1	13.909 to 1
10—30	7.9	6.8	5.1	4.3
20—40	9.5	7.3	5.5	—
30—50	10.0	7.9	6.6	—
40—60	11.9	8.8	—	—
50—60	13.6	10.6	—	—
60—80	16.6	—	—	—

From rest through gears to :

M.P.H.	sec
30	4.6
50	10.1
60	15.5
70	22.0
80	32.7

Standing quarter mile, 20.0 sec.

SPEED ON GEARS :

Gear		M.P.H. (normal and max.)	K.P.H. (normal and max.)
Top	(mean)	91.25	146.89
	(best)	91.50	147.28
3rd		64—78	103—126
2nd		40—51	64—82
1st		25—30	40—48

TRACTIVE RESISTANCE : 22.5 lb per ton at 10 M.P.H.

TRACTIVE EFFORT :

	Pull (lb per ton)	Equivalent Gradient
Top	255	1 in 8.75
Third	320	1 in 6.9
Second	420	1 in 5.2

BRAKES :

Efficiency	Pedal Pressure (lb)
86 per cent	100
68 per cent	75
46 per cent	50

FUEL CONSUMPTION :
18 m.p.g. overall for 376 miles, (15.7 litres per 100 km).
Approximate normal range 17-20 m.p.g. (16.6-14.1 litres per 100 km).
Fuel, First grade.

WEATHER : Fine, dry ; very slight wind.
Air temperature 68 degrees F.
Acceleration figures are the means of several runs in opposite directions.
Tractive effort and resistance obtained by Tapley meter.
Model described in *The Autocar* of October 10, 1952.

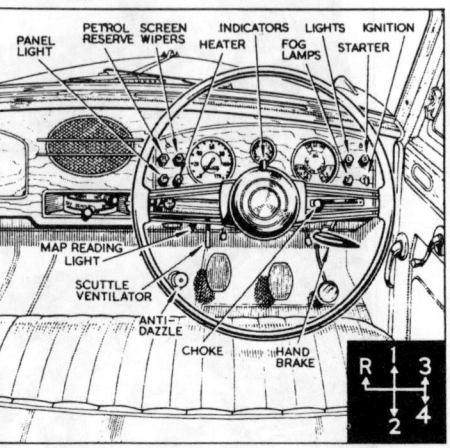

SPEEDOMETER CORRECTION : M.P.H.

Car speedometer			10	20	30	40	50	60	70	80	90	91
True speed			10	20	29	39	49	59	68	79	89	91

The Pedigree Car
with the
Jet-Bred Engine

The new Armstrong Siddeley Sapphire has the performance of a very fast car—the appearance and appointments of a luxury carriage.
The engine is a new 120 B.H.P. 'square-type'—built on the same production lines as the Sapphire jet that powers the world's fastest aeroplanes. Top speed is 95 m.p.h., acceleration is very responsive, yet *fuel consumption is amazingly low — over 20 m.p.g.!* Special anti-roll bars are fitted front and rear to give far faster, and safer cornering. Gears may be either synchromesh or new "Selectric". Both give ready racing changes. Externally, the lines of the coachwork are sweeping and elegant. Inside, the fittings are quietly luxurious . . . with deep-piled carpets, polished walnut panelling, finely grained hide upholstery.
The price is £1,215 plus £507 P.T., total £1,722. "Selectric" gearbox £43 extra.
You will find the Sapphire at your local showroom, ready for your inspection and your demonstration drive.
After you have driven it you too will agree
"There is no finer car on the road today than the Armstrong Siddeley Sapphire".

Anti-roll bars . . . for smooth cornering.

Now 120 B.H.P. "Square-type" engine. — top speed 95 m.p.h. — amazing fuel economy . . . over 20 m.p.g.!

Extra large boot . . . holds all family's luggage.

ARMSTRONG SIDDELEY *Sapphire*

MEMBER OF THE HAWKER SIDDELEY GROUP / PIONEER . . . . AND WORLD LEADER

The Car of Character

Here is a British thoroughbred . . . comfortable, fast and safe, graceful yet practical and roomy.
There is finger-tip Preselector Gear Change or Synchromesh The Hurricane is a car for the Connoisseur
Earls Court Motor Show—Stand No. 149

Armstrong Siddeley
Member of The Hawker Siddeley Group
COVENTRY · ENGLAND

The Autocar, September 30, 1949

Introducing
THE WHITLEY

A four-door saloon, with ample room without the external appearance of an unduly large car. The semi razor-edged style is both smart and practical. The front seat is of the single-bench type, with folding arm rest. Altogether a luxurious motor car in the best Armstrong Siddeley tradition.

Price £975. Purchase tax £271.11.8.

At the Motor Show · September 28th to October 8th · Stand 153

ARMSTRONG SIDDELEY
MOTORS LIMITED · COVENTRY · WARWICKS

Member of the Hawker Siddeley Group

The Car of Character

The Whitley Saloon is a four-door, five-seater luxury British thoroughbred in every sense of the word. It combines the best of tradition with the finest of modern lines

ARMSTRONG SIDDELEY

Make: Armstrong Siddeley.   **Type:** Sapphire 2-Carburetter Saloon.
Makers: Armstrong Siddeley Motors Ltd., Coventry.

Dimensions and Seating

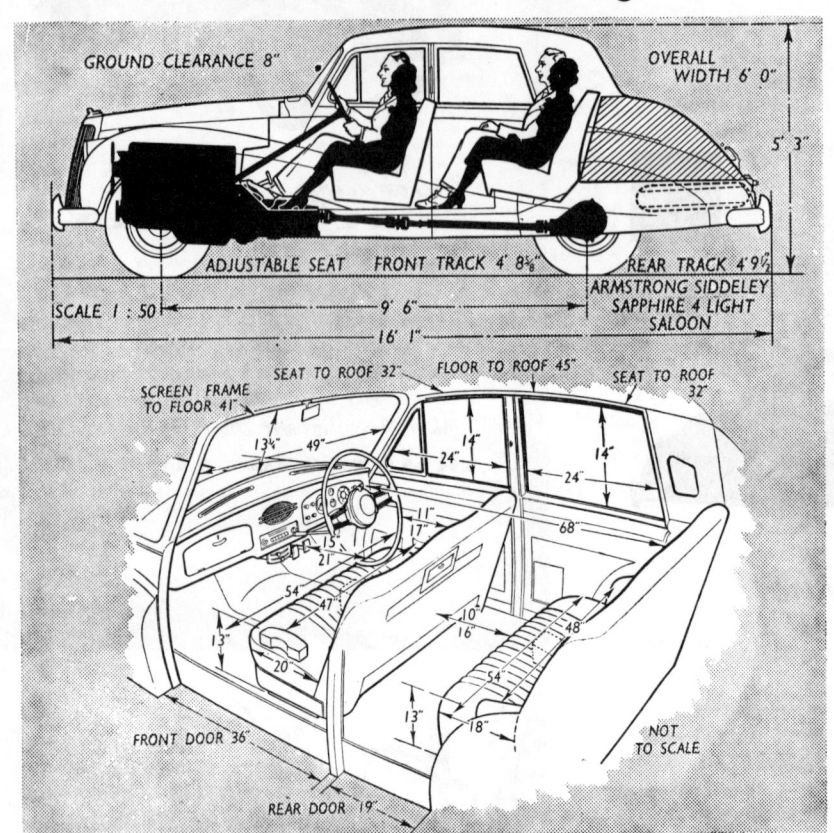

ARMSTRONG SIDDELEY SAPPHIRE 4 LIGHT SALOON

In Brief

Price (2 carburetters, synchro-mesh transmission, bench seating) £1,240 plus purchase tax £517 15 10 equals £1,757 15 10.
Capacity .. .. .. 3,435 c.c.
Unladen kerb weight .. 32¼ cwt.
Fuel consumption.. .. 18.7 m.p.g.
Maximum speed .. 100.1 m.p.h.
Maximum speed on 1 in 20 gradient .. .. 88 m.p.h.
Maximum top gear gradient 1 in 7.6

Acceleration.
10-30 m.p.h. in top .. 8.5 sec.
0-50 m.p.h. through gears 8.9 sec.

Gearing: 20.2 m.p.h in top at 1,000 r.p.m., 85.5 m.p.h. at 2,500 ft. per min. piston speed.

Specification

Engine
Cylinder 6
Bore .. .. 90 mm.
Stroke .. .. .. 90 mm.
Cubic capacity .. .. 3,435 c.c.
Piston area .. .. 59.2 sq. in.
Valves, pushrod o.h.v. inclined at 70°
Compression ratio 7/1
Maximum power .. 130 b.h.p.
at .. .. .. 5,000 r.p.m.
Piston speed at max. b.h.p. 2,960 ft./min.
Carburetters Stromberg DAA36
Ignition .. .. Lucas B14 Coil
Sparking plugs ..Champion N8B long reach
Fuel pump .. .. AC mechanical
Oil filter .. AC or Purolator
Transmission
Clutch Borg & Beck 10" s.d.p.
Top gear (s/m) 4.091
3rd gear (s/m) 5.81
2nd gear (s/m) 8.55
1st gear (s/m) 13.80
Propeller shaft .. ..Hardy Spicer, divided
Final drive .. Hypoid bevel, 45/11
Chassis
Brake Girling hydraulic, two leading shoe front
Brake drum diameter .. .. 11 in
Friction lining area .. .. 184 sq. in.
Suspension: Front, Coil and backswept wishbone I.F.S., with anti-roll torsion bar Rear, Semi-elliptic, with anti-roll torsion bar.
Shock absorbers .. Double-acting telescopic
Tyres .. .. .. Dunlop 6.70–16
Steering
Steering gear Burman, recirculatory ball type
Turning circle .. .. 39 ft.
Turn of steering wheel, lock to lock .. 4
Performance factors (at laden weight as tested)
Piston area, sq. in. per ton 33.1
Brake lining area, sq. in. per ton .. 103
Specific displacement, litres per ton mile 2,850
Fully described in " The Motor " October 8, 1952.

Test Conditions

Warm, dry weather with strong cross wind. Smooth concrete surface (Ostend-Ghent Motor Road) Premium grade petrol.

Test Data

ACCELERATION TIMES on Two Upper Ratios

	Top	3rd
10-30 m.p.h.	8.5 sec.	5.9 sec.
20-40 m.p.h.	8.5 sec.	5.9 sec.
30-50 m.p.h.	8.4 sec.	6.1 sec.
40-60 m.p.h.	10.0 sec.	7.1 sec.
50-70 m.p.h.	12.8 sec.	9.7 sec
60-80 m.p.h.	14.9 sec.	—

ACCELERATION TIMES Through Gears
0-30 m.p.h. .. .. 4.3 sec.
0-40 m.p.h. .. .. 6.4 sec.
0-50 m.p.h. .. .. 8.9 sec.
0-60 m.p.h. .. .. 13.0 sec.
0-70 m.p.h. .. .. 17.7 sec.
0-80 m.p.h. .. .. 24.9 sec.
Standing Quarter Mile .. 19.3 sec.

FUEL CONSUMPTION
28.5 m.p.g. at constant 30 m.p.h
26.5 m.p.g. at constant 40 m.p.h
22.0 m.p.g. at constant 50 m.p.h
20.0 m.p.g. at constant 60 m.p.h
17.5 m.p.g. at constant 70 m.p.h.
14.5 m.p.g. at constant 80 m.p.h.
Overall consumption for 860 miles, 46 gallons equals 18.7 m.p.g.

MAXIMUM SPEEDS
Flying Quarter Mile
Mean of four opposite runs .. 100.1 m.p.h.
Best time equals .. .. 100.8 m.p.h.

Speed in Gears
Max. speed in 3rd gear .. .. 75 m.p.h.
Max. speed in 2nd gear .. .. 50 m.p.h.
Max. speed in 1st gear .. .. 33 m.p.h.

WEIGHT
Unladen kerb weight .. .. 32¼ cwt.
Front/rear weight distribution .. 52/48
Weight laden as tested .. .. 35¾ cwt.

INSTRUMENTS
Speedometer at 30 m.p.h. .. accurate
Speedometer at 60 m.p.h. .. 1% slow
Speedometer at 90 m.p.h. .. 2% fast
Distance recorder .. .. 1% fast

HILL CLIMBING (At steady speeds)
Max. top gear speed on 1 in 20 .. .. 88 m.p.h.
Max. top gear speed on 1 in 15 .. .. 83 m.p.h.
Max. top gear speed on 1 in 10 .. .. 64 m.p.h.
Max. gradient on top gear .. .. 1 in 7.6 (Tapley 290 lb/ton)
Max. gradient on 3rd gear .. .. 1 in 5.5 (Tapley 400 lb/ton)
Max. gradient on 2nd gear .. .. 1 in 4.0 (Tapley 535 lb/ton)

BRAKES at 30 m.p.h.
0.80 g retardation (=37½ ft. stopping distance) with 150 lb. pedal pressure.
0.74 g retardation (=40½ ft. stopping distance) with 100 lb. pedal pressure.
0.52 g retardation (=58 ft. stopping distance) with 50 lb. pedal pressure.
0.28 g retardation (=107 ft. stopping distance) with 25 lb. pedal pressure.

Maintenance

Fuel tank: 16 gallon. (including 1½ reserve.) **Sump:** 10 pints, S.A.E. 30 (Summer), S.A.E. 20 (Winter). **Gearbox:** (Synchromesh) 5 pints, S.A.E. 30. **Rear axle:** 2½ pints, S.A.E. 90 hypoid gear oil. **Steering gear:** S.A.E 90 gear oil. **Radiator:** 28 pints (2 drain taps). **Chassis lubrication:** By oil gun every 1,000 miles to 23 points. **Ignition timing:** 7° B.T.D.C. **Spark plug gap:** 0.028-0.033 in. **Contact breaker gap:** 0.012 in. **Valve timing:** I.O., 8° B.T.D.C : I.C., 62° A.B.D.C.: E.O., 46° B.B.D.C.: E.C., 18° A.T.D.C. **Tappet clearances:** (Hot) 0.006 in. inlet and exhaust. **Front wheel toe-in:** 3/16 in. **Camber angle:** 2°. **Castor angle:** Unladen 0°, laden 1°. **Tyre pressures:** normal running, Front and Rear, 24/26 lb. according to load, (for fast driving, increase by 4-6 lb.) **Brake fluid:** Girling crimson. **Battery:** Lucas 12 volt, 63 amp.hr. type GTW 11A. **Lamp bulbs:** 12 volt. Headlamps 48/48 watt. No. 302. Foglamps 38 watt. No. 326. Side, boot and number plate lamps, 6 watt. No. 989. Stop/tail lamp, 18/6 watt. No. 361. Reversing lamp 18 watt. No. 221.

The ARMSTRONG SIDDELEY Sapphire

town carriage, infuriatingly slow to settle down after the engine had been started from cold and with its top-gear flexibility marred by a bad carburation flat-spot a 10 m.p.h. in top gear: for most of our test mileage we accepted these shortcomings as perhaps unfortunate characteristics of the engine in its optional twin-carburetter form, but after our main tests had been completed we ventured to experiment with the carburetter slow-running adjustments, finding that the former trouble could be greatly reduced and the latter entirely eliminated at, we would imagine, a neglig-

A Dual-personality Car at a Highly Competitive Price

IF such a person as a "typical" Armstrong Siddeley owner may be said to exist, he is undoubtedly an individual of rather conservative tastes, a motorist who is less concerned with dazzling performance and flashy styling than with the more practical virtues of roominess, comfort, smoothness and durability. The new Armstrong Siddeley "Sapphire" is a car which will not disappoint such motorists, but it will also obviously appeal to another class of buyer. Driven normally, it can be the most docile of touring cars, but handled in sporting fashion the twin-carburetter version also reveals quite remarkably fast acceleration right up to a maximum speed of 100 m.p.h.

By the standards of Europe, this Armstrong Siddeley is a large car, although it does not have the gargantuan proportions which characterize vehicles built in the western hemisphere. It is a genuinely spacious five-seater car, spoilt as a six-seater only by proximity of the heater controls to the centre of the front seat, yet somehow its considerable dimensions do not feel excessive for the narrow, embanked lanes which are such a feature of the English landscape. Modern cars are almost invariably roomy in the front compartment, but this car also provides spacious surroundings for the occupants of the rear seat, the doors being wide, the floor low and (apart from a slight camber) flat without needing to be dropped below the door

sills, and the leg room ample to allow passengers to stretch out during a long journey. Generally speaking, the interior is extremely pleasingly furnished, with polished walnut veneer woodwork, leather upholstery, pile carpets, and a rather light-coloured roof lining in washable plastic material: the air of solidity is, however, rather spoilt by one or two details such as disappointingly flimsy interior door handles.

An owner-driver will certainly appreciate the good view from the driving seat, through a wide windscreen which is flanked by reasonably slender pillars and over a bonnet which drops sharply enough to leave the sidelamp on each wing clearly visible. The positions of such items as the control pedals and the armrests are comfortable, although the seat cushion extends rather far forward under the knees of any but a tall driver: the combination of a steering-column gear control with a telescopic steering-wheel adjustment is, however, not quite happy, the gear lever at times coming too close to a driver's knees or (in reverse gear) to knobs on the facia panel.

As submitted to us from the factory for test, the Sapphire was a disappointing

RECESSING of the counterbalanced lid leaves ample height above the wide and deep luggage platform. The tools are accommodated in sponge-rubber, inside a drawer to the right of the spare wheel.

ible sacrifice of economy in comparison with the published figures. Contrary to our first impressions, this car can, in fact, be supremely flexible in top gear, and will accelerate smoothly and rapidly away from 10 m.p.h. in this ratio even up to considerable gradients. At almost any time, second gear can be used for starting from rest, and for leisurely driving top gear may be engaged almost so soon as the car is moving. Driven thus, the car will reveal itself to many owners simply as a docile model which runs quietly and smoothly at anything between 20 and 60 m.p.h. and has a very nice surge of top gear power for hill-climbing or for overtaking other traffic.

An experiment into the effect of making "proper" use of the indirect gears instantly reveals a very different aspect of the Sapphire's character. When the traffic

DUPLICATION of the carburetters fitted to the six-cylinder engine is an optional extra, giving enhanced performance but also leaving the engine entirely docile at low r.p.m.

DRIVER AND PASSENGERS can both appreciate virtues of the Sapphire. The instruments are set directly in front of the driver on a walnut facia panel, forward vision being excellent: genuine roominess and luxurious seating combine with good suspension to make this a comfortable car for rear-seat passengers also.

The Armstrong Siddeley Sapphire - - - - Contd.

signal on a de-restricted road changes to green, it is possible to rush straight up to 30 m.p.h. in 1st gear, go on up to about 50 m.p.h. in 2nd ratio, and only change from 3rd into top when a speed of over 70 m.p.h. has been attained within about 20 seconds and a quarter of a mile of the start from rest. We expected this car to perform well, but were a little surprised when, for example, the 0-60 m.p.h. acceleration time proved to be better than anything which we have recorded since the war in a five-six-seat saloon car. By no means free from wind noise, this car seems happy to cruise indefinitely at 80 m.p.h. on modern continental motor roads. One point which must, however, be mentioned is that, as the ignition timing was set on the test car, only the highest-octane premium petrols completely eliminated pinking below 40 m.p.h. in top gear.

Unusual in this country, the suspension system of the Sapphire has been planned to give what has been described in America as a "boulevard ride," but the flexible springs and relatively gentle-acting dampers are supplemented by anti-roll torsion bars at both front and rear so that there is the freedom from exaggerated roll on corners which European motorists would expect from this low-built and wide chassis. Really atrocious road surfaces, of rough gravel or of Belgian cobblestone, can be negotiated in exceptional comfort at speeds of the 20-40 m.p.h. order, and the car is also beautifully sprung for negotiating the minor irregularities of good main roads at speeds up to its maximum, but the lesser continental roads with open yet badly surfaced straights do invoke rather a lot of movement from this type of suspension if the car is driven fast.

Handling characteristics on any car vary with tyre pressures, and whilst 24 lb./sq. in. front and rear suits this car for leisurely touring, the owner who uses it rather more as a sports car will prefer an all-round increase of 4-6 lb./sq. in. in order to

obtain quicker steering response and almost complete freedom from tyre-squeal during fast cornering. Very satisfactory rather than brilliant steering characteristics are provided by this chassis, gearing of four turns from lock to lock giving light control at any but the lowest speeds, and slight flexibility (as distinct from lost motion) in the steering linkage eliminating shock without robbing a keen driver of "feel" of the road. Although needing some correction in a gusty cross-wind, the car proved very stable right up to its maximum speed, and could be driven quite fast on a winding road without swaying or showing much body roll.

Concerning the brakes of the test car, it must be said that whilst they were eminently satisfactory for touring conditions they left a little to be desired when the high performance of the engine was fully exploited. Even from a very high

CAPACIOUS glove or map compartments are provided in each of the four doors, concealed by spring-loaded lids. Arm-rests on the doors are comfortably positioned, but the interior door handles are disappointingly flimsy.

speed, the brakes would stop the car firmly in a straight line, but the impression was formed that repeated stops from high speeds would soon make brake adjustment necessary. The handbrake was open to more definite criticism, needing considerable effort to apply or release if the car had to be held on a hill although the pull-out control moved at almost a natural angle.

Fuel consumption figures on a car which is docile yet extremely fast depend to an immense extent upon driving methods, and our overall figure of 18.7 m.p.g. represents a compromise between fast and gentle running conditions. No doubt there are owners who will consistently better 20 m.p.g., and sometimes approach the 26½ m.p.g. which we recorded at a steady speed of 40 m.p.h. on level road, but there are also hustlers who will use up a gallon of fuel in 15 miles or less.

Combining great comfort with very high performance at no disproportionate consumption of fuel, the Sapphire is quickly appreciated as offering notably competitive value for its price of £1,240 (exclusive of the purchase tax which is levied in Britain). As befits a quality car, various alternative specifications are offered, such as a six light saloon body at the same price as the four light body fitted to the test car, individual front seats instead of the usual bench seat for an extra £25, a pre-selector gearbox and automatic clutch at £30 additional cost, or a single-carburetter engine of rather less sporting performance at £25 less cost. In the autumn it is seasonable to comment on the inclusion in the standard specification of quite a powerful car interior heater, a unit which draws fresh air from a forward-facing vent just ahead of the windscreen and which does not collect dust and fumes from other traffic as do some low-level air intakes. Two foglamps are inbuilt items, the instruments are comprehensive, the counter-balanced lid of the big luggage locker lifts up high enough to make loading up an easy task, and the spare wheel and tools are accessibly stowed on a lower shelf of the luggage locker.

Performance characteristics which suit either lazy or impatient moods, plus the considerable range of specification options available, quite evidently make the Sapphire suitable for a wide variety of motorists in many parts of the world. Attractive even in the first year of its life, this model should provide a sound basis for detail improvement up to yet higher standards of performance and refinement in the future.

MOTOR TRADER

ARMSTRONG SIDDELEY

Sapphire 3.4-litre, 1953

*Manufacturers: Armstrong Siddeley Motors Ltd.,
Parkside, Coventry.*

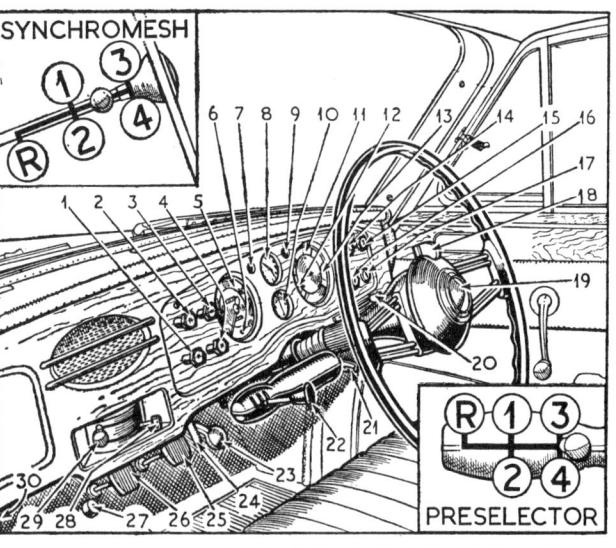

REPRESENTING a radical departure from previous Armstrong Siddeley practice, the Sapphire was introduced at the 1952 Earls Court Motor Show, and came into production soon after.

Bore and stroke are equal on the six-cylinder engine, which has hemispherical combustion chambers, and inclined valves operated through two sets of rockers by inclined push-rods from a high camshaft.

As on previous models, the gearbox is epicyclic, but to obviate the difficulties associated with mechanical linkage from the preselector control on the steering column, an electrical system is used. A small preselector switch, working in a gate, operates a separate solenoid for each gear through a master switch connected to the normal gear change pedal. Apart from the preselector system, which is bolted to the side in place of the normal camshaft, the gearbox is quite standard. A centrifugal clutch is fitted.

A synchromesh gearbox with orthodox steering column control is offered as an optional alternative to the preselector. The gearbox is similar to that fitted to the Humber Super Snipe Mark IV.

Front suspension is independent, by coil springs and double wishbone links. Anti-roll bars are fitted at front and rear The all steel body is built by Armstrong Siddeley, and is mounted on an orthodox chassis frame.

There have been no changes affecting service up to the present. A change in the type of Salisbury rear axle, from 2HA to 4HA, took place at chassis No. 340994. The difference is dealt with in the text.

Chassis numbers, prefixed C, and engine numbers, prefixed E, started at 340001, the first two figures indicating

Instruments and controls:

1. Panel light switch
2. Petrol reserve switch
3. Screenwiper switch (two-speed)
4. Heater switch
5. Speedometer
6. Ignition warning light
7. Main beam warning light (when fitted)
8. Clock
9. Flasher warning light (when fitted)
10. Ammeter
11. Oil pressure gauge
12. Water temperature gauge
13. Petrol gauge
14. Lighting switch
15. Starter push
16. Fog lamp switch
17. Ignition switch
18. Trafficator switch
19. Horn push
20. Starter mixture control
21. Handbrake lever
22. Gear preselector switch
23. Accelerator
24. Scuttle ventilator control
25. Brake pedal
26. Clutch pedal
27. Dipper switch
28. Demister control
29. Heater control
30. Bonnet lock (under scuttle on near side)

Note—Preselector witch on left-hand drive cars is inverted

the model and the rest being a serial number. The chassis number is stamped on top of the nearside chassis frame member alongside the starter motor, and the engine number on the off side of the crankcase behind the distributor drive housing. Chassis and body numbers are stamped on a plate fixed to the nearside wing valance.

No special tools are needed except a spring compressor, which can be made up in the workshop, and tools and fixtures recommended for Salisbury rear axles. All threads and hexagons are B.S.F. except on the rear axle and the synchromesh gearbox, which use S.A.E. or Unified threads.

ENGINE DATA

No. of cylinders	...	...	...	6
Bore × stroke : mm				90 × 90
in				3.5433 × 3.5433
Capacity : c.c.	...		...	3435
cu. in				209.6
R.A.C. rated h.p.	...		...	30.13
Max. b.h.p. at r.p.m. :				
single carburettor			...	125 at 4700
twin carburettor	...			150 at 5000
Max torque (lb/ft) at r.p.m. :				
single carburettor			...	182 at 2000
twin carburettor			...	194 at 2000
Compression ratio	...	...	...	7 :1
Compression pressure at starter speed		...	...	130lb/sq.in

ENGINE

MOUNTING

Front: Trunnion on bracket bolted to front of cylinder block spigots in bonded rubber bush in flanged housing bolted to front of inverted U-member, lower ends of which are bolted to chassis frame. Trunnion retained in bush by Allen screw with taper collar and split collet.

Rear: Bracket bolted to rear of gearbox rests on rubber mounting units on brackets bolted to chassis

DISTINGUISHING FEATURES—An alternative body style is the four-light saloon, otherwise identical. Inset: Bonnet safety catch

frame cross-member. Bolts extended downwards through rebound buffers. Top nuts must be tightened fully. Bottom self-locking nuts must be tightened until there is $\frac{1}{8}$in clearance between rebound buffers and cross-member.

REMOVAL

Gearbox should be removed first. Detach bonnet top from hinges (two setscrews each side). Detach radiator grille (two bolts at top, four at bottom). Disconnect radiator hoses and water temperature gauge bulb, and remove drain tap from front of radiator. Disconnect and remove bonnet lock cross-shaft and brackets (four setscrews each side). Take off two castellated nuts at bottom of radiator core, and lift out. Note rubber mounting blocks and do not overtighten nuts on reassembly.

Disconnect exhaust down pipes from manifold, and detach front silencer from bell-housing. Disconnect all pipes, wires and controls, remove air cleaner, and take weight of engine on slings under front and rear of sump.

Slide front seat back. Remove carpet and detach pedal pads from levers. Remove front floor pressing (toeboards, floorboards and gearbox cowl in one piece).

Disconnect front propeller shaft from gearbox, take off two centre bearing mounting nuts and push shaft assembly back. Disconnect gear or clutch pedal link, speedo drive and selector wiring or gear change linkage. Take off top nuts on rear mounting bolts (holding bolts by centre hexagon). Bolts, with rebound buffers, will then drop out. Lift engine slightly and remove rear mounting brackets from cross-member (three bolts, one Allen head screw each). Take out 10 bolts and two nuts round bell-housing flange, draw gearbox back and lift out through door. Take out bolts (three

each side) holding front mounting bracket to frame and lift engine out.

When reassembling engine in chassis, before tightening rear mounting top nuts (self-locking), move engine-gearbox unit backwards or forwards until dimension from rear face of gearbox driving flange to line between body mounting dowels is $2\frac{1}{2}$in for preselector, or $4\frac{1}{2}$in for synchromesh gearbox. If front engine mounting bracket has been removed, rock engine and allow to settle before tightening centre Allen screw.

MANIFOLDS

Inlet manifold in two parts. Outer four-branch pipe has water heated hot spot. Water fed from head through transfer port consisting of union screwed into head with fibre washer. Hot-spot plate fits against outer end of union, sealed by soft rubber ring. Water is returned to suction side of pump through external pipe.

Inner section of manifold is cast and bored in head. Ends sealed by plugs. Rear plug flange-bolted, front plug plain, retained by water pump. Balance plug fits in centre of manifold, retained by plate with dowel and spring washer. Plug has $\frac{1}{4}$in B.S.F. drawhole.

CRANKSHAFT

Four main bearings. Thin steel-backed, white metal-lined shells located by tabs. End float controlled by half thrust washers located in crankcase on either side of rear main bearings, and retained by cap. No hand fitting permissible. Nos. 1, 2 and 3 bearing shells interchangeable. All caps have $\frac{5}{16}$in B.S.F. drawhole.

Main bearing shells can be changed with engine in chassis, but practice is not recommended except in emergency.

CRANKSHAFT and CONNECTING ROD DATA			
	Main bearing journals		Crankpins
	Nos. 1, 2 and 3	No. 4	
Diameter...	2.7505in*	2.7505in*	2.1250in*
Length ...	1½in	1.85in	1$\frac{7}{16}$in
Running clearance :			
main bearings			.001–.0025in
big ends			.001–.0025in
End float : main bearings...			.002–.010in
big ends ...			.005–.008in
Undersizes			.010, .020, .030, .040in
No. of teeth on starter ring			
gear/pinion			142/10
Con. rod centres			6.500 ± .001in
* Machining limits plus .0005 minus .0000in.			

Flywheel, with shrunk-on starter ring gear, spigoted on end of crankshaft, located by two dowels (one offset) and retained by six setscrews. On cars with synchromesh gearbox, different flywheel is fitted, with sealed ball spigot bearing pressed into centre and retained by special flywheel setscrew locking plates.

Timing sprocket (chamfered bore to rear) and pulley, with oil thrower between, keyed on front end of shaft with separate Woodruff keys and retained by hand starter dog setscrew. Pulley hub passes through lipped oil seal pressed into front of timing cover.

Flywheel housing fits round oil return thread on rear end of crankshaft. Clearance must be .003-.005in all round.

CONNECTING RODS

Big ends thin steel-backed, white metal-lined shells located by tabs. No hand fitting permissible. Big ends split diagonally, caps located by hollow dowels. Fit with caps towards off (camshaft) side.

Small ends bronze bushed for floating gudgeon pins.

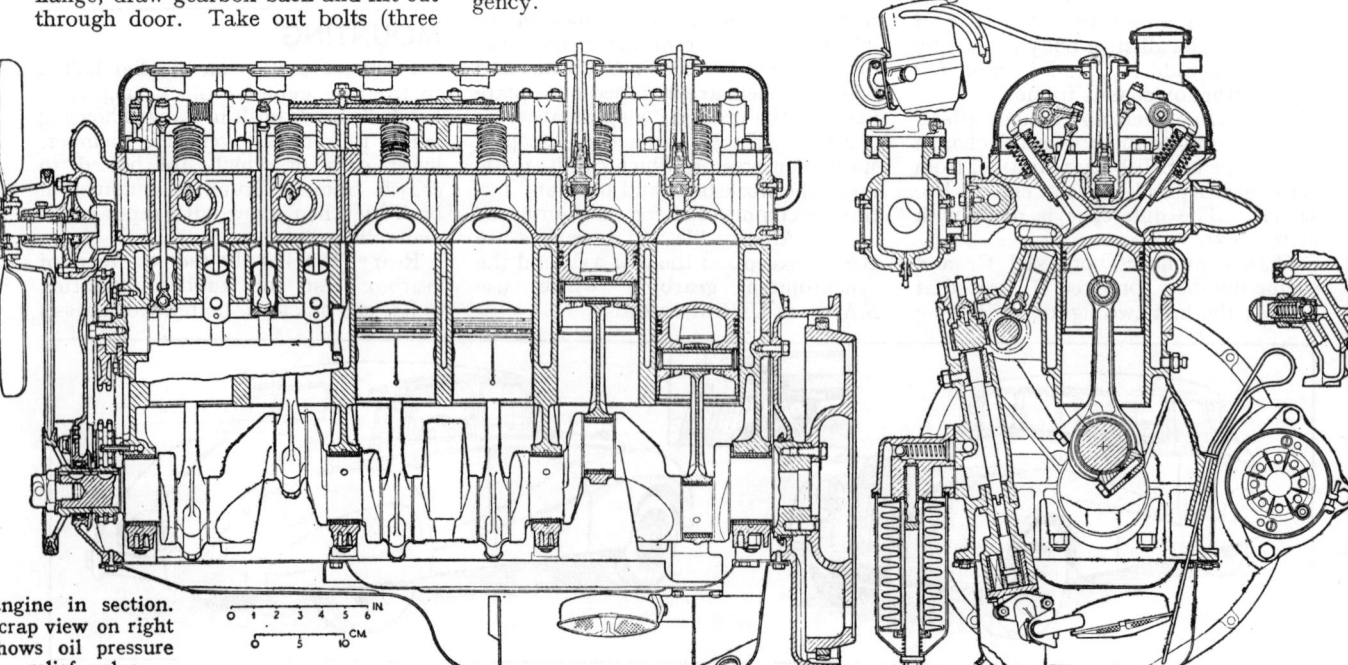

Engine in section. Scrap view on right shows oil pressure relief valve.

PISTON DATA	
Clearance (skirt)...	.0014–.003in
Oversizes ...	.010–.050in in .005in steps
Gudgeon pin :	
diameter ...	.8751 ± .0001in
oversizes	.002, .004, .006in
fit in piston	.0001in clear. to .0003in interf.
fit in rod	.0000 to .0004in clear.
Compression height (to top of dome)	2.545 ± .002in

	Compression	Oil Control
No. of rings ...	2	1
Gap ...	.010–.015in	.010–.015in
Side clearance in grooves	.0015–.0035in	.0015–.0035in
Width of rings ...	$\frac{1}{32}$in	$\frac{5}{32}$in

PISTONS

Aluminium alloy, T-slot. Fit with slot to near side. "Front" stamped on crown. Gudgeon pins located by spring rings.

Top compression ring chromium plated. Second compression ring taper faced. Fit with side marked "T" to top.

Big ends will pass through cylinder bores. Remove and assemble through top.

CAMSHAFT DATA		
Bearing journals : diameter	...	1.870in
length	...	1.1in
Bearing clearance ...	...	.001–.0028in
End float	...	.001–.005in
Timing chain : pitch...	...	$\frac{3}{8}$in
no. of pitches	...	74

CAMSHAFT

Duplex roller endless chain drive with eccentric tensioner sprocket. Spindle of tensioner sprocket, with eccentric hub pressed on and drilled for oil feed from crankcase, spigoted in crankcase, passes through rubber seal in timing cover. Outer end of spindle serrated for quadrant plate, which is retained by spring ring.

To adjust tension, slacken locking setscrew, move quadrant plate clockwise until tension is felt, back off slightly and lock. If chain is too tight it will whine, if too loose it will rattle.

Camshaft sprocket spigoted on end of shaft, located by dowel and retained by setscrew. No adjustment for timing.

Camshaft runs in four white metal-lined steel bushes pressed into crank-

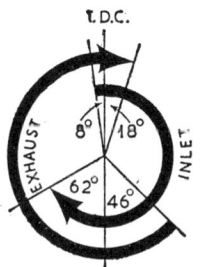

Left: Valve timing diagram, with cold tappet clearance, inlet .016in, exhaust .014in

Below: Diagram showing order of tightening of cylinder head nuts

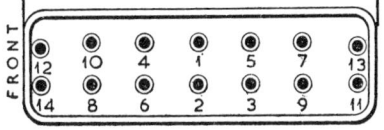

case. End float controlled by horse-shoe collar locating in groove behind sprocket, and bolted to front of crank-case with .005in shims for chain alignment.

Camshaft can be withdrawn with engine in place, but easier to remove engine. Remove cylinder head and extract tappets. Remove fuel pump, sump and oil pump. Detach front mounting bracket and draw off pulley. Extract spring ring from chain adjuster, releasing quadrant plate. Remove timing cover, draw out tensioner spindle and sprocket, and remove chain. Extract thrust collar setscrews through holes in sprocket, and draw out camshaft with sprocket.

To retime valves, turn crankshaft until keyway is at top, and fit chain so that punch mark on crankshaft sprocket and "O" on camshaft sprocket are towards each other and in line with centres when chain is tensioned.

VALVE DATA		
	Inlet	Exhaust
Head diameter ...	1.700in	1.490in
Stem diameter ...	.340–.341in	.340–.341in
Face angle	45 deg	45 deg
Tappet clearance (hot)	.006in	.006in
	Inner	Outer
Spring length : free ...	2.10in	2.44in
full lift	1.085in	1.214in
at load	46.5–49.5 lb	91–93 lb

VALVES

Overhead set at 70 deg included angle. Not interchangeable, inlet larger than exhaust. Split cone cotter fixing, double springs with cups between springs and head.

Valve guides shouldered, interchangeable.

TAPPETS AND ROCKERS

Plain cylindrical tappets sliding directly in cylinder block. Cylinder head must be removed for access to tappets. Push rods are cupped at both ends, and work on $\frac{1}{8}$in steel balls inset in bases of tappets.

Push rods can be removed singly when adjustment is slackened fully.

Rockers are in two sets on separate shafts, exhaust on near side with valve tips offset to front, inlet on off side with valve tips offset to rear. Each shaft carried in seven pillars and located by end pillar studs, which pass through shaft. Exhaust rockers (straighter than inlet) have springs in front, inlet rockers have springs behind. Washers between rockers and pillars and at both ends of springs.

Oil feed from No. 2 camshaft bearing to No. 3 inlet rocker pillar through drillings in head and block. Cross-pipe to exhaust rocker pillar.

All rockers are bushed. If new bushes are fitted, note that small bleed hole in flank ($\frac{1}{32}$in) must be drilled after bush is pressed in.

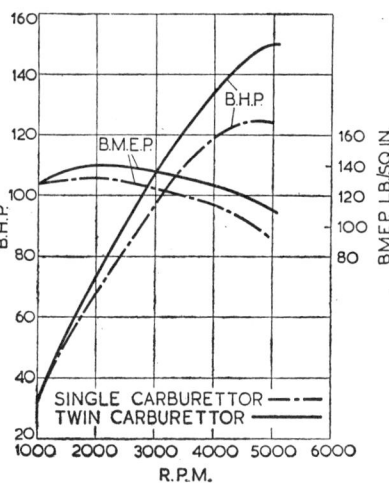

SINGLE CARBURETTOR	- - - -
TWIN CARBURETTOR	——

LUBRICATION

Hobourn-Eaton eccentric rotor pump spigoted and flange-bolted to crankcase, and driven by separate tongued shaft integral with skew gear. Drive shaft runs in bronze-bushed sleeve spigoted in crankcase below gear and located by taper-ended grubscrew and locknut on outside.

Pump can be removed from below without disturbing drive shaft, but if drive shaft is removed from above it must be reassembled first, with slot for distributor drive in position shown in sketch when crankshaft is at T.D.C.1/6 (as slot is not offset it does not matter which cylinder is firing).

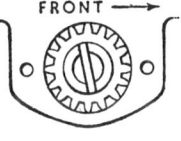

FRONT →

Oil drawn through floating gauze intake strainer and delivered through drive housing and drillings in crankcase to full flow filter on off side of crankcase. Filter may be AC No. 1530761 (element FF20) or Purolator MF606 (element MF26A). From filter oil is delivered to gallery feeding main and camshaft bearings, and rocker gear.

Adjustable spring-loaded ball relief valve under cap nut on off side of crankcase in front of filter. Pressure 40lb at normal speed.

IGNITION

Anti-clockwise distributor, with centrifugal and vacuum control, spigoted in long drive housing and retained by clamp plate with two setscrews. Drive housing spigoted and

IGNITION DATA		
Advance range: centrifugal (crank deg.) ...	...	32–36
vacuum (crank deg.) ...	...	8–12
Advance starts (crank r.p.m.) ...		200–420
Max advance (crank r.p.m.) ...		3800
Cam angle (closed period)...		35±2 deg
Contact spring tension ...		20–24 oz
Condenser capacity ...		.2 mf
Firing point		7 deg B.T.D.C.
Firing order		1 5 3 6 2 4
Contact breaker gap ...		.012in
Plugs : make		Champion N8B
type		
size...		14 mm
gap...		.028–.033in

flange-bolted to crankcase with thrust washer inset in lower end. Distributor driven by loose quill pinned to shaft, lower end dogged to engage in slot in oil pump drive skew gear. Slot is not offset.

Set contact points to break 5-7 deg before T.D.C. by setting at T.D.C. (Notch on pulley and pointer on timing cover visible only when engine is out. With engine in place, find T.D.C. by rod through plug hole.) and advancing on micrometer adjustment.

COOLING SYSTEM

Pump and fan. Bellows thermostat in housing on radiator header tank. System pressurized to 4lb. Pump has carbon and rubber seal unit.

To remove pump, remove radiator and detach pump body from cylinder head.

To dismantle pump, detach fan and pulley. Separate body from bearing housing, take out bearing locating setscrew, and press shaft and sealed ball bearing assembly out of impeller. Seal unit pressed into back of impeller. Pulley hub pressed on to shaft with peg, retained by pulley.

When reassembling, press bearing and shaft assembly into housing, and press on impeller with seal until impeller is flush with end of shaft. Fit bearing housing assembly to body, and insert two long setscrews in body before fitting pulley.

Adjust fan belt by swinging dynamo until there is about $\frac{1}{2}$in movement either way on offside run of belt.

FUEL SYSTEM DATA

	Single	Twin
Carburettor: make	Stromberg d.d.	Stromberg d.d.
type	DAV 36	DAA 36
Settings :		
Choke ...	$1\frac{3}{16}$in	$1\frac{3}{16}$in
Main jet ...	.060in	.058in
Power jet (by-pass) ...	.054in	
Main discharge tube ...	L 1802	
Idle feed holes	No. 62 left and right	
Idle discharge :		
top	No. 60	
bottom ...	No. 68	
High speed bleed	No. 68	
Idle tube : top	75	
bottom	68	
Pump jet ...	No. 70	
Pump lever ...	A	
Pump stroke ...	Short inner hole	
Needle valve seat	.100in	
Fast idle setting	.028-.032in	
Fuel level ...	$\frac{3}{4}$in	
Economy spring	L 1205	
Air cleaner: home:		
make	AC oil wet	
type	7222408	
export : make	AC oil bath (single carb. only)	
type	1579997	
Fuel pump: make	AC	
type	UE-1524885	
pressure	$1\frac{1}{2}$-$2\frac{1}{2}$ lb/sq in	

TRANSMISSION

CLUTCH

Centrifugal, with Newton driven plate.

To remove clutch assembly from flywheel, remove gearbox and extract pins from bobweight levers. Wire levers to prevent them dropping inside flywheel, and detach assembly of backplate, pressure plate and actuating plate from flywheel. Three outer springs will stay in cups in flywheel.

To dismantle assembly, take off three adjusting nuts and locknuts. Extract split pins from driving pin nuts, take weight of springs on press, and undo driving pin nuts gradually. Backplate, actuating plate and six pressure springs can then be lifted off pressure plate.

To reassemble clutch, reverse order of dismantling, making sure that balancing marks on various parts correspond. Tighten driving pin nuts fully and back off if necessary so that distance between face of pressure plate and three bobweight lever thrust pads is equal all round. Assemble clutch to flywheel and screw in three stop screws (setscrews with locknuts) until clearance between pressure plate and driven plate is about .002in. Turn adjuster nuts (small nuts with locknuts) until spring plates are parallel with pressure plate, and lock. Then readjust stop screws until clearance between pressure plate and driven plate is .015-.020in all round.

To lock clutch in emergency, screw down three stop screws (reached through opening in top of bell-housing). Bobweights will then be free to rattle.

Borg & Beck single dry plate clutch with graphite thrust release bearing is fitted to cars with synchromesh gearbox. Only external adjustment, to give 1in free movement at pedal pad, is by disconnecting ball joint at either end of pull rod and screwing joint along rod.

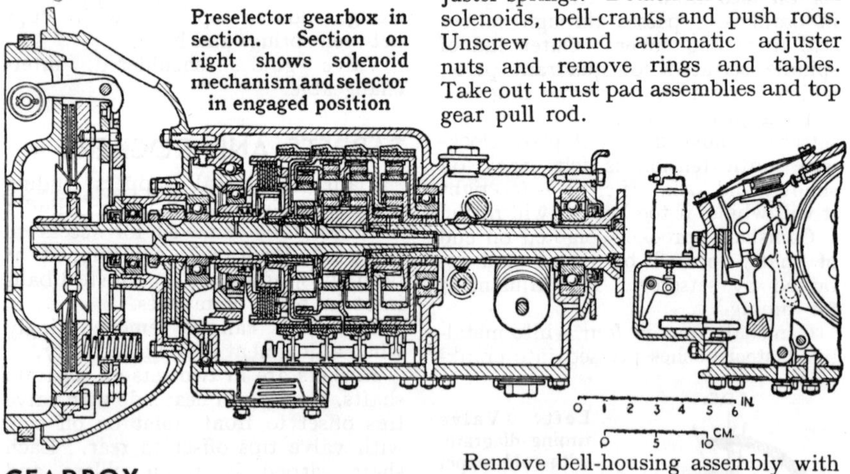

Preselector gearbox in section. Section on right shows solenoid mechanism and selector in engaged position

GEARBOX

Four-speed epicyclic self-changing, with electrically operated preselector. Four-speed synchromesh gearbox alternative.

To adjust gearbox, if gear slips, increase toggle action. Detach top cover and engage a gear other than one being adjusted (if working on 1st or reverse select 2nd, 3rd or top, *not* neutral, as this partially engages both 1st and reverse). Slacken locknut on stop screw at edge of opening in box, and screw stop screw *in* $\frac{1}{4}$ turn. Unhook top eye

TRANSMISSION DATA

	Newton		Borg & Beck
CLUTCH			
Make	Newton		Borg & Beck
Type	Centrifugal		10A6-G
Springs :	inner	outer	
No.	6	3	12
colour	—	—	Cream
free length ...	$2\frac{3}{4}$in	$2\frac{5}{16}$in	2.68in
fitted length ...	2.125in	2.175in	—
at load	163lb	103lb	—
Centre springs :			
colour	—		Red/cream
Linings : thickness	$\frac{5}{32}$ in		.145-.155in
dia.ext....	$9\frac{1}{2}$in		$9\frac{7}{8}$in
dia.int....	6in		$6\frac{3}{4}$in
GEARBOX ...	Preselector		Synchromesh
No. of speeds ...	4		4
Final ratios : 1st...	13.91		12.80
2nd	8.15		8.55
3rd...	5.56		5.81
Top	4.09		4.09
Rev	19.47		13.54
Crown wheel/bevel pinion teeth ...	45/11		

and loop of automatic adjuster spring, and unscrew round nut $\frac{1}{2}$ turn (Use $\frac{3}{8}$in B.S.F. bolt and locknut). Refit spring eye and loop, and select gear being adjusted. Mark round nut with pencil and pump pedal until nut stops turning. If gear still slips, repeat operation, screwing in stop screw $\frac{1}{4}$ turn at a time.

If gear engagement is harsh or pedal action heavy, decrease toggle action by screwing stop screw *out* $\frac{1}{4}$ turn at a time. No need to slacken round nut as for increasing toggle action.

To remove gearbox. See under "Engine—Removal."

To dismantle preselector gearbox, detach top cover and bus bar spring cover, screwing three setscrews out evenly to release spring. Note two aluminium shims under spring cover. Lift out bus bar spring and guides. Unhook and lift off five automatic adjuster springs. Detach side cover with solenoids, bell-cranks and push rods. Unscrew round automatic adjuster nuts and remove rings and tables. Take out thrust pad assemblies and top gear pull rod.

Remove bell-housing assembly with driving shaft, oil pump, top gear actuating ring and clutch, breaking joint with hide mallet. Pick out running gear parts, noting position of bushes and thrust washers for reassembly. Take off rear cover nuts and tap driven shaft out to rear with driving flange and rear cover, which carries ball bearing and lipped oil seal. If reverse gear drum has stayed in centre bearing, tap out to front. Base plate with brake gear and bus bar can then be removed. Note pump valve ball, on seat at front of base plate.

To reassemble gearbox, reverse dismantling procedure.

If gear change pedal is operated when selector wires are disconnected or current "off," all struts will fall away from bus bar, and pedal will return beyond normal position. With neutral selected, selector master switch should be adjusted to $\frac{1}{16}$in clearance from bus bar operating cross-shaft lever. If switch is too close, current may continue to flow through solenoid, causing it to heat up.

PROPELLER SHAFT

Hardy Spicer, two-stage, Series 1300. Needle roller bearing universal joints with nipples for lubrication.

Rear end of front section supported in sealed ball bearing pressed on shaft in front of driving flange (taper and Woodruff key). Outer race of bearing pressed into flanged sleeve mounted on centre of cruciform bracing by two rubber bushed shouldered bolts (tighten fully).

REAR AXLE

Salisbury 2HA hypoid bevel drive, semi-floating shafts. Final drive housing integral with axle tubes, rear cover detachable. Type 4HA coming into production on latest cars is similar, but dimensions are slightly different.

To remove axle from car, draw off hubs and detach backplate assemblies. Disconnect propeller shaft, handbrake linkage and hydraulic pipes (can be unclipped from axle and left on chassis), shock absorbers, anti-roll bar and U-bolts. Draw axle out sideways through springs. When reassembling note shims between axle flange and backplate, and paper washers on either side of stiffening plate between backplate and oil seal housing.

Hubs keyed on tapered half-shafts (interchangeable). Taper roller bearings in axle tube ends, retained by backplates with shims behind (.003, .005, .010, .030in thick) to adjust end float (.006-.008in). Inner ends of half-shafts butt on floating thrust block round planet bevel spindle.

To remove half-shaft, draw off hub, detach brake backplate assembly with lipped oil seal in housing, and shims. Draw out shaft and bearings carefully through inner oil seal (lip inwards). If both shafts are withdrawn, when refitting see that shims on both sides are of about equal thickness, so that thrust block remains central.

Bevel pinion shaft carried in taper roller bearings. Outer races pressed into final drive housing from front and rear. Distance-piece between inner races on 2HA, shouldered shaft on 4HA. Shims (.003, .005, .010, .030in thick), between distance-piece and inner race of front bearing for bearing adjustment. Shims (.003, .005, .010in thick) between outer race of rear bearing and housing for mesh adjustment.

Pinion setting marked on face of pinion may be zero, plus or minus.

This indicates amount in "thous" above or below nominal distance (2.750in on 2HA, 2.625in on 4HA), of face from centreline of crown wheel. Use mesh adjusting shims to obtain setting marked, and assemble pinion in bearing with original bearings shims, but *without* oil thrower or oil seal. Tighten driving flange nut and test for preload (8-12lb/in).

Crown wheel spigoted and bolted to flange of one-piece differential cage. Side bevel gears run directly in cage with flat thrust washers behind. Planet bevel pinions have spherical thrust washers, and run on spindle retained by pin peened to lock. Axle shaft thrust block round spindle.

Differential assembly carried on taper roller bearings in split housings with shims (.003, .005, .010, .030in thick) between inner races and cage for bearing and mesh adjustment. Install differential assembly *without shims* and with bevel pinion removed, and mount dial gauge on axle casing with button against back face of crown wheel. Move differential assembly to one side of housing with lever, and set gauge to zero. Lever assembly over to other side and note gauge reading (A). This figure indicates play in bearings, and thickness of shims needed to take up play. Add .008in to total to give pre-load. This total must be divided to obtain correct crown wheel mesh as follows:—

After installing bevel pinion, reassemble differential, again without shims. Lever away from pinion, set indicator to zero, and lever assembly towards pinion. Note reading (B). This, minus backlash figure etched on crown wheel, is thickness of shims to go behind crown wheel side bearing. Remainder of shims from total (A + .008in) go behind offside bearing.

When assembling differential with shimmed bearings, use spreader (Salisbury tool No. SE104) to open housing or, if this is not available, cock outer races slightly and tap lightly into place with lead hammer.

When assembly is complete, check for backlash (.004in minimum). Change shims from one side to other of differential bearings if necessary.

CHASSIS

BRAKES

Girling hydraulic. Two leading shoe front brakes with separate cylinder for each shoe. Rear brakes have single cylinder incorporating wedge expander operated by handbrake lever through separate cables in conduits to compensator on chassis frame.

Snail cam adjustment for front

BRAKE DATA		Front	Rear
Drum diameter ...	...	11in	11in
Lining : length : leading	...	10$\frac{1}{4}$in	10$\frac{1}{4}$in
trailing		—	9$\frac{3}{8}$in
width	...	2$\frac{1}{4}$in	2$\frac{1}{4}$in
thickness	...	$\frac{3}{16}$in	$\frac{3}{16}$in
No. of rivets per shoe	...	12	12

brakes. Jack up car, turn each adjuster (*two per wheel*) until shoe touches drum, and back off until free.

Square ended adjusters on rear brakes. Jack up, tighten and back off one or two clicks.

Handbrake adjustment at compensator to take up cable stretch.

REAR SPRINGS

Semi-elliptic. Bonded rubber shackle and anchorage bushes. Tighten all bolts fully with two people in back seat. Centrebolts offset to front.

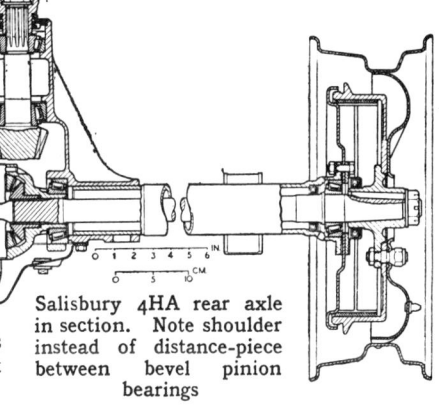

Salisbury 4HA rear axle in section. Note shoulder instead of distance-piece between bevel pinion bearings

FRONT SUSPENSION

Independent. Coil springs and double wishbone links with screwed bushes at all pivot points except inner ends of lower links, which have bonded rubber bushes. Anti-roll bar linked to front arms of lower links.

To remove spring, remove top nuts and bottom plate attaching shock absorber to spring plate (two setscrews) and lower shock absorber through hole in spring plate. Make up spring compressor with high tensile steel rod 24in long, threaded $\frac{9}{16}$in B.S.F. for 12in at upper end, 1in at lower end. Fit plate at lower end large enough to cover shock absorber hole and preferably to register in it. Thread rod through shock absorber location and screw long nut on upper end. Jack up under front cross-member (avoiding centre steering arm), take out four setscrews attaching spring plate to lower link arms, and slacken compressor nut until spring and plate are free. Note rubber seat for spring in plate.

Complete assembly of stub axle, king pin and upper and lower links with inner pivots can be detached from cross-member. Upper link inner pivot bracket bolted to cross-member by three bolts, and lower link pivot bracket by four bolts.

SPRING DATA		
	Front	Rear
Length (eye centres, laden)...	—	50½in*
Width	—	2in
No. of leaves	—	10
Free camber (length, coil)...	16in	7-7½in
Loaded camber (length, coil)	9½in	1¼-1½in neg.†
at load	1195lb	950lb

* Centrebolt offset. Front to centre 23in
† Export rear springs have ¼-½in negative
  loaded camber

To dismantle assembly, take out bolt joining halves of upper link, and take nuts off inner pivot pin. Front arm can then be pulled off. Pull inner pivot pin and bracket out of rear arm and screw pin out of bracket to front. Rear end of pin is carried in plain bush in bracket.

Take nut off rear end of outer pivot pin, releasing rear arm, and screw pin out of bush to rear. Bush is eccentric for camber adjustment and is inserted in king pin upper eye from front, and cotter-clamped.

Take nuts off lower link inner pivot pin at both ends and outer pin at rear. Rear arm, with bushed outer eye, will then come off with rubber bush assembly at inner end. Note packing washer behind inner sleeve. Outer pivot pin can then be screwed out of bush in king pin lower eye, which is pressed in.

All pivot pins have special wide pitch thread (except those on earlier cars, which have normal thread). This gives greater bearing surface for radial loads.

When reassembling pivot pins,

screw in until eye or bracket is central between arms. Do not omit rubber sealing rings.

King pin lower eye spigoted on lower end of pin and retained by nut. King pin turns in bronze bushed stub axle, which has sealing sleeve pressed in between bushes. Roller thrust bearing assembly between stub axle and upper king pin eye, with shims for preload adjustment.

When assembling king pin in stub axle, build up without shims and tighten lower nut fully. Measure end float with feeler, and rebuild with shims (.002, .003, .006in) of thickness equal to end float *less* .002in to give slight preload.

Hubs run on taper roller bearings. Adjust by castellated nut to give .004-.006in end float (back off nut one slot). Lipped oil seal pressed into hub behind inner bearing.

Inner ends of two-piece track rod carried by centre swinging arm connected to short transverse drag link. Ball joints have shanks threaded left- and right-hand for adjustment, screwed into tubes and clamped. Drag link and track rod joints not interchangeable. Track rod joints have nipple in cap.

Centre swinging arm, with thrust washers above and below, carried in bushed bracket bolted to cross-member. Pin cottered in arm.

Adjust track on both track rods so that they are kept of equal length.

Front suspension, with hub and king pin in section. Scrap views show upper link assembly and lower link pivots in section. Note wide pitch thread on pivot pins

STEERING DATA		
Castor : unladen		0 deg
laden		1 deg
Camber		2 deg
King pin inclination		5½ deg
Toe-in		$\frac{1}{16}$in
No. of turns lock to lock		3

When turning rod to adjust, grasp with both hands and pull in direction opposite to twist, so that ball joints stay in line.

To adjust camber, slacken cotter-clamp bolt on upper king pin eye and turn eccentric bush by large hexagon at front.

STEERING GEAR

Burman F type worm and nut with recirculating balls.

To remove gear from car, detach preselector switch or synchromesh gear control, handbrake lever and steady bracket from column. Disconnect column wiring at push-in connectors. Slacken two grubscrews in steering wheel hub and pull out control head with short tube and wires. Extract spring ring and pull steering wheel off parallel serrations (after slackening adjuster). Draw off drop arm, slacken clamp bolts on steering box bracket and nut on outside of chassis frame. Steering box can then be drawn out of bracket, and assembly lifted out over wing. If car is over pit it may be more convenient to lower assembly out under front suspension. On R.H.D. cars petrol pump must be removed first. On L.H.D. cars remove brake pedal pad.

Worm and lower end of column supported in cup-and-cone ball bearings ($14 \times \frac{3}{32}$in loose balls in each race), adjusted by shims under lower end plate. Column tube flange-bolted to box. Nut has 14 loose $\frac{3}{8}$in recirculating balls.

End play in rocker shaft adjusted by grubscrew and locknut in top cover. Adjust in straight ahead position so that there is no end play, but no tightness. On either lock there should be slight play. Upper end of column supported in Tufnol bush with oil seal and washer behind.

SHOCK ABSORBERS

Front: Girling telescopic type DAS6. Rear: Girling telescopic type DAS8. No attention needed.

BODY

Body and front wings form integral assembly mounted at four points each side in body, one each side inside boot (lift matting at front corners) and one each side of spare wheel tray. One bolt at front to chassis frame on each side of radiator carrier. All wiring harness carried on body.

To remove body take up front floor, disconnect all wiring, pipes and controls to chassis (including radiator temperature gauge tube and steering column top bracket). Detach rear bumpers, detach brackets from frame, separate and draw out inwards through grommets. Take out two mounting bolts and 12 setscrews, and lift body over steering wheel. Sling by poles through door openings after removing fillets, or by hooks under door sills.

When reassembling body note Kautex pads at all mounting points, and locating dowels on mountings at rear of front floor opening.

Door locks—Rotary claw locks controlled by Bowden cable behind trim panels. Adjust cable so that safety catch operates before door is shut.

Instrument panel—For access to wiring, twist two screws at top ¼ turn and lift panel out (located by two lugs at bottom). When speedo drive and oil gauge pipe are disconnected, panel can be pulled further out.

Petrol tank—Mounted on chassis by four bolts. Remove petrol reserve tap and disconnect wire at push-in connector (access through trap in boot floor).

ARMSTRONG SIDDELEY SAPPHIRE WIRING DIAGRAM

Tap can be removed without tank being disturbed.

Gear change switch—If switch is removed, cut wires to reverse lamp and fuse box (green and yellow) and replace with push-in connectors. Wires are difficult to change on terminal block.

Boot lid—If lid is slammed, air pressure inside may prevent one side from catching. Lower gently and push at centre.

TRAILER ATTACHMENT

No special provision for towing bracket.

Towing capacity 30cwt.

GENERAL DATA		
Wheelbase		9ft 6in
Track : front		4ft 8⅜in
rear		4ft 9½in
Turning circle		42ft 6in
Ground clearance (laden) ...		8in
Weight (dry)		31 cwt (approx)
Tyre size		6.70-16
Overall length		16ft 1in
Overall width		6ft 0in
Overall height (laden) ...		5ft 3in

ELECTRICAL DATA Lucas Equipment		
	Model	**Service No.**
Dynamo	C45PV5	22456
Starter	M 45 G	26041
Starter solenoid switch ...	ST950	76411
Lighting, fog lamp switches ...	PPG2	31114
Ignition switch	S45	31287
Control box	RB 106/1	37139
Fuse box (Accessories) ...	SF6	033240
Battery	GTW 11A	—
Distributor	DMX 6A	40392
Coil	B 12	45012
Headlamps : Dip left ...	RF770	056601
Dip right ...	PF770	057101
Vertical dip ...	PF770	057102
3-pin bulb (France) ...	PF770	51484A
Side lamps : Standard	490	052863
Flasher	488	052631
Stop/tail, reversing lamps...	464	052654
Number plate lamp ...	469	052442
Screenwiper (R.H.D.) ...	DR1	072947
Screenwiper and heater switches	PRS 5	31302
Trafficators	SF 80	54044A
Horns : low note ...	WT 614	69011
high note ...	WT 614	69012
PRESELECTOR SYSTEM		
Gear change relay ...	SB40/2	33116
Fuse box	SF 5	37130
Gear change master switch	KDS1	31397
Gear change solenoids ...	TGS2	76501
Column control: R.H.D. ...	PGS1	31398
L.H.D. ...	PGS1	31414

BULBS			
	Voltage	**Wattage**	**Cap**
Headlamps :			
Dip left ...	12	48/48	Prefocus
Dip right ...	12	48/48	Prefocus
Vertical dip ...	12	45/40	Prefocus
Fog lamp ...	12	38	Prefocus
Side lamps :			
Standard ...	12	6	m.c.c.
Flasher ...	12	18/6	s.b.c.*
Stop/tail lamps ...	12	18/6	s.b.c.*
Reversing and rear flasher lamps ...	12	18	s.c.c.
Number plate and boot lamps ...	12	6	m.e.e.
Panel and ignition warning lamps ...	12	2.2	m.e.s.
Roof lamp	12	6	s.c.c.
Main beam and flasher warning lamps ...	2.5	0.2	m.e.s.
Map reading lamp and trafficators ...	12	3	festoon
* Offset pin			

FUSES	
Accessories	35 amperes
Horns and roof lamp	50 amperes
Preselector gearbox	25 amperes

ARMSTRONG SIDDELEY SAPPHIRE MAINTENANCE DIAGRAM

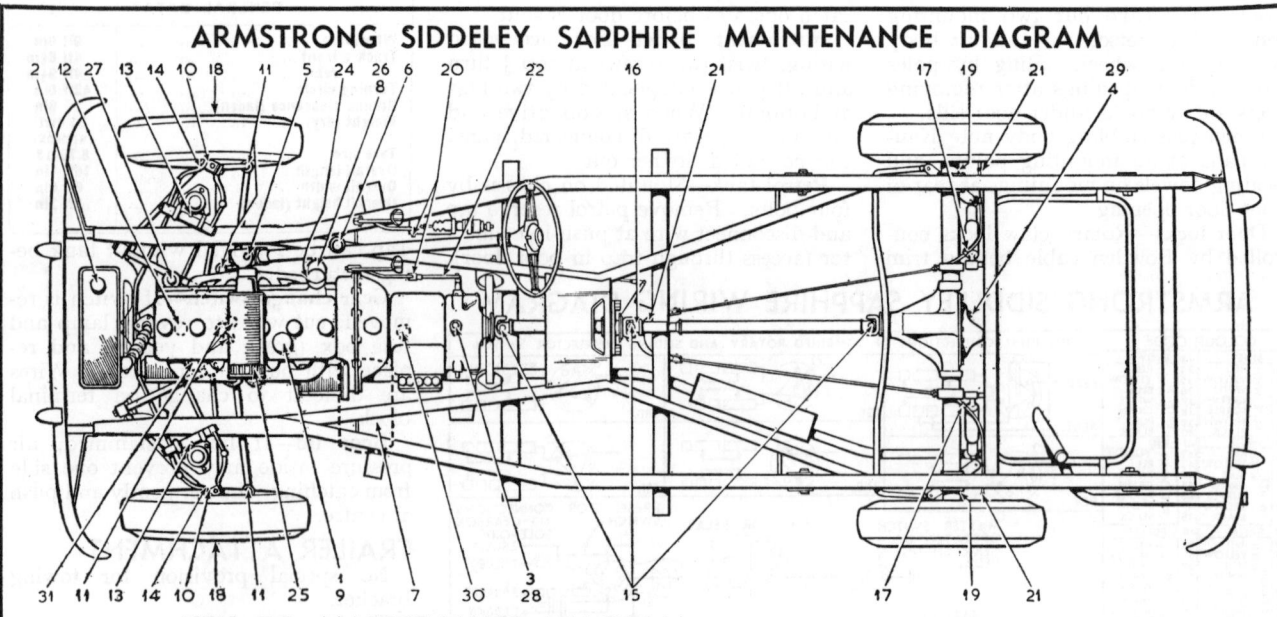

KEY TO MAINTENANCE DIAGRAM

WEEKLY
1. **Engine sump** } Top up
2. **Radiator**

EVERY 2,000 MILES
3. **Gearbox**
4. **Rear axle**
5. **Steering box** } Top up
6. **Brake fluid reservoir**
7. **Battery**
8. **Engine oil filter**—Clean element and canister
9. **Engine sump**—Drain and refill
10. **King pin bearings** (2)
11. **Steering ball joints** (6)
12. **Centre swing arm pivot** (1)
13. **Front suspension upper link inner pivots** (2)
14. **Upper and lower link outer pivots** (4)
15. **Propeller shaft universal joints** (3)
16. **Propeller shaft splines** (1)
17. **Handbrake cable** (1)
18. **Front hubs**—Pack with bearing grease through plug
19. **Rear hubs**—Grease gun, bearing grease
20. **Brake and clutch or gear pedals**
21. **Handbrake linkage**
22. **Gear change linkage** (synchromesh)
23. **Accelerator controls**

} Oil gun

} Oil can

EVERY 3,000 MILES
24. **Distributor**—Oil shaft bearing, auto advance and contact breaker pivot. Smear cam with engine oil. Repack grease cap with bearing grease.

EVERY 5,000 MILES
25. **Air cleaner**—Clean in petrol and re-oil or refill bowl
26. **Engine oil filter**—Renew element (AC type FF 20 or Purolator MF26A)
27. **Engine breather filter**—Clean in petrol and re-oil
28. **Gearbox** } Drain and refill
29. **Rear axle**
30. **Gearbox filter** (preselector)—Clean gauze in petrol

EVERY 10,000 MILES
31. **Dynamo**—Refill lubricator with petroleum jelly

FILL-UP DATA

			Litres
Engine sump	... ...	10 pints	5.7
Extra for filter	... ...	1 pint	0.6
Gearbox : preselector		6 pints	3.5
synchromesh		5 pints	2.8
Rear axle	... ...	2½ pints	1.4
Cooling system	... ...	28 pints	16
Fuel tank	... ...	16 gallons	73
Tyre pressures : front	...	24 lb	
rear	...	24-26 lb	

DRAINING POINTS

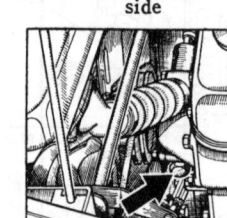

Water pump body is drained by plug on near side

Radiator drain tap, reached from below front of car

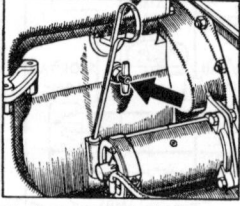

Cylinder block drain tap on near side. System is pressurized

RECOMMENDED LUBRICANTS

		S.A.E. No.	Filtrate	Shell	Vacuum	B.P. Energol	Wakefield	Esso
Engine	Above 90° F ...	40	—	—	—	—	—	—
	90° to 30° F ... (Home Summer)	30	A.S. Filtrate 30	X-100 30	Mobiloil A	Energol S.A.E. 30	Castrol XL	Essolube 30
	30° to 10° F ... (Home Winter)	20	A.S. Filtrate 20	X-100 20/20W	Mobiloil Arctic	Energol S.A.E. 20	Castrolite	Essolube 20
	10° to —10° F ...	10	—	—	—	—	—	—
Gearbox ... (Preselector and synchromesh)	Above 30° F ...	30	S.C. Filtrate	X-100 30	Mobiloil A	Energol S.A.E. 30	Castrol XL	Essolube 30
	30° to —10° F ...	20	—	—	—	—	—	—
Rear axle, Steering box	Above 10° F ...	90	Hypoid Filtrate 90	Spirax 90 EP	Mobilube GX 90	Energol EP S.A.E. 90	Castrol Hypoy	Esso Expee Compound 90
	Below 10° F ...	80	—	—	—	—	—	—
Chassis nipples, Propeller shafts	...	140	EP Filtrate Gear Oil 140	Spirax 140 EP	Mobilube C-140	Energol S.A.E. 140	Castrol D	Esso Gear Oil 140
Front and rear hubs, Distributor grease cap		—	Filtrate Solidified Oil	Retinax A	Mobilgrease No. 4	Energrease C3	Castrolease Heavy	Esso Grease
Brake fluid reservoir	... ...	—	Filtrate Hydraulic Brake Fluid	Donax B	Mobil Brake Fluid	—	Girling Brake Fluid Crimson	Esso Hydraulic Brake Fluid

A Twin-carburetter Sapphire

Styling of the Armstrong Siddeley Sapphire four-light saloon combines a traditional radiator with the fashionable, flowing front wing line extending the length of the car. Below is the twin-carburetter manifold, an optional extra which increases the power output from 120 b.h.p. to over 150 b.h.p., as shown in the accompanying power curve.

The Armstrong-Siddeley Range for the Coming Season

IN spite of its most interesting high-efficiency engine, the Armstrong Siddeley Sapphire was not designed primarily as a sports saloon. Introduced just before the 1952 Motor Show, the car was regarded by its makers as a modern development of past Armstrong Siddeleys, and was intended to appeal to just the type of owner who had bought these cars previously.

It was thought that too much emphasis on performance might well have an adverse effect on the class of owner to which this make has hitherto appealed, and the potentialities of the new power unit were therefore deliberately not exploited to the full.

What was not expected, however, was that the Sapphire would be so eagerly welcomed in overseas markets, particularly in the United States. The result has been that ever since the introduction of the new model the Armstrong Siddeley works have had to adopt the three-shift system, and to work the clock round in an attempt to satisfy the insatiable demand from overseas for the cars. Another result has, of course, been that Sapphires are but rarely seen on English roads, for over 90% of the output is being exported.

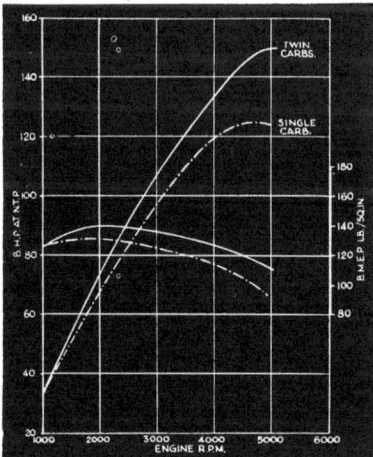

Overseas, the traditional Armstrong Siddeley owner is practically non-existent, and a twin-carburetter induction system has therefore been developed for export models which increases the maximum power output from 120 b.h.p. to over 150 b.h.p. This system, which has been fitted as standard to all cars shipped to the United States—as have also white-walled tyres and blinking direction indicators—has more effect on top gear

acceleration than on maximum speed.

This we were able to experience for ourselves during the course of several laps of the Le Mans circuit in the twin-carburetter Sapphire owned by Briggs Cunningham which was in use as an équip car by the Cunningham team.

The twin-carburetter induction system incorporating two Stromberg downdraught carburetters type DAA 36 is now available in the home market as an optional extra, as also are twin bucket seats at the front instead of the standard bench-type seat. These are also the result of overseas demand.

Apart from these optional additional items, the specification of the cars remains unchanged for the coming year, save for an increase in the compression ratio from 6.8 to 1 to 7 to 1.

The 1954 range of Armstrong Siddeleys therefore consists of a six-light and a four-light Sapphire saloon, both based on the interesting 3.4-litre chassis with its six-cylinder engine having overhead valves operating in hemispherical combustion chambers and actuated by pushrods of different lengths for inlet and exhaust.

ARMSTRONG SIDDELEY SAPPHIRE SPECIFICATION

Engine.—Dimensions: Cylinders, 6; bore 90 mm.; stroke 90 mm.; cubic capacity, 3,435 c.c.; pushrod o.h.v. in hemispherical combustion chambers; carburetter, single or twin Stromberg downdraught; four-bearing crankshaft.

Transmission.—Clutch, either Armstrong Siddeley centrifugal and electrically operated pre-selector epicyclic gearbox (overall ratios 4.091, 5.564, 8.153, 13.909) or a dry single plate and synchromesh gearbox (overall ratios 4.091, 5.807, 8.540, 12.800). Final drive, hypoid.

Chassis details.—Brakes, Girling hydraulic (2 l.s. front); friction lining area, 184 sq. in.; suspension: front, independent with coil springs and wishbones and anti-roll bar; rear: semi-elliptic springs with anti-roll bar; shock absorbers, Girling telescopic; steering, Burman recirculating ball.

Dimensions.—Wheelbase. 9 ft. 6 in.; track: front, 4 ft. 8⅝ in.; rear, 4 ft. 9½ in.; overall length, 16 ft. 1 in.; overall width, 6 ft.; overall height, 5 ft. 5½ in.; ground clearance, 8 in.; turning circle, 42½ ft.; dry weight, 32½ cwt.

ARMSTRONG SIDDELEY ADOPT AMERICAN HYDRA-MATIC SYSTEM

Two-tone paintwork is particularly well suited to the Armstrong Siddeley body style. New external features include rubber stone guards on the leading edges of the rear wings, and flashing direction indicators which are mounted low down at the sides of the fog lamps.

ALTHOUGH the external appearance of the Armstrong Siddeleys for 1955 is unchanged except for minor details, the range of two six-light saloons—one with synchromesh and the other with a preselector gear box—has been increased by the inclusion of a third model fitted with automatic transmission, all three cars being available in this country.

The transmission, manufactured in this country under General Motors' patents and known as Hydra-Matic when fitted to cars in its country of origin, is similar to that used in two other makes of British car. The principles of this transmission have been previously described in *The Autocar*; it consists of a four-speed epicyclic gear box together with a fluid coupling, the latter being used to provide a smooth take-up from rest. For normal operation the control is automatic but the driver can modify the normal change up and down arrangements to a limited degree by varying the position of the selector lever, which has five positions: from top to bottom of the " gate " these are neutral, normal, fast, fixed second, and reverse. These correspond to the perhaps more familiar American terms of neutral, drive range, third, low range, and reverse.

For normal driving the lever is placed in the position bearing that label, and as the throttle is opened the car accelerates in first gear; as the road speed increases it automatically changes up through the gears until it is in top. The change-up speeds can be varied according to the

Automatic Transmission

throttle position, providing a range for the gears as follows :

1st to 2nd	.....	6 to 15 m.p.h.
2nd to 3rd	.....	11 to 30 m.p.h.
3rd to Top	.....	20 to 64 m.p.h.

while the change down can occur at

Top to 3rd	....	14 m.p.h.
3rd to 2nd	....	8 m.p.h.
2nd to 1st	....	4 m.p.h.

If the lever is moved to the next position (labelled " Fast ") the change-up speed from third to top, regardless of throttle position, is 64 m.p.h., while the next notch limits the ratios available to first and second gear, and limits the speed of the car to 35 m.p.h., corresponding to 4,580 r.p.m.

With any car fitted with a transmission providing automatic take-up as the engine speed increases, it greatly assists driving and manoeuvring in confined spaces if there is a progressive ratio on the throttle pedal, and a new cam action arrangement is fitted to the Armstrong Siddeley which provides a variable ratio between the pedal and butterfly valve, so that a relatively large movement of the pedal is required to open the throttle a very small amount initially, the required movement becoming progressively less the more the pedal is depressed.

Perhaps the most important chassis modification is to the brake system, which now utilizes a vacuum servo in conjunction with

Rubber bushes are used for the outer wishbone bearings of the suspension : brakes have two-trailing shoes in front.

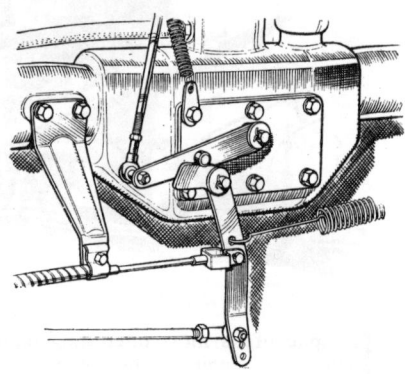

To assist the driver when manoeuvring in a confined space, a cam type progressive throttle linkage is used.

12in diameter brakes having two-trailing shoes at the front and leading and trailing shoes at the rear; the object of using two-trailing shoes is to obtain a brake that is less susceptible to a loss of efficiency or balance under arduous operating conditions.

The independent front suspension, by upper and lower wishbones trailing at an angle of 25 deg, has been modified in detail to reduce routine maintenance, and rubber bushes are now used for both upper and lower outer wishbone fulcrum bearings.

The 3.4-litre six-cylinder " square " engine continues virtually unchanged. This unit has hemispherical combustion chambers and inclined valves operated by a single side camshaft mounted high up on the right-hand side of the block, the valves being operated by push rods and rockers. There are two rocker shafts running parallel to the centre line of the engine, and the exhaust valve push rods are longer than those used to operate the inlet valves, and run diagonally across the engine; this arrangement eliminates the need for twin camshafts.

Minor modifications to the engine

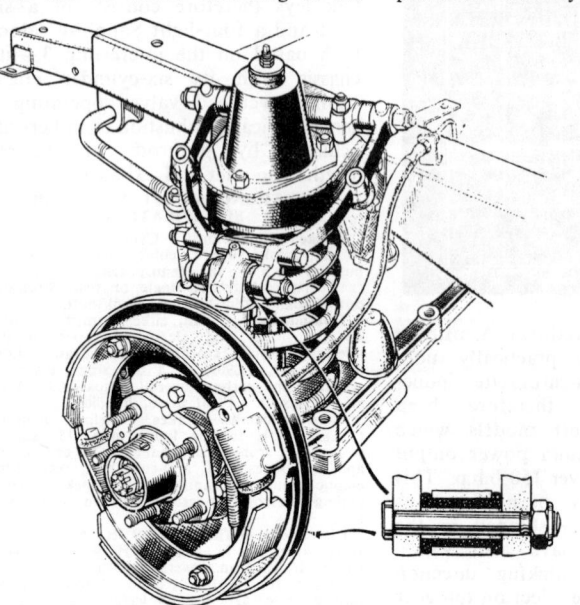

include the use of a five-blade fan—a seven-blade one is also available for export models if required—and this, together with the dynamo and water pump, is driven by a new narrow-section fan belt. The bulb for the water temperature gauge, previously in the top of the radiator header tank, has been replaced by an electrical unit housed in the top of the water pump at the point where the hot water leaves the cylinder head; by placing it in this position the possibility of obtaining a false reading owing to a drop in water level in the radiator header tank is eliminated. The standard engine with a single carburettor develops 125 b.h.p. at 4,700 r.p.m., but on all models twin carburettors are available as an optional extra and their use increases the b.h.p. to 150 at 5,000 r.p.m.

Rubber stone guards are used on the leading edges of the rear wings, and semaphore direction indicators have been replaced by flashing units built into the front and rear of the car.

The interior is very neatly finished and there is an abundance of polished hardwood. The layout of the facia has been rearranged and includes larger-

for Sapphire

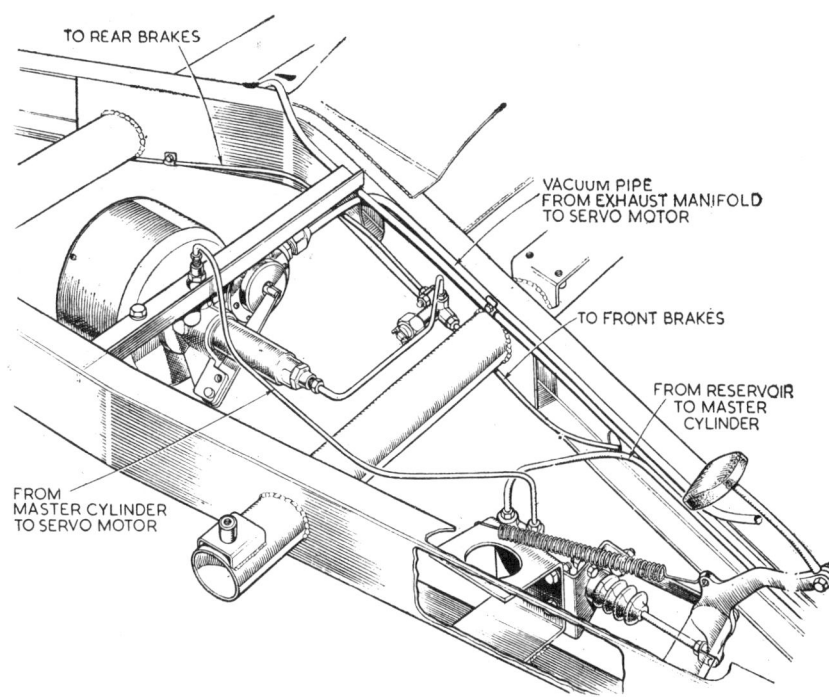

The vacuum servo motor used to energize the brakes is mounted behind the master cylinder and between the frame members.

diameter instrument units. A group of four warning lights is placed between the instruments and below the clock, and these indicate to the driver that the choke is in operation, that he has forgotten to release the handbrake, that the direction indicators are working, and that the head lamp main beam is switched on. All these warning lights show red.

SPECIFICATION

Engine.—6 cyl, 90×90 mm, 3,435 c.c. Compression ratio 7 to 1. 125 b.h.p. at 4,700 r.p.m. Maximum torque 182 lb ft at 2,000 r.p.m. Twin carburettor engine, 150 b.h.p. at 5,000 r.p.m. Maximum torque 194 lb ft at 2,000 r.p.m. Four-bearing crankshaft. Hemispherical combustion chambers. Inclined valves operated by single side camshaft, push rods and rockers.

Transmission.—Synchromesh: 10in diameter dry single-plate clutch. **Gear box:** Overall ratios, top 4.091; third 5.81; second 8.55; first 12.8 to 1. Reverse 13.54 to 1. Synchromesh on all forward ratios. **Preselector gear box:** 9½in diameter dry single-plate centrifugally operated clutch. Overall ratios, top 4.091; third 5.564; second 8.153; first 13.909 to 1. Reverse 19.473 to 1. **Automatic transmission:** Fluid coupling and four-speed planetary gear box. Overall ratios, top 4.091; third 5.932; second 10.776; first 15.625 to 1. Reverse 17.609 to 1.

Final Drive.—Hypoid axle (11:45). Ratio 4.091 to 1. Two-pinion differential.

Suspension.—Front, semi-trailing (25 deg). Wishbones, coil springs, telescopic dampers, anti-roll bar. Rear, half-elliptic leaf springs, telescopic dampers, anti-roll bar.

Brakes.—Girling vacuum servo assisted, hydraulically operated two-trailing shoe, front;

leading and trailing shoe, rear. Drums: 12in diameter, 2¼in wide, front; 12in diameter, 2¼in wide, rear. Total lining area, 181 sq in (80 sq in front).

Steering.—Burman recirculating ball; ratio 22 to 1. Three turns from lock to lock.

Wheels and Tyres.—6.70-16in tyres on 5.50 × 16in rims. Five-stud steel disc wheels.

Electrical Equipment.—12-volt; 64 ampère-hour battery. Head lamps, single or double dip, 48-48 watt bulbs.

Fuel System.—16 gallon tank (including 1½ gallons reserve). Oil capacity 11 pints.

Main Dimensions.—Wheelbase 9ft 6in, track (front) 4ft 8⅜in, (rear) 4ft 9½in. Overall length, 16ft 1in. Width 6ft 0in. Height (unladen) 5ft 5½in. Ground clearance 8in. Frontal area 25.7 sq ft. Turning circle 42ft 0in. Weight (with 16 gallons fuel) 32½ cwt. Weight distribution, 50 per cent front.

These three photographs show the alternative arrangements used to accommodate the three types of transmission. On the left can be seen the dry single-plate clutch for the synchromesh gear box, in the centre is the centrifugally operated clutch used in conjunction with the preselector gear box, and on the right is the flywheel to which is mounted the fluid coupling for the automatic transmission.

AUTOMATIC

A PURPOSEFUL blend of tradition and modernity in appearance is now allied to a choice of "conventional," pre-selector or automatic transmission on the Sapphire.

THE six-cylinder 3.4-litre Armstrong Siddeley Sapphire has hitherto been available with either a normal four-speed synchromesh gearbox with steering-column gear-change or with an electrically-operated pre-selector box. For 1955, however, potential Sapphire purchasers will be offered a third choice, for this model is now being fitted with a British-built version of an American automatic transmission which has already been incorporated in two of Britain's best-known cars. Known, when fitted to the Sapphire, as the No-clutch gear-change, this transmission eliminates the clutch pedal, but enables the driver to retain some measure of control over its automaticity by means of a gear lever moving in a quadrant beneath the steering wheel, the lever also being employed for selecting neutral and reverse.

The No-clutch transmission consists of a fluid coupling, which acts as a clutch, two epicyclic gear trains each providing two forward speeds, and a third epicyclic gear train to provide reverse. Engagement of the appropriate gear to suit the road conditions of the moment is carried out hydraulically as a result of the counter-action of two opposing high-pressure oil streams from two pumps, the output of one pump depending on the position of the

accelerator pedal, and the output of the other being controlled by the road speed of the car.

Overall gear ratios provided by the No-clutch transmission are 4.091, 5.932, 10.776 and 15.625 to 1, with 17.609 to 1 reverse.

Another alteration to the Sapphire specification for 1955 applies to all models, namely servo operation for brakes of increased diameter. The new drums have a diameter of 12 in. compared with the 11 in. drums previously fitted, and the result of this change has been to increase the brake lining area from 184 sq. in. to 206 sq. in. Girling Autostatic operation is employed, the front drums having two trailing shoes which are self-adjusting. A spring in each operating cylinder develops just sufficient pressure to hold the shoe in contact with the drum, this pressure being counteracted in part by a bias-reducing spring which ensures that the shoe remains just in contact with the drum without any braking effect. It will be appreciated, therefore, that since the shoes have to move through a much smaller distance than normally when the brakes are applied, there being no clearance to take up first, the quantity of fluid which has to be displaced to apply the brakes is also greatly reduced. It has therefore

EASY TO REACH, the coil is now bolted to the side of the air cleaner, a position which much reduces the length of the ignition leads and cuts down interference with television. Also seen here is the reservoir for the screen-washer which is now standard equipment

TRANSMISSION for the
Armstrong Siddeley Sapphire
Also Bigger Brakes with Servo Assistance

THE FACIA panel has been slightly restyled, the circular speedometer being matched by a similar-sized dial containing gauges for fuel, oil pressure, water temperature and battery charge, while between them are a clock and four warning lights. Shown below is the quadrant and selector lever by which the driver may exercise some control over the now-optional automatic transmission.

been possible to reduce the size of the master cylinder and increase the size of the brake operating cylinders, with a consequent increase in the hydraulic leverage applied to the brakes, without increasing the pedal pressure.

This increase in part makes up for the lack of servo effect of the trailing shoes, which, of course, do not tend to wrap themselves ever more tightly round the drum as do leading shoes when applied. In actual fact, the new Sapphire braking system provides greater stopping powers with lighter pedal pressures, thanks to the inclusion of a Clayton-Dewandre vacuum-operated booster unit in the system. This booster unit is located between the hydraulic master cylinder and the distribution point of the fluid to the individual wheel cylinders. The vacuum to operate the booster is obtained by connecting it to the induction manifold, and the degree of vacuum boost applied is controlled by the pressure of the hydraulic fluid in the pipeline linking the booster to the master cylinder. The degree of servo action supplied by the booster is therefore directly related to the pressure applied by the driver to the brake pedal.

Should no vacuum be available to operate the booster

owing to the engine having stalled or for any other reason, there is still direct communication between the master cylinder and the brake cylinders, and the brakes can therefore still be applied, More pressure will naturally then have to be exerted on the brake pedal to make up for the missing servo action, but the system has been so designed that the pressure required is not beyond the capabilities of the average driver.

Refined in Detail

A number of other modifications have also been incorporated in the latest Sapphires now in production. The throttle linkage on the two-carburetter models, for instance, has been considerably revised, and instead of the two carburetters being linked by a somewhat complicated arrangement of rods and bell cranks, they are now operated by a simple shaft connecting the two throttle spindles, thereby greatly simplifying any adjustments that may be required. Moreover, they are now connected to the throttle pedal by a linkage of rods instead of by a cable. On all models, incidentally, the throttle pedal is now of the organ type.

Two alterations have been made to the cooling system; a five-blade, pressed-steel fan has replaced the two-blade type (a seven-blade fan now being fitted to export models) and the water pump has been redesigned to incorporate the thermostat in its housing. In this position, the thermostat is able to exercise a more direct influence on the water circulation than was the case when it was mounted in the radiator header tank.

One minor modification to the ignition system is the removal of the coil from its previous location on the bulkhead to a new mounting at the side of the air cleaner, thereby considerably shortening the ignition leads with a consequent reduction in the interference caused to television sets. CONTINUED ON PAGE 107

ARMSTRONG SIDDELEY

The *Sapphire*

By JOE WHERRY

PHOTOS BY AUTHOR

One of the world's great industrial organizations is the Hawker-Siddeley Group of England, a sort of mutual benefit amalgamation. The "Group" includes such well know firms as Hawker Aircraft, A. V. Roe, Ltd., Air Services, Ltd., Flight Refueling Corp. and others of equal import as well as Armstrong Siddeley Motors Ltd. with the main works at Coventry. One might liken this latter old line manufacturing firm to our own General Electric, for instance, in that Armstrong Siddeley manufactures an array of products encompassing almost every purpose known to machine age man. Probably the outstanding current product is the firm's "Sapphire" jet engine, one of the most powerful anywhere, and currently in great favor among military aviation authorities in our own country.

We mention this bit of background because wherever we went during 900 miles of road testing, we were queried about this car's origin. Several persons who were familiar with aircraft matters readily understood the connection between the two small jet engine-like earbobs on the miniature radiator cap Sphinx ornament. Of course the little jets signalized the blood relationship between the SAPPHIRE car and the jet engine, and the Sphinx denotes silence, a quality proudly stressed by Armstrong Siddeley

representatives when they speak of the new and powerful six-cylinder overhead-inclined-valve engine found under the attractive, classical hood.

Very British George Wheeler, service manager for H. L. Arnes, Inc., the sole American concessionaires, told me to drive the Sapphire as far and as hard as I liked (the test car was already thoroughly broken in) just before leaving Fergus Motors service station on West 55th Street in Manhattan where the Arnes organization has space. Told to expect something between the handling of an out-and-out sports car and a better type of American family sedan, the writer still didn't anticipate the kind of results indicated in the accompanying PERFORMANCE DATA box.

The reader will better understand the following comments if he will turn to page 61 and run through the Sapphire's specifications. Note that two carburetors, an 8.0 to 1 compression ratio and 160 horsepower characterize the test car. A single carburetor, 120 hp engine with a conservative 7.0 to 1 compression ratio is optional. Virtually all of the Sapphires now coming into the USA through the Port of New York are the higher powered model. Incidentally, according

Performance Data

ACCELERATION THROUGH GEARS	0-30 mph:	4.8 secs.
	0-50 mph:	9.2 secs.
	0-60 mph:	12.8 secs.
HIGH GEAR	30-50 mph:	7.2 secs.
STANDING ¼ MILE		18.6 secs.
MAXIMUM SPEED		103 mph.
BRAKE TEST	From 30 mph:	35 ft. 2-in.
	45 mph:	68 ft. 5-in.
	60 mph:	132 ft. 11-in.

FUEL CONSUMPTION

Under all traffic conditions and including all tests: 16.7 mpg.

SPEEDOMETER CORRECTION

At 40 mph, read 41 mph: 2.5% fast
50 mph, read 53 mph: 6.0% fast
60 mph, read 64 mph: 6.6% fast

Sapphire	GOOD	AVERAGE	SLIGHT	POOR	BLIND SPOT	EXCESSIVE	NIL
Hard cornering—lean			✔				
Panic stops—nosedive		✔					
Spring rebound—rough road		✔					
Steering wheel road shock							✔
Steering wheel lost motion							✔
Right front fender vision				✔			
Left windshield pillar vision					✔		
Rear window vision	✔						
Rear view mirror				✔			
Legibility—instruments	✔						
Driver's seating position	✔						
Rear leg room	✔						
Rear head-room	✔						
Restfulness—long trips	✔						
Windshield reflection							✔
Sun glare protection	✔						
Headlight effectiveness	✔						
Wind noise						✔	
Luggage space	✔						
Detail finish		✔					
Running economy	✔						

to George Wheeler, over four dozen Sapphires have already been sold in the Northeast even though introduced only a few months ago.

Definitely a fine car, the Sapphire is descended from a long line of Armstrong Siddeley vehicles. The marque is rare in the USA but widely known in Europe, India, etc. among car loving and prestige-wise buyers. Delivering FOB at any US Port of Entry for $4250, this Sapphire has all the luxury and quality of any of the (*Continued on page* 88)

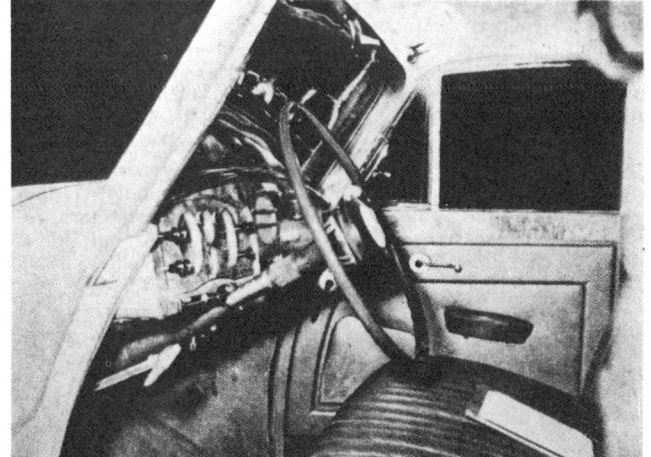

Below is the Sapphire's luxurious walnut and leather interior. At right, the engine, showing husky air cleaners of dual Stromberg carburetors. Note also spark plug location and split exhaust manifold.

Cornering hard on gravel at 30 mph, car came through with no slide.

Armstrong-Siddeley
The Sapphire

fine domestic cars plus a sensible middle size and very superior performance. The 114 inch wheelbase makes this a shorter car than either of the so-called small Big Three sellers over here; the weight is two or three hundred pounds greater, but is offset by an amazing power plant that gets the Sapphire over the road without the slightest strain for hours on end at well over 80 mph. The Sapphire may well give the Jaguar Mark VII sedan a rugged run for the buyers' money since it easily exceeds 100 mph!

Perhaps the best way to summarize the car's capabilities would be to recount the Sapphire's time on Thompson Raceway, a 1½ mile closed course at Thompson, Connecticut specifically laid out for sports car competition. The Sapphire was cleared by the well-known George Weaver, formerly SCCA Regional Executive for the New England Region, and was lapped twice around in practice by the author. With an official track record of 1 minute and 16 seconds the shooting mark at that time, we took off on the run after the second practice lap. George Weaver and friend Tom McClung, a Remington Rand research technician, were on the stop watch as we went through the first long, well banked corner at 65 mph, hit a shade over 85 mph on the back straight, rounded the next corner at about 35 mph, power drifting nicely, and nearly touched 90 mph on the next straight stretch. The smooth, Wilson type Preselector gear box really helps turn in a performance. Family car suspension is well stiffened by double acting Girling shock absorbers and antisway bars (coil springs in front, semielliptical springs in the rear). Other features include a fast Burman recirculatory ball type steering system with only three turns lock-to-lock and excellent balance in spite of rather heavy weight. All these factors make the Sapphire corner unbelievably well for its size and designed purpose. At any rate the car turned in 1 minute, 39 seconds around the Thompson track—certainly fast for a six passenger family car. As a stock racing car, the Sapphire might present a threat to domestic makes running in NASCAR events.

Such speed and roadability is fine for those of us who like sports cars and the sort of superior handling and safety factors exemplified by these little-understood imports that are causing such a migraine headache in Detroit. But how does the Sapphire stack up as a good value to the family car driver who wants something different, yet thoroughly

practical, durable, and within his means if he has arrived at the 4,000 buck car class? Here are details on both sides:

Appearance often accounts for more favorable public response to a new car than it deserves; on the other hand Americans frequently fail to look beneath the glossy enamel surface at details of engineering and craftsmanship. Belonging to the semi knife-edge classical school of design, the Sapphire will appeal to those who genuinely love fine cars more for their quality, stamina and roadworthiness than for line. So we must place the Sapphire's design in the same category occupied by the incomparable Rolls Royce, the beautiful Bentley, and others like the Delahaye and the rarer Bugatti. Chrome is used sparingly but tastefully, in the right places, and like the enamel finish, the chrome appears to be of excellent quality and quite frankly better than anything we are getting on our native cars. Details, such as instrument panel controls and the fine quality, highly rubbed burr walnut dash panel and window frames, all reflect the sort of craftsmanship at which England's coachbuilders excel.

THE metal body and fender panels are excellently fitted and one must go over the Sapphire with a fine tooth comb to reveal any but minor imperfections. After our complete tests, there were no rattles—the Sapphire is a very sturdy car. In rain we found no leaks—an improvement over several European jobs.

Driver and passenger safety has played an important part in the development of the Sapphire. Fully hydraulic brakes with two leading shoes, 11 inch diameter drums that are 2¼ inches wide, and an effective lining area of 184 square inches allow for very fast braking, and the reasonably firm suspension causes little nosedive during panic stops. We have rated the Sapphire as *average* on panic stops, but I must hasten to add that this is only average as concerns European cars—the Sapphire brakes very much better than American family cars of equal weight. The same comment attaches to spring rebound—it's very slight compared to domestic softsprung, overpowered, under-braked cars.

As for passenger comfort there is only one omission that occurred to the writer: there is no lighter, and it seems logical to expect one in a fine $4,250 car. This brings up another point of objection: ventilation is just so-so—cruising along at 75 mph on open highways is commonplace today, but in the Sapphire the wind

noise and disturbing blasts of air cause not only undue discomfort but make it impossible to enjoy the radio, an "His Master's Voice" model of excellent tone and receptive qualities. Ash trays are three, one on the back of the bench type front seat and one on each front door panel well forward. Long distance comfort would be enhanced if the front seat were about one inch lower. Truly chair high, the front seat has a tendency to cramp the legs beneath the knees.

Upholstery is excellent top grain cowhide dyed in colors complementary to the exterior finish. Retractable front and rear seat center armrests (unnecessarily hard to pull down) are nearly six inches wide. When these are folded, there is plenty room for three average sized persons on either front or rear seat. The side armrests in front are adjustable for height. The headliner is of a plastic fabric matching the leather work; this plastic material, which appears very serviceable, extends down to meet the leather door panels. Inasmuch as *four light* (two windows on each side) and *six light* (three to a side) sedan models are available, we should mention small additional parcel holders immediately aft of each rear side window in the former. Additional "cubby boxes" supplementing a large dash glove case are in each door panel.

Actually the Sapphire has the look and interior roominess of a much longer wheelbase car, so we were pleasantly surprised to find as much leg and knee room as in almost any American car. Driving comfort and safety would get a boost if one did not have to stretch one's neck to see the right front fender—even the parking lights at the fender crown help little and none but the very tall will be able to see this important aid to delicate maneuvering. The adjustable Burman steering wheel is excellent. The existence of a blind spot caused by the left windshield pillar was irritating though not as bad as on many cars, also, the extremely small rear view mirror, common to many European cars, is little better than none. Visibility, otherwise, is good, especially on the *three light* model. All instruments, in addition to warning lights, are readily visible. The speedometer, incidentally, is not nearly so optimistic as in most cars, regardless of origin. Twin signal lights, self cancelling, are controlled by a switch on the horn button.

Beneath the hood one is impressed by the ready accessibility of all vital parts. Because the valves are inclined, the spark plugs are located high on top of the head. The exhaust manifold is of the dual header type culminating in a single large muffler and tail pipe. American Stromberg carburetors are used rather than the usually present S.U. or Solex types. We would rather have seen an electric fuel pump than a mechanical type. However, the AC pump is fitted with a hand primer, useful for the fellow who likes to work on his own car. This fuel pump is of the single diaphragm variety (because of the electric windshield wipers) and is, hence, much more durable and easier to maintain. An AC "Sphinx" full flow oil filter is fitted as standard equipment, and the oil capacity of the sump is a generous 12 (U.S.) pints. As regards oil consumption, we noted virtually none in spite of hard driving and hot August weather.

WE have touched only briefly on the actual driving of the Sapphire desiring rather to bring out a few salient points. We may add that the Sapphire is a true sports sedan for the driver who likes to combine touring comfort, space for his family, plenty of luggage space (17 cubic feet), very high performance, and unusual road holding and cornering ability. The fine cornering is not immediately evident; while strange to the car, one has the feeling of leaning, but examination of action photographs and several hundred miles of hard, fast driving over all kinds of roads and under all traffic conditions impresses one with the roadability of this vehicle. In fact, one day's driving of 301 miles which included all accelerating and raceway activities, much idling, etc. resulted in an average of 16.7 miles per gallon, exceptional for the weight of car, engine size and the tests encountered. The fuel ca-

pacity is 19.2 U.S. gallons of which 1.8 gallons are in a reserve section. When a sputtering engine warns of the empty fuel tank, you merely pull the "R" switch (reserve) on the left side of the dash and go on for another 25 miles. Such refinements are one small reason why there are ever increasing numbers of European car fans in this country where more cars are built for better comparable prices than anywhere else on Earth.

In conclusion a word about the little known (in the U.S.A.) Preselector transmission: this is a fast and flexible system in the hands of an experienced person. Similar in operation to the Daimler and Lanchester unit (see AUTO AGE for June '53), the only real difference is that gear changes are selected on a small column gear shift pattern in which slides a miniature shift. The gear is selected by moving the small lever into the correct position for the next expected shift; when you desire to complete the shift, the left pedal (actually a gear change pedal—not a clutch) is depressed and released rapidly. The skill required to down shift at high speeds is not difficult to acquire. The clutch is of the fully automatic centrifugal type, and the gears are operated by solenoids. The advantage of this system, used before World War Two on the outstanding E.R.A. competition sports cars for example, and as far back as 1932 by Daimler, is that the driver can keep both hands on the steering wheel if shifting time comes during a precarious driving operation.

Though the Sapphire is not without small faults, it is also well worth the price. We predict for it a successful future in the U.S. when the nationwide sales organization now being formed gets under way. ✐✐✐

NEW ARMSTRONG-SIDDELEY SAPPHIRE

CONTINUED FROM PAGE 65

Steering, of the Burmann recirculating ball type, is light and reasonably accurate, but drivers who wish to make full use of the car's performance may prefer a more direct type of steering.

Any driver will feel comfortable in the car because the steering column as well as the bench seat is adjustable for reach. Lateral support is provided by a folding armrest and the cushion is deep enough to support the driver under the legs.

The Girling hydraulic brakes, with two leading shoes in front, are most efficient, require light pedal pressure and show no sign of fade on long descents. A pistol-grip handbrake, operating on rear wheels only, will bring the car to a slow stop on steep grades.

The facia is efficiently and attractively laid out. The instruments are set in black dials with white figures; the speedometer has a trip recorder inset in addition to the usual total mileage recorder. Other instruments include clock, oil, petrol, water-temperature and ammeter gauges. A large glove box is situated in front of the passenger.

ARMSTRONG SIDDELEY "SAPPHIRE" 3-4 LITRE SPECIFICATIONS

Number of cylinders	6
Bore	3.54 in.
Stroke	3.54 in.
Displacement	209.64 cu. in. (3435.35 cc.)
Compression ratio	8.0:1
Maximum output	160 bhp at 5,000 rpm
Bore/stroke ratio	1:1
Bhp per cu. in.	.763
Valves	70°-Overhead inclined, pushrod operated
Carburetors	Two Stromberg downdraft
Transmission	Electrically operated Preselector. (Manual Synchromesh optional)
Overall ratios	4th: 4.091 2nd: 8.153 3rd: 5.564 1st: 13.909
Rear axle ratio	4.091
Weight (car tested)	3,640 pounds
Power/weight ratio	22.75 lbs/bhp
Wheelbase	114 in.
Turning circle	42 ft. 6 in.
Turns (lock to lock)	3
Tire size	6.70 x 16
Tread	Front: 56⅝ in.; Rear: 57½ in.
Overall height	63 in.
width	72 in.
length	193 in.
Ground clearance (min.)	8 in.

ALL THROUGH THE NIGHT.— In order to acquire a great deal of experience in the shortest possible time, one Sapphire prototype was driven all over the country for 24 hours a day by a team of test drivers working in three shifts. These early Sapphires looked very much like the Whitley but with the Sapphire wing treatment.

The Saga of

ARMSTRONG SIDDELEY cars have always occupied an unusual position in the world of motoring, probably because the philosophy behind their production has for so long differed from the line of thought of most other manufacturers. Right from the very early days of motoring it was the paramount aim of their creator, John Siddeley, the first Baron Kenilworth, to produce a car which was the natural successor to the gentleman's carriage and pair in which "carriage folk" could travel with dignity and in comfort. Even in 1904 the Siddeley cars which were the ancestors of the present models were being advertised as "durable, quiet and economical" while the pre-Kaiser War Siddeley-Deaseys with their coffin-shaped bonnets foreshadowing the present Armstrong Siddeley radiator were described on the front covers of copies of *The Motor* of that period as "comfortable carriages." In brief, Siddeley-inspired cars have always been comfortable means of travel rather than pieces of engineering to which bodies were added somewhat as an afterthought.

Not that the cars have been lacking in technical excellence; the Siddeley-Deaseys were among the earliest cars to be fitted with self-starters, had dry-sump lubrication and used much light alloy in their construction. The first Armstrong Siddeley, the massive 1919 "Thirty," owed much to the experience gained by the company in the manufacture of Siddeley Puma aircraft engines which were produced at the rate of 700 a month during the first world war. In 1928 the company pioneered the use of the preselector gearbox and in 1933 the fabulous Siddeley Special with its Hiduminium light-alloy engine was placed in production. Nevertheless, the Armstrong Siddeley had come to be regarded as a highly respectable and rather sober carriage, inhabited exclusively by the best county families and by the directors of banks.

Additional Virtue

The Sapphire seemed to be a complete break with this tradition when it was introduced in the autumn of 1952, for here was a car with a performance matched by very few contemporary sports saloons and unrivalled by most pre-war out-and-out sports cars. In actual fact there had been no such break for the Sapphire is still the perfect gentleman's carriage, dignified and superbly comfortable. Its exceptional performance may be regarded as the natural result of the application to a car of the engineering knowledge possessed by a company which has recently

produced the most powerful aircraft gas turbine in the world—also a Sapphire—to complete its type tests.

The fascinating story of how the car came to be designed and built was told to me recently by Mr. H. T. Chapman, Armstrong Siddeley's managing director. He said the genesis of the Sapphire went back to 1947, when it was decided that a successor to the 2.3-litre Whitley was required. The Whitley, it may be recalled, was the first completely new post-war British car. It was new throughout owing to enemy bombs having destroyed not only all jigs and tools for the pre-war models but all the car division's drawings and records as well.

THE HEART OF THE CAR.—This sectioned drawing of the highly interesting Sapphire power unit shows the unusual valve gear and its chain drive, and the manner in which the plugs are sunk in wells in the cylinder head.

The directive from the Board to the Engineering Department called for a six-seater saloon of semi-traditional lines which, while not possessing sports-car aspirations, would yet have an adequate performance to satisfy overseas requirements. Moreover, the car had to be built to a price which would ensure a sufficient demand to enable it to be produced in reasonable quantities.

As Maurice Olley laid down in that highly significant paper he gave to the Institution of Automobile Engineers in 1938, cars, like vegetables, sell at so much a pound. Therefore, if the weight can be reduced without the employment of highly expensive materials, the selling price can also be reduced. It was therefore realized that if the weight of the new car could only be kept down, the problems of both a reasonable selling price and adequate performance would be a long way towards solution.

Weight and its reduction, however, is a constant night-

he Sapphire

By Philip A. Turner

How the Most Outstanding Armstrong Siddeley Model in the History of the Company came to be Designed and Built

mare to all design departments, for it is far more difficult to produce a reasonably light car than to endow it with a good performance or excellent road-holding. It is so much simpler to make everything so substantial that there is no likelihood of it breaking than to study each and every bracket and component minutely in order to reduce its weight.

As a starting point, a chassis frame was built by hand and mounted at three points in a special rig to test its stiffness. Readings were then taken of the deflection of the frame along its length when a load was applied, and the frame was stiffened where necessary until the minimum deflection was recorded at each point. The result of this experimental work is a frame of light weight yet remarkable stiffness, for although it weighs only 245 lb. compared with 289 lb. for the Whitley frame, a load of 1,145 ft. lb. is required to produce one degree of deflec-

PUT TO THE TEST.—It was an anxious time for the engineering department when the unconventional new engine was first run on the test bed, but anxiety rapidly gave way to delight when the figures obtained exceeded all expectation.

tion, whereas the same deflection of the Whitley frame can be produced by a load of only 615 ft. lb. By comparison, the frame of a popular American car weighs 269 lb. and is deflected through one degree by a load of 777 ft. lb.

A considerable research programme was also carried out on the engine for the new car—known to begin with in the works as the Three Litre—and not only was an engine with normal pushrod and rocker-type valve actuation built, but also one with twin overhead camshafts. The twin overhead camshaft unit, however, was finally abandoned owing to the difficulty of silencing the yards of chain required to drive the camshafts. It was also felt that servicing such a unit would prove difficult for the average garage, a point of considerable consequence in a car designed to be exported to all parts of the world and which would therefore find itself operating in districts with

ON TRACK.—Just outside the big aircraft hangars where the Sapphires receive their finishing touches is the company's own test track whose purpose is not to allow the new cars to be tested at speed but rather to enable the testers to concentrate on listening for unwanted noises and to try the brakes, steering and general handling of the car without having to worry about other traffic.

somewhat primitive ideas on servicing and maintenance.

The present most interesting valve gear was therefore decided on, for it seemed to combine the simplicity of the normal pushrod system with most of the advantages to be gained by the use of inclined valves in a hemispherical combustion chamber. Pushrod actuation was found to function very satisfactorily up to engine speeds giving a road speed of 120 m.p.h., and as at this time the maximum speed envisaged for the new model was some 85-90 m.p.h. this seemed to provide an ample margin for future development. Moreover, the use of a high-mounted camshaft meant that only a short chain drive was required, and the retention of pushrods meant that the valve gear would present no problems to the average garage mechanic. Moreover, experimental units employing this type of valve gear proved exceptionally quiet, a very important point when the type of car the Sapphire is intended to be is borne in mind.

Rigid Unit

Although the crankshaft runs in only four bearings, the shaft itself is exceptionally stiff, its main journals being no less than 2¾ in. in diameter and 1½ in. long. A break with recent Armstrong Siddeley practice was the abandonment of wet cylinder liners for the new engine. Experience had shown, however, that it was difficult to mount wet liners in such a way that they retained their roundness, with a consequent increase in oil consumption owing to blow back. It was felt that if the cylinder block of the new engine could be made sufficiently rigid, then the bores were bound to remain round, and such has proved to be the case. In spite of the use of a cast iron cylinder head, which, however, was found to give satisfactory results and to cost much less to produce than a light-alloy head, this 3.4-litre engine producing 150 b.h.p. weighs only 70 lb. more than the 2.3-litre Whitley engine developing 75 b.h.p.

The immense torque of the new engine meant that a divided propeller shaft was required, for a single shaft capable of transmitting it would have been impossibly big. A Salisbury hypoid final drive was also decided upon to lower the transmission line, and has proved very satisfactory and given no bother.

Another departure from post-war Armstrong Siddeley

practice that has caused some comment was the abandonment of torsion bars for the front suspension in favour of coil springs. This step was taken for various reasons, including cost reduction, weight saving and the difficulty that had been experienced in obtaining matching pairs of torsion bars, both made from the same quality steel and having received the correct heat treatment, for any discrepancies between the two bars resulted in the car having a set to one side. Moreover, owing to their length, torsion bars are difficult to accommodate in the chassis and any inaccuracy at one end is greatly magnified by the time it reaches the other end. It has been found in practice that coil springs give just as good a result and have the additional advantage that they can be located near to the wheel they are suspending.

Intensive Road Test

The design of the Sapphire was begun early in 1950, and in spite of the amount of research work carried out before the design was finalized, two cars were on the road by the end of the year. To begin with, they were fitted with Whitley bodies, and were therefore somewhat disguised. In order to gain running experience as rapidly as possible, one car was driven for 24 hours a day by three teams of test drivers operating over three different routes, and by this means a mileage of 75,000 was rapidly accomplished.

On the whole, the new design gave very little bother, such troubles as were experienced being confined mainly to chassis brackets. However, this was not unexpected, for in order to keep the weight down, these had been made from sheet metal and had been fabricated as light as possible in the knowledge that they could readily be stiffened should the road test programme reveal any failures. So well had the engineering staff carried out their task of keeping the weight down that the Sapphire chassis minus its heavier wheels and battery weighed only 20 lb. more than the Whitley.

Body Design

Meanwhile, the design of the body was being carried out by Lord Kenilworth—or Col. Siddeley as he was at that time. From the beginning it had been determined that a traditional radiator would be maintained bearing at least a similarity to previous Armstrong Siddeley radiators, and that the lines of the body would be those of a gentleman's carriage, rather than a sports saloon. When the general shape of the body had finally been decided, the usual Armstrong Siddeley practice was followed of building a wooden mock-up which was then mounted on a turntable. Much further discussion then ensued on the details of the body, and finally Motor Panels (Coventry), Ltd., began the task of sinking the dies for the new steel bodies.

In spite of the fact that the design had been started early in 1950, the Sapphire did not appear until the 1952 Motor Show. This was partly due to the very difficult materials position at that time, for it was originally intended to introduce the new model at the 1951 Show, but although the car itself was ready by that date, the tools for producing it were not, and so its début was reluctantly postponed for a year. The delay was not without its compensations, however, for it enabled a car to be shipped out to East Africa, a part of the globe notorious for its ability to wear out new motorcars in an astonishingly short space of time. There, the car was driven hard for thousands of miles and proved itself very suitable for overseas conditions.

First Announcement

In due course, however, the tooling difficulties were overcome and early in October, 1952 the Press were summoned to meet the new car at a country-house style of hotel outside Coventry. The car was an immediate success, for it appealed—just as had previous Armstrong Siddeleys—to men who had reached a position in life where they are able to appreciate the good things of this world and can afford to obtain them.

Development of the Sapphire has proceeded steadily since its introduction, a twin carburetter version with a maximum of 100 m.p.h. being introduced at the 1953 Motor Show and a fully-tested form of automatic transmission being made available towards the end of 1954.

Although the high performance of which the car is capable has been regarded in the nature of a bonus by many of its owners, the potentialities of the Sapphire as a competition car were not overlooked. Two cars were entered for the 1954 Monte-Carlo Rally and both finished, the one driven by W. M. Couper being awarded the Grand Prix d'Honneur for Road Safety in the Rally Concours and the R.A.C. Challenge Trophy for the best-equipped car placed highest in the rally.

Tuned for Competition

The Sapphire engine has also made many notable appearances during the 1954 season on racing circuits in a special car created by Tom Sopwith and christened the Sphinx. With three twin-choke carburetters and a compression ratio of 8.5 to 1, the Sapphire engine in its new surroundings has been developing more than 200 b.h.p. at 5,200 r.p.m.

It is obvious, therefore, that this engine has by no means reached the limit of its development, and no doubt much of the Saga of the Sapphire still lies in the future.

IN PRODUCTION.—Although the Sapphire is assembled on a production line, the line moves at the speed of the men and not the men at the speed of the line, for great care is taken to ensure that each individual car is well made.

Armstrong Siddeley present two new 2.3 litre

Sapphires

to join the famous *Sapphire 346*

Sapphire 236

with the amazing MANUMATIC no-clutch pedal gear change

Armstrong Siddeley have set a high standard of refinement in their new 2.3 litre 6 cylinder saloon. There is no clutch pedal. You simply move a centrally placed gear lever straight into the gear you want at the precise moment you want it—and you're in! No snatch. No clashing of gears. Just a continuous smooth flow of power. It is a great thrill to make perfect changes easily and quickly with this new type of control.

You get unmatched smooth performance at all speeds up to 85 m.p.h. Yet you will average 30 m.p.g. on the open road. The Sapphire 236 costs £1104 (plus £461 P.T.).

Sapphire 234

OVER 100 M.P.H. Synchromesh gearbox and central gear lever

The new Sapphire 2.3 litre 120 b.h.p. 4 cylinder saloon is a car that allies exceptional performance to the greatest possible refinement in styling and finish. Using the 4-speed synchromesh gearbox you can accelerate from 0 to 60 m.p.h. in 12.8 secs. and in top there is over 100 m.p.h. at your command.

Wonderfully responsive. Superbly safe, with its large size vacuum servo assisted brakes, it will give you immense pleasure to drive under all possible road and traffic conditions. The Sapphire 234 costs £1065 (plus £445 P.T.).

BOTH the Sapphire 236 and 234 are identical in exterior appearance, refinement and luxury. Both are full 5-seater saloons with 13½ cu. ft. luggage boots. Both come straight from the drawing boards, workshops and testing grounds that produce the brilliantly successful Sapphire 346 and the world famous Sapphire jet which powers many of the world's fastest aircraft.

Both have NYLON FINISHED UP-HOLSTERY, very durable and easy to clean.

Outstanding features include:

double bulkhead for super silence, extra wide bucket seats in front; full four-point visibility from the driver's seat, and quick-lift front offside window; air conditioner unit; instrument dials have ultra-violet lighting; windscreen washers; right-angle opening doors with concealed forward hinges for safety; non-corrosive body; luxury walnut instrument panel. An overdrive can be fitted as an optional extra on both cars. Wire wheels can be fitted as an optional extra on the Sapphire 234.

There is a choice of seven exceptionally attractive body colours in plain and two-tone versions. Drive whichever model you prefer, you will be more than impressed,

Write to **ARMSTRONG SIDDELEY MOTORS LIMITED, COVENTRY,**
for catalogue No. 236 or No. 234.

 MEMBER OF THE HAWKER SIDDELEY GROUP

Sapphire Limousine Introduced

Armstrong Siddeley Announce New 7-seater Chauffeur-driven Model on Extended Sapphire Chassis

Two occasional seats are provided in the rear compartment, folding down into the floor and division when not required. West of England cloth, polished walnut, and pile carpet give an air of luxury.

THE announcement this week of a limousine edition of the Armstrong Siddeley Sapphire marks the re-entry of the makers into a field in which they have had much successful experience in the past. Mechanically, the new model closely follows the specification of the existing Sapphire except for a lengthening of the wheelbase from 9 ft. 6 in. to 11 ft. 1 in. and the inclusion of such minor changes as are called for by this increase in size.

The new model is listed at a basic price of £1,910 which, with a purchase tax increment of £796 19s. 2d., gives a total of £2,706 19s. 2d.

As a seating dimensions diagram reproduced on this page indicates, the increased length of this model has been used to provide ample space for occasional seats in the rear. The latter are arranged so that, when not required, they fold into recesses formed in the floor and the dividing partition; when in use, they line up closely to make, in effect, a bench-type seat. The normal rear seat provides accommodation for two or three passengers and has both a central and side arm-rests. In the driving compartment, the seat is also of the usual bench-type and, as at the rear, both side and central arm-rests are provided. Upholstery is carried out in leather in the front compartment, with rubber floor covering, whilst the rear compartment trim is in West of England cloth, with pile carpeting, a mohair rug being offered as an extra if required.

Two Heaters

Special attention has been paid to heating and ventilation, there being separate units for the two compartments. At the front, the heater and de-mister is of the same type as on the normal Sapphire saloon and the separate unit at the rear is provided with a

control lever in one of the rear arm-rests and supplies warm air via grilles in the partition.

In order to provide maximum ease of access, all four doors are hinged at the rear and both the rear doors and the driver's door have key-operated locks.

At the rear, the doors conceal recessed steps which make for easy entry or exit, which are further aided by grab handles on the dividing partition. The latter has sliding safety-glass panels arranged to lock in any desired position.

As one would expect from a car of this type emanating from the Armstrong Siddeley factory, the whole interior finish and equipment are of the highest quality. Walnut veneer is used for the facia board, whilst polished walnut is also used for all window and door fillets.

Interior lighting is by a single roof light in the front with two additional lamps arranged above the rear doors

and operated by courtesy switches, supplemented by an overriding control. Blinds are provided for the rear window and, if required as an optional extra, for both the partition and the rear quarter-lights. Other items of equipment include a washer unit for the curved windscreen, two ashtrays in the front doors and two in the rear arm-rests, an electric clock in the partition, rope pulls of the spring-back type on the rear pillars and a pair of wing mirrors.

In the interests of silence, the pressed-steel body is mounted on special insulating pads. The chassis frame follows the same general design as that of the Sapphire and the standard 6-cylinder, o.h.v. single-carburetter 3.4-litre engine developing 125 b.h.p. is used. For this model, the makers have

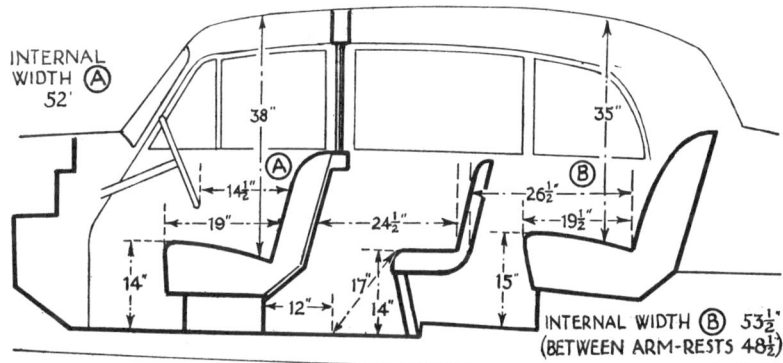

Interior dimensions of the Sapphire limousine. A photograph of the complete car appears on page 273.

chosen the standard four-speed pre-selector transmission, operated by an electric control and incorporating a centrifugal clutch, but a heavy-duty Salisbury hypoid-bevel axle is used providing the lower overall ratio of 4.45 : 1.

No changes have been made in the independent front-suspension system apart from the provision of coil springs with an increased rate, whilst the rear suspension also follows standard practice except that the semi-elliptic springs are fitted with overload leaves. Apart from 7-16-in. tyres and larger hubs, the remainder of the specification is standard except for the overall dimensions which are: length, 17 ft. 8 in.; width, 5 ft. 11½ in.; height, 5 ft. 8½ in.

Make : Armstrong Siddeley. **Type :** Sapphire (Automatic Gearbox)

Makers : Armstrong Siddeley Motors, Ltd., Parkside, Coventry

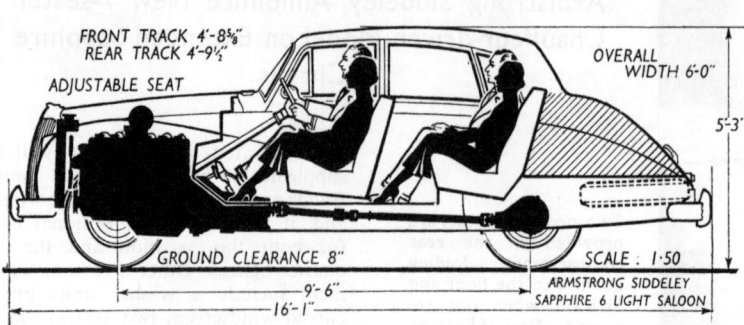

FRONT TRACK 4'-8⅝"
REAR TRACK 4'-9½"
ADJUSTABLE SEAT
OVERALL WIDTH 6'-0"
5'-3"
GROUND CLEARANCE 8"
SCALE : 1·50
9'-6"
16'-1"
ARMSTRONG SIDDELEY SAPPHIRE 6 LIGHT SALOON

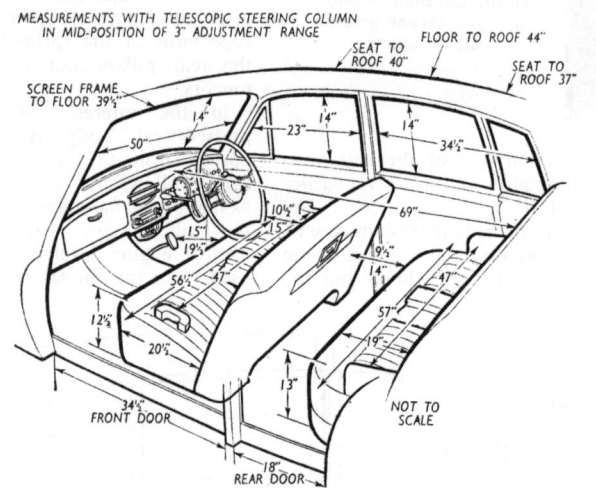

MEASUREMENTS WITH TELESCOPIC STEERING COLUMN IN MID-POSITION OF 3" ADJUSTMENT RANGE
FLOOR TO ROOF 44"
SEAT TO ROOF 40"
SEAT TO ROOF 37"
SCREEN FRAME TO FLOOR 39½"
34½" FRONT DOOR
18" REAR DOOR
NOT TO SCALE

Test Data

CONDITIONS. *Cool, dry weather with little wind (Barometer 30.0-30.2 in., temperature 40°-46°F.). Smooth concrete road surface (Ostend-Ghent motor road). Premium-grade pump fuel. Tyre pressures raised 2 lb./sq. in.*

INSTRUMENTS

Speedometer at 30 m.p.h.	1% slow
Speedometer at 60 m.p.h.	Accurate
Distance recorder	Accurate

MAXIMUM SPEEDS
Flying Quarter Mile

Mean of four opposite runs	95.9 m.p.h.
Best time equals	96.8 m.p.h.

Speed in Gears (Settled by automatic gearbox)

Max. speed in 3rd gear	58 m.p.h.
Max. speed in 2nd gear	28 m.p.h.
Max. speed in 1st gear	12 m.p.h

FUEL CONSUMPTION

26.0 m.p.g. at constant 30 m.p.h.
24.5 m.p.g. at constant 40 m.p.h.
22.0 m.p.g. at constant 50 m.p.h.
18.5 m.p.g. at constant 60 m.p.h.
16.0 m.p.g. at constant 70 m.p.h.
14.0 m.p.g. at constant 80 m.p.h.
Overall consumption for 1,464 miles, 87½ gallons, =16.8 m.p.g. Fuel tank capacity 16 gallons, including 1½-gallon reserve

ACCELERATION TIMES Through Gears

0-30 m.p.h.	5.4 sec.
0-40 m.p.h.	8.3 sec.
0-50 m.p.h.	11.4 sec.
0-60 m.p.h.	16.3 sec.
0-70 m.p.h.	23.1 sec.
0-80 m.p.h.	32.6 sec.
Standing Quarter Mile	20.7 sec.

ACCELERATION TIMES in Normal range

	Top
10-30 m.p.h.	3.7 sec.
20-40 m.p.h.	4.2 sec.
30-50 m.p.h.	6.0 sec.
40-60 m.p.h.	8.6 sec.
50-70 m.p.h.	11.7 sec.
60-80 m.p.h.	16.3 sec.

WEIGHT

Unladen kerb weight	33 cwt.
Front/rear weight distribution	52/48
Weight laden as tested	36¼ cwt.

HILL CLIMBING (at steady speeds)

Max. speed on 1 in 20	78 m.p.h.
Max. speed on 1 in 15	73 m.p.h.
Max. speed on 1 in 10	61 m.p.h.
Max. speed on 1 in 5	36 m.p.h.

BRAKES at 30 m.p.h. (Tested in neutral with fast tick-over)

0.87g retardation	(= 34½ ft. stopping distance) with 96 lb. pedal pressure
0.82g retardation	(= 36½ ft. stopping distance) with 75 lb. pedal pressure
0.73g retardation	(= 41 ft. stopping distance) with 50 lb. pedal pressure
0.41g retardation	(= 37½ ft. stopping distance) with 25 lb. pedal pressure

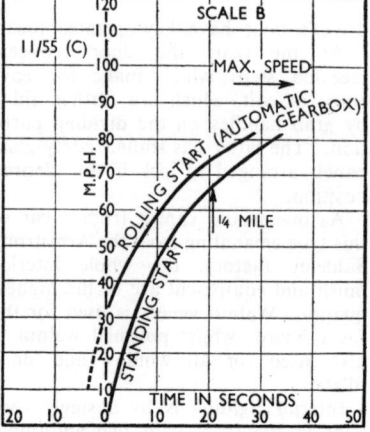

SCALE B
11/55 (C)
MAX. SPEED
ROLLING START (AUTOMATIC GEARBOX)
STANDING START
¼ MILE
M.P.H.
TIME IN SECONDS

Drag at 10 m.p.h. .. .. .. 64 lb.
Drag at 60 m.p.h. .. .. .. 160 lb.
Specific Fuel Consumption: when cruising at 80% of maximum speed (i.e., 76.7 m.p.h.) on level road, based on power delivered to rear wheels. .. .. 0.95 pints/b.h.p./hr.

Maintenance

Sump and oil filter : 11 pints, S.A.E. 30, (10-30° F, S.A.E. 20.) **Gearbox :** 20 pints, Automatic transmission fluid, Type A. **Rear Axle :** 2½ pints 90 E.P. **Steering gear :** 1 pint .90 E.P. **Radiator :** 28 pints, (2 drain taps and drain plug on water pump.) **Chassis Lubrication :** By oil gun every 2,000 miles to 19 points. **Ignition timing:** 5° B.T.D.C. **Spark Plug gap :** .028-.033 in. **Contact breaker gap :** .014-.016 in. **Valve timing :** I.O., 8° B.T.D.C.; I.C., 62° A.B.D.C.; E.O., 46° B.B.D.C.; E.C., 18° A.T.D.C. **Tappet clearances :** (Hot) Inlet and Exhaust .006 in. **Front wheel toe-in :** ⅛ in. **Camber angle :** 2°. **Castor angle :** Nil. **Tyre pressures :** Front 24 lb. Rear 24 lb. (26 lb. with heavy luggage.) **Brake fluid :** Girling. **Battery :** 12v., 64 amp.-hr. (Lucas GTW 11A), Lamp bulbs 12v., Head lamps (R.H. drive), 48w. and 48/48w. Side, boot and number plate lamps, 4w. Reversing light 21w. Tail light 6/18w. Fog lamps 38w. or 48w.

Ref. B/35/55.

—The Armstrong Siddeley Sapphire Saloon

(Automatic Transmission)

A High-grade Large Car with Modern Driving Aids

UNTIL quite recently the market for large cars, in contrast to the field of small family saloons, offered two distinct classes of vehicle from which the intending purchaser might choose. On the one hand there were those cars, of which the popular American was typical, which might be described as of "pressed steel all over"; and, on the other, the products of the British luxury motor industry, hand-built and hand finished, and to some extent traditional in specification as well as

WELL proportioned and undating in line, the Sapphire is at its best in two colours. (*Left*) Prominent features of the test car are the two pedals and quadrant control for the automatic gearbox.

appearance. Rarely did the twain meet. The latest Armstrong Siddeley Sapphire which has covered more than 1,500 miles in our hands is an example of the increasing post-war progress in marrying these extremes, for its unmistakably British coach-work goes with a maximum speed a shade under 96 m.p.h., power assisted brakes and an optional fully-automatic gearbox which is alternative to previously used Armstrong Siddeley transmissions.

The two last-named features are technical developments new to the Sapphire since one of these cars, with the alternative twin-carburetter version of the engine, was tested by *The Motor*, the maximum speed of the car just tried proving to be only 4 m.p.h. less than with that model. With cars of such performance it is part of our

normal procedure to cross the Channel in order to take stop-watch figures on a motor road suitable for sustained high speeds, and on this occasion the opportunity arose to judge the car more qualitatively on a rapid excursion through a variety of roads in Belgium and Holland.

It may be said straight away that the refined and rather staid carriage which used to characterize products of this company has been transmuted mainly in those elements concerned with its going and stopping. Bodily, the Armstrong Siddeley holds fast to a traditional style in which only faired-in headlamps and the line of the front wings continued rearwards concede to modern practice. In Continental countries especially, where last year's model frequently looks out of date, the style was remarkable for its un-ageing quality, and performance tests moreover indicate that neither lines nor such items as external door hinges are as much a handicap to "streamlining" as might be casually supposed.

An initial approach to the car in a confined space reveals one disadvantage in rather thick forward-opening doors, and hinges on the leading edges of the front doors would make a large car much more practical for many owners. Nevertheless, given space to open them, the easy access they allow is appreciated. The floor is high (and, incidentally, can be easily brushed out as it has no sill), and the driver finds himself sitting well above the road in the best of traditional fashion. This is continued in a long bonnet on each side of

In Brief

Price: £1,404 plus purchase tax £586 2s. 6d. equals £1,990 2s. 6d.

Capacity	3,435 c.c.
Unladen kerb weight ...	33 cwt.
Fuel consumption	16.8 m.p.g.
Maximum speed	95.9 m.p.h.
Maximum speed on 1 in 20 gradient	78 m.p.h.
Maximum top gear gradient	Not applicable

Acceleration:
   10-30 m.p.h. in Normal range   3.7 secs.
   0-50 m.p.h. through gears   11.4 secs.

Gearing: 20 m.p.h. in top at 1,000 r.p.m.; 85.5 m.p.h. at 2,500 ft. per min. piston speed.

SLIM pillars allow excellent visibility in all directions, and the wings are easily seen, topped by separate side lamps and mirrors. An annoyance on such a large car are rear-hinged front doors made bulky by the bulge of the wing line.

which the tops of the wings, with blended-in side lamps and, on the test car external mirrors, are plainly visible, unmasked by a driving mirror fitted at the top of the windscreen. The bench front seat is softly upholstered, adjustable for wide variations in length of leg, and deep enough to border on awkwardness for anyone short in the thigh. This is mitigated by a reclining seat squab, again not to everyone's taste but accommodating to most with a large steering wheel on a telescopic column.

From the driving seat, the most obvious departure from orthodox practice is the absence of a clutch pedal, and the gear selector lever on the steering column, moving in a quadrant marked Neutral, Normal, Fast, Fixed Second and Reverse. The features of this automatic transmission, basically of American origin and in the case of the Armstrong Siddeley built with certain detail developments by a well-known British constructor, will already be familiar to many readers. Briefly, it consists of a fluid flywheel and epicyclic gearbox which allows either fully automatic control between rest and maximum speed, or certain degrees of driver control to meet exceptional conditions.

A REALLY big boot and spare wheel in a separate compartment are provided, together with a foot pump and tools in a fitted, rubber-lined tray. The weight of the lid is balanced by torsion bar springs.

With the lever at "Normal" a forward gear is engaged, and there is enough drag in the flywheel to need a foot on the brake in order to keep the car at rest. If the brakes are released, gentle pressure on the throttle accelerates the car successively through second and third gears, into top at a pace barely registered on the speedometer, while full throttle from a standing start raises the upward gear-change points to approximately 12, 28 and 58 m.p.h., and control anywhere between these limits is possible with practice.

Selection of the "Fast" position has only one effect on the workings of the gearbox, preventing a change into top below 58 m.p.h., and in "Fixed 2nd" only first and second gears can be engaged, no matter how fast the car is driven. The latter range is useful as an auxiliary brake on steep hills, and may also come into play if the car has

to be "rocked" out of soft ground, where the fluid flywheel and adjacent positions of "Fixed 2nd" and "Reverse" make an excellent combination. In the hands of an enthusiastic driver the "Fast" range may be used a great deal, as in overtaking main road traffic when a momentary hesitation might cause the fully automatic mechanism to make an unwanted change into top. The same effect at slower speeds can make for smoother progress in a continuous traffic stream.

On the particular Sapphire supplied to us for test the combination of engine and transmission seemed in some ways an unhappy one. Even in its single-carburetter form the engine was very responsive (pinking a little on premium grade fuel), and the gearbox controls were apparently adjusted on more sporting lines than this single-carburetter model seemed to justify. At full throttle, upward changes were on the harsh side, although changes down from third to second were possible only below about 13 m.p.h., at which speed the "thinking" mechanism is distinctly slow to respond to snap opening of the throttle.

Throttle Changes

It is undoubtedly for the more restrained driver that this car is best suited, and a great deal can be learnt by experience of the art of changing smoothly up or down

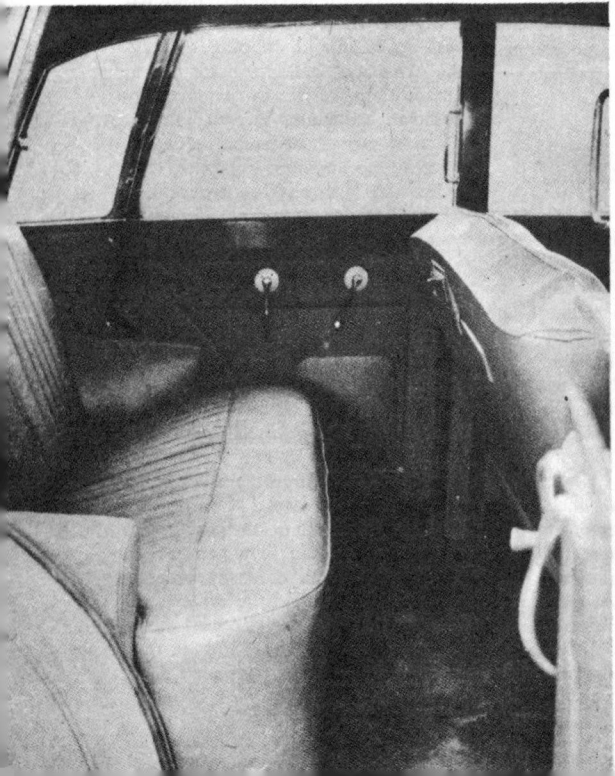

QUIET comfort, good finish and an almost flat floor for rear seat passengers. With the heater fan switched on, a good deal of heat passes under the front seat.

THE PETROL filler is concealed, and rear wheels enclosed in spats which may be removed by undoing a couple of Dzus fasteners.

by the use of the accelerator. This finding is further borne out by the character of the Sapphire as a whole. Firm to the extent of allowing much less roll than most modern large cars, the suspension achieves excellent riding comfort over most types of surface likely to be encountered in Great Britain or the Continent of Europe, with the impression of overriding irregularities in the road by sheer weight. "Export" shock absorbers were fitted to the model tested, and proved satisfactory in damping oscillations on both Belgian pavé and fast motor road where softer suspensions are apt to produce a disconcerting "boulevard ride."

Although springing and the absence of mechanical fuss (in top gear) permit almost any cruising speed up to 90 m.p.h. on straight roads most drivers even in these conditions find themselves settling down at about the 70 m.p.h. mark, owing both to a rise in wind noise above that speed and to a degree of steering wander if there is much cross wind. The steering as a whole leaves something to be desired in precise control, particularly with the recommended tyre pressures, but it is reasonably light and direct for the size of the car, and transmits little shock from the road surface. In fast cornering there is pronounced understeer which is not helped by the rather flexible feel of the steering, and a tendency for the more lightly loaded rear wheels to slide earlier than is expected. At a very small loss of comfort, a considerable improvement in roadholding and handling for the faster driver can · be made by increasing the pressures in all tyres.

Vacuum Brakes

A big car driven energetically, not only on Alpine roads but in the crowded conditions of this country, requires frequent and powerful stopping, a factor very adequately provided by the excellent vacuum servo brakes fitted to the Sapphire. A certain "treacliness" in the action of the brake pedal needs a little getting used to. Brisk use in admittedly flat country produced no sign of fade. A handbrake of the usual pull-out type is supplemented by a more positive arrangement for parking on a hill, when engaging reverse with the engine at rest will lock the transmission.

Turning to matters of greater interest to five of the six people who can comfortably occupy this car, a high standard of finish and furnishings is found, well in the Armstrong Siddeley tradition. The front seat, already remarked upon, can be adjusted to suit almost any length of leg, and even in its extreme position leaves plenty of room for passengers in the back. To say that the upholstery is of leather seems almost superfluous, while both facia and door cappings are in pleasantly grained polished wood. A most desirable feature is a powerful interior heater which draws fresh air from the top of the scuttle or recirculates warm air within the car by a two-speed fan, and with the help of the latter directs a blast of warm air as far as the feet of rear seat passengers. Some improvement in draught sealing around the front doors would be welcome in the coldest weather.

Fully Equipped

Light and airy to sit in by virtue of big side windows and slim pillars, the interior is further brightened by a washable plastics headlining, and at night the roof light can be switched on manually, or automatically upon the opening of the doors. For the driver, there are sensible circular instruments, of which the speedometer actually reads slightly slow, with two stages of "black light," and a cluster of four small red lamps on the facia gives warning that flashing indicator, choke, handbrake or headlamp main beam is on. Standard external lamps include a pair of long-range headlamps and two auxiliary lights of spreading beam on either side of the grille. Two-speed electric windscreen wipers are fitted, supplemented by a vacuum-operated windscreen washer, and there is a facia switch for the 1½-gallon reserve of fuel.

Comprehensive equipment extends to a boot of huge dimensions, with a counter-balanced lid, spare wheel in a separate compartment where it can be withdrawn independently of luggage, and a set of hand tools in a fitted, rubber-lined tray. In addition to jack and wheelbrace there is a foot pump.

As an indication of the manufacturer's ability to combine traditional coachwork quality and technical progress, the automatic-gearbox Sapphire is an encouraging sign of the times. It should do much to widen an already profitable market, where modern aids to easy driving make a useful backing for a car with "old-fashioned" comfort.

Mechanical Specification

Engine

Cylinders	6
Bore	90 mm.
Stroke	90 mm.
Cubic capacity	3,435 c.c.
Piston area	59.2 sq. in.
Valves ... inclined o.h.v. (pushrod)	
Compression ratio	7.0/1
Max. power	125 b.h.p.
at	4,700 r.p.m.
Piston speed at max. b.h.p. 1,775 ft. per min.	
Carburetter ...	Stromberg DAV-36
Ignition	Coil
Sparking plugs	Champion N8B
Fuel pump	AC mechanical
Oil filter	Full-flow

Transmission

Clutch	Fluid coupling with automatic transmission
Top gear	4.091
3rd gear	5.932
2nd gear	10.776
1st gear	15.625
Propeller shaft ...	Hardy Spicer, divided
Final drive	Hypoid bevel
Top gear m.p.h. at 1,000 r.p.m.	20
Top gear m.p.h. at 1,000 ft./min. piston speed	34.2

Chassis

Brakes Girling hydraulic, with vacuum servo	
Brake drum diameter	12 in.
Friction lining area ...	206 sq. in.
Suspension:	
Front ... Coil springs, trailing wishbones	
Rear ... ... Semi-elliptic leaf springs	
Shock absorbers ... ... Girling telescopic	
Tyres	6.70—16

Steering

Steering gear Burman re-circulating ball	
Turning circle (between kerbs):	
Left	47 feet
Right	44 feet
Turns of steering wheel, lock to lock	3¼

Performance factors (at laden weight as tested)

Piston area, sq. in. per ton ...	32.2
Brake lining area, sq. in. per ton	112
Specific displacement, litres per ton mile	2,800
Fully described in The Motor, October 6, 1954.	

Coachwork and Equipment

Bumper height with car unladen:
Front (max.) 22½ in., min. 13 in.
Rear (max.) 22½ in., min. 11 in.

Starting handle	Yes
Battery mounting	Under bonnet
Jack	Screw type

Jacking points: Front bumper and rear springs
Standard tool kit: Screwdriver, 3 box spanners, tommy bar, adjustable spanner, 2 O/E spanners, tyre pressure gauge, tyre valve key, 2 tyre levers, nave plate remover, grease gun, distributor screwdriver and feeler gauge, pliers, carburetter jet key, tyre pump, starting handle, jack, wheelbrace.
Exterior lights: 2 headlamps, 2 sidelamps, 2 auxiliary driving lamps, 2 tail lamps, number plate and reverse lamp.
Direction indicators: Flashing type, self cancelling.
Windscreen wipers: Electric, 2-speed, self-parking.
Sun vizors ... ... 2, universally pivoted.
Instruments: Speedometer with decimal trip distance recorder, fuel gauge, oil pressure gauge, water thermometer, ammeter, clock.
Warning lights: Headlamp main beam, choke, handbrake, direction indicators.

Locks:

With ignition key	Ignition, driver's door
With other key ...	Luggage locker
Glove lockers	1, not lockable
Map pockets	4 in doors
Parcel shelves ...	1 behind rear seat
Ashtrays	2 front, 1 rear
Cigar lighters	None

Interior lights: 1 roof light with interior switch, 1 map-reading light under facia, boot light, under-bonnet light.

Interior heater	Fresh air type with screen de-misters
Car radio	Optional extra

Extras available: Radio, twin carburetters, separate front seats, synchromesh or preselector gearbox.

Upholstery material	Leather
Floor covering	Carpet

Exterior colours standardized: 10 single or dual colour combinations of black, fawn, elephant grey, silver grey, Langham grey, Corinthian green, dark blue.

Alternative body styles ...	4-light saloon, limousine

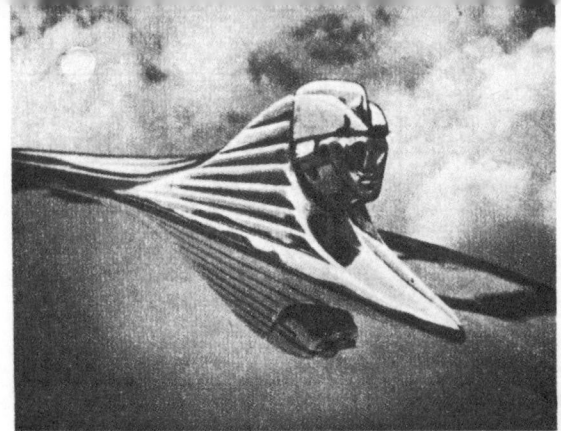

PROFILE:

by K. E. JOLLES

One of the first cars to appear after the war with modern styling, the Armstrong Siddeley quickly built for itself a name for refinement and sound workmanship

THE old proverb has it that beauty is in the eye of the beholder. Certainly, to me, DAG 595 is beautiful, but I do not expect everyone to agree with me. A wise old University professor in my student days dampened my somewhat unjustified self-congratulatory attitude after end-of-term examinations by remarking, almost sadly, "Blessed is he who expecteth nothing, for he shall not be disappointed." If I never learned much about chemistry, I am, at least, forever indebted to him for one of life's greater wisdoms.

The object of my admiration, then, is an Armstrong Siddeley Hurricane drop-head coupé, with the 2.3-litre engine rated at 18.22 h.p. by the old R.A.C. method, its six cylinders developing 75 b.h.p. at 4,200 r.p.m., a fairly modest output for an o.h.v. unit of 2,309 c.c. capacity with the low compression ratio of 6.5 to 1, all of which denotes a touring engine designed for reliability, smoothness of running and longevity rather than maximum performance.

Hydraulic tappets further aid in achieving this object—they are virtually inaudible in operation, and one of my favourite parlour-tricks is to take an unsuspecting friend out in the car and, when we momentarily stop, as perhaps at traffic lights, to ask whether he thought, in the absence of any noise or vibration from the idling unit, that the engine had stalled? If he obliges me by saying yes, I "accidentally" touch the accelerator pedal with my foot whilst pretending to fumble for the starter button on the dash, and so discover that the engine is still with us. Childish, perhaps, but to me subtly gratifying in an age when you can see the owners of most cars rudely shaken out of tranquility by the vibration of their engines whilst idling.

A solid-tappet conversion is available for those who want it, and some of the later engines of this type are thus equipped but, whilst they gain a few m.p.h. in top speed, they are noisier and, of course, need periodical adjustment if they are to retain a smooth tick-over.

The wings and body are finished in smooth, deep, shiny black relieved only by a double white line to pick out a flash moulding along the side. The wheels are black with one concentric white line, and the upholstery is in high-grade green leather. The dash and door fillets are what our American friends wonderingly describe as "real tree wood," and highly polished to endow the interior with an aura of quiet and unostentatious luxury. Maybe I am a sybarite, but is there anything wrong in that, and must our generally hard modern times destroy our appreciation of such of the fine things in life as are within our grasp? The hood is the original rubberized canvas in a light fawn colour, but a replacement, in battleship-grey Vynide, is shortly to be fitted.

It is my firm belief that certain cars look their best in certain colours, and the ageless, aristocratic lines of this car are best displayed in black, just as both my wife and I unhesitatingly awarded highest place, in our private *concours d'élégance*, to an ivory-coloured Jaguar XK120 drop-head with a black hood, as being the best colour combination for that car.

Speaking of hoods, I consider the modern type of convertible body not only equal but, in fact, superior to the saloon. Weather sealing is able to cope with the worst that this country can offer, and I think it would prove fully efficient anywhere, although I am unable to speak from personal experience on that point.

THE LADY IN BLACK

1950 ARMSTRONG SIDDELEY HURRICANE DROP-HEAD COUPÉ

There are no draughts, and detachable zip fasteners along the upper edges of the cant rails prevent the hood from ballooning up when the car is travelling fast, and so creating an aperture between the hood and the top of the window on each side. To be fair, this particular model has rather blind rear quarters, where the corresponding Whitley saloon has quarter windows, so that side vision is somewhat restricted for rear-seat occupants. This is a small price to pay for the ability to furl the top down and out of the way on fine days and so enjoy the greatest of all commodities, and free at that—God's own fresh air.

Surprising, too, when once you start looking for them, how many opportunities there are for putting the top down. The exhilaration of open-car motoring is a sensation to which words cannot do justice. Other fresh-air types will know what I mean, and to those unfortunates who have never tasted this supreme joy I can only say, " If you haven't been in an open car, you haven't lived ! "

Furling the hood, and re-erection when really bad weather threatens, are simple operations, but cannot be accomplished entirely from the driving seat. There is a half-way, de ville position where the canopy is rolled back and secured, the rear portion of the hood remaining erect, so that with side windows wound up the effect is obtained of a saloon car with a sliding roof panel in the open position. I hardly ever run the car in that trim, for having got that far, I am always itching to dispense with a top altogether and push it right down.

The car is fitted with a heater which is, however, rather a poor specimen. Actually it suits us very well, as neither my wife nor I dislike the cold but react badly to excessive warmth, yet I could imagine a lot of people shivering at the very thought of us setting out on a long run in freezing mid-winter, with the top down and the heater just keeping our toes warm, but otherwise relying on normal winter outdoor clothing. And yet such a run is just about the best tonic I know, and we always return feeling as though we had been away on holiday, instead of only one day in the fresh air. Suitable headgear would seem to be the most controversial subject, and my wife's experiments in that direction would supply enough material for another article. . . .

The famous and old-established Wilson type of preselector gear box of Armstrong Siddeley manufacture is fitted to my car, but a manual synchromesh gear box is available optionally. I regard mine as an unequalled method of driver-controlled gear changing, for both simplicity and speed of operation. This epicyclic gear box, together with the centrifugal clutch, constitutes a well-tried unit and, whilst it is admittedly heavy, I would say it more than pulls its weight in any car to which it is fitted. This unit has been used in pre-war E.R.A.s, Tommy Sopwith's Sphinx, and also the latest Connaught Formula I car, to mention but a few, so it seems I am not alone in my approval.

Aircraft firms have a reputation for building their cars just that little bit better than their competitors, and the Hurricane worthily upholds this tradition. The beautiful panel work, fine detail finish, engine layout, and clear circular instruments with their edge-lit black dials and white figures, deeply recessed into the wooden dash to avoid reflections—all these point their story. Even in the choice of names for its post-war models, this firm proudly refers to its connection with the aircraft industry—Typhoon, Lancaster, Whitley, Hurricane, and, most recent arrival on the scene, the Sapphire. The last, whilst still designed and

In " converted " form the Hurricane becomes a truly open car ; with the roof up it is as draught-free and waterproof as a saloon

glad that this is so; an automatic choke is available for the lazy. Fitted on the steering column is a manual hand throttle control which I find invaluable for warming-up, keeping the centrifugal clutch engaged whilst descending steep hills, reversing in confined spaces, or even just to give my right foot a rest once in a while on a long run.

The side lights were originally fitted inside the head lamps, and not as separate " bubble " lamps beneath them as on later models. This gave me an opportunity simply to remove the side light bulbs from their holders, and to mount neat, chromium-plated Lucas side lamps on the front wings, which I consider to be the proper place for side lamps anyway. Slipped in between the wing and the base of each of these lamps is the slotted and flattened end of the stem of a wing mirror, and this has the double advantage of making the mirror-and-lamp combination look like one unit, and avoiding extra holes drilled into the very strong wings.

I do not like wing mirrors, but I confess I find them essential on this car, for the blind rear quarters otherwise render observation of the world behind very difficult—and this can be expensive! Besides, these mirrors enable me to reverse confidently whilst apparently looking straight ahead —and if this gives the uninitiated onlooker a pain in the neck, I cannot help it.

A manually operated twin-jet screen washer was fitted some time ago, and proved such a worth-while addition that I now wonder how I ever got on without one before. A radio was also installed, but is used only when I am driving slowly, or during stops. During fast runs, wind noise interferes with enjoyable listening.

Our big Airedale is an enthusiastic motorist, and has

Though its owner does not take an active part in competitive motoring, the badge bar indicates where his interests lie

THE LADY IN BLACK . . . . continued

built to their established high standards in comfort, smoothness and reliability, has almost surprised its own makers by the enthusiastic reception it has been given not only by their usual type of buyer but also by the sportsman, and I think that the 2.3-litre chassis has helped pave the way for its bigger brother. Immediate post-war production was centred around a chassis similar in general layout to that of my Hurricane, but powered by an engine of just under 2-litre capacity, which was perhaps lacking in acceleration. The introduction, late in 1949, of the 2.3-litre engine with a few other modifications, remedied this by improving the power-to-weight ratio considerably, and produced a touring car capable of putting up deceptively high averages.

My car seemed so " right " in its general conception that I thought it reasonable to tailor it even more to my personal taste, and I found the manufacturers' service department ever ready to assist. The torsion bar i.f.s. was stiffened by fitting auxiliary piston-type dampers to eliminate frontend pitch at high speeds over certain surfaces, and this further improved the already high cornering powers of the car, whilst not giving rise to scuttle-shake as was once feared.

Very comfortable individual bucket seats with rounded back squabs provide firm location and support the shoulders, but I had the base springs reinforced in deference to the combined weight of myself plus heavy overcoat, and the seats show no sign of sagging.

When the original rear spring dampers were due for replacement at about 30,000 miles, a set of heavy-duty units was fitted which has almost gilded the lily where road holding and riding comfort are concerned; yet I can still traverse rough surfaces in smoothness usually associated with much softer suspensions, and irrespective of speed.

Instruments originally included gauges for oil pressure, water temperature, fuel contents, an electric clock, and speedometer with total mileage and also separate trip recorders, the latter reading to decimals, but to my surprise there was no ammeter fitted. I took out the clock and fitted a matching ammeter, and then replaced the original interior driving mirror with one which incorporated an electric clock in its tinted anti-dazzle glass. Warning lights on the dash for the ignition circuit and also to indicate side lamp failure complete the information bureau.

On my car the choke is manually controlled, and I am

come to regard the rear seat as his own. To protect the leather from his claws, I have had it covered in matching green Rexine with ivory piping, and so successfully was this done that the cover looks like the original upholstery.

Performance figures are very difficult to give as, with an ordinary owner like myself, it is more a matter of impressions than exact stop-watch readings, and driving methods as well as traffic conditions affect the result. However, when contemplating a long run, say from the Midlands to South Cornwall, a distance of some 270 miles, I usually find that,

De ville position; the roof can be fully stowed or rolled to the half-way position, leaving the occupants of the front seats to enjoy the open air

calculations based on an average of 38-40 m.p.h., including short stops, are confirmed in actual fact, Considerably more than 40 miles can often be put into every hour, but traffic density has increased so greatly of late that I have noticed a definite and marked decline in my averages over well-known runs. The speedometer is not unduly optimistic, and indicated maximum speeds on the gears are 1st 24 m.p.h., 2nd 40, 3rd 60, and top just above 93 on the clock; the car cruises comfortably with the needle at 65-70 m.p.h.

Petrol consumption, again, depends on driving methods but, running on Esso Extra, I never seem to drop below 20 m.p.g. With a compression ratio of only 6.5 to 1, the black lady will run on lower-grade fuel, but this is my way of rewarding her. Incidentally, there is that blessed fitting, a reserve petrol tap controlled from the dash.

Oil consumption, at a total mileage of about 35,000, is very reasonable, and I use perhaps 2 or 3 pints of oil for topping-up, between draining and refilling the sump at regular intervals of 1,500 miles.

On Course

With a wheelbase of 9ft 7in, the turning circle of 37ft is adequate rather than outstandingly good. Quite low-geared steering facilitates operation at low speeds, yet the car steers very accurately at all times, with just enough understeer to help maintain stability at high speeds and in cross winds, and responds readily and smoothly to the helm. There is no lost motion at the wheel, and changes in road surface can be felt. I remember a run to the North last winter, when the steering suddenly acquired that characteristic lightness which indicates ice on the road. The car, however, had remained so steady that I could hardly believe this, and stopped to investigate. No sooner had I stepped down than I went into a wild—and uncontrolled—"two-foot drift," so icy was the road! As with most well-balanced cars, steering characteristics can be subtly influenced by experiments with the tyre pressures.

Nothing is perfect, so I must admit Dag's main fault—her tendency to brake squeal. The brakes themselves—of Girling hydro-mechanical type—are excellent and do not fade or grab, although they require fairly heavy pedal pressures, but they do at times emit the most piercing squeal. This generally happens when the car is about to come to rest, but the noise suggests abrupt termination of a supersonic rate of travel, and we collect black looks from all and sundry. Different brake linings have been tried, slotted brake shoes, carbon inserts, and a host of other remedies, but the squeal continues. I hope to try the effect of a coil spring round the brake drum, as seen on certain vintage Bentleys. The silver lining of this particular cloud is that my squealing brakes have taught me to rediscover the gentle art of deceleration without use of the pedal!

The use of the personal pronoun "she" when referring to Dagatha, or Dag as we usually call her, has been fully intentional—I firmly believe that cars have souls, and voices, and their own personalities. To me, she represents a sophisticated lady, elegant in black, aloof at first sight, but warm and alive and eager when you know her.

I use her only for long journeys and touring—preferring a small 803 c.c. convertible (guess which?) for my local "stop-and-start" trips—and for that purpose the Hurricane has proved herself well-nigh our ideal. My wife likes the classic lines of the car, the smooth silence, comfort, and the feeling of safety inspired in the occupants. I completely endorse this, but, as the driver, I must say how much I always enjoy driving Dag. She fits in with my moods and instantly adapts herself to any change; quite happy to go silently drifting along some country byway with never a murmur to betray her passage, she will equally readily break into a smooth gallop, the six long-stroke cylinders emitting a joyous hum to indicate their contentment, and share our pleasure that once more we're going places—and how better?

Stiffened torsion bar i.f.s. has improved the cornering abilities of the car—already a strong point with the Hurricane

John Trowell finds that automatic transmission hasn't robbed this famous British car of any of its zest

SAPPHIRE

GIVEN 300 miles of hard treatment, which included several laps of the Phillip Island racing circuit, the new Armstrong Siddeley Sapphire, fitted with the new fully automatic transmission, proved that this type of unit can be designed so that there is still plenty of fun left in driving.

When first taking over the Sapphire for road test, I had my left foot floundering around looking for the clutch pedal—it took quite a few miles to get used to the idea that there were only two pedals required to keep all under perfect control.

On the left-hand side of the steering column is the quadrant, marked out in neutral, normal, fast, fixed second and reverse. There is a long selector lever, and the mechanism can be easily worked by fingertip control, without having to shift the left hand from the wheel.

To start the car, the selector must be placed into the neutral position; if it is left in any other of the four drives, the starter will not operate. This has been designed as a safeguard to the transmission as well as to the driver.

Selector on "Normal"

Once the engine is ticking over, the normal position can be selected simply by moving down the lever, and the car will move away as engine speed is increased by pressure on the throttle. If the idling speed of the motor is rather fast, there will be a slight amount of "transmission creep." In other words,

QUADRANT, with long fingertip-controlled selector lever, is mounted left of the steering column, needs no effort to operate.

BOOT (below) has spare housed under shelf, with the tool kit in a nested drawer alongside. Boot lid curves down at the sides.

GOES AUTOMATIC

the car will move forward slowly as the vanes in the gearbox take up. This can be stopped just by keeping a light pressure on the brake pedal.

The harder a driver accelerates, the quicker the car will move off from rest. With only a light foot, and a slight release of throttle pressure as one requires a change-up in the four forward gear ratios, top can be selected at speeds as low as 15 m.p.h. From this one can gather the sensitive control that can be had with the "normal" position on the quadrant.

Normal is the drive which can be selected at the start of a run, and at no time would it be necessary to move the selector lever. All up and down changes take place fully automatically, and as the car comes to rest, say at traffic lights, the action both in starting and stopping is as smooth as could be desired by the most fastidious motorist.

Now, if hard acceleration off from rest is the order of the day and some keen owner is trying to hit his 0-50 m.p.h. time in the 10 seconds, then the accelerator is pressed to the floor and left there. The car will quickly move away, gather speed in first, shift into second at about 15 m.p.h., before the power unit can be over-revved, build up to 34 m.p.h. in second, and after changing into third will hold 55 m.p.h. before top gear is selected.

I wondered at first whether these changes were not a little early to obtain the best acceleration, but there are no tricks that can be applied to the transmission which will

better 0-50 m.p.h. in 10 seconds. Of course, no matter how much of a speed fiend a driver happens to be he just cannot over-rev the Sapphire in any gear bar the fixed second. More about the latter ratio later.

The mechanical "brain" is designed to give a certain take-off, and in the words of the prophet, that's that.

This Sapphire had the hot twin carburettor kit which can be fitted as optional equipment to any car of the new Armstrong Siddeley range, and I recalled that on previous tests of the standard synchromesh gearbox and clutch two-carb version, 0-50 m.p.h. could be hit repeatedly in less than 9.0 seconds. In that car the speeds attained in various gears were 33 m.p.h. in first, 50 in second, and 75 in third.

"Fast" Really Means it

Bringing some real entertainment back into the driving of the automatic Sapphire is the next drive, which lives up to its name—"fast."

In "fast" position third will not change up until 63 m.p.h. is reached, and whenever road speed falls back to this third-gear maximum the transmission will change down automatically.

By the same token, if you are driving in "normal," and some extra boost is required in a hurry, dropping the selector lever down in "fast" will make an immediate change into third gear. This obviously means that the driver remains in reasonable control of the

JOHN TROWELL

With this able road test, Victorian John Trowell joins the staff of Modern Motor's expert contributors. Well known as a competitor in the last Redex Trial and motoring writer for newspapers and periodicals, John has tested most cars that have reached Australia in the past five years. You will like his truthful, accurate reports on all aspects of motoring.

gear-changes, to meet the sudden requirements arising when negotiating a winding road with high averages from point to point in mind.

When taking-off in "fast," first and second will change up at the same speeds as with the "normal" drive, but third is held for an extra 8 m.p.h., showing an improvement of 1.0 second in the 0-60 m.p.h. acceleration.

If at any time it becomes necessary to hold second gear, such as in loose sand or in very hilly country, the fixed second drive can be engaged. Also, to take the loading off the brakes, this ratio will re-

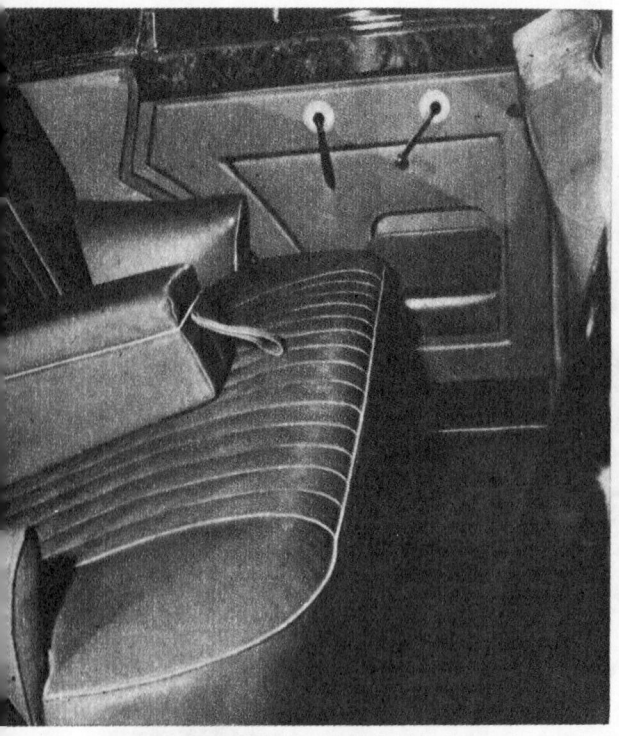

REAR SEAT has permanent armrests at sides, pull-out armrest in middle. Comfort is A-1.

ENGINE VIEW shows twin Stromberg downdraught carburettors, each with its own cleaner, and twin manifolding (right).

main engaged no matter how high the engine revs build up.

At all times the transmission was completely silent, adding to the feeling of effortless power built into this luxury machine.

Safe, Powerful Engine

The twin Stromberg carburettors build up the power output from the 125 b.h.p. at 4700 r.p.m. of the standard Sapphire to 150 b.h.p. at 5000 r.p.m. These revs are pretty high for a 3.4-litre engine, but from what I can find out the unit is robust enough and able to take many miles of strong, healthy driving. In England there is a sports car using this motor with a power output over 200 b.h.p., and lately it has been quite successful.

Another factor which should keep down the "wear bug" is the square design of the engine, with bore and stroke of 90 mm. At the piston speed of 2500 ft. per min., claimed as the theoretical safe limit for any car engine, the Sapphire's road speed is 85.5 m.p.h.—fast enough for anyone, including the law.

Engine design is right up to the minute, with hemispherical combustion spaces and spark plugs set down through the centre of the cylinder-head. The valves are inclined at an angle of 70 degrees and operated by long and short push-rods from a camshaft set high in the right-hand side of the cylinder-block casing.

Sports-car Handling

When it comes to the handling department, the latest Sapphire is just so far ahead of any previous model that it bears no comparison. On loose-surface work this car can be thrown around like a full-bred sports car. On some of the long, fast bends of the new Phillip Island racing circuit, which are still covered with loose metal prior to sealing, I held this car in 60 m.p.h. slides, using the throttle to steer.

Steering is light and surprisingly accurate, and there is just enough reaction at the wheel to spell away any "dead" feeling.

Turns from lock to lock of the 13in. steering wheel total 3¼, which

is very good for a large car. There is also ample self-centring action—a definite assistance when parking. Turning circle is average at 42½ feet.

Over the bitumen the Sapphire retains its good manners, but on sharp corners taken at average speeds a fair amount of tyre squeal can be heard. However, the tyres are large—6.70 x 16 inches—so I suppose some noise is to be expected, considering the weight of the car (33 cwt.).

Body roll is kept down to a minimum by the addition of heavy anti-sway bars at both front and rear, and they check any tendency for the "mushiness" sometimes associated with luxury vehicles.

In the front there are conventional coil springs, independently set with backswept wishbones. Large telescopic shock absorbers are mounted inside the coils. At the rear are long leaf springs of the semi-elliptic type, again with telescopic shock absorbers.

The chassis is good and solid, well braced by tubular cross-members. Its rigid construction is largely responsible for the rock-like stability we enjoyed when travelling at high speed.

Those Two Pedals

On the test car the accelerator was rather too stiff, and on long trips I developed an uncomfortable feeling in the right leg. On checking through the linkage we discovered

PERFORMANCE DATA

ACCELERATION through gears: 0-30 m.p.h., 4.4 sec.; 0-50 m.p.h., 10.0 sec.; 0-60 m.p.h., 14 sec.

MAXIMUM SPEED: 101 m.p.h.

SPECIFICATIONS

ENGINE: 6-cylinder, o.h.v. Bore, 90 mm., stroke, 90 mm. Capacity,

3435 cc. Develops 150 b.h.p. at 5000 r.p.m. Compression ratio, 7.0 to 1.

TRANSMISSION: Fully automatic, with two-pedal control.

WEIGHT: 33 cwt.

PRICE: £2850 (including sales tax).

Test car supplied by Stokoe Motors Pty. Ltd., Melbourne.

SAPPHIRE GOES AUTOMATIC

that there were unusually heavy return springs fitted to the carburettor spindles. Some slight modification here should prove quite simple and would be well received by owners.

In contrast to the heavy accelerator were the delightfully light pressures required to bring the Sapphire to a screaming halt from any speed up to the maximum. If hard pressure was applied to the brake pedal at anything below about 40 m.p.h., the braking action was most violent and all four wheels locked. Just a light caress on the pedal brought the car smoothly to a halt— a lighter pressure than the accelerator needed, believe it or not.

These latest-type brakes are servo-assisted by a Hydro-Vac system, and the brake-drum size has been increased from 11in. to 12in. x 2¼in. all round. Giving a severe test (which frankly I would not attempt on every car) by applying full pedal pressure from near the maximum speed of 100 m.p.h. brought this Armstrong Siddeley to a halt in a dead straight line, without any need for correction at the wheel. No fade was noticed.

Luxury Plus Comfort

My test car was black and cream, with tan upholstery, and it certainly looked the last word in luxury. Cruising around the city brought many a long look from passersby, a good indication of the inbuilt "snob appeal."

The bodywork is well tailored, and where the bonnet, doors, rear-wheel cover and luggage compartment lid fit, the seams are fine and regular. The trailing edge of the front wings is finished with a "knife-edge," and the sides of both front and rear wings are relieved by a neat swept fairing. Plenty of sparkle

is given off by the chrome around the side windows and on the traditional radiator.

The doors open wide to give ample ease of entry and exit, and close with a soft click. At the base the front doors are about 7in. wide, and when stepping from the car there is no dirty sill over which a woman must drag a new evening frock.

The driver has an excellent view forward, the bonnet sloping away so that both front mudguards can be clearly seen. The test car was purchased in England and was fitted with the twin mudguard-mounted rear-vision mirrors which are now compulsory over there by law.

Corner pillars are swept well back, and I did not notice them to be annoying blind spots at any stage. To the rear, vision is adequate for reversing out of narrow drives.

Always a good test for the seating in a particular car is a journey of 100 miles or more. With two passengers, I tried every seating spot in both front and rear, and we came back with the unanimous opinion that here was one of the most comfortable six-seaters we had ever ridden in. The bench-type seats are soft, yet have sufficient resilience to give a fatigue-free support for lengthy periods. Leg-room in both front and rear is ample, and there is generous room for three across both seats.

Genuine leather has been used for all the trim, and the roof lining is done out in a practical washable plastic. Some people complain that plastic headlinings are poor sound insulators, but to me there was no cause for complaint on this score. When three people can converse in normal tones at 80 m.p.h., it seems

clear that wind, engine and road noise are kept down to a low enough level.

The instruments are in the right place, being set out in front of the driver. They consist of a speedometer (with trip mileage recorder) graduated up to 110 m.p.h., clock, water temperature gauge, oil-pressure gauge, ammeter, and fuel gauge. Warning lights are fitted for headlamp-beam indication, winking-light trafficators, handbrake on, and choke in operation. Windscreen washers are fitted as standard, and there is a control marked "R" which operates a 1½-gallon fuel reserve.

One small detail which is quite an annoyance in this car is the location of the front ashtrays underneath the window vents. If the vent is opened while the ashtray is in its out position, the contents blow straight out into the driver's face.

Folding armrests are set in the centre of both front and rear seats, and there are additional armrests on the front doors.

At the rear, the luggage compartment lid is counterbalanced and reasonably easy to lift. When raised, it will stay in any position without the need of support. Spare wheel and tools are neatly stowed in a separate compartment beneath the boot floor. This leaves an unimpeded luggage area 46½in. deep, 56in. wide and 20in. high—a total space of 17 cubic feet.

Altogether the Armstrong Siddeley Sapphire appealed to me as a well-made luxury saloon retaining such features as excellent handling, high performance, and a restrained dignity in both design and trim which is characteristic of the "classic" British car. For all this the potential buyer must pay £2850 (including sales tax).

Armstrong Siddeley Sapphire

CONTINUED FROM PAGE 85

The instrument panel has also been restyled and now has two five-inch dials, the left-hand one for the speedometer and odometer while the right-hand face combines the fuel gauge, oil pressure gauge, water temperature gauge and ammeter. Between these two main dials are an electric clock and four indicator lights to show when the flashing direction indicators are in use, when the hand brake is on, whether the headlamp beam is dipped and whether the choke is in or out of operation. Incidentally, the choke on this car is controlled by a lever sliding horizontally across its gate instead of by the normal pull-out knob. The instruments are now illuminated by ultra-violet light.

Two modifications to the electrical equipment are the substitution of winker-type direction indicators for the semaphore pattern, and a reversion to single dipping for the headlamps, although those drivers who prefer double-

dipping can have the second headlamp made to dip instead of being extinguished, by a very simple service operation.

A further modification which has reduced the number of grease points requiring attention is the substitution of Metalastik rubber bushes for the normal bearings previously fitted at the two outer ends of the top arms of front suspension wishbone links.

Additional equipment now fitted as standard to all Sapphires includes a windscreen washer, an under-bonnet lamp and an interior lamp of the courtesy pattern which lights up automatically whenever a door is opened.

Prices of the 1955 Sapphire are as follows: With synchromesh gearbox, £1,215 plus £507 7s. 6d. purchase tax, a total of £1,722 7s. 6d.; with pre-selector gearbox, £1,285 plus £536 10s. 10d. purchase tax, a total of £1,821 10s. 10d.; with No-clutch automatic gear change, £1,404, plus £586 2s. 6d. purchase tax, a total of £1,990 2s. 6d.

How it works

Once on the move the SAP-PHIRE changes gear without thought or action on your part at precisely the right moment without jar or tremor, according to your accelerator pressure and the road requirement. Accelerate hard and you change into 2nd, 3rd and top at precisely the right moment for maximum performance. Accelerate gently and, by slightly relaxing the pedal, you move through the gears into top as low as 15 m.p.h. if you wish.

★

At a check or in traffic you merely brake the SAPPHIRE to a standstill, then accelerate away again. No clutch to disengage, no worry about changing down or up, or rolling back. And always the exhilarating sense of full control and the knowledge that by mere accelerator pressure you can either flash through the gears to 50 m.p.h. in 10.9 sec., and on up to the 100 m.p.h. mark, or move away silently and sedately.

★

When only top or 3rd are likely to be needed, use the position marked "fast". This gives automatic changes up and down through 1st, 2nd and 3rd gears at the same speed as "normal", but top is not engaged until 65 m.p.h. Similarly, if speed drops below 65 m.p.h. 3rd gear re-engages. When driving in "normal" you can engage 3rd for extra acceleration at any stage by shifting the lever to fast.

★

For parking or backing there is a position marked "reverse" on the quadrant. You will find that the no-clutch SAPPHIRE is most docile and easy to handle in every situation, as easy to park as a much smaller car. Without a clutch to control, movement can be gauged to a hair's breadth, by using the left foot on the brake and the right foot on the accelerator.

30.13 h.p. .. developing 150 b.h.p.

gives the Sapphire a blended character which places it well above the box-happy character is not recommended to buy a car fitted with an automatic transmission. Therefore, the Sapphire is one with which all, with the exception of our friends in the Vintage Car Clubs, should be happy.

both the top gear and the sportingly inclined motorist, although the gearbox suits ruck. The automatic gearbox is not recom-

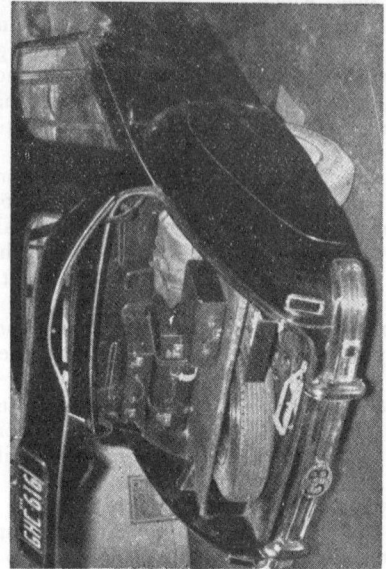

ABOVE: Two medium size suitcases, an overnight bag and a large portable typewriter hardly make any impression on the stowing space in the Sapphire's boot. BELOW: Slim, elegant window surrounds and supports can be seen here together with wide-opening rear door.

Sapphire

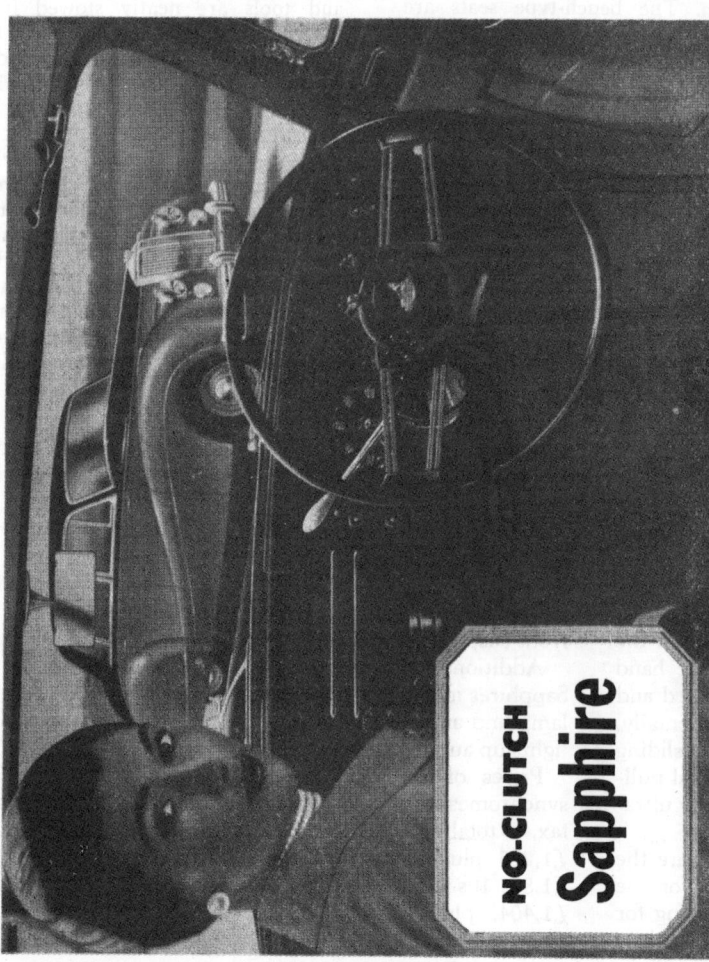

NO-CLUTCH **Sapphire**

THE SIDDELEY THAT THINKS FOR ITSELF

It Was Easy Road Testing . . .

MANY makes of cars have been and will be sold to the Australian buyer. Few of these are remembered some years after they are first introduced. However, there are exceptions, particularly some of the English and American cars of the thirties that are today still looked upon with great admiration and respect. In a class with these never-to-be-forgotten cars Motor Manual rates the latest Armstrong Siddeley Sapphire, fitted with automatic transmission. This saloon has power, grace and distinctive lines, greatest bulwarks against obsolescence and the march of time.

The Sapphire saloon is probably the ultimate of the well-designed base that had its start in the days immediately following the Second World War. At the conclusion of a test run in which over 500 miles were covered, the Motor Manual test staff was well satisfied that the cost of £2,850 represented good value.

Unmistakable English coachwork coupled with high performance and a top speed of 101 miles per hour

MOTOR MANUAL Road Test

108

GEARBOX THINKS.

Although being fully automatic when the driver wishes, more ambitious use of the gearbox can be made by placing the indicator on the neat steering column mounted selector quadrant into fixed second gear or the "fast" ratio. This fixed second means that only first and second gears can be engaged no matter how fast the car is driven. It proves most useful when descending steep hills or in passing main road traffic. "Fast" range takes the car up to seventy miles an hour and is most useful for fast touring and when running through a continuous traffic stream. All normal motoring is done with the gear selector in the "normal" position on the quadrant. In this position forward gear is engaged and there is enough drag in the fly wheel to need a foot on the brake in order to keep the car at rest. Acceleration is smooth and rapid up to 80 miles an hour—any speed after this being the result of "winding up" rather than true acceleration.

FIRM SUSPENSION.

Not altogether happy on roads containing deep potholes, crossways, gutters and other irregularities the Sapphire gives a stable and comfortable ride on good dirt and bitumen roads. The desired amount of under steer is present when cornering fast although cross winds when the car is travelling fast induce some wander and keep the driver constantly alert. Body roll is not pronounced although fast cornering may give this feeling to the passengers as the seating position is high off the road. An excellent driving position is provided and in association with light pedal pressures (the brakes are vacuum assisted) long distances may be covered with little fatigue to the driver.

Turning now to the more homely aspects of the car, the bench seats take six persons in comfort with ample leg room. A heater is provided and a deep glove box is situated in the beautifully finished wood veneer facia panel. The forward opening doors provide easy entry to both front and rear compartments, although they tend to be rather thick if approached in a confined space.

The floor is high and flat and can be easily cleaned out as there is no sill. Another practical feature of the interior is the washable plastic material used in the roof lining. Slim windscreen pillars considerably aid all-round vision whilst the instruments are lit at night by two stages of "black light" which does not reflect on the windscreen. Two speed electric windscreen wipers are fitted, supplemented by a vacuum-operated windscreen washer, and there is a facia switch for the 1½ gallon reserve of fuel.

Comprehensive equipment extends to a boot of huge proportions with a counterbalanced lid. The spare wheel is in a separate compartment, where it can be withdrawn without disturbing luggage and there is a set of hand tools in a fitted rubber-lined tray.

Sapphire has Silky Power

Six cylinders in line of "square" dimensions, overhead valves, twin carburetters and a compression ratio of 7.0/1 are blended together to produce 150 b.h.p. at 5,000 r.p.m. This is relayed to the road wheels in a manner that is quite disconcerting to the first-time driver. Practically the only knowledge the drivers or passengers of the car have that the Sapphire is mobile apart from passing scenery is the almost imperceptible click as the gearbox adjusts itself to the various road speeds and loads.

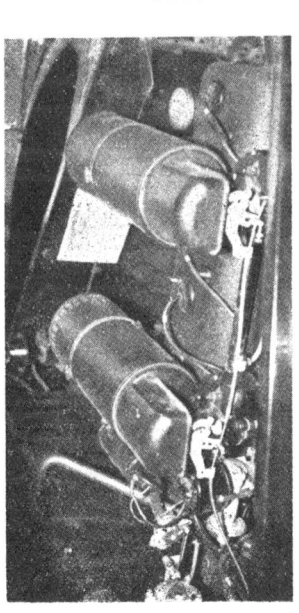

The large six-cylinder engine showing the air cleaners of the two carburetters.

MOTOR MANUAL ROAD TEST

Car ARMSTRONG SIDDELEY SAPPHIRE (automatic transmission)
Other Cars in same price class: Bristol 403, Jaguar Mk. VII, Lancia Aurelia.—

Test mileage: Out, 4,150; In, 4,653; Total, 503.
Weather .. .. Windy, wet roads
Price £2,850

ENGINE
6 cylinder. Bore: 90 mm. Stroke 90 mm.
Capacity: 3,435 c.c. Comp. ratio: 7.0/1.
Valves: Overhead. Rated horsepower: 30.
B.H.P.: 150 at 5,000 r.p.m.
Top gear m.p.h. per 1,000 r.p.m.: 20.

TRANSMISSION
Automatic.
Gearbox Ratios: 1st, 15.625; 2nd, 10.776;
3rd, 5.982; 4th, 4.091.
Propellor shaft: Open.
Final drive: Hypoid bevel.

SUSPENSION
Front: Coil springs, trailing wishbones and telescopic dampers.
Rear: Semi-elliptic leaf springs and telescopic dampers.

STEERING
Burman re-circulating ball.
Turning circle: 47 ft. (left), 44 ft. (right).
Turns of steering wheel (lock to lock): 3½.

DIMENSIONS
W'base: 9 ft. 6 in. Length: 16 ft. 1 in.
Width: 6 ft. 0 in. Height: 5 ft. 3 in.
Ground clearance: 8 in. Tyres: 6.70 x 16.
Weight: 33 cwt. Petrol tank: 16 gallons.
Track: Front, 4 ft. 8-5/8 in.; Rear, 4 ft. 9½ in.

PERFORMANCE SUMMARY
Acceleration: 0-50m.p.h., 10.9 sec.
Normal range: 10-30, 3.7 sec.; 20-40, 4.3 sec.; 30-50, 6.1 sec.; 40-60, 8.4 sec.
Max. speed: 101 m.p.h. Average m.p.g.: 18.
Maximum speeds in gears selected by automatic gearbox: 1st, 12 m.p.h.; 2nd, 28 m.p.h.; 3rd, 58 m.p.h.; 4th, 101 m.p.h.
Brakes (from 30 m.p.h. to stop): 34½ ft.

SCORE	Av. for Group	Score for this Car
Styling: Pleases all tastes	4	5
Bodywork: Finely finished	5	5
Interior fittings: Excellent	5	5
Instruments: Well placed — easily read	5	5
Passenger comfort: Not quite up to average	5	5
Riding comfort: Particularly stable	5	5
Driving position: Very good	5	4
Boot capacity: 17 cu. ft.	4	5
Spare tyre position: Below boot deck	5	5
Toolkit: Good, well placed	4	5
Jacking: Average	4	5
Max. speed: 101 m.p.h., good	5	5
Acceleration: Smooth and rapid	5	5
Braking: Very good	5	5
Roadholding: Excellent for big car	5	5
Flexibility: Could not be better	4	5
Turning circle: Poor	3	3
Parking ease: Average	4	5
Miles per gallon: 18, fair	4	4
Tank range: 288 miles	5	5
Steering: Heavier than average	5	4
Price per b.h.p.: £19		4
Depreciation: Large initial drop	4	8
Delivery: 6 weeks	3	8
Lbs. per b.h.p.: 24.64	118	112

POWER STEERING for the

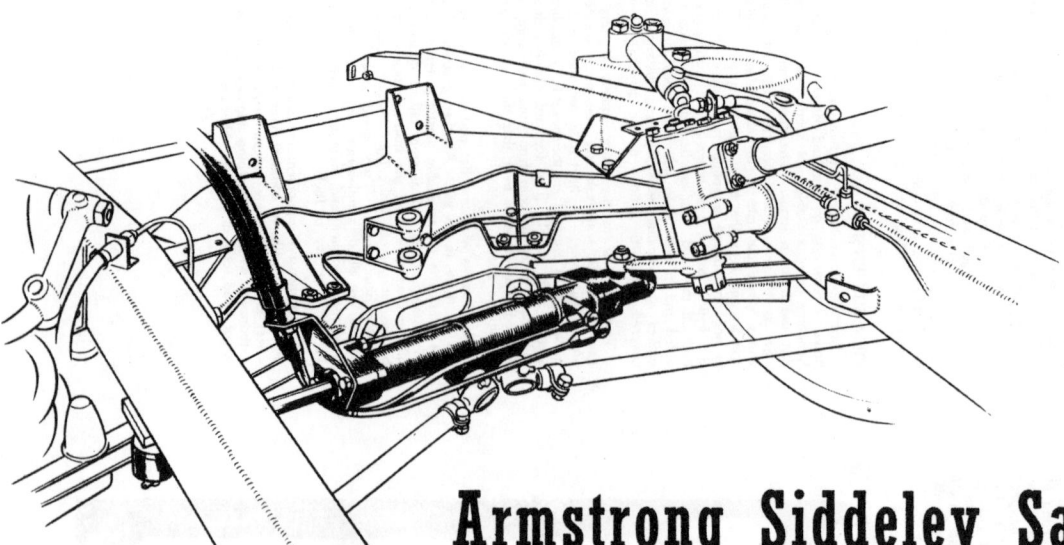

Armstrong Siddeley Sapphire

Also adjustable ride control and power-operated windows

Unchanged in external appearance, the Sapphire is offered with significant refinements for 1956, while retaining the option of three different types of transmission.

THE 1956 Armstrong Siddeley Sapphire makes motoring history by being the first British car to be offered with power steering and the first car in the world to incorporate assisted steering with variable power controlled by the driver. Further refinements now available for this model are rear dampers with adjustable ride control, enabling the damping to be varied between very wide limits, and power-operated windows of the press button type.

Apart from these three striking innovations which are all available as optional extras and which can be installed on any Sapphire at present on the road, no changes are being made to the car for 1956. The range, therefore, continues as before and will consist of the Sapphire saloon and the Sapphire limousine, both being available with a choice of three types of transmission, a clutchless automatic gearbox, an electrically controlled preselector gearbox or a normal four-speed synchromesh gearbox with steering-column gear change.

The Girling power steering system now available for the Sapphire consists of three units, a hydraulic fluid reservoir mounted on the left front wing valance, a Hobourn Eaton pump mounted on a bracket on the left of the engine at the front and driven by a belt from a double pulley on the nose of the crankshaft, and the actuator which is a hydraulic jack and its control valve and is incorporated in the steering linkage.

Hydraulic fluid under pressure from the rotor type pump—a pressure limited to a maximum of 600 lb. per sq. in. by a relief valve incorporated in the pump circuit—is fed to the actuator by a flexible hose and is admitted by the control valve to one or other face of the hydraulic piston in its cylinder. The piston rod terminates in a bracket attached to the left-hand chassis side-member, and the cylinder in a ball and socket joint with the steering-box drop-arm. It may be recalled that the Sapphire steering linkage consists of a two-piece divided track rod whose inboard ends are attached to a centre swinging arm pivoted at the centre of the chassis front crossmember. This swinging arm is itself connected to the steering box by a short transverse drag link. When power steering is installed, the centre swinging arm and the drag link are removed and the inboard ends of the two track rods are attached to brackets on the hydraulic cylinder.

The control valve for the actuator is situated in the end of the hydraulic cylinder and is connected

by a universal joint to the socket forming part of the ball and socket joint with the steering-box drop arm. The valve is highly sensitive and admits oil under pressure to the piston as soon as it is displaced from its neutral central position by movement of the steering wheel. As the ball is maintained in position in its socket by a powerful spring, however, the valve is not displaced from its central position until a force sufficient to compress the spring is applied to the steering wheel—two to three pounds in the case of the Sapphire. The power steering system does not automatically come into operation, therefore, as soon as the steering wheel is moved.

A most interesting further refinement of the system as applied to the Sapphire

Full power-assistance for the steering, part assistance, or none: a selector on the facia gives the driver this choice.

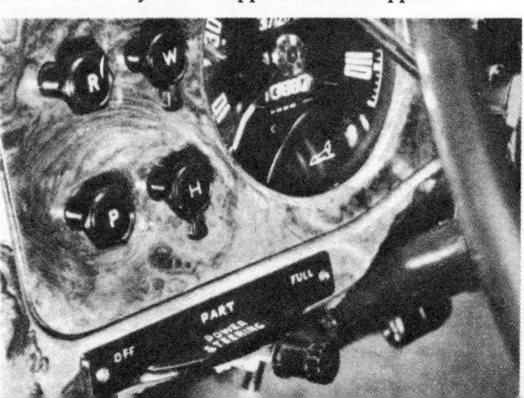

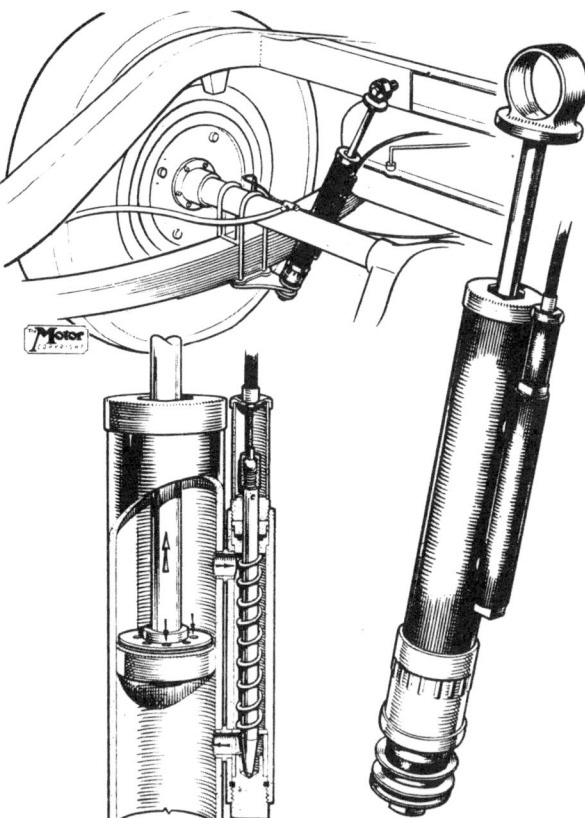

is the provision of a facia-mounted control by means of which the driver can not only put the power steering system out of operation completely should he so desire but he can also, by moving the lever in its horizontal slide, apply the degree of power steering which seems best to suit the requirements of the moment. The facia-mounted lever is connected to a spool-type valve incorporated in the pump body which controls the amount of hydraulic fluid passed on to the actuator by the pump. When in the "Full Power" position, the total output of the pump is passed on to the actuator, but in the "Half Power" position some of the fluid passes through the restricted passage to the actuator while the rest of the pump output is by-passed straight back to the inlet side of the pump again. This refinement is found of special benefit by drivers who have not hitherto driven a car fitted with power steering, for it enables them to become accustomed to the new feel of the car gradually by employing, for instance, full power in town driving or when parking but only half power when the car is running freely on the open road. In this connection, it has been noted that members of the Armstrong Siddeley staff unaccustomed to the very light steering given by full power usually drive a power steering car with the lever at mid-position while those who have grown accustomed to the feel move the lever to the full power position as soon as they enter the car and then leave it there the whole time.

Owing to the way purchase tax is calculated, the cost inclusive of tax of fitting power steering to a new car before delivery is £75 15s. 2d. (£53 9s. 6d. basic plus £22 5s. 8d. tax) but the cost of having power steering fitted to a car already in service is only £65 incuding tax.

The second refinement now available for all Sapphires is adjustable ride control which is provided by fitting a pair of new Telaflo Hi-duty telescopic dampers to the

Ride control for the rear suspension is achieved by using Telaflo shock-absorbers with a valve-operated by-pass for the working fluid attached to the side of the damper body. Opening the valve (by remote cable control) lessens the damping.

rear axle. Made by Telaflo, Ltd., an associate company of Universal Dampers, Ltd., the new dampers have an external housing on the side of each damper in which is located a spring-loaded piston-type valve which is pulled open against its spring by a Bowden cable connected to a control knob mounted on the facia. When the valve is open it permits the mineral oil with which Telaflo dampers are filled to flow along a passage which by-passes the damper piston. The wider the valve is opened the more oil flows along the by-pass and, therefore, the less damping there is of the piston. The two ports giving access from the main cylinder to the by-pass passage are carefully positioned to ensure that the by-passing effect takes place only over the central four inches of the damper's eight-inch stroke.

Automatic Over-rider

Thus even when the by-pass valve is wide open and the ride is, therefore, made as soft as possible by minimum damping of the piston, any circumstances—such as an exceptionally deep pot-hole or a humpback bridge taken at speed—which result in an exceptional degree of wheel travel, and therefore of damper piston travel, move the damper piston beyond this central four-inch, lightly-damped section and at once bring into operation the normal valving control built into the damper, with the result that the dampers then re-assume their normal characteristics and are completely unaffected by the position of the ride control.

When driving a car fitted with the new

dampers, it was found that with the control in the extreme "Soft" position, the ride given was markedly less damped than that provided by the rear dampers normally fitted to the Sapphire as standard equipment, with the result that car and passengers floated over the roughest roads. With the ride control on "Hard" however, a complete change in the character of the car took place and it acquired the taut, rigid feeling of a sports saloon, and it could then be cornered at considerable speed without tyre squeal or instability. The car could also be braked hard from fast speeds without worry or undue dipping of the nose. For normal main road motoring, setting the control to its mid-position provided an excellent compromise ride, the big saloon still feeling fully under control when cruising fast and proving itself capable of sudden changes in direction without becoming unstable.

The cost of having the adjustable ride control fitted to a new Sapphire before delivery is £32 11s. 8d. (£23 basic and £9 11s. 8d. tax), while the cost of converting a Sapphire already in use by the replacement of its present dampers with the new Telaflos is £26 5s. including tax.

Press-Button Windows

Power-operated windows are the third new refinement now available for the Sapphire. The Piper system is employed which uses small electric motors built into each door and controlled by two conveniently-mounted press buttons, one button being pressed to raise a window and the other to lower it. The push buttons for the window of the near-side front door are situated on the facia panel in front of the driver instead of on the door, for it is felt that the driver often wishes to adjust the amount of fresh air entering the car by raising or lowering this window as well as his own, and by locating the buttons on the facia within his reach he does not have to reach for them right across the wide front seat.

The cost of installing the system in a new Sapphire before delivery is £119 9s. 7d. (£84 6s. 8d. basic and £35 2s. 11d. tax), while the cost of converting an existing car to the system is £88 10s. inclusive.

Push-buttons for "up" and "down" movement of the driver's window are mounted on the door; a similar pair on the facia control the front passenger's window.

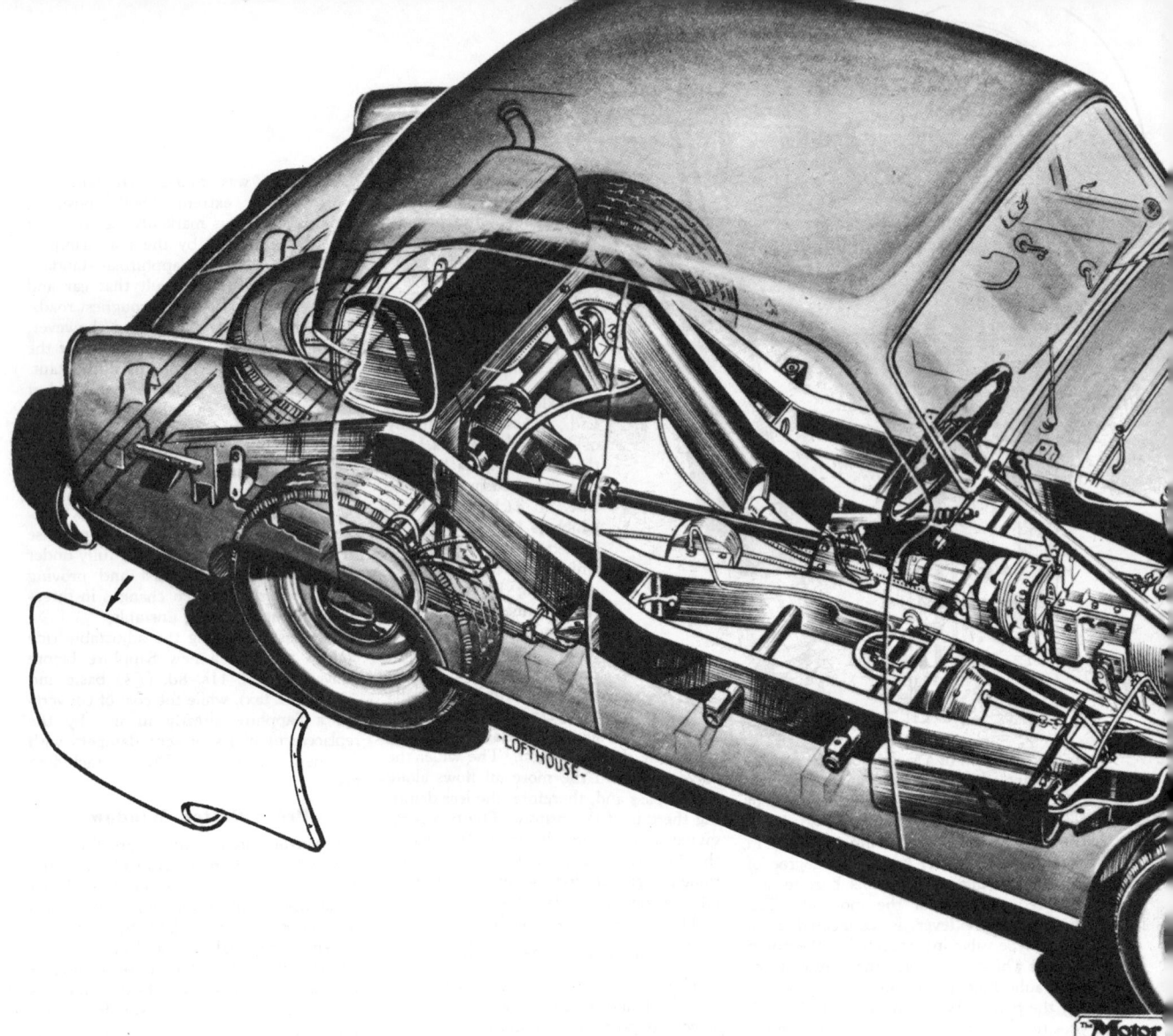

ARMSTRONG SIDDELEY SAPPHIRE 236 and 234

Prices of all models in the Sapphire range are shown on page 489

	Sapphire 236	Sapphire 234		Sapphire 236	Sapphire 234
Engine dimensions			**Chassis details**		
Cylinders	6	4	Brakes	Girling hydraulic servo assisted	Girling hydraulic servo assisted
Bore	70 mm.	90 mm.	Brake drum diameter ...	11 in.	11 in.
Stroke	100 mm.	90 mm.	Friction lining area ...	189 sq. in.	189 sq. in.
Cubic capacity	2,309 c.c.	2,290 c.c.	Suspension: Front	Independent (coil and wishbone) with anti-roll torsion bar	Independent (coil and wishbone) with anti-roll torsion bar
Piston area	35.80 sq. in.	39.44 sq. in.			
Valves	Pushrod o.h.v.	Inclined Pushrod o.h.v.			
Compression ratio ...	7.5 to 1	7.5 to 1	Rear	Semi-elliptic with anti-roll torsion bar	Semi-elliptic with anti-roll torsion bar
Engine performance			Shock absorbers	Girling telescopic	Girling telescopic
Max. power	85 b.h.p.	120 b.h.p.	Wheel type	Disc	Disc
at	4,400 r.p.m.	5,000 r.p.m.	Tyre size	6.40—15	6.40—15
Max. b.m.e.p.	126 lb./sq. in.	150 lb./sq. in.	Steering gear	Burman	Burman
at	1,750 r.p.m.	3,500 r.p.m.	Steering wheel	17 in.	17 in.
B.H.P. per sq. in. piston area	2.20	3.04			
Peak piston speed ft. per min.	2,900	2,950			
Engine details			**Dimensions**		
Carburetter	Stromberg Down-draught.	Twin S.U. H.D.6.	Wheelbase	9 ft. 3 in.	9 ft. 3 in.
Ignition	12-volt High Duty Coil	12-volt High Duty Coil	Track		
			Front	4 ft. 7⅛ in.	4 ft. 7⅛ in.
Plugs: make and type ...	Lodge HLN	Lodge HLN	Rear	4 ft. 6 ⁵⁄₁₆ in.	4 ft. 6 ⁵⁄₁₆ in.
Fuel pump	AC mechanical	AC mechanical	Overall length	15 ft. 0 in.	15 ft. 0 in.
Fuel capacity	11 gallons	11 gallons	Overall width	5 ft. 8½ in.	5 ft. 8½ in.
Oil filter	Full flow	Full flow	Overall height	5 ft. 1¾ in.	5 ft. 1¾ in.
Oil capacity	11½ pints	16 pints	Ground clearance	6⅜ in.	6⅜ in.
Cooling system	Pump, fan and thermo-stat	Pump, fan and thermo-stat	Turning circle	39 ft.	39 ft.
			Dry weight	26 cwt.	26 cwt.
Water capacity	20 pints	21 pints			
Electrical system	12-volt Lucas	12-volt Lucas			
Battery capacity	51 amp.-hr.	51 amp.-hr.			
Transmission			**Performance data**		
Clutch	Manumatic	Single dry plate	Piston area, sq. in. per ton ...	27.6	30.4
Gear ratios:			Brake lining area, sq. in. per ton	145	145
Top	4.545 (o'drive 3.536)	4.545 (o'drive 3.536)	Top gear m.p.h. per 1,000 r.p.m.	17.1 (o'drive 21.9)	17.1 (o'drive 21.9)
3rd	6.450	6.450			
2nd	9.703	9.703	Top gear m.p.h. at 2,500 ft./ min. piston speed ...	65.2 (o'drive 83.2)	72.4 (o'drive 93.0)
1st	15.692	15.692			
Rev.	13.555	13.555	Litres per ton-mile, dry ...	3,140 (o'drive 2,440)	3,120 (o'drive 2,420)
Prop. shaft	Open	Open			
Final drive	Hypoid bevel	Hypoid bevel			

112

Two New 2.3-litre Armstrong Siddeley Sapphires

The Refined Six-cylinder Model "236" with Manumatic Transmission and the 120 b.h.p. Four-cylinder "234" with 100 m.p.h. Maximum

ALTERNATIVE engines are available for the new 2.3-litre Armstrong Siddeley, the smooth six-cylinder unit shown in these drawings or an inclined-valve four-cylinder engine of 41% higher b.h.p. Luxurious bodywork is mounted on an X-braced chassis, separate wing sections localizing the effects of damage in minor traffic accidents.

THE Armstrong Siddeley Sapphire range has now been extended by the introduction of a brace of 2.3-litre cars resembling each other in external appearance but with very different road characteristics. The big 3.4-litre, six-cylinder Sapphire—now known as the Sapphire 346—continues in its 1956 form as described in our issue of August 17.

The overall length of the new cars is 15 ft., compared with the 16 ft. 1 in. of the big 346 and although width is down from 6 ft. to 5 ft. 8½ in., they can still take five people in comfort. One of the new cars, the 234, has a four-cylinder version of the six-cylinder 346 Sapphire engine with its hemispherical combustion chambers and unusual valve gear, and as it develops 120 b.h.p. and the car weighs only 26 cwt., the performance is outstanding, with a claimed maximum of 100 m.p.h.

The second of the new models, the 236, has been designed to incorporate the refinement and silence of a big car in one of medium size. It has a simple six-cylinder overhead valve engine developing 85 b.h.p. and is the first car in the world to be marketed with the Automotive Products Manumatic transmission, which provides two-pedal control and simple but not automatic gear-changes.

The new four-cylinder engine has benefited not only from experience gained with the standard six-cylinder unit which powers the big 346 Sapphire but also from the development work carried out on the special version for the Sphinx sports-racing car which Tommy Sopwith, the son of the chairman of the Hawker-Siddeley Group, Sir T. O. M. Sopwith, drove in numerous events during the

Scale 1 : 30

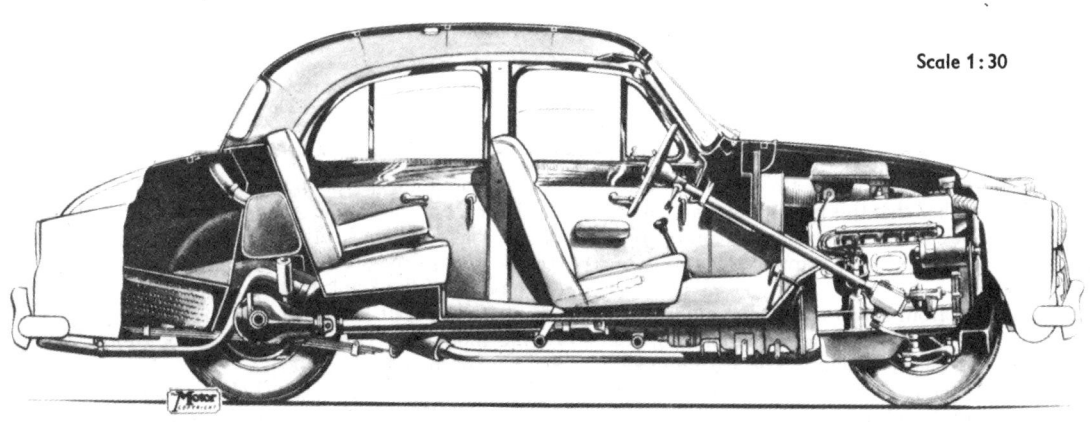

THE new 2.3-litre cars retain the familiar Armstrong Siddeley radiator grille, complete with sphinx mascot, in combination with a full-width body which makes considerable use of corrosion-proof light alloys in its panelling.

1954 racing season. This engine developed more than 200 b.h.p. at 5,200 r.p.m. and the stiffer connecting rods, sturdier valve rockers and thicker valve stems carrying bigger heads, found necessary to attain these figures, have all been incorporated in the new engine, thereby once again most forcibly demonstrating that production designs still stand to gain directly and considerably from being subjected to a racing programme.

Apart from these modifications, the new engine by its very compactness is inherently stiffer than the bigger unit. Four extra longitudinal stiffening ribs have been incorporated in the crankcase casting along the crankshaft centre line and above it, and the crankcase has further been strengthened by the elimination of the big opening on the right where the fuel pump was mounted on a cover plate.

The fully counterbalanced three-bearing crankshaft has main bearings of the same dimensions as the 3.4-litre unit and runs in thin, steel-backed white-metal lined shells, although indium lead bronze bearings are available as an optional extra for owners contemplating using their cars for competition work. The connecting rods have been stiffened by increasing the depth of the web on one side of the diagonally split big ends. The strength of the fully floating gudgeon pins has also been increased by a reduction of their internal bores. The aluminium alloy pistons have two compression and one scraper ring, the top compression ring being chromium-plated.

Dual Manifolding

Both inlet and exhaust valves have been increased in size by 0.1 in. compared with the 346 Sapphire. They operate in fully machined hemispherical combustion chambers and are actuated by the same system of unequal-length, inclined pushrods and tappets from a camshaft situated high up on the right of the cylinder block. The rockers have also been increased in stiffness to withstand with equanimity the high r.p.m. of which this engine is fully capable. It will be recalled that this type of valve actuation enables inclined valves in an hemispherical combustion chamber to be used without the complications of twin overhead camshafts.

Lubricant is drawn from a two-gallon cast aluminium sump by a Hobourn Eaton eccentric rotor pump of the same size as on the bigger engine. The exceptionally generous flow of oil thereby obtained ensures that even when the engine is hot the oil pressure does not fall below 60 lb. per sq. in.

Cooling water is fed from the pump into a gallery tube running along the left of the cylinder block and is then directed into the head and on to the exhaust valve guides. The water leaves the head at the front and passes via a thermostat back to the radiator. A by-pass conveys hot water to the water-jacketed induction manifolds to provide a hot spot for the twin S.U. type HD6 carburetters which are inclined at an angle of 30 deg. on their two short manifolds, taking the mixture to siamesed inlet ports in the cylinder head. The two inlet manifolds are linked by a big diameter balance pipe, and the carburetter air intakes are enclosed in an air box which has a central pipe crossing the head to a single large air cleaner. The throttle linkage is rod-operated throughout.

The twin exhaust manifolds couple 1 and 4 ports and 2 and 3 ports, then merge into a single tail pipe. This

DIFFERING from the 234 in having control buttons in place of a tachometer in the centre of the pleasing facia panel, the 236 seen here has two-pedal control—brake and accelerator—but a conventional gear lever.

exhaust manifold was found to yield an additional 11 b.h.p.

The front of the engine is the same as the big 346 engine except that the fan is not mounted on the water-pump spindle but is driven by a separate belt from a twin pulley on the nose of the crankshaft, a change made necessary to reduce the overall height of the power unit. The front engine mountings consist of Metalastik rubber bobbins inclined at an angle.

The cast-iron flywheel—slightly smaller than the Sapphire 346 flywheel—carries the 9-in. Borg and Beck clutch with hydraulic actuation. A special competition clutch, which does not object to being withdrawn at

PROMINENT rear wings with shrouded tail-lamps in their raked extremities, a wide boot and large rear window are seen in this view of the new car.

r.p.m. above 5,500, is available as an optional extra.

A four-speed gearbox, with Warner balk ring synchromesh on all four forward gears, is controlled by a short central lever located at the rear of the gearbox top. Behind the gearbox is an extension piece the same length as the optional Laycock-de Normanville overdrive unit. The rear axle casing houses the Salisbury 3HA hypoid bevel final drive unit.

Scaled-down Chassis

The chassis frame, with its channel section side-members boxed at front and rear and its cruciform bracing, resembles that of the Sapphire 346, but is, of course, scaled down. As in the case of the bigger frame, it was developed with the assistance of Armstrong Siddeley's special test rig in which the chassis was mounted at three points and then loaded while readings of its deflections along its length were taken, the frame being progressively stiffened at weak points until the minimum deflection at each point was recorded. The result is a frame which is both exceptionally light and also remarkably stiff. The 234 frame differs from the bigger chassis in having the cross-member carrying the front suspension welded instead of bolted into position to provide greater front end rigidity, and it lacks the central stiffening box which was found to be unnecessary in this smaller and more compact frame.

The unequal length wishbone arms for the independent front suspension consist of two separate forgings at both top and bottom, whose inner ends all pivot in rubber bushes. The two-piece track-rod type of steering linkage follows Sapphire 346 practice, the inner ends of the track rods being attached to a slave arm whose other end pivots on a centre mounting on the front cross-member. The slave lever is linked by a tubular rod to the drop arm of the Burman recirculating ball steering gear.

Semi-elliptic eight-leaf springs for the rear suspension have a rubber bush at the front spring eye and rubber bushes for the rear shackle, their purpose being (as with the rubber bushes in the front wishbone links) to prevent road noise from reaching the chassis. Girling telescopic dampers are fitted at front and rear, the front dampers being located inside the coil springs and the rear dampers inclined inwards with their tops attached to a cross-member forward of the rear axle. An anti-roll is also fitted at both front and rear.

The Girling hydraulic brakes with 11 in. by $2\frac{1}{4}$ in. drums at front and rear provide no less than 189 sq. in. of lining area. They are servo assisted by a Clayton Dewandre booster unit, which is mounted towards the rear of the chassis and boxed in to protect it from corrosion caused by salt spread by local authorities on ice-covered roads. The unit breathes via a pipe leading into the body under the rear seat, thereby ensuring it does not suck in dust or water. The brake master cylinder is also shielded to protect it from water and sand. The handbrake lever is located between the front seats and is of the pull-up pattern.

One of the advantages in belonging to a group of companies is that other members in the group may have the knowledge required to solve certain problems. For instance, the lightweight body for the new cars has been made possible by the experience possessed by High Duty Alloys, Ltd., in the production of Hiduminium 22 sheet, and by the fact that the Sir W. G. Armstrong Whitworth Aircraft Co., Ltd., had both the plant and the know-how for pressing such sheet into body panels: both these companies are members of the Hawker-Siddeley Group.

The body has a main bulkhead, floor, main pillars, door inner frames and box-section sills of steel, but the rest of

IN-LINE overhead valves and a single downdraught Stromberg carburetter are used on the six-cylinder engine, seen above installed in the car, and this model has the Manumatic transmission of which the operating solenoids are visible on the left of the picture. Twin S.U. carburetters and a divided exhaust system on the opposite side of an inclined-valve cylinder head may be seen (left) on the alternative four-cylinder power unit.

it is panelled throughout in Hiduminium and is, therefore, proof against corrosion. Both front and rear wings are also of steel and, being bolted to the main body structure, can be detached for repair should they be damaged. The body is mounted on the chassis on rubber pads to ensure there is no metal-to-metal contact between the two, thereby eliminating road noise and drumming. It is also insulated from both noise and heat from the engine compartment by a double-bulkhead, for in front of the steel bulkhead is a hardwood false bulkhead sprayed with synthetic foam rubber on its rear face. The main steel bulkhead is also covered with Fibreglass and felt insulating material.

The 11-gallon petrol tank, which has a built-in 1-gallon reserve, is at the front of the boot, which has a cubic capacity of 13½ ft, the spare wheel being separately mounted below.

Six For Smoothness

All four doors open to 90 deg. and the driver's window is controlled by a quick lift type handle. The front seats are of the bucket type and have spring cases with a hair overlay trimmed with Nylon and leathercloth upholstery, the same materials being used for the rear-seat upholstery. The rear seat has a centre armrest and armrests are also provided on all four doors.

The polished wood instrument panel has three 5-in. instruments in the centre, namely a speedometer with trip, a rev. counter driven from the distributor drive and a four-in-one instrument for the oil, fuel and water gauges, and the ammeter. All instruments are lit by ultra-violet lighting. Standard equipment includes a heater, a screen washer and an electric clock.

The Sapphire 236 differs from the 234 in two major particulars (it has a six-cylinder engine driving a Manumatic transmission) and in some minor body details. The 65 by 100 mm. overhead valve engine is based on experience gained with the power unit used in the Whitley saloon, but differs from the older engine in a great many ways, having a new cylinder block casting, a new head casting, a different front end and a modified crankshaft, to name but a few of the changes that have been made. It follows Whitley practice in using wet cylinder liners, however, but these now have their rubber sealing rings grooved into the liners instead of into the block, with a consequent gain in cylinder-block strength.

The forged steel counterbalanced crankshaft has four integral balance weights and runs in four indium lead bronze bearings. The connecting rods carry aluminium alloy pistons with floating gudgeon pins and four rings (two compression and two scraper). The inlet valves have been increased in size from 1.325 in. to 1.425 in. and in conjunction with a new camshaft with modified profiles and an increase in the compression ratio from 6.5 to 1 to 7.5 to 1 have combined to produce an increase of more than 10 b.h.p. in the engine's power output. Special anti-surge valve springs, close-coiled at one end, also play their part by permitting higher r.p.m. to be obtained.

Although the cylinder head casting is new—the thermostat for instance, having been moved from the previous housing in the head to a new position at the radiator end of the water delivery pipe—the general layout remains the same with the pushrod-operated overhead valves set vertically. The head retains the interesting inlet porting devised by Weslake when he gas-flow tested the engine. The single downdraught Stromberg carburetter on a short external manifold feeds mixture into a longitudinal passage cast into the top nearside of the cylinder head and from this passage tracts incline steeply downwards to the inlet valves. Both the hot spot and the exhaust manifold have been slightly modified, mainly in order to make room for the steering gear on left-hand drive cars.

Front engine mountings are of the Metalastik bobbin type placed horizontally, while the rear mounting—as on the 234—is of the Metalastik sandwich type with the rubber in shear and is situated at the rear of the gearbox.

The Manumatic transmission fitted to the 236 is dealt with more fully on page 459 of this issue. It will thus suffice to say here that it enables the clutch pedal to be eliminated but at the same time is not an automatic transmission, for the driver retains full control of when and where he will change gear, the actual movement of the lever from gear to gear still remaining his responsibility.

The only other detail in which the Sapphire 236 differs from its companion 234 model is that the switches as well as the instruments are ultra-violet lit and no rev. counter is fitted, the car being designed as a refined gentleman's carriage rather than as a sports saloon. Nevertheless, as chassis, suspension and brakes are identical to those fitted to the sports saloon, it is a car with roadholding and braking powers superior to potential performance, and it should, therefore, prove to be a very safe car.

In this connection, it is of interest that both models were extensively tested not only on the high-speed circuit at Lindley but also over many hundreds of laps of Silverstone where weaknesses were brought to light (and cured) which did not make their appearance when the cars were driven flat out on the high-speed circuit. It is also of interest that the test programme for the cars was the responsibility of Tommy Sopwith, for drivers with racing experience are apt to demand above average roadholding before they are satisfied with a car, nor is a car in their hands likely to suffer in development through not being driven hard enough.

Optional extras available for both models include the Laycock-de Normanville overdrive unit, radio and an electric demister for the rear window, while for the 234 model only, wire wheels may also be obtained.

A ROOMY, tasteful and well-appointed interior follows Armstrong Siddeley tradition. The front seats are separate and the rear seat has a wide central armrest in addition to side rests shaped as door-pulls. Leathercloth and an attractive woven Nylon are used to upholster the seats.

Entirely new lines distinguish the Sapphire 234 and 236 models. The rear wing treatment is bold and there is a plated strip at the bottom door sill line. Auxiliary flashing indicators are placed on the top of each front wing, just forward of the windscreen

A Cluster of

SAPPHIRES

New Armstrong Siddeley Chassis Has Four- or Six-cylinder Engine

FOLLOWING the success of the 3½-litre Sapphire saloon (which is now to be known as the Sapphire 346), the Armstrong Siddeley company has introduced a smaller model which is to be available with either a four- or six-cylinder overhead-valve engine, both types having a capacity of 2.3 litres. The cars will be known as the Sapphire 234 and 236, according to the engine.

Both cars are fitted with the same four-speed, all-synchromesh gear box. The 234 has a normal central gear change lever, with Laycock-de Normanville overdrive unit and foot-operated clutch. The type 236 has the Lockheed Manumatic gear

The bonnet line slopes sharply downwards towards the Sphinx mascot. Air for the heater unit is fed through the grille in the left front valance. Very small parking lights are placed below the flashing direction indicators

change—a full description and road impressions appear on pages 650-1—which requires no clutch pedal.

The four-cylinder engined car is the more potent of the two, and the specification would appear to make it a potential rally car.

In outward appearance the four-cylinder unit strongly resembles the larger 3½-litre unit, and when the valve cover is removed the resemblance is even stronger. Internal bearing surfaces are of good proportions and the whole unit should be very rigid and able to stand up to hard work with the minimum of maintenance.

The crankshaft has three main bearings, front and centre bearings having a width of 1.25in, the rear main being 1.625in; the diameter in each case is 2.75in and steel-backed micro-babbit forms the bearing surfaces. An oil return ring is formed on the rear end of the crankshaft, which is also flanged to support the flywheel. The forged H-section connecting rods have diagonally split big ends, the two halves being held together by set bolts. The big-end bearing diameter is 2.125in with a width of 1.125in, while the bearing material is identical with that used for the mains.

Cast iron is used for the combined crankcase and cylinder block. The light alloy pistons have domed tops, and they are provided with two compression rings —the top one being chromium plated— and one oil control ring; the compression ratio is 7.5 to 1. The floating gudgeon pins are located by circlips. Lubrication is by a rotary vane type pump which is skew gear driven from the rear of the camshaft. The oil pressure is in the neighbourhood of 60 lb per sq in when the engine is hot.

Resemblance to the original Sapphire is evident in the valve gear of the 234. The camshaft is mounted in three bearings high up on the right-hand side of the cylinder block and is chain driven from the front of the crankshaft. The hollow tappets are located at an angle in the block and the bottom of the push-rods have a hardened steel ball as a bearing surface. A separate rocker shaft is used for inlet and exhaust valves.

The valve guides are cast iron and the valves seat direct on the cylinder head, which is of the same material; they are closed by duplex coil springs. The inlet valve diameter is 1.80in and that of the exhaust is 1.59in. Each rocker shaft has five pedestal bearings, and the rockers are retained by lightly loaded coil springs.

Fed by a camshaft-driven mechanical fuel pump, the twin S.U. HD6 carburettors are mounted at an angle of 30 degrees on the two cast alloy manifolds. The two induction manifolds, connected by a balance pipe, are water jacketed. The inlet ports are of Siamese configuration. On the left-hand side of the engine are two separate exhaust manifolds, one connecting numbers 1 and 4 cylinders, and the other numbers 2 and 3. The twin downpipes merge and enter a common silencer.

The distributor is mounted high up at the back of the inlet side of the cylinder block and the leads go to sparking plugs fitted vertically in the front of the hemispherical combustion chambers.

A belt-driven water pump is bolted direct to the front of the cylinder head; the same belt drives the dynamo which is on the left-hand side of the engine. A separate belt drives the four-bladed fan which is mounted on a spindle below the water pump.

In the 234 the clutch is an hydraulically operated Borg and Beck 9in unit with a single dry plate; a competition type clutch is, however, available as an optional extra. Synchromesh is used on all forward ratios of the four-speed gear box and the change is made with a neat central gear lever. As stated earlier, the 236 has an entirely different arrangement, but it is based on a 9in Borg and Beck centrifugal unit

The gear box ratios of the two models are identical.

In comparison with the 90 × 90 mm bore and stroke of the four-cylinder engine, the six has a bore and stroke of 70 × 100 mm and develops 85 b.h.p. at 4,500 r.p.m. which, the manufacturer claims, is produced with fan, dynamo and exhaust system fitted. The crankshaft bearing sizes vary slightly and lead bronze is used for the main bearings. The pistons have two compression and two oil control rings, and one of the most outstanding internal differences between the two engines is the use of centrifugally cast iron cylinder liners in the 236 (these are of the wet variety sealed by rubber rings), while on the four the bores are integral with the block.

The camshaft is located in four bearings in the right-hand side of the cylinder block, and there is a single rocker shaft operated by vertical push-rods. Inlet and exhaust valve diameters are 1.425in and 1.3in respectively, and the sparking plug orifices into the bathtub combustion chambers are in the right-hand side of the cylinder head. The single Stromberg D136 carburettor is fitted to a cast alloy inlet manifold on the opposite side. An A.C. oil-wetted air cleaner is used.

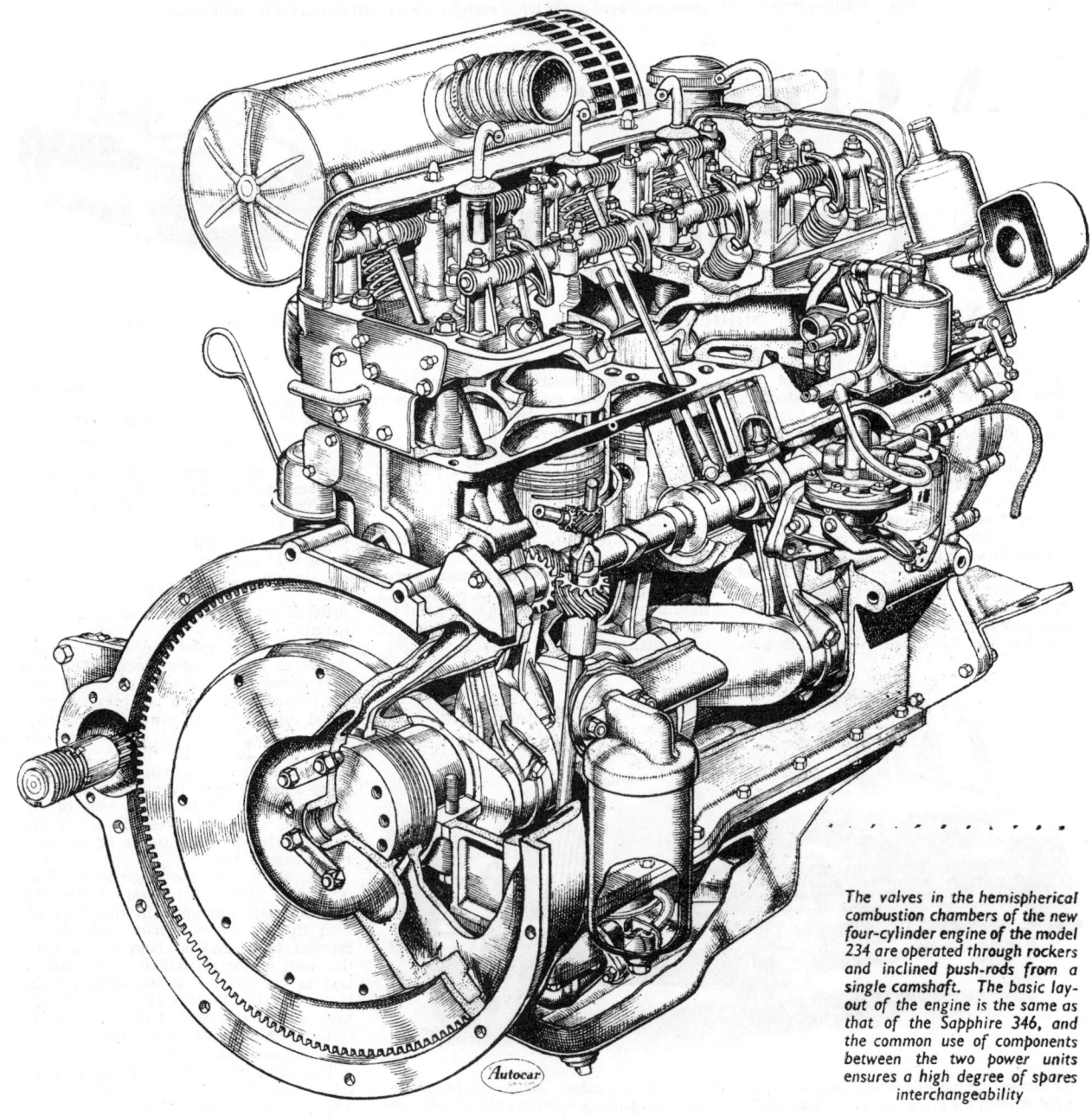

The valves in the hemispherical combustion chambers of the new four-cylinder engine of the model 234 are operated through rockers and inclined push-rods from a single camshaft. The basic layout of the engine is the same as that of the Sapphire 346, and the common use of components between the two power units ensures a high degree of spares interchangeability

A strong but simple chassis frame has been designed to accommodate either of these power units. It consists of channel and box section members of 14-gauge steel welded together. The front cross-member is a steel pressing of generous dimensions, and it is extended on each side of the frame to house the independent coil spring suspension, which is similar to that used on the Sapphire 346. Built-up forged steel semi-trailing wishbones are used, the coil spring seating in a steel pressing bolted to the lower wishbone. Girling

The chassis frame is light but rigidly braced. The inner members have gusset plates welded down half their length, and outrigger brackets are provided for body mounting

telescopic dampers operate within the coils of the springs. Extensive use is made of rubber bushes in the suspension bearing surfaces, thus eliminating the need for lubrication.

Long, half-elliptic leaf springs are used for the rear suspension, again with rubber bushes, and the Girling telescopic dampers are splayed outwards from their anchorage points on a rectangular chassis cross-member. Anti-roll bars are fitted at front and rear.

Burman Douglas recirculatory ball steering gear is fitted and there are approximately $3\frac{1}{4}$ turns from lock to lock. The track rod is split, a slave lever being mounted behind the front cross-member.

The manufacturers have matched the performance of both models with a Girling hydraulic braking system using Clayton vacuum servo assistance. Two-trailing shoes are used in the front drums, with leading and trailing at the rear; the effective lining area is 185 sq in. The hand brake lever, which is coupled to the rear drums by cable, is centrally mounted on the rear tubular cross-member.

6.40×15in Dunlop tubeless tyres are used on the 15in steel disc wheels, but if wire wheels and knock-on hubs are specified by the purchaser, conventional tyres and tubes are supplied. The disc wheels have a five-stud fixing.

(Left) Forged wishbones are used for the front suspension. Conventional king pins with cross pivots accommodate wheel movement. Arc welding is used for all joints on the chassis frame members. (Right) The vacuum servo cylinder for the hydraulic brake actuation is mounted towards the rear of the chassis. A rectangular cross-member provides support for the spring dampers, and the anti-roll bar is in front of the rear axle

A
Cluster
of
SAPPHIRES

Hydraulic actuation is used for the clutch on the 234, the piston mechanism being bol ed on to the right side of the gear box. A separate casing is used for the clutch housing

Mounted on this chassis is an equally interesting saloon body of composite alloy and steel construction. The alloy used is Hiduminium, a product of the Hawker-Siddeley group of companies, and it plays a large part in keeping the weight of the two models down to 26½cwt. The bonnet, roof panels, outer panels of the doors, the luggage locker and its lid, are some of the body components which are constructed of this material.

Steel is used in the construction of the body pillars, cant rail, the front bulkhead, the floor and the inner panels of the doors.

A great deal of attention has been devoted to making the body as sound- and draught-proof as possible. Rubber insulation pads are placed between the chassis outrigger brackets and the body mounting points and there is a double bulkhead between the engine and driving compartment, with a facing of foam rubber and carpet. In addition to the customary anti-rust treatment, the interior of the floor is lined with thick felt and carpeting.

The fuel tank is placed between the back of the rear seat and the luggage locker and has a capacity of eleven gallons, of which one is in reserve. The luggage locker has a capacity of 13½ cubic feet. Spare wheel and tools are housed in a separate compartment below the locker floor.

Separate front seats are fitted in the

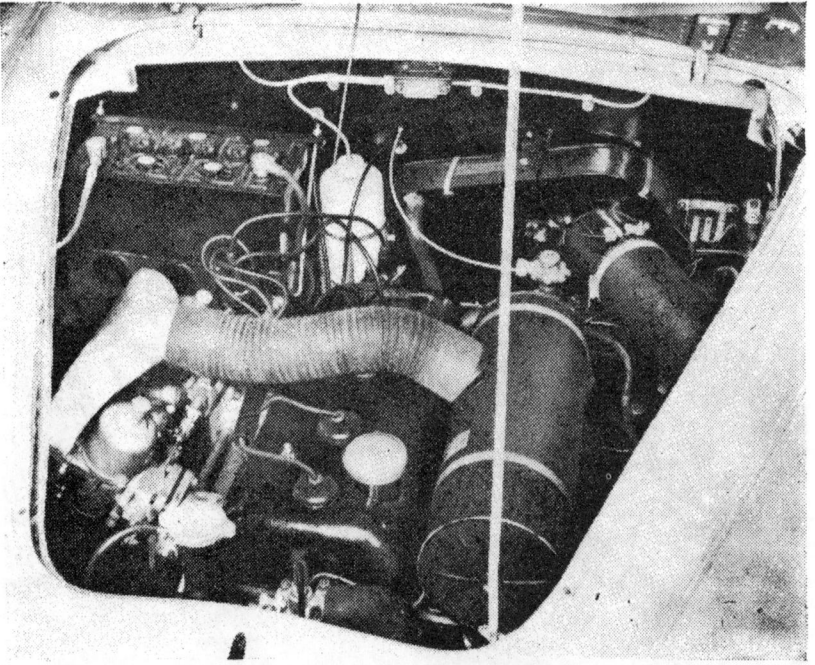

The four-cylinder engine of the 234 is immediately recognized by the valve cover. A hinged stay supports the bonnet in the open position

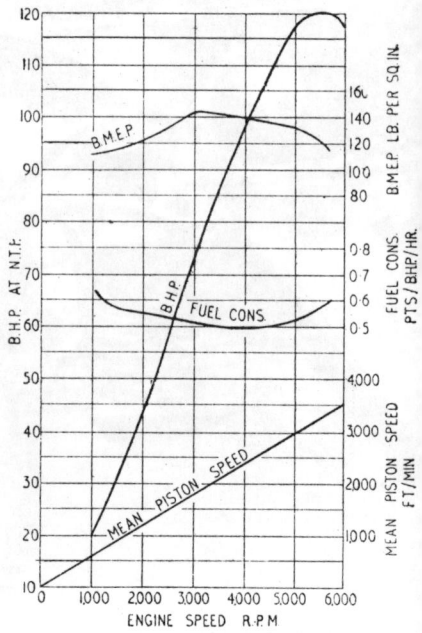

A Cluster of SAPPHIRES

Doors open to the right-angle and the well-appointed upholstery gives an air of luxury to the interior of the smaller Sapphire. There are opening quarter lights in the front doors, and a quick-action lever for the driving window

driving compartment. These and the bench seat at the rear are covered in nylon cloth and Vynide.

The facia panels of the two models differ slightly in the layout of the instruments. The rev counter is omitted on the 236 and it has ultra-violet lighting for the instruments; the control switches are also illuminated by this means. Facias of both models are well finished in polished wood; there is a cubby hole at each side and provision for a radio. Heating and demisting equipment is standard equipment on both cars, as also is a screen washer.

The performance of the new Sapphires should be as interesting as their construction, and the manufacturers are to be commended for their enterprise in introducing two new high quality cars for the world markets.

SPECIFICATION
Model 234
Engine.—4-cylinder, 90×90 mm (2,290 c.c.). Max. b.h.p. 120 at 5,000 r.p.m. Compression ratio, 7.5 to 1. Three-bearing crankshaft. Side camshaft operating o.h.v. by push-rods.

Transmission.—9in diameter Borg and Beck dry single-plate clutch, 9 springs, carbon block. 4-speed all-synchromesh gear box with central lever. Overall ratios, overdrive (when fitted) 3.536, top 4.545, third 6.45, second 9.703, first 15.692 to 1; reverse 13.555 to 1. Hypoid final drive; two-pinion differential. Axle ratio, 4.545 to 1.

Model 236
Engine.—6-cylinder, 70×100 mm (2,309 c.c.). Max. b.h.p. 85 at 4,500 r.p.m. Max. B.M.E.P. 126 lb per sq in at 1,750 r.p.m. Compression ratio, 7.5 to 1. Four-bearing crankshaft. Side camshaft operating o.h.v. by push-rods.

Transmission. — Lockheed Manumatic with four-speed synchromesh gear box. 9in dry single-plate clutch, centrifugally operated. Servo operated withdrawal mechanism. Overall gear ratios same as Sapphire 234. Axle ratio, 4.545 to 1.

Suspension. — Front, independent by semi-trailing wishbones and coil springs. Rear, half-elliptic leaf springs. Girling tele-scopic dampers and anti-roll bar front and rear. Suspension rate (at the wheel) front, 90 lb per in; rear, 95.5 lb per in.

Brakes.—Girling hydraulic, vacuum servo assisted; front, two trailing shoes; rear, leading and trailing. Drum size, $11in \times 2\frac{1}{4}in$ front and rear. Total lining area, 185 sq in.

Steering.—Burman Douglas recirculatory ball. Ratio in straight ahead position, 22 to 1. Turns from lock to lock, $3\frac{1}{4}$.

Wheels and Tyres.—Dunlop 6.400×15 tubeless on five-stud 15in steel disc wheels.

Electrical Equipment.—12-volt 51 ampère-hour battery. Double dip head lamps.

Fuel System.—11-gallon tank. Mechanical feed pump.

Main Dimensions.—Wheelbase, 9ft 3in. Track, (front) 4ft $7\frac{1}{8}$in; (rear) 4ft $6\frac{7}{16}$in. Overall length, 15ft; width, 5ft $8\frac{1}{2}$in; height, 5ft $1\frac{1}{2}$in; ground clearance, $6\frac{3}{4}$in. Frontal area, 21 sq ft approx. Turning circle, 39ft 8in. Weight with 5 gallons of fuel, $26\frac{1}{2}$ cwt (2,968 lb).

Price.—Sapphire 234, £1,065 plus British purchase tax £445; total in Great Britain, £1,510. Sapphire 236, £1,104 plus British purchase tax £461; total in Great Britain, £1,565.

Left: Type 234 facia. Apart from the addition of a rev counter, the driving compartment of the four-cylinder model can be recognized by the clutch pedal. The overdrive switch is on the right of the steering column. On the 236 (right), the switches are recessed in the centre of the facia and illuminated by ultra-violet lighting. The hand brake lever on each car is between the seats

236 MANUMATIC

Which is your *Sapphire?*

236 Manumatic. Most compact, most economical, most refinement for the price plus
the ease of two-pedal driving and 30 m.p.g.

234 Synchromesh, its twin. Most verve - and over the 100 mark in top.

346 Limousine seven-seater. Most luxury and space at the price.

346 Automatic. Most brilliant 100 m.p.h. performance. No-clutch control and 22 m.p.g. on the open road.
The only car in the world with controlled power steering.

Sapphire brilliance springs from the engineering 'know-how' behind the
Sapphire jet aero engine - power unit for many of the world's fastest aircraft.

346 LIMOUSINE

346 AUTOMATIC

Sapphire 236 Manumatic £1469.17.0 (Incl. £490.17.0 P.T.)
Sapphire 236 Synchromesh £1439.17.0 (Incl. £480.17.0 P.T.)
Sapphire 234 Synchromesh £1411.7.0 (Incl. £471.7.0 P.T.)
Sapphire 346 Automatic £2107.7.0 (Incl. £703.7.0 P.T.)
Sapphire 346 Limousine £2866.7.0 (Incl. £956.7.0 P.T.)

Write to **ARMSTRONG SIDDELEY MOTORS LTD** *Coventry, for Catalogue No. 346, 236 or 234*

Used cars on the road

1953 ARMSTRONG SIDDELEY HURRICANE DROPHEAD COUPÉ

Price new .. £1,000 0s 0d
Purchase tax .. £417 15s 10d
Price secondhand £850 0s 0d

Acceleration from rest through gears :
to 30 m.p.h. .. 6·7 sec
to 50 m.p.h. .. 16·6 sec
to 60 m.p.h. .. 26·8 sec
20-40 m.p.h. (*top gear*) 9·7 sec
30-50 m.p.h. (*top gear*) 11·4 sec
Petrol consumption: 20-22 m.p.g.
Oil consumption: negligible
Speedometer reading: 10,357
Car first registered: November, 1953

The appearance of the Hurricane was in keeping with the character and quality of the car, and hood and paintwork had to be examined closely to observe any traces of previous use

AMONG the first new models to appear in the immediate post-war period were the Armstrong Siddeley Hurricane and Lancaster, which were continued until 1953, when they were replaced by the Sapphire. The Hurricane which is the subject of this test must have been one of the last to be built before the model was discontinued; it was provided by Welbeck Motors, Ltd., 107, Crawford Street, London, W.1, who are official retailers for this make. This car had covered little more than 10,000 miles, and was therefore expected to be in really good condition. This was confirmed on the test.

Even when working very hard the engine was smooth, but while quiet at low speeds it was more obtrusive in its cruising range than some other cars in this class. Starting, with the automatic choke, was instantaneous from cold, but less certain when the engine was really hot. The preselector gear box with which this make of car is normally associated was not standard equipment on the Hurricane; on the car tested the gear box was controlled by an orthodox centrally placed lever. The synchromesh was weak, but in other respects the mechanical condition of the car was up to the standard expected in a new model, and the transmission was silent.

An impression that the car had been carefully used was made by the excellent external and internal appearance.

The chromium and black cellulose were practically unblemished, and the brown floor carpets and leather upholstery showed little sign of wear. Careful examination of the polished wood facia and surrounds revealed slight weathering and cracking, but the general appearance was particularly good, and the hood had also suffered remarkably little in two years' use.

The car provided an extremely comfortable ride, though there was a certain amount of pitching at the front. This up and down movement was not sufficient to indicate that the dampers were seriously worn. Considering the size and relatively soft suspension of the car, the road-holding was good; there was a tendency to oversteer when corners were taken fast, but this could be corrected easily and did not give any suggestion of lack of control.

On this model the steering is very low-geared, resulting in considerable lack of feel; manœuvring the car in confined places involved the driver in quite a battle with the steering wheel to change the lock, and at speed the control was not precise. However, on the car tested there was actually very little lost movement.

All other driving controls were good; wipers, lights and instruments were sound. The brakes were satisfactory although rather insensitive to light pedal pressure. It was understood before the test, however, that they were to be overhauled by the vendors upon the arrival of spare parts. Under arduous conditions it was possible to provoke clutch slip in spite of the unusually strong clutch springs; the take-up was very smooth at all times.

The Hurricane was particularly pleasant with the hood in the *coupé-de-ville* position. Lowering or raising the hood was a fairly lengthy procedure, but when the weather promised to remain fine it was well worth the effort. There were none of the rattles which besiege many open cars, and only over one or two of London's roughest road surfaces was there any tendency towards shaking and flapping of the hood. The penalty for open-air motoring—bad visibility to the rear—was particularly marked on this car, and a wing mirror would be desirable for safety in traffic.

The original Dunlop tyres were less than half worn and the spare was unused; the toolkit was complete. The car was fitted with a recirculatory heater built neatly into the bulkhead. This proved adequate in the relatively mild weather in which the car was tested but the radiator was then running at only 100 deg F, so that the efficiency of both engine and heater could undoubtedly be improved by reducing the cooling area of the radiator.

This car gave the impression that it had enjoyed a fairly leisurely and comfortable existence and had been well preserved. It was easy to forget that the car was being offered for sale at £150 less than the original *basic* price. Certainly its condition had not depreciated to this extent.

There were few indications that this car was two years old; the facia panel included a switch for the reserve fuel tank, a warning light to indicate side or tail light failure, and a clock. All the instruments were in working order

Swiss Movement — One Jewel

by RONALD BARKER

The grey Sapphire Countryman pauses by a typical farm in the French village of Chavannes, a few miles west of the Swiss border between Belfort and Basle.

NOW and then a particularly tasty plum falls from the Editor's tree, and this one contained no common kernel, but a shiny, new Sapphire 346. Waldo Price-Owen, who now manages the export affairs of Armstrong-Siddeley Motors, was bound for Switzerland with a Radford Countryman conversion of the standard saloon — to be used as a demonstrator during the Geneva Show — and offered first-class accommodation and all modern conveniences to a navigator and co-driver for the trip. The Editor suggested to me that this seemed an admirable opportunity to add to my knowledge and experience of the 346, which shows what understanding people Editors are. (Flannel noted.—Ed.)

We had no tight time schedule to maintain, which was just as well in view of the special nature of the car and the almost Arctic conditions prevailing on the highways of the European Continent, in the grip of the severest winter for many years past. Thus we planned to cross by the Dover — Dunkirk night ferry one Sunday evening and spend two days crossing France, to arrive in Berne for the Tuesday night; thereafter I would make some practical use of my presence in Switzerland and return by B.E.A. Viscount from Geneva on the Thursday afternoon.

Our rendezvous in London allowed us plenty of time to pay heed to treacherous road surfaces along A20 and to pause for a late dinner in Ashford, where we ate most appreciatively at the George; during the last few years there has been a tremendous improvement in both the selection and quality of food

offered by reputable hostelries in this country, but it is good to know of at least one such which keeps its kitchen ovens hot later than most on this much used route.

The pale grey of the Sapphire blended well with its snow-covered setting, and it looked as natural as would a white fox in an Arctic ice-field; inside, it was snug and warm, and with the inner man satisfied, one sank back into those deep, red leather cushions with that mellow sense of well-being synonymous with the Club armchair after an evening gluttony. Yet perhaps no single item of equipment contributes more to this sense of luxury than an efficient heater unit, not so very long ago a rare provision indeed, yet now commonplace on the cheapest cars.

The Armstrong-Siddeley was by no means free of draughts, insidious jets of sub-zero air betraying chinks in the rubber armour of the door seals and adding to one's appreciation of the heater. On the dry, dirt roads of the tropics dust is a persistent foe, and we

still have some lessons to learn from our American and Continental rivals in the matter of efficient sealing; some of these cars are now slightly pressurised in the driving compartment to combat this nuisance—but pressurisation cannot be achieved if there are too many punctures.

The long hill out of Folkestone, virtually unclimbable without tyre-chains when conditions are really bad, was surmounted with wheelspin and little reserve traction, and before long we were lost in the murky maze of Dover's docks. A final obstacle, after the A.A. and customs officials had cleared us, was the steep and slippery ramp leading up to our boat, the Hampton Ferry, and a dock-hand encouraged us: "Give 'er all you got, sir, and she'll make it". She did—just. We parked her beside a streamlined maroon Lotus, which members of the ship's company were examining without much appreciation. "Home-made job, I suppose", said one, and another thought it would only do 80, because that was the maximum on the

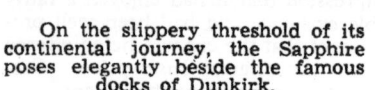
On the slippery threshold of its continental journey, the Sapphire poses elegantly beside the famous docks of Dunkirk.

speedometer; so I defended Colin Chapman by explaining about tachometers, and suggested a maximum speed which Colin would have blushed to hear.

Any expectations of a good night's rest in preparation for an early start were soon rudely shattered, when a Channel swell took charge of our transporter and gave us all the thrills of the big dipper at a seaside fun fair. Water, trapped in the U of the cabin wash-basin, gurgled gleefully all night, our cupboard doors slammed and the cabin walls creaked and groaned with constant flexing of the structure. One even had to crank the knees to prevent one's body from rolling out of the bunk, and by morning we were ready for a good night's sleep. I sighed for the smooth expediency of a Silver City Bristol freighter.

Dunkirk welcomed us with roads glazed with a transparent film of ice, on which the Armstrong's new Dunlops found about as much grip as a dog's pads on waxed linoleum. It was strange to see front-drive Citroens, sure-footed Peugeots and thundering French diesels reduced to a common 15 m.p.h., their powers of acceleration and arrestation practically non-existent. The steep camber of the roads added to the sport, and there was no alternative to a patient, alert progress at this rate for many miles.

It was during this morning run that we gradually became aware of Gaston; he was driving a small van—Citroen, Renault or Berliet, perhaps—and he was the press-on type. Waldo was worried about having Gaston on our tail, so we waved him on to overtake us on a slight downgrade, and he swung out to pass. He never made it; instead, he kept on swinging and followed us for quite a distance sideways, like a tinned crab. Poker-faced, he waited until inertia had played itself out, then turned once again in our direction and renewed the chase.

whilst we were reversing to the bottom of the hill that a triumphant, but still poker-faced Gaston overtook us, his little van now bellowing like an asthmatic cow. That was the last we saw of him.

Mercifully, there are few steep slopes in this part of France, and we progressed through Cassel, Bethune, Arras and Bapaume to reach Peronne for lunch, having covered some 90 miles at the inconsiderable average of 18 m.p.h.

Here the A.A. Foreign Touring guide agreed with that invaluable French guide to good eating-places, Les Auberges de France, published by the Club Des Sans Club, in recommending L'Hostellerie des Ramparts, and where we consoled ourselves with a first-class meal, brought to perfection by a modest bottle of Beaujolais.

From Peronne, the road surfaces changed almost miraculously into hard-packed snow, with only occasional patches of dangerous ice to demand constant caution, and we were able to bowl along at much better speed. An overload of good things had, however, taxed our unaccustomed stomachs, which for several hours went about their work with more vigour than efficiency. This discomfort from over-indulgence, combined with the rough state of the roads, accentuated an impression that the front end of the Sapphire is insufficiently restrained, in that it plunges up and down more than it should if encouraged by inequalities in road surface of a certain frequency. An adjustment for the setting of the rear shock absorbers is provided, the hardest setting possible seeming to match all conditions; but the pitching motion is always more pronounced at the front.

Berne, Federal Capital of Switzerland, has some fine old arcaded streets, and the Zytglogge Turm (Clock Tower), containing a 16th century chiming clock, is one of the city's most precious early buildings.

A Swiss garage mechanic and passer-by are intrigued by the Countryman's picnic set, here seen resting on the sliding table included in the special equipment of this model

After a lunch-time halt at Péronne, Waldo Price-Owen selects an afternoon route beside the frozen waters of the Somme

Next time Waldo pulled well off the road, and Gaston, grim with determination, sped by on a steady course.

A few miles further on we came across something long and rusty lying in the road, then Gaston proceeding at a fair pace, but in the opposite direction; he had shed his exhaust system. Another ten miles, and we were confronted by a vast lorry charging down a hill towards us, passing a small saloon. "Off the road, Waldo!" I urged, and he steered the Armstrong into thick snow at the road's edge. The danger past, we regained the road but could not get sufficient adhesion to restart, and it was

Rivers and canals were frozen solid and carpeted with snow; everywhere were barges and boats of all kinds trapped and held fast with little prospect of being freed to resume their trade for many weeks. We wondered whether their owners were compensated for their idleness by insurance, and how their timbers would react to the compressive forces trying to crush them; and we thought what fun it would be to drive the Countryman on to one of these wide rivers, and speed along its surface free of anxiety about steep gradients, cross-roads and the opposing traffic stream.

The 346, which had been as sweet and docile as a lamb at the lower speeds, welcomed the improvement in conditions as much as we did, and with a very light touch on the throttle pedal upward changes of its automatic gear box were scarcely discernible; more vigorous treatment produced the slight snatch one has come to expect of this type of instrument, and it was always found preferable to change down by means of the manual lever rather than by the "kick-down" method. This large Sapphire can, of course, be obtained with either the Wilson pre-selector or a plain synchro-mesh box, and my own preference would still be for the manual box for its cheapness, simplicity and closer gear ratios. Nevertheless, the fully automatic box with two-pedal control does contribute a lot to the ease and simplicity of handling this relatively large car, and would best suit the majority of drivers.

One of the places to remember for a night halt on this route is the Hotel d'Angleterre at Chalons-sur-Marne, some 30 miles S.E. of Rheims on N.44 and about 195 miles from Dunkirk. Chalons is a spacious and attractive town, and the Hotel d'Angleterre is almost brand-new, an earlier building next door still being used for meals until the new restaurant is completed. It is modern, attractive in decor and spotlessly clean, whilst the cuisine is in the best traditions of France. Edelweiss was the title of a masterpiece consisting of a watery vanilla ice in the form of a hollow ring, filled with Chartreuse and decorated with fresh whipped cream to represent the Alpine bloom.

Whilst in Chalons, I determined to obtain for my kitchen two appliances manufactured by the old-established firm of Peugeot Freres—a wooden pepper-mill and a coffee grinder. These I found at a quincaillerie in the market square, and Waldo was also unable to resist a pepper-mill for his dining-table. I am now able to grind my breakfast coffee, pepper my breakfast egg and drive to work with mechanical contrivances from a common source. Such an affectation would be quite meaningless were any of these items less than first-class, but each

serves its purpose admirably.

Our second day's motoring began with qualms about crossing the Vosges into Switzerland, bearing in mind that the Armstrong must not suffer the least surface reminder of its journey. It proved difficult to get any two natives to agree on the easiest route, but on balance it seemed that the most favourable would be the short Belfort-Basle crossing along N19 in the lower ground between the Vosges and the Jura. In front of the 346's driver is a battery of four warning lights, for handbrake, choke, headlamp full beam and ignition, and the hand-brake lamp would not now extinguish. We satisfied ourselves that the brakes had in fact freed, but made a mental note that lamps of different colours would simplify identification of the service indicated, especially at night. Since the handbrake cables were obviously inclined to freeze up in their outer housings, there was clearly a necessity to pack these with low freezing point grease.

From Chalons onwards the roads were more or less constant in quality, with a predictable surface of hard packed snow which enabled us to make relatively good time. There were even occasional clear stretches where the speedometer could be allowed to approach 80 m.p.h., at which speed this single-carburettor car seemed quite happy, indeed relatively quieter and smoother than at 40. On these brief bursts of speeds the suspension seemed more at home, stiffening up in line with the greater demands on it, and one longed for 20 clear miles in which to get the true feel of the car.

One of the more significant features of this model is its adjustable power steering, which can be set by a simple manual control to give any degree of assistance from nil to 100 per cent power. Experience indicated that no power assistance was required except for manoeuvring at a walking-pace, and the merit of this control would be much greater if there were less reduction in the steering gear box. Without assistance there is less definition and feel than is desirable, and the ratio is such that the more acute bends require a considerable amount of arm movement. I should like to try the 346 with, perhaps, 2½ turns from lock to lock instead of 3½, and would expect then to appreciate 50 per cent. power assistance for normal use.

After lunching lightly, quickly and without distinction in Vesoul, we were soon through Belfort and enjoying the picturesque timbered farmhouses of the border country, where many village names emphasise the German origins of those parts, and reached the Swiss border in full daylight; but by the time we entered Olten, lamps were lit along the

famous old wooden footbridge, built at the beginning of the last century to carry pedestrians over the River Aare—a magical, fairyland sight.

Stopping near Olten for petrol, we had to content ourselves with commercial grade because the Super pump had frozen up. Again, when we asked our Berne garage to wash the Sapphire, we were told that the water supply had suffered l i k e w i s e — in Switzerland! Berne was, in fact, so cold that it was a mild torture to leave the warmth of our carriage, and many citizens were equipped with woolly ear-muffs. It is the Federal capital of Switzerland, and not so international in character and gay as the larger centres such as Geneva, Zurich and Basle; but it is a fine old city full of ancient buildings and arcaded streets, standing on high ground within a loop of the Aare, with no fewer than five high-level bridges radiating over the river.

In Berne we stayed at the Hotel Bellevue-Palace, a wonderfully equipped and managed establishment which merits every one of its five stars, and from here Waldo travelled on in the grey Sapphire to Zurich. He had quite a full pro-gramme of visits to make in the larger cities of Switzerland prior to the Geneva Salon, whereas I had one day in which to follow up various contacts be-fore finding my way home by other means. The Sapphire had provided restful and efficient transport, and its special equipment, including seats which let down into beds, a tape-recorder and all the paraphernalia required for wash-ing, shaving, eating and drinking (hot and cold), attracted lots of attention wherever Waldo chose to display it.

Swiss trains are fun; the primitive campanology of their little bells con-trasts with the modern might of their electric locomotives, equipped with snow deflectors and massive headlamps and driven by ordinary little men dressed in civilian clothes. Inside, they are com-fortable, overheated and well furnished, all metal fittings being in nicely-worked aluminium, and between halts an atten-dant pushes a clattering aluminium trolley along the corridors, selling hot tea and coffee, rolls, chocolate and cigarettes. Train fares are, however somewhat expensive, my second-class journey from Berne to Geneva, about 100 miles, costing 23 francs (at 11½ to the pound sterling). For the same journey, a third-class seat would have cost 16 francs, and a first-class 32 francs.

As the Viscount rose from Geneva's snow-covered airfield, I glanced back over the city and saw a steam train pass-ing through, laying in its wake the thickest and dirtiest smoke trail there ever was—a reactionary blackleg in the cleanest and tidiest country in the world.

Near the ancient city of Lâon, we struggled to remove heavy accumu-lations of ice from beneath the wings

The **Autocar**
ROAD
TESTS

No. 1611

ARMSTRONG
SIDDELEY
234

A low body line is used, in conjunction with a fairly high roof. There are winking indicators on the sides, as well as at front and rear

SOMETHING of a stir occurred in motoring circles twelve months ago when Armstrong Siddeley, renowned for their emphasis on comfort and dignity, introduced a big four-cylinder engine of 2.3-litre capacity rated at a formidable 120 b.h.p. at 5,000 r.p.m., and installed it in a compact five-seater saloon. Evidently the company was setting its sights on performance additionally. The original announcement of this engine was followed by further development work, but now a 234 has been provided for full Road Test.

The designation 234 indicates the engine size (2.3) and the number of cylinders, and the model should not be confused with the outwardly similar 236, which has the older, six-cylinder engine and Manumatic two-pedal transmission.

A short drive in the 234 makes it evident that the model is hard to drop into any specific category in the motoring scene. In some ways the conception of the car is contradictory, yet it does fulfil two separate functions. One is the rôle of high performance saloon; the other the dignified carriage appropriate to executive transport. Yet in some respects the characteristics appropriate to the one rôle detract a little from the value of the other. There is some conflict between the engine design and details of the chassis and coachwork.

To understand and appreciate this unusual car it is necessary first to get to know the engine, which is almost a minus-two-cylinder version of the largest Sapphire unit, the 346. In common with most four-cylinder units of 2-litre capacity or more, tuned to give a high power output, there is a certain amount of harshness which can be felt from a tick-over upwards through the speed range, accompanied by a noise level more appropriate to the purely sports

saloon. The unit, which has twin S.U. carburettors, is responsive but not tuned to a degree that results in any temperament or difficulty with starting, although there was brief running-on. Owing to some clutch drag the tick-over is set fairly fast, which means that the engine can be heard and felt in traffic hold-ups. When starting from rest with maximum acceleration the flexibly mounted unit shakes sufficiently to cause some transmission judder, but this certainly does not occur in normal acceleration from a standstill. During the test this vibration revealed, but did not actually cause, a fault in the distributor. The engine is exactly "square," with bore and stroke both of 90mm; there are overhead valves operated by push rods and the compression ratio is 7.5 to 1.

This power unit provides a cruising speed in the eighties, and 80 m.p.h. itself is reached within half a minute. The car tested was fitted with the optionally extra overdrive which operates on the upper two ratios of the four-speed gear box. Normally, acceleration is achieved with the use of the orthodox gears, overdrive top being brought into play (by a switch conveniently mounted near the steering wheel rim) when the desired cruising speed has been reached. Alternatively when overtaking at speed in third, the overdrive may be switched in on this ratio to prolong acceleration and a change made subsequently direct into overdrive top. In practice there is no appreciable gain by changing from overdrive third to normal top, which involves movement of the gear lever with the left hand and at the same time the overdrive switch with the right.

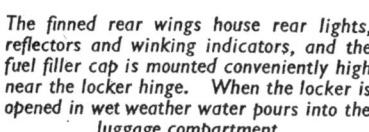

The finned rear wings house rear lights, reflectors and winking indicators, and the fuel filler cap is mounted conveniently high near the locker hinge. When the locker is opened in wet weather water pours into the luggage compartment

The car tested was fitted with a badge bar (which had to be removed before the starting handle could be inserted). Below the head lamps are the front winkers and the side lights. Windscreen washers are standard, but the chromium-plated wire wheels are an extra

Bumper overriders are standard fittings at front and rear. The smooth contours of the low bonnet enable the nearside front wing to be seen from the driving seat

ARMSTRONG SIDDELEY 234 . . .

During rapid acceleration through the gears each new ratio takes up with a forward surge unless a pause is made during the change. One senses considerable flywheel inertia playing a part. When running free the engine revs up quickly but drops back to idling more slowly.

There is no lack of engine flexibility. On top gear the car will pull away smoothly from substantially under 20 m.p.h., and the loads imposed by the lazy driver during hill climbing are accepted without rebuke. In heavy traffic there is no need to make regular use of the gear box, orthodox third gear looking after most of the speeds involved. The gear ratios are well chosen when allied to engine flexibility. The maxima were checked at 5,250 r.p.m., where there is a red line on the rev counter, and proved to be 25, 41 and 62 on first, second and third gears respectively. On overdrive third the maximum is 81 m.p.h. The red line on the rev counter is intended to limit the r.p.m. used in ideal, prolonged open road conditions, but it may be passed briefly without fear of "expensive noises"; thus the speeds mentioned could be increased in the interests of safety in certain circumstances or in competitive acceleration.

In the ordinary run of Road Tests the speeds quoted on the gears as normal are those which the test driver considers are advisable for use in the ordinary way by owners: with the 234 4,000 r.p.m. was selected as a likely maximum r.p.m. for everyday use for drivers not in a hurry, and even at this quite modest engine speed first, second and third gears gave 20, 33 and 49 m.p.h. on the electric test speedometer Overdrive third gave 64 m.p.h. at the same r.p.m.

The speedometer recorded most speeds with greater accuracy than that of the majority of other speedometers,

except that it was unusually slow at low speeds. At 70, 80 and 90, however, it was but a mile an hour optimistic, and exactly accurate at 50 and 60 m.p.h.

Such is the pattern of the sheer performance of the 234; now to the transmission and steering. Although the car can undoubtedly be driven very fast, the suspension and steering characteristics are not ideal for a performance model. The steering has a lock to lock movement of the wheel of 3⅓ turns, which provides quick control at speed without unreasonable heaviness in parking manœuvres. But it gives a feeling of slight sponginess which leaves the driver a little in the dark about what is going on at road level. The insulation of the wheel from road shock is good, and no conscious effort is demanded by the steering in normal driving.

The suspension matches the steering in some respects. Again there is a slightly rubbery feeling, although roll is firmly limited. On poor surfaces there is some vertical movement of the body, and the springiness of the seats adds to the vertical movement of the occupants. Passengers are not bounced about even at high speed, but the ride could be more level, a little more "dead". The fairly high seating position gives good forward visibility and the car is easy to place on the road. The nearside front wing can be seen and this, added to the compact overall dimensions, aids handling in heavy traffic.

The limitation of roll already mentioned adds to comfort when cornering fast, and also to the stability. The 234 can be pushed round corners hard, particularly on dry surfaces: beyond the obvious considerations of the additional slipperiness of wet surfaces, the car shows some tendency to slide if pressed in wet weather. On poor surfaces this is the more noticeable because the rear suspension permits some wheel hop.

In describing the character of the engine and of the transmission and steering one has the two sides of this model's nature to consider. On the one hand high performance, on the other comfort and docility.

Vacuum-servo assistance is provided for the braking

Wide use is made of cloth in the interior to provide non-slip surfaces that will not make clothes shiny. There are ashtrays in the backs of the separate front seats

The dials are central in the polished wood facia, cowled to reduce reflections in the screen. The sturdy central gear and brake levers are conveniently placed and operate easily. The overdrive switch is on a column projecting from the facia, out of sight, in this view, behind the steering wheel hub

system, and on the car tested the optionally extra wire wheels, which aid cooling of the drums in addition to improving the appearance, were fitted. The slight delay associated with most servo mechanisms can be felt, but the overall efficiency is satisfactory. It is possible to hold the road wheels just short of locking on a dry road for as long as may be necessary when extreme retardation is required, and the car does not pull to either side. During hard driving there was no trace of fade. The hand-brake lever is mounted between the separate front seats, where it is easy to reach. It works efficiently.

Apart from its failure to take full throttle from a standing start, the transmission is good. The clutch is light to operate and it takes up smoothly. There is no axle noise, and the whine from the indirect gears is hardly detectable. The four-speed gear box has a central, floor-mounted change lever which, although a little stiff, is pleasant to use. There is first class synchromesh action on all forward

The intrusion of the spare wheel compartment and the sharp slope of the lid reduce the luggage accommodation somewhat. The comprehensive tool kit is housed beside the spare wheel

gears which is virtually unbeatable. Gears are selected with precision, and a fairly long movement to the accompaniment of a workmanlike snicking sound. No difficulty is found in engaging any gear up or down, and unorthodox changes from, for example, top to second or bottom to third, can be made as if the gears were successive. The experienced driver will find, to his academic satisfaction, that there is no difficulty in making clutchless changes. In the transmission there are vibration periods.

When cruising the noise is not obtrusive and the generally smooth body shape prevents wind roar when the windows are closed. Most of the sound at speed comes from the engine and when travelling fast occupants have to speak up.

The driving position is particularly good, as owners of almost any size can make themselves comfortable even though there is no adjustment of the steering column. The steering wheel is close—but not too close—to the facia, so that one can get well back if desired, but even sitting back one can still reach the pedals comfortably without interference from the ample support for the thighs provided by the front of the seat. For short legs the seat length may even be too generous. Those who value a lively performance yet desire a roomy body, with unusually easy entry to the front seats, will appreciate this model. But

Engine accessibility is fair, but the dipstick handle is placed very close to the exhaust manifold. The distributor is located near the battery so that removal of the cap is difficult without damage to one clip

for the thick screen pillars, visibility is better than from most cars of this performance class.

The instruments are grouped centrally but those looked at most frequently are easily read, and the left hand on the steering wheel does not obscure vision of the right hand dial which is the speedometer. Oil pressure, water temperature, amps and fuel level all have their own gauges in a dial on the left, the rev counter taking up the centre of the three large dials. Minor controls include a petrol reserve of one gallon, according to the handbook, but it was found that this was good for only about 17 miles with quiet driving; but useful nonetheless. Two-speed windscreen washers are a standard fitting. At each side of the polished facia there is an open glove locker.

Coachwork details are well thought out, and a particularly convenient feature is the quick-operating lever for the driver's window. This works smoothly, so that the (safety) glass can be raised or lowered fully in an instant. Other window mechanisms are orthodox. The upholstery is part bright nylon cloth to help prevent passengers sliding about and to reduce any tendency to make clothes shine, and part leather cloth. Slipperiness is certainly reduced by the combination of these materials. A further improvement could be made by shaping the separate front seats to give better lateral support. There is a central armrest for the rear seat and armrests on the rear doors. A clever safety

ARMSTRONG SIDDELEY 234 . . .

device on each door lock makes the rear compartment safe for children.

Ashtrays are fitted to the rear of the front seats, but the front, facia mounted ashtray must be removed to make room for the optionally extra radio. The interior light works automatically when a door is opened, and there is a light in the luggage locker which comes on as the lid is opened, provided the side lights are on. The heater is a standard fitting which works well.

Under-bonnet components which need regular attention are reasonably accessible, but the dipstick urgently requires to be lengthened as it is very difficult to see and to reach, and the handle is close to the exhaust manifold. Also, the distributor is so close to the battery that disengagement of one of the clips is almost impossible without damage to the clip itself. The water and oil fillers, and the carburettors are easily reached.

Luggage room is limited by the space taken up by the separate spare wheel compartment, the intrusion of the wheel arches, and the sharply sloping locker lid. Nevertheless, a good deal of luggage can be carried.

To summarize, the 234 performs well, reaching 80 m.p.h. quickly, even if not very quietly. The handling characteristics are satisfactory, the absence of roll commendable, and the quality of construction high. It offers an intriguing blend of motoring that will appeal to many drivers whose requirements favour a chameleon form of transport—now dashing, now sedate.

ARMSTRONG SIDDELEY SAPPHIRE 234

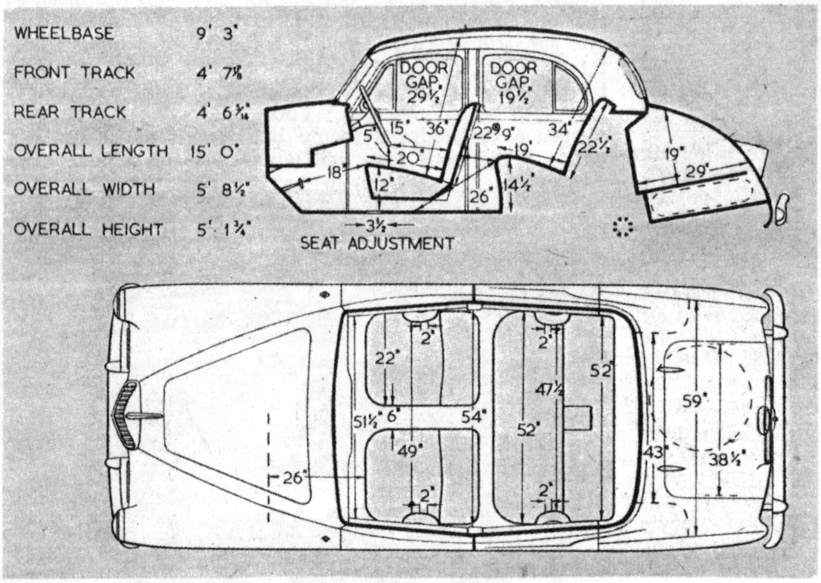
WHEELBASE 9' 3"
FRONT TRACK 4' 7⅜"
REAR TRACK 4' 6¾"
OVERALL LENGTH 15' 0"
OVERALL WIDTH 5' 8½"
OVERALL HEIGHT 5' 1¾"
DOOR GAP 29½"
DOOR GAP 19½"
SEAT ADJUSTMENT 3½"

Measurements in these ¼in to 1ft scale body diagrams are taken with the driving seat in the central position of fore and aft adjustment and with the seat cushions uncompressed

PERFORMANCE

ACCELERATION: from constant speeds
Speed Range, Gear Ratios and Time in sec.

M.P.H.	*3.54 to 1	4.54 to 1	*5.02 to 1	6.45 to 1	9.70 to 1	15.69 to 1
10—30	—	—	—	6.9	4.5	—
20—40	15.5	9.3	9.2	6.7	4.9	—
30—50	14.6	9.5	9.8	7.1	—	—
40—60	16.2	11.3	10.8	8.0	—	—
50—70	20.2	12.7	11.8	—	—	—

* Overdrive.

From rest through gears to:

M.P.H.	sec.
30	4.7
50	10.9
60	15.5
70	21.8
80	29.6

Standing quarter mile, 20.2 sec.

SPEEDS ON GEARS:

Gear	M.P.H. (normal and max.)	K.P.H. (normal and max.)
Top (mean)	**96.5**	**155.3**
(best)	**97.0**	**156.1**
O.D. 3rd ..	**64—81**	**103.0—130.4**
3rd	**49—62**	**78.9—99.8**
2nd	**33—41**	**53.1—66.0**
1st	**20—25**	**32.2—40.2**

TRACTIVE RESISTANCE: 30 lb per ton at 10 M.P.H.

TRACTIVE EFFORT:

	Pull (lb per ton)	Equivalent Gradient
Top	240	1 in 9.3
Third	320	1 in 6.9
Second	440	1 in 5.0

BRAKES:

Efficiency	Pedal Pressure (lb)
41.0 per cent	25
61.0 per cent	50
79.8 per cent	75

FUEL CONSUMPTION:
21.6 m.p.g. overall for 567 miles (13.0 litres per 100 km.).
Approximate normal range 19.1-27.2 m.p.g. (14.7-10.3 litres per 100 km.).
Fuel, Premium.

WEATHER: Mild breeze.
Air temperature: 55 deg F.
Acceleration figures are the means of several runs in opposite directions.
Tractive effort and resistance obtained by Tapley meter.
Model described in *The Autocar* of October 21, 1955.

SPEEDOMETER CORRECTION: M.P.H.

Car speedometer	10	20	30	40	50	60	70	80	90	98
True speed	15	23	32	41	50	60	69	79	89	97

DATA

PRICE (basic), with saloon body, **£940.**
British purchase tax, **£471 7s.**
Total (in Great Britain), **£1,411 7s.**
Extras: Overdrive **£45** plus **£22 10s** purchase tax.
Radio, **£31** plus **£15 10s** purchase tax.
Rim embellishers **£6 10s** plus **£3 5s** purchase tax.
Wire wheels (chromium) **£70** plus **£35** purchase tax.

ENGINE: Capacity: 2,290 c.c. (140 cu in).
Number of cylinders: 4.
Bore and stroke: 90 × 90 mm (3.54 × 3.54in).
Valve gear: o.h.v., pushrods.
Compression ratio: 7.5 to 1.
B.H.P.: 120 at 5,000 r.p.m. (B.H.P. per ton laden 78.7).
Torque: 140 lb ft at 3,500 r.p.m.
M.P.H. per 1,000 r.p.m. on top gear, 17.0.
M.P.H. per 1,000 r.p.m. on overdrive, 21.8.

WEIGHT (with 5 gals fuel): 27½ cwt (3,080 lb).
Weight distribution (per cent): F, 54.3; R, 45.7.
Laden as tested: 30½ cwt (3,416 lb).
Lb per cc. (laden): 1.4.

BRAKES: Type: Girling. F, two-trailing shoe; R, leading and trailing.
Method of operation: Hydraulic, vacuum servo-assisted.
Drum dimensions: F, 11in diameter; 2¼in wide. R, 11in diameter; 2¼in wide.
Lining area: F, 74 sq in. R, 94.5 sq in (110.5 sq in per ton laden).

TYRES: 6.40—15in.
Pressures (lb per sq in): F, 24; R, 24-26 (normal).

TANK CAPACITY: 11 Imperial gallons.
Oil sump, 10½ pints.
Cooling system, 20 pints.

TURNING CIRCLE: 39ft (L and R).
Steering wheel turns (lock to lock) 3¼.

DIMENSIONS: Wheelbase: 9ft 3in.
Track: F, 4ft 7⅜in; R, 4ft 6¾in.
Length (overall): 15ft.
Height: 5ft 1¾in.
Width: 5ft 8½in.
Ground clearance: 6¾in.
Frontal area: 23.5 sq ft (approximately).

ELECTRICAL SYSTEM: 12-volt; 51 ampere-hour battery.
Head lights: Double dip; 48 watt bulbs.

SUSPENSION: Front, independent, coil springs, trailing wishbones. Rear, semi-elliptic. Anti-roll bar front and rear.

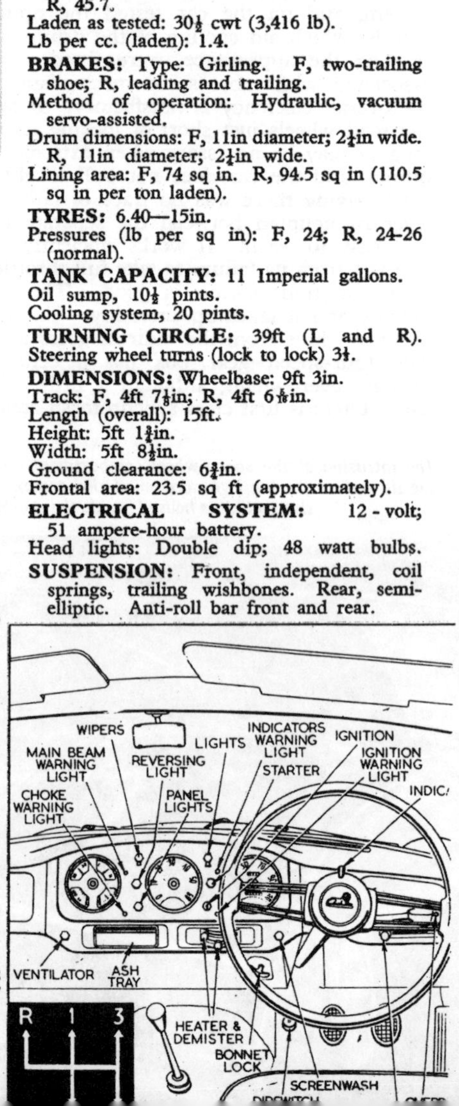
WIPERS
INDICATORS WARNING LIGHT
IGNITION
LIGHTS
MAIN BEAM WARNING LIGHT
REVERSING LIGHT
STARTER
IGNITION WARNING LIGHT
CHOKE WARNING LIGHT
PANEL LIGHTS
VENTILATOR
ASH TRAY
R 1 3
HEATER & DEMISTER
BONNET LOCK
SCREENWASH

This Sapphire is a remarkable example of the value which can be obtained in the luxury class of car. Its low price is a result of its heavy fuel consumption—which is often regarded as a greater factor in overall running costs than it actually is

Used Cars on the Road—108

1953 ARMSTRONG SIDDELEY SAPPHIRE 346

Basic price new	£1,110	0	0
Total price new	£1,573	12	6
Price secondhand	£685	0	0

Acceleration from rest through gears:

to 30 m.p.h.	6.0 sec
to 50 m.p.h.	12.9 sec
to 60 m.p.h.	18.1 sec
to 70 m.p.h.	26.4 sec
20 to 40 m.p.h. (top gear)	7.8 sec
30 to 50 m.p.h. (top gear)	8.6 sec

Petrol consumption	15-24 m.p.g.
Oil consumption	1,600 m.p.g.
Mileometer reading	15,975
Date first registered	July, 1953

Provided for test by The Spur Garage, Ltd., Bushey Road, Raynes Park, London, S.W.20

QUALITY cars, of such size, weight and power that fuel economy is not among their sales points, are in little demand among used car buyers. The result is rapid and heavy depreciation, typified by this Armstrong Siddeley Sapphire (with preselector gear box and centrifugal clutch), which is now offered at considerably less than half its original purchase price, including tax. Yet at the same time the Sapphire is a splendid example of the sort of value which can be obtained in this class by those whose annual mileage is small.

First impressions on sitting at the wheel are of the excellent forward visibility through the deep, curved windscreen, and the comfort of the seat and driving position. Instruments and controls are neatly and sensibly placed, and the tiny preselector gear lever is conveniently near to the driver's left hand.

The engine is not as silent as would be expected, but the noise does not develop appreciably as the revs increase, and the sound is not obtrusive. There is also the familiar whine of the Wilson gear box when taking up the drive, but when the car is on the move the gears are very quiet. In the usual way, the next ratio to be needed is selected electrically with the little lever, and the change is not made until the "clutch"—in fact, the gear change pedal—is depressed. The clutch automatically disengages when the engine is running at idling speed; thus, to stop the car only the brake pedal need be pressed.

The transmission worked well and was very pleasant to use. The sole cause for criticism was that it was difficult to move away from rest smoothly, particularly in low speed manœuvring. The car would sometimes creep unless it was held on the brakes at traffic halts, and at other times the clutch would fail to disengage when stopping, but both these faults were because the idling speed was too fast when the engine was really hot.

The Sapphire's steering, was heavy at low speeds, and the lock poor, but control became pleasantly light when the car was under way. The directional stability also was good, and the steering was positive, so that little effort was necessary to keep to the line chosen on the road. Cornering also was well up to the standard necessary in a car which will cruise at 75 m.p.h.; the understeering tendency was slight, and the car willingly hurried round bends without excessive tyre squeal or roll. Allied to this, the suspension was a little firmer than expected, yet it was well damped and gave a comfortable ride.

The Sapphire weighs 32 cwt, so that when it is driven fast the brakes have to work hard. They do so without signs of fade, and in response to commendably light pedal pressures. Less efficient, but still adequate, is the umbrella-type handbrake which was about due for adjustment.

Because of a fault in the dipswitch, it was not possible to try the car's head lamps on main beam, but in their absence it was found that the two built-in pass lamps gave a good spread of light. These, and a powerful heater, are standard equipment, but among additional accessories were an excellent radio, with aerial underneath the car; map-reading light under the facia; two very useful movable interior lamps; two wing mirrors, and, in the luggage locker, a set of green seat covers.

Also in the luggage locker was a fitted tool tray, almost complete, and a starting handle. The tyre on the spare wheel was a Dunlop, about two-thirds worn; the other four tyres were all Goodyears, approximately half-worn.

The appearance of the Sapphire was first-class, both inside and out. The beige leather seats had lasted remarkably well, and the plastic roof lining was practically unmarked. Slight cracking was apparent on the polished woodwork of the facia and trimmings. Outside, the black cellulose and chromium were in outstandingly good condition for a four-year-old.

The Armstrong proved to be both pleasant to drive and capable of covering the ground deceptively rapidly without apparent effort. On the open road the reasonably accurate speedometer rested at 70 m.p.h. for much of the time, but high average speeds were achieved only at the expense of a fuel consumption in the vicinity of 15 m.p.g. The higher figure of 24 m.p.g. resulted when acceleration was used sparingly and speeds above 45 m.p.h. were avoided.

The total mileage covered by the car may well be appreciably above the mileometer reading, but it was considered that many more should be covered without need for major overhauls. Undoubtedly this is another example of a used car in which the rate of its deterioration has been left far behind by the galloping progress of its depreciation.

Among the neat array of instruments are speedometer; clock (gaining slightly); ammeter; water thermometer; oil pressure gauge; and fuel gauge. The windscreen wipers are two-speed, and there is a facia control for the one gallon fuel reserve

Meet A. Siddeley, Jr.

Smallest car of new Armstrong-Siddeley range follows "gentleman's carriage" tradition, says Bryan Hanrahan

GOT an introduction to the new "small" Armstrong-Siddeley the other day—the Sapphire 236. It came out in England 18 months ago, but didn't reach Australia till now.

This handsome six-cylinder saloon does everything well; but, apart from its beautiful finish, it has no outstanding characteristic.

For instance, a 2.4-litre Jaguar has everything the Sapphire's got — beauty, luxury, flexibility, superb road-holding, PLUS a hunk more performance-wise. And it's slightly cheaper, too.

Crux of the matter, I think, is that Armstrong-Siddeley still build, primarily, "gentlemen's carriages."

But I defy anyone with a feeling for motor-cars to stay out of love with the 236. If the "gentleman" happens to be a driver, too, he'll only agree with me more.

The test car is (or was at the time) the only one of its kind in this country. It should have been stiff, but didn't feel so. The figures re-

turned are pretty accurate—and nothing to be ashamed of if you study them.

Speed Tests First

So let's go down to the test strip first, just for a change. Instruments hooked-up and stopwatches cocked for a preliminary dash over the flying quarter.

Found her quite fast through a slight curve on the run-up. Click on the watch . . . click again, and the reading checks out at 87 m.p.h. Back again and it's 86 m.p.h. Mean of four runs was 86.

The 236 would certainly do 2 to 3 m.p.h. better when fully run-in.

From a standing start, the runs to 50 m.p.h. turned in an average of 13.2 sec.

Second gear was very lusty, with third taking over eagerly.

Cornering was largely a matter of willing the car round. It sits firmly on bitumen, and with third gear capable of 66 m.p.h. there're bags of torque available if you're really in a hurry.

Laycock-de Normanville electric overdrive, working on the upper three of the four forward gear ratios, is standard equipment. Apart from its main wear-and-tear-saving function of reducing engine revs for a given road speed, it can be used to help general performance.

The steering-column-mounted fingertip switch and gear lever command seven forward speeds. Pop it in on the indirect ratios, and the al-

WOOD panelling for the dash, of course. Floor gearshift, steering-column overdrive control give choice of seven forward speeds. BELOW: Streamlining is a little bolder at the rear than at the front of the new car.

MAIN SPECIFICATIONS

ENGINE: Six-cylinder, o.h.v.; bore 70mm., stroke 100mm., capacity 2634 c.c.; compression ratio 7.5 to 1; maximum b.h.p. 85 at 4500 r.p.m.; Solex downdraught carburettor mechanical fuel pump, 12v. ignition.

TRANSMISSION: Single dry - plate clutch, 4-speed gearbox synchromeshed on top three; hypoid bevel final drive.

SUSPENSION: Front independent, by coil springs and wishbones; semi-elliptics at rear; telescopic hydraulic shock-absorbers all round.

STEERING: Recirculating-ball type,

3 turns lock-to-lock; turning circle 36ft. 8in.

WHEELS. Disc type, with 6.00 by 15in. tyres.

BRAKES: Hydraulic, two-leading-shoes front.

CONSTRUCTION: Separate chassis and body.

DIMENSIONS: Wheelbase 8ft. 3in.; track, front 4ft. 2½in., rear 4ft. 3in.; length 14ft 3in., width 5ft. 8in., height 5ft.; ground clearance 7in.; seat widths, front 52in., rear 54in.

KERB WEIGHT: 29cwt.

FUEL TANK: 11¾ gallons.

PERFORMANCE ON TEST

CONDITIONS: Cool, dry, no wind; smooth bitumen, two occupants, premium fuel.

MAXIMUM SPEED: 88 m.p.h.

FLYING quarter-mile: 86 m.p.h.

STANDING quarter-mile: 20.9s.

ACCELERATION from rest through gears: 0-30, 5s.; 0-40, 7.3s.; 0-50, 13.2s.; 0-60, 18.1s.; 0-70, 25s.; 0-80, 34s.

ACCELERATION in top gear: 10-30,

5.9s.; 20-40, 8s.; 30-50, 10.1s.; 40-60, 11.2s.; 50-70, 14.3s.; 60-80, 19.5s.

MAXIMUM SPEEDS in indirect gears: 1st, 30 m.p.h.; 2nd, 51; 3rd, 66.

BRAKING: 34ft. 2in. to stop from 30 m.p.h.

CONSUMPTION: 31 m.p.g. at 30 m.p.h., 21 at 60, 25 overall.

SPEEDOMETER: Accurate at 30, 3 m.p.h. fast at 60.

PRICE: £2287 including tax

most instantaneous change gives you quite a few more m.p.h. without touching the clutch; you can often switch it out to save braking for a corner.

Most impressive use is to select the right overdrive gear for a tight corner, switch the high ratio out as the car is coming out, and press the loud pedal.

In the Rough

So much for that sort of performance—now for a bit of rough stuff.

Twenty-nine cwt. is a fair kerb weight, and I wasn't surprised to find that the body acquired a bit of momentum that the shockers couldn't quite deal with on a potholed earth section.

This spells reduced shocker life.

But the 236 never looked like developing a pitch, and the rear wheels rarely lost traction.

Plenty of power was in hand to drift the car, and otherwise push it through twisting and undulating sections.

It seems to have a zest for being energetically driven.

Largely responsible, I think, are the beautifully precise steering and that handy little floor gear lever, which commands the nicest of second and third gear ratios.

All forward ratios are instantaneously synchronised. A point for the ladies.

Also, the driving position can be tailored to suit. The semi-bucket seats give quite a bit of lateral support, and everything in the "office" is well-placed and light in operation. Vision all round is particularly good. There's a quick-action lever-wind for the driver's window.

Not so pleasing was the small dash-mounted reducing rear-vision mirror. I can never get used to judging distance by one of those.

For sheer power and lightness of action, the brakes are outstanding. I made six crash stops from 30 m.p.h. after a 21-mile run through hilly country, and every reading was between 33 and 34ft.

The handbrake is central, easy to lock on, and you needn't give the car any anxious backward glances if you leave it on a hill.

Main impression after the test was how smoothly and quietly the car did what it was asked. It's not a potential Le Mans winner, but it's utterly safe and no sluggard.

About the Car

For those who haven't heard much about the 236, it is the lower-powered of Armstrong-Siddeley's two newest models.

BOOT is fair-sized and free of spare and tools, housed under the floor.

A very smooth six-cylinder engine, developing 85 b.h.p. at 4500 r.p.m., trots it along. Compression is 7.5 to 1.

The other model, not yet out here, mounts a four-cylinder unit and semi-automatic transmission in a similar chassis. It develops quite a piece more power and is said to be capable of 100 m.p.h.

The interior of the car is well-equipped and meticulously finished. Leather, plastic and wood (not veneer) are sensibly combined.

Back seat (with armrest retracted) will take three, and head and leg-room are adequate.

There's a comprehensive set of instruments fitted centrally, but convenient to read. Heater and demister are standard.

Front and rear suspensions are conventional, but anti-roll bars are fitted at both ends. These certainly are responsible for much of the 236's good cornering powers, although weight distribution has been studied, too.

The relatively long stroke of the motor (70 x 100 mm.) is the only out-of-ordinary point about it. Valves are overhead, pushrod-operated. Carburation by one Solex.

The unit is laid out cleanly, with not too much top-hamper. Strange that the most-used under-bonnet gadget — the dipstick — should be buried in the very vitals.

Boot is quite handsome, with spare carried on a tray beneath. There's a light here, and under the bonnet, too.

Fuel consumption over 200 miles was 25 m.p.g.—good in a stiff unit of the 236's calibre. Long runs in overdrive would probably shoot it over 30 m.p.g.

And there's your Sapphire 236—for £2287 including tax. A pleasant and elegant motor-car that likes to be put through its paces.

Testing it has whetted my appetite for an acquaintance with its more powerful brother, the 234. But no one can tell me whether that car will ever reach Australia. ● ● ●

SEATS are well-sprung, comfortable; wide-opening doors make entry easy.

Improved Armstrong Siddeley Limousine

Concentration on 3.4-litre Models

Without any increase in actual body size, seat width and leg-room have been usefully improved in the latest Sapphire limousine. One of the two occasional seats is seen unfolded here.

A MINOR but useful increase in the passenger accommodation of the Armstrong Siddeley Sapphire 346 limousine is the only change which is being made for 1958 in the Armstrong Siddeley 346 range. The smaller 236 and 234 Sapphire types will be discontinued, although a full supply of spare parts will, of course, be kept available.

The change in the limousine has been brought about by an alteration in interior arrangements without change in external size, the width across the rear seats between arm rests having been increased from 47½ in. to 50 in. In addition, knee room has also been improved, the distance between the rear squab and the backs of the occasional seats having gone up from 26½ in. to 29½ in., and the distance between the occasional seat squabs and the interior partition now being 26 in. instead of the former 24½ in.

The limousine, it will be recalled, is of similar general specification to that of the 3.4-litre saloon except that the wheelbase is 11 ft. 1 in. instead of 9 ft. 6 in., to accommodate the seven-passenger limousine body. A normal synchromesh transmission system is used.

The saloon model, on the other hand, is available either with a synchromesh gearbox or with the British-built version of the Hydra-Matic fully automatic transmission. The engine is notable for the way in which the advantages of hemispherical combustion chambers and inclined overhead valves are obtained with a single highly placed side camshaft, which operates the valves by means of short push-rods passing diagonally through the block and head castings.

Both single- and double-carburetter versions of the engine are obtainable, the former giving 125 b.h.p. at 4,700 r.p.m., and the latter 150 b.h.p. at 5,000 r.p.m.

All models are large, very comfortable and well finished, whilst such refinements as power-assisted steering, adjustable ride control and power-operated windows can be specified as extras.

ARMSTRONG SIDDELEY PLANS FOR 1958

Limousine coachwork on the long wheelbase (11ft 1in) Sapphire chassis. When a pair of occasional seats is raised, five can be accommodated in the rear, which is upholstered in cloth

A RMSTRONG SIDDELEY'S range of 346 saloons and limousines has been consolidated for the coming year. The 3½-litre saloon, a good-looking car, can carry six persons, the width of the seats being in the region of 53in. The customer has the choice of a bench front seat or separate bucket seats. Upholstery is in good quality leather, and polished walnut facia panel and window rails give the interior the quality finish expected of this manufacturer.

The six-cylinder engine has a compression ratio of 7 to 1, and, while the single carburettor model develops 125 b.h.p. at 4,700 r.p.m., a twin carburettor induction system is offered which steps up the power output to 150 b.h.p. at 5,000 r.p.m. An automatic transmission, offered as an alternative to the four-speed all-synchro-mesh gear box, consists of a four-speed epicyclic box in conjunction with a fluid flywheel. A selector lever is placed close to the steering wheel, and gear changes are made automatically according to load and engine speed.

Girling 12in dia brakes, with two trailing shoes at the front and leading and trailing at the rear, have vacuum servo assistance. Another optional extra on Armstrong Siddeleys is the Girling-Hydrosteer power-assisted steering. The amount of assistance applied can be varied by the driver by moving a facia-mounted lever. Driver control of the rear damper settings is a further item of extra equipment.

The 346 limousine now has more space for rear seat passengers. Leg room has been increased from 26½in to 29½in, and occupants of the two folding occasional seats also benefit by an extra 2in.

Rear seat width between armrests is now 50in.

ARMSTRONG SIDDELEY

We drive a brand new example of the new small Sapphire; find it an impeccably finished car of refinement with plenty of power, excellent visibility, smooth silence, and superlative brakes.

This newcomer to the range of smaller luxury cars will appeal to the discerning driver.

We were impressed by this quick-action control for the driver's door window. A brief push downward opens the window, while quick lift on the lever closes it. Note quality finish of interior fitments shown in this picture.

▶

Penalty paid for a low bonnet line is a deep-set engine which appears rather over-cluttered with accessories. Accessibility of vital service components, however, is good.

FAIRLY recently, sales managers have noticed a demand for a medium-sized car with the luxury of a limousine, and at a price roughly around the two and a half thousand pound mark.

These buyers seem to want a car which their elderly aunts wouldn't baulk at riding in, yet which packs much of the punch of a sports car.

The new Armstrong Siddeley Sapphire 236 series car seems to be the answer. It's snappy, but it's also very, very stylish! And there's a range of three different models, all within a few pounds of each other.

Drivers wanting sports car performance will pick the 234 with its twin carburettors, 4-cylinder engine and speed of 100 m.p.h. The standard model 236 with a 6-cylinder engine and a four-speed synchromesh gearbox with optional overdrive provides instead a moderate abundance of both power and decorum. And for the ladies, the 236 with "manumatic"

◀

Sapphire 236 has pleasant, distinctive line, with rear fenders quite unlike those of any other car. Car is a 4/5 seater; has good visibility, excellent brakes, a rare degree of refinement.

gear change and two pedal control seems the obvious choice.

Although luxuriously styled and powerful, all these cars, in typically British restraint, are far from radical. But they do have a lot of interesting features.

Held on a leash . . .

The model we tested was a conventional 236, straight off the ship and with only 400 miles on the "clock". Trying out any new marque with so little mileage is always, to say the least, frustrating. Throughout the drive, we felt that the Sapphire had always to be held firmly on a leash.

On the road the car is comfortable and quietly luxurious, as becomes a fully imported car priced at £2287, including tax. Its new styling (our model was all black with dove grey interior) drew much admiration from bystanders and passengers both.

Once or twice we nearly forgot our pledges and for a second or two really surprised a couple of drivers who thought they'd show us their tails — but we were, after all, only looking for impressions and did not try to record any test figures from a car which had not been run-in.

Just the same, we took the Armstrong Siddeley over some of the roughest local roads (and in Mel-

bourne they are really rough!), through potholes and over corrugations; as well as up hills of all gradients. At all times the car went along with all the ease and decorum of its larger brothers.

Despite its 27 cwt., light pressure on the accelerator always gave a prompt and responsive pick-up. The speedometer-marked gear change maximums of 1st to 2nd at 15 m.p.h., 2nd to 3rd at 35, and 3rd to top at 55 seemed appropriate.

On the sharpest corners, there was only a very slight tendency to sway, and the tail seemed almost unshiftable.

Super brakes . . .

No family saloon can have a better claim to "stop on a zac" than has the Sapphire. Its power-boosted brakes must be tested to be believed! Whether stopping from 15 to 50 m.p.h., slight pressure on the pedal was sufficient to actuate the system, which could be felt building up its pressure almost without any further effort on the pedal. A heavy-footed driver could, we feel, throw an unwary front seat passenger through the windscreen!

Our model had not been into the workshop since leaving the ship and it consequently was suffering from a few minor troubles. The steering

SAPPHIRE 236.

Superb finish is apparent in the front compartment, with its polished wooden facia, quality carpets, and comfortable, luxurious seats. Stubby gearshift falls easily to hand; handbrake (between seats) proved really effective. (All pictures by Edward Steet Studios, Melbourne).

wheel had excessive play and the steering itself had a tendency to bear to the left. Steering was stiff, too, on the corners, and needed a lot of effort to pull it across against a strong self-centreing action.

The clutch pedal had a deceptively long travel and needed taking up. Gear change was stiff at low speeds but moved easily at higher revs. But all these minor problems could be fixed during the car's initial service period.

Happy Sapphire . . .

Body style of the 236 is a happy breakaway from the traditional squarish Armstrong Siddeley lines. There still remains a hint of the company's original conservatism, but the car can now be described as being truly modern without being in any way ostentatious.

Head-on, the sloping bonnet leading down to a faired-in grille set in a square front give the car an almost squat appearance, with a distinct impression of width. From the side, the rear wings faired into the doors add a distinctive line, which is a welcome change from the dreary monotony of many contemporary slab sided designs.

Headlights sit above the front "winkers" and parking lights, while the tail-lights are recessed into an inverted chrome Vee at the end of each rear wing.

Direction indicator telltales are mounted on the side wings, but the driver is more likely to notice the clicking light on his facia panel. All doors are fitted with push-button handles, feel solid, and close easily. They open wide to give easy access to the car's interior, and metal guard strips are fitted over the front "steps". Front doors operate the inside dome light, and the facia is lit by restful ultra violet lighting.

Interior furnishing is a happy compromise of both the traditional and the modern. A walnut facia retains the dignity of hand finish, while the comfortable seats are upholstered very practically in nylon fabric and plastic. The roof and sides, in turn, are upholstered with washable plastic material.

Thick carpets, with a permanent rubber mat for the driver, add to the Armstrong Siddeley's opulence, although some degree of cheeseparing is apparent in the two open glove boxes, one at either end of the facia.

On a car worth over £2,000, these, we feel, ought to be made from something stronger than pressed cardboard, and at least one of them should be fitted with a lockable lid.

Both independent front seats are high, wide and extremely comfortable. Both are easily adjusted with the car either stationary or on the move and are well countersprung.

Pedals are comfortably situated, but the deceptive clutch pedal made us tend to place the driver's seat further forward than we would normally have liked. The dip switch, too, is unduly close to the clutch pedal, and could be accidentally pressed by anyone wearing heavy shoes when making a quick gear change.

Stubby gearshift . . .

The makers have placed a short gear lever centrally between the two front seats and, set further back than on most cars, it falls conveniently to hand. Placed as it is on the floor between the seats, the handbrake is also quickly reached and acts efficiently (a very pleasant discovery) even on the steepest hills.

Instruments are centrally grouped on the wide walnut facia panel. These are comprehensive and include a speedometer, clock, oil pressure gauge, petrol gauge, water temperature gauge, and ammeter. Between the two large dials a recessed panel holds the ignition switch and five knobs which operate the starter, windscreen wipers, facia lights, petrol reserve and headlamps. The choke control is handy, set as it is somewhat unusually, beneath the wide steering wheel.

Perhaps the most useful interior feature is the driver's window control. Unlike the other three movable windows which are fitted with the usual winder mechanism, this has a short chromed rod which moves through only thirty degrees. A short push down on the rod closes the window instantly, a slight upward pull opens it again, and in the same motion, the hand can continue on to give a hand signal!

All doors are fitted with interior safety locks.

Four/five seater . . .

The floor is split by the tailshaft housing at both front and rear and although classed as a five-seater, the Sapphire is really a luxury conveyance for four. Rear seat passengers can place their feet beneath the front seats, a necessary feature since, when the front seats are fully back, their legroom would otherwise be restricted.

Two ashtrays at the back of the front seats and a large one on the left of the facia are sufficient to cater to even the heaviest smokers. Unfortunately the driver must use his window, since the front ash tray is rather a long reach from his seat and, with the polished walnut nearby, it is doubtful whether the proud owner would risk butting out his cigarette on the facia instead of in the tray.

Windscreen washers, a heater and air conditioning are standard fittings and are of good quality.

Visibility is excellent. The sloping bonnet and high front seats contribute to perfect vision, and the pillars, although wide, provide little interference to visibility when cornering. The convex rear-vision mirror has perhaps too great a reduction, although, coupled with the wide rear window, it shows an extremely clear view of everything going on to the rear. Windscreen wipers overlap and sweep cleanly, while the twin horns are tuned to a loud, satisfying and harmonious note.

Beneath the sloping bonnet, the penalty paid for good visibility is apparent in a deeply-set engine somewhat over-cluttered with accessories. The six cylinders set in line have a deep stroke of 100 mm., with a bore of 70 mm. Rated at 18.22 h.p., the engine develops a maximum of 85 b.h.p. at 4,500 r.p.m., and is fed by a single downdraft Stromberg carburettor. The fuel tank holds ten gallons and an extra gallon is held in reserve. This can be switched in by touching a knob on the facia.

The boot is clean and roomy, with the spare wheel mounted in a separate compartment beneath that for the luggage. It is both accessible and well-finished, although a car of the Sapphire's size could perhaps do with a shade more luggage space for long trips.

Driving the Sapphire . . .

At the wheel of a car like the Sapphire, the test driver feels that he is faced with a mixed blessing. While he can view tolerantly the failings of a small, cheap car, on a model which costs over £2,000 he is inclined to be rather more critical.

However, the Sapphire came through with flying colours!

Starting is positively ghostly, and the only indication that the engine is ticking over is the extinguishing of the ignition light! Pulling away, the car is always effortless, and handles easily, even in heavy traffic. Over the very worst road surfaces, we never once heard a single body noise.

Very slight vibration was noticeable at the steering wheel, but this was so mild and apparent only on the roughest sections, and our impression was that it was preferable to no road feel at all. It had no effect on the steering, which, with the exception of the adjustment troubles mentioned earlier, had a precise feel under all conditions. The car's front suspension appeared to be a little on the firm side, but rear seat riding was of the best. Severe bumps could be felt, although the combination of good suspension and comfortable seating allowed the passengers to remain perfectly comfortable.

On some harshly undulating surfaces the car showed a very slight tendency to bounce, but when cornering sharply, side sway was negligible.

The forty foot turning circle is perhaps unduly large, but this proved no handicap when parking.

Despite its having had limited use, the motor felt remarkably free. Once moving, it was just loud enough to permit of gear changes at correct revolutions, yet was never intrusive.

On our own very special Melbourne hill, a pinch of well over 1 in 5, approached over a rough section of potholed gravel, the Sapphire began its ascent in top gear and finally went over the top in second. Most cars change down to second or even low before attempting this hill, which is some indication of this car's latent pulling ability.

Gear changing is easy enough and there is good synchromesh on all forward gears. Quick changes can therefore be made from one cog to another at will. The overdrive, operated by a switch on an arm just below the right hand side of the steering wheel, comes in and goes out smoothly and without lag. A worthwhile reserve of power always seems to be on hand, and the engine pulls away smoothly from low top gear speeds.

The clutch engaged smoothly with moderate pedal travel, and although some initial adjustment would have been in order, the impression was that this component is rugged enough to stand up under even the heaviest pedalling for extremely long periods.

Generally speaking, the Armstrong Siddeley is a distinct cut above the ordinary, and obviously a lot of forethought and planning has gone into the design and production of this car.

The finish is typical of high standard British craftsmanship. The Sapphire gives little impression of being a production car, and is solidly made and well put together. It should provide discerning buyers with refined, yet fast motoring in above-average comfort and silence.

* * *

Driver's seat comment . . .

Totting up pros and cons after a day at the wheel of this engaging, almost ghostly car, my main impressions came from its excellent visibility and magnificent brakes. Couple these with the pinpoint way it steers and goes around corners as if its tail were tied down, and I cannot help but feel that this car goes a long way towards providing a safety standard seldom achieved.

I approved the practical touches, too, such as the washable plastic hood lining and that wonderful driver's window mechanism (something we could do with on *all* saloon cars!).

The Sapphire, of course, had its little irritations—as have practically all cars regardless of size, type or price. I disliked the "cheap" glove boxes. The centralising of the instruments on the facia is not in keeping, I feel, with the best modern trend; just as the dip switch, though doubtless very accessible on the two-pedal models, is badly positioned when one has to use the clutch pedal. Nor did I care greatly for the rearward positioning of the central gearshift lever —although this, I feel, was more just a matter of personal taste.

I'm looking forward to an opportunity of taking the four-cylinder Sapphire 234 on tests, as soon as one becomes available. If the 236's refinement, good road holding, and general tractability has been retained— and I see no reason why it should not be—the extra punch provided by the revvable twin-carb engine should make the 234 an exciting car indeed.

Certainly the quality of interior finish, the riding comfort, and that delightful polished wood facia are in keeping with the high grade Armstrong Siddeley tradition, even though there are a few detail improvements yet to be made, as mentioned in our text above.

But taken all-in-all, I thoroughly enjoyed driving the Sapphire 236, and its riding qualities are such that I feel I could take it on long journeys over Australia's roughest roads without either slackening speed unduly or having to worry about some component falling to bits.

It's a fairly expensive car, to be true, but such is the standard of finish and attention to detail generally — and such is the level of smoothness, quietness and refinement —that I feel one desiring a car something above the ordinary would cheerfully pay the extra for this Armstrong Siddeley.

Fuel consumption, incidentally, is claimed (we were unable to check) to be in the region of 30 m.p.g., a worthwhile figure for anybody's money.

John Goode. ●

SPECIFICATIONS
ARMSTRONG SIDDELEY SAPPHIRE 236

Armstrong Siddeley Sapphire 236, 4/5 passenger saloon. *Our test car from Stokoe Motors Ltd., Melbourne. Price, £2,287 (including tax). Availability, six to eight weeks.*

Engine: *6-cylinder 2309 c.c., O.H.V., 70 x 100 mm., compression ratio 7.5 to 1. Single Stromberg carburettor, mechanical A.C. fuel pump, 12 volt electrical system, 51 amp./hour battery.*

Transmission: *Borg and Beck clutch driving through four speed overdrive, and reverse gearbox with synchromesh on all forward speeds. Hardy Spicer one-piece tailshaft, 4.545 to 1 final drive. Gear ratios: 4.54, 6.45, 9.70, 15.69 to 1. Rev, 13.55 to 1 Overdrive top, 3.53 to 1,*

Chassis: *Heavy cruciform frame with boxed in side members.*

Brakes: *Girling hydraulic with Vac-hydro assist. Front, 11" diameter with 2¼" shoes; rear, 11" diameter with 2¼" shoes. Handbrake on rear wheels only.*

Suspension: *Front — Independent by coils and wishbones. Rear — Conventional semi-elliptic springs. Girling double acting telescopic shock absorbers front and rear.*

Dimensions: *Length, 15 ft.; wheelbase, 9 ft. 3 ins.; width, 5 ft. 8½ ins.; height, 5 ft. 1½ ins.; weight, kerbside, 27 cwt Track, front, 4 ft. 7½ ins.; rear, 4 ft. 6 5/16 ins.*

The

S

ALTHOUGH the new Armstrong Siddeley Star Sapphire—which will be seen by most people for the first time at Earls Court today—is a direct development of the well-known 346 Sapphire, the changes which have been made go far beyond mere detail improvements and, in fact, place the car in the more-exclusive high-powered luxury class.

Most important mechanical innovations are an enlarged engine of 4 litres capacity, built-in power-assisted steering, disc front brakes, improved suspension and Borg-Warner fully-automatic transmission.

Body changes include detail modifications to external appearance and a complete revision of interior trim and appointments, which are now carried out on a lavish scale and include such luxury items as an independent heating system for the rear compartment, with de-misting for the rear window.

Naturally there has been an increase in price compared with the 346 Sapphire, the new Star Sapphire saloon selling for £1,763, which, with British purchase tax of £882 17s. gives a total of £2,645 17s.

* * *

To deal first with the mechanical changes, the Star engine has an enlarged bore of 97 mm. (instead of 90 mm.) but the stroke remains as before at 90 mm. and the unit is thus considerably "over-square," with a capacity of 3,990 c.c. in place of 3,435 c.c. In the new cylinder block the bores have been siamesed in pairs, but to ensure adequate cooling, larger water spaces are now provided at the sides of the bores.

Two Stromberg downdraught carburetters are fitted as standard and the arrangement is similar to the installation on the twin-carburetter version of the "346" model, but the carburetters are larger (42 mm. in place of 36 mm.) whilst the manifolds have larger tracts and are improved in shape.

Considerable development work has been carried out on the valve gear. As before, the layout embodies inclined valves situated in hemispherical combustion chambers and operated by inclined rockers from a single, high, side camshaft driven by Duplex roller chain from the nose of the crankshaft. In the Star engine, a Reynolds hydraulically operated chain tensioner is fitted and there is also a Neoprene damper to cut out flutter. The timing has been modified to give better idling without loss of power, and lightweight push-rods constructed of Bundy tubing are used to reduce reciprocating weight. The valves themselves are of larger size, the head diameter of the exhausts being 1.59 in. (instead of 1.49 in.) and the inlets 1.80 in. (in place of 1.70 in.). KE 965 steel is now used for the exhausts and the stems have Stellited tips.

Lubrication improvements include the fitting of a Hobourn-Eaton oil pump of 60% greater output, enlarged oil galleries throughout, a larger filter and a sump increased in capacity from 10 to 14 pints. Both the big-end and main bearings are of lead-indium and the webs carrying the intermediate bearings have been made deeper to provide added stiffness, whilst a Metalastik torsional vibration damper is now fitted to the nose of the crankshaft.

Other engine changes include a higher compression ratio (7.5/1 instead of 7/1), the transference of the thermostat from the radiator to the cylinder head (so relieving the hose of pressure), the use of a twin-belt drive for the dynamo (to cope with the extra power required to drive the power-steering oil pump, which is mounted on the back of the dynamo), the use of a ball race for the distributor drive shaft (in place of an impregnated bronze type of plain bearing), and the provision of a separate large-size, oil-wetted air filter for each carburetter to minimize induction noise.

Modifications have also been made to the exhaust silencing system to reduce noise to a minimum. As before, twin manifolds are used, and from these a pair of separate pipes lead to a union, whence a large-diameter pipe conveys the gases to a long cylindrical expansion chamber which is inclined upwards to

WHITE-ON-BLACK instrument dials are set in a panel of walnut veneer, matched on the passenger's side by a large cubby; switchgear is placed centrally. The steering column is adjustable.

rmstrong Siddeley
AR SAPPHIRE

New Model with Enlarged Engine, Power-assisted Steering, Disc Brakes at the Front, and Luxury Bodywork

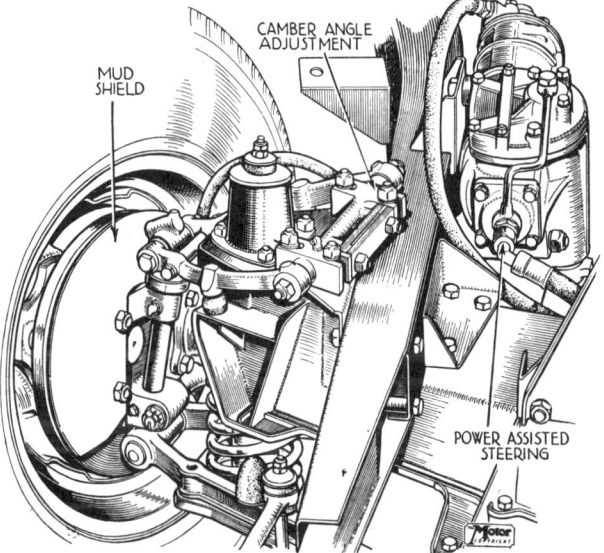

REVISED frontal appearance stems from the use of a shallower plated grille, small circular intake grilles, and fog and driving lamps mounted on the bumper apron.

avoid a sharp bend in the tail pipe. The large-diameter intermediate pipe is to provide for preliminary expansion of the gases before reaching the silencer proper.

In effecting these changes, the primary objective has been to produce an exceptionally quiet power unit with high torque at low engine speeds rather than to concentrate on maximum output. The latter has, however, been increased considerably, the new gross figure of 165 b.h.p. at 4,250 r.p.m. comparing with the 150 b.h.p. at 5,000 r.p.m. of the "346" engine in twin-carburetter form. Torque has been increased to 260 lb. ft. gross at 2,000 r.p.m. from 194 lb. ft. at the same speed.

In unit with the engine is a Borg-Warner fully-automatic transmission with intermediate gear hold. A high top gear giving 21.8 m.p.h. per 1,000 engine r.p.m. is used to take full advantage of the improved torque.

The Burman power-assisted steering is of the new built-in re-circulating ball type as fully described in *The Motor* a fortnight ago. A further steering improvement results from an increase of $1\frac{1}{4}$ in. in front track, which has enabled wheel movement to be increased and the turning circle thereby reduced from $42\frac{1}{2}$ ft. to 38 ft.

Girling disc brakes with quickly detachable segmental pads have been adopted at the front, normal drum brakes working in 12 in. diameter drums being retained at the rear. The system includes a vacuum servo of the Girling suspended vacuum type and a vacuum reservoir is incorporated in the system as a safety measure. A notable adjunct to the front disc brakes is a sheet-metal shield close to the inner side of each disc to protect the surface from mud thrown up by the opposite wheel.

Several minor changes have been made in the suspension system. In the first place, the front suspension cross-member has been stiffened and a new mounting adopted for the upper of the two trailing wishbones;

CHASSIS INNOVATIONS on the Star Sapphire include Girling disc brakes at the front with special mud-deflector shields, a stiffened front-suspension cross-member with an upper wishbone incorporating an adjustment for camber, and the latest built-in Burman power-assisted steering.

TREMELY OMY, as these ographs show, interior of the Sapphire is shly equipped furnished with -quality leather polished walnut er. The front is of the split-bench type.

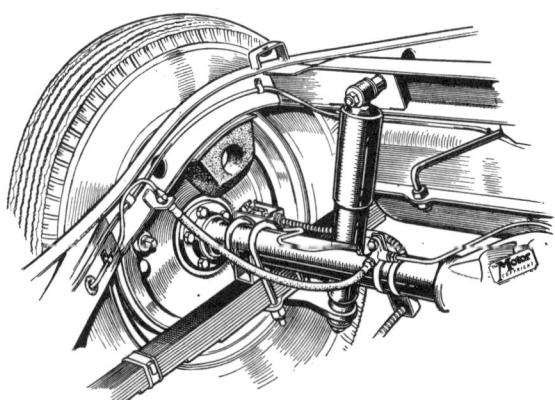

PROGRESSIVE ACTION of the rear suspension is obtained by the use of special pierced bump stops which have a similar effect to spring helper leaves but are stated to be more progressive in action. The rubbers are capable of absorbing from 30 lb. on initial contact to over 1,000 lb. when fully compressed.

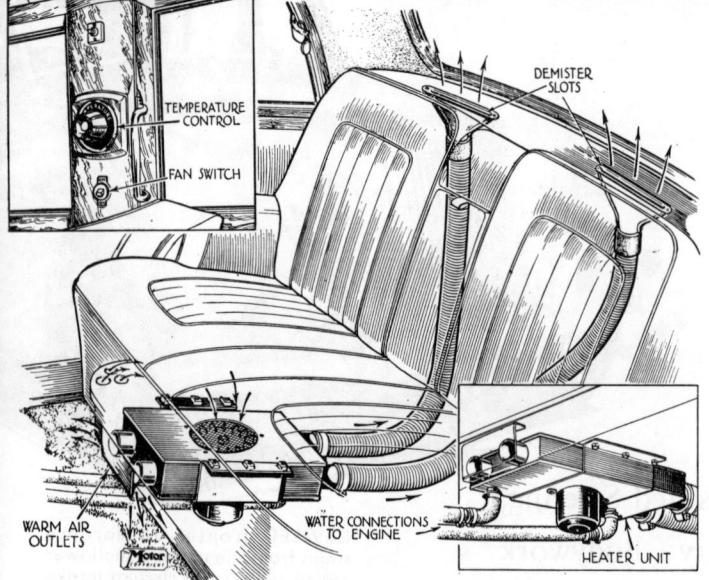

REAR SEAT COMFORT in bad weather is assured on the new Star Sapphire by a separate heater system under the rear seat, with demisting ducts to prevent condensation on the rear window. How the system is arranged can be seen from this drawing, which shows both the air circulation and the controls. A normal heater-and-demister system is fitted for the front compartment in addition.

Armstrong Siddeley STAR SAPPHIRE

bumpers of new section with completely boxed over-riders are used, this change applying also to the rear, where a bumper apron has been added.

The most noticeable changes which will be observed from the side lie in the use of cut-away rear wheel spats and a re-arrangement of the doors which are now all hung from the front and have concealed hinges. In addition, concealed door sills are provided and there is a chromium rubbing strip along the sill line.

It is in the interior, however, that the greatest body developments are noticeable, the trim and equipment having been revised throughout. The facia board is entirely new and beautifully carried out in walnut veneer. On the passenger's side there is a large glove locker with table-type lid and the main instruments occupy a corresponding position in front of the driver. The instruments themselves have clear circular faces and a large-dial speedometer is matched by a combination dial with segments for the ammeter, oil gauge, thermometer and fuel gauge. Between the two is a clock, and on the right are the screen washer switch and warning lights for the headlamp main beam, ignition, and choke (the control for which is of the segment type just below the board).

The other small controls are nicely disposed on a centre panel, with provision for radio, and details worth mentioning include a cigar lighter, petrol reserve switch, two-speed wiper control, starter (adjacent to the ignition switch), and a pull-and-twist switch for separate operation of the fog and road lights. The Borg-Warner automatic transmission control is mounted on the steering column, which is now cowled, and the gear position indicator is illuminated.

Walnut veneer is also used for the door cappings and, more unusual, for the surrounds of the windscreen and windows and for the centre door pillars. In conjunction with the beautifully carried out leather upholstery (two-tone if required) and high grade carpeting, the effect is one of luxury and comfort. The front seat is of the divided bench type to provide individual adjustment or three-abreast seating and is split off-centre to allow a folding central arm rest to be incorporated in the passenger's section. The front side arm rests are now adjustable and a folding rear arm rest is, of course, provided. Useful spring-loaded pockets are built into the backs of the front squabs.

Perhaps the most notable new body feature is the rear-compartment heating. An entirely separate heater unit is located beneath the rear seat and this serves both to provide warmed air at floor level and to demist the rear window. Of the recirculating type, this heater is controlled from the central door pillar on the driver's side. The whole system is quite independent of the fresh-air heating and demisting arrangement for the front compartment.

Other innovations of note include carpeting for the large rear luggage boot, improved draught sealing, flush-fitting recessed sun vizors and large ash trays conveniently placed for all occupants.

this incorporates shims so that the camber angle can readily be adjusted. In addition, Armstrong heavy-duty telescopic hydraulic shock absorbers with $1\frac{1}{8}$ in.-diameter pistons have been standardized all round.

Semi-elliptic springs are used at the rear as before, but a notable change lies in the adoption of special progressive bump stops in place of the more conventional helper-leaf system. As will be seen from the drawing on page 3, the bump stops are of large size and pierced with a hole which is tapered towards the centre. In the normal laden condition, these rubbers are close to the axle and, unlike normal bump stops, come into operation on anything beyond quite small spring deflections. Initial contact causes the lower portion of the rubber to compress and tends to flatten and elongate the hole, further pressure serving to collapse the hole entirely and offer increasingly greater resistance. The action is stated to be much more progressive than helper leaves, the rubbers being capable of absorbing from 30 lb. on initial contact to over 1,000 lb. when fully compressed.

To turn now to the body, the general lines remain unchanged, but the whole body has been lowered by 1 in. and numerous detail changes made. At the front, the bonnet top has been extended over the grille and a new type of Sphinx mascot placed slightly farther back than before. Circular intake grilles take the place of the former built-in fog and road lamps, the latter now being mounted separately for easier adjustment. In addition,

ARMSTRONG SIDDELEY STAR SAPPHIRE

Engine Dimensions			
Cylinders	...	...	6
Bore	...	...	97 mm.
Stroke	...	...	90 mm.
Cubic capacity	...	...	3,990 c.c.
Piston area	...	...	68.72 sq. in.
Valves	...	...	Overhead (inclined push rods)
Compression ratio	...		7.5/1

Engine Performance			
Max power	...	...	165 b.h.p. (gross)
at	...	...	4,250 r.p.m.
Max b.m.e.p.	...	...	142 lb./sq. in.
at	...	...	2,000 r.p.m.
B.H.P. per sq. in. piston area	...	...	2.4
Piston speed at max. power	...	...	2,510 ft./min.

Engine Details			
Carburetters	...		Two Stromberg downdraught DAV 42
Ignition timing control	...		Vacuum and centrifugal
Sparking plugs	...	...	Lodge HLN 14
Fuel pump	...	...	AC mechanical
Fuel capacity	...	...	16 gallons (incl. 2 reserve)
Oil filter	...	...	Purolator full-flow

Oil capacity	...		14 pints (plus $1\frac{1}{4}$ for filter)
Cooling system	...		Pump, fan and thermostat
Water capacity	...		26 pints (incl. heaters)
Electrical system	...		12-volt Lucas
Battery capacity	...		64 amp. hr.

Transmission			
Borg-Warner	fully	automatic with torque convertor	
Gear ratios:			
Top	...	...	3.77
Intermediate	...		5.41-10.82
Low	...	...	8.674-17.348
Rev.	...	...	7.574-15.148
Prop. shaft	...	...	Open, divided
Final drive	...	...	Hypoid bevel

Chassis Details			
Brakes	...		Front, Girling disc; rear, Girling drum (with servo and reservoir)
Brake sizes	...		Front, 11.82 in. dia. disc, rear 12 in. drum
Friction lining areas			Front pads, 30.48 sq. in.; rear shoes, 90 sq. in.
Suspension:			
Front	...	...	Independent (coil) with anti-roll bar
Rear	...	...	Semi-elliptic

Shock absorbers	...		Armstrong telescopic hydraulic
Wheel type	...	...	Dunlop disc
Tyre size	...	...	6.70-16 tubeless
Steering gear	...		Burman power-assisted recirculating ball

Dimensions			
Wheelbase	...	...	9 ft. 6 in.
Track:			
Front	...	...	4 ft. $9\frac{7}{8}$ in.
Rear	...	...	4 ft. $9\frac{1}{2}$ in.
Overall length	...	...	16 ft. 2 in.
Overall width	...	...	6 ft. 2 in.
Overall height	...	...	5 ft. 2 in.
Ground clearance	...	...	$8\frac{1}{2}$ in.
Turning circle	...	...	38 ft.
Dry weight	...	...	35 cwt. (approx.)

Performance Factors (at dry weight)			
Piston area, sq. in. per ton	...	...	39.3
Brake lining area, sq. in. per ton	...		69.0 (disc front, drum rear)
Top gear m.p.h. per 1,000 r.p.m.	...	...	21.8
Top gear m.p.h. per 1,000 ft./min. piston speed	...	...	29.6
Litres per ton-mile	...	...	3,180

More Powerful Armstrong Siddeley With Automatic Transmission

1959 MODELS

Star Sapphire

FIRST examples of Armstrong Siddeley's new Star Sapphire have started to leave the works at Coventry; a substantial production programme has been planned. While the car may seem familiar at first sight in its general outline, mechanical changes, general development and important new items of equipment have all combined to transform this model for 1959.

Principal feature of the Star Sapphire is the new, more powerful 4-litre engine, designed to give high torque at low r.p.m., ensuring exceptional flexibility and good matching with the characteristics of the Borg Warner automatic transmission which is now standard equipment. Additional standard fittings are servo-aided brakes with discs for the front wheels, and integral, power-assisted steering. Among important detail changes are the provision of an independent heating system for the rear passengers, and demisting of the rear window.

The 346 Limousine continues as previously with synchromesh gear box, but automatic transmission becomes available at extra cost.

Engine

A revised cylinder block, cast in one with the crankcase, is used for the new 3.9-litre over-square engine. This accommodates the increased bore diameter and provides water passages between each cylinder. Vandervell lead-indium is used for the big end and main bearings, and the connecting rods, derived from those of the 3,435 c.c. engines, have been stiffened at the webs and radii. The bearing caps have also been strengthened, and a vibration damper is fitted at the front end of the crankshaft. The pistons are fitted with two compression and one oil control rings. A larger capacity sump carries 14 pints, compared with the previous engine's 11 pints, and the oil pump feed has been increased by 60 per cent.

Exhaust valves, which have stellited stem tips, are of KE.965 steel; compared with those of the 346 engine, the valve head diameters have been increased by 0.1in, making the sizes 1.80in inlet and 1.59in exhaust. They are closed by double coil springs, and to cut down reciprocating weight, the pushrods are formed of drawn steel tubing of 0.028in wall thickness.

A six-port induction system is cast internally in the cast iron cylinder head, and separate, water-heated alloy manifolds carry the twin downdraught Stromberg carburettors, which are fed from the 16-gallon tank by an A.C. mechanical pump. A dual exhaust system is used. The manufacturers claim that the new Star engine, in addition to a greatly increased power output, also has an improved fuel consumption range when compared with the 346 engine.

Steering

Burman power-assisted steering is fitted; the operation of this new system was fully described in last week's issue of *The Autocar*. On the Sapphire the pump for the steering gear is located on the back of the generator, to which it is connected by a flexible coupling. They are driven by a double belt from the crankshaft.

Brakes

Hydro-Vac servo assistance is applied to the Girling braking system; a reservoir is incorporated to allow up to five braking applications with a dead engine. Disc brakes are fitted at the front, and 12in diameter drums with two-trailing shoes at the back—this combination gives ample stopping power for the performance of the Star Sapphire and also enables a powerful hand brake to be fitted. Splash guards are placed on the insides of the discs, to keep grit and water off the surfaces. The friction pads are wedge-shaped; with a total friction area of 30.5 sq in, the pads sweep a 280 sq in area of disc, compared with the 170 sq in of the rear drum brakes, which have a friction linings area of 90 sq in.

Suspension

Provision has been made to adjust the camber angle of each front suspension by means of steel shims, and this should ease servicing problems. The long half-elliptic rear springs have reverse camber, and the rear shackles are mounted beneath the frame, instead of with the shackle pin pass-

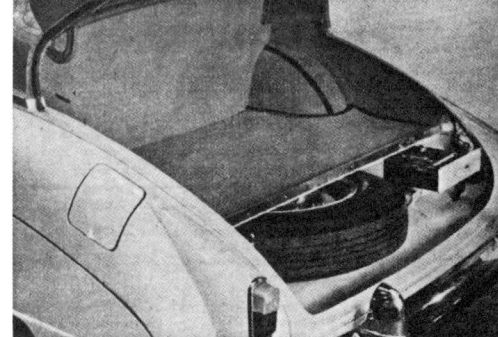

Below left: Entry is easy to the deeply upholstered seats, which may be had covered with two-tone leather. There is a hinged pocket in the back of each front seat. Below right: Highly polished veneer covers the facia and window surrounds. Right: The luggage locker is lined and the spare wheel is housed beneath its floor, with a tray containing a kit of small tools.

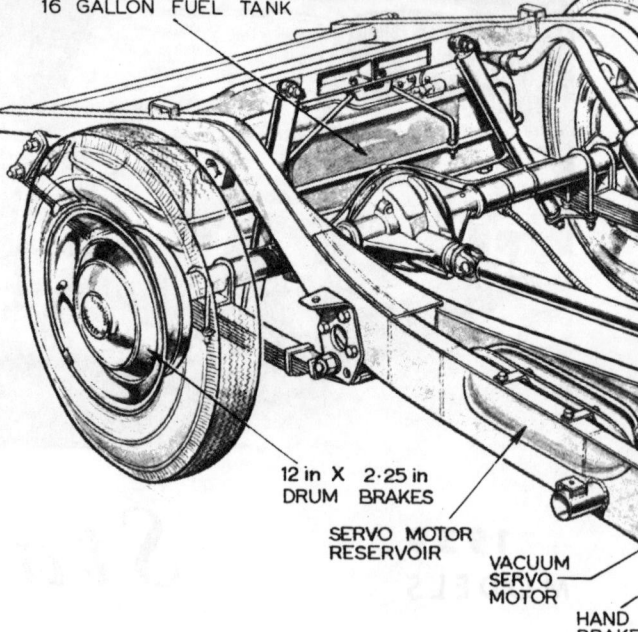

16 GALLON FUEL TANK

12 in X 2·25 in DRUM BRAKES

SERVO MOTOR RESERVOIR

VACUUM SERVO MOTOR

HAND BRAKE

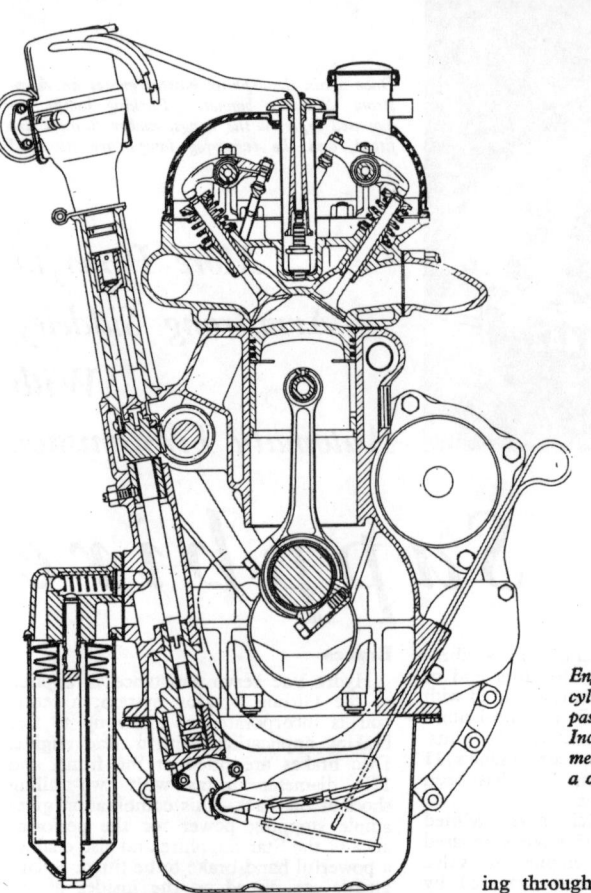

Engine cross-section showing the new cylinder block with generous water passages around the enlarged bores. Inclined valves of increased head diameter are operated by push-rods from a camshaft carried high in the block

On the right door pillar is the control for the rear compartment heater. The switch operates the heater fan. Grab handles are fixed to each pillar and on the left of the facia

ing through the frame members as was the former practice. "Helper" spring leaves have been omitted, and a thick rubber pad is secured to the underside of the chassis frame on the centre line of the axle; compression of this pad provides progressive damping under load. Armstrong telescopic dampers are fitted front and rear.

Transmission

Automatic transmission is provided by a normal Borg-Warner box. The gear control lever is mounted on the left of the steering column and the positions are indicated on an illuminated quadrant; a manual control permits the intermediate gear ratio to be held up to its maximum speed of approximately 60 m.p.h. The divided propeller shaft has a rubber-mounted steady bearing.

Body

The all-steel body, built by Armstrong Siddeley at Parkside, Coventry, is rust-proofed, and all its undersurfaces are sprayed with sound-deadening material before the body is painted. The doors are hung on their forward edges, and they

seat on double rubber sealing strip. A wide choice of colour schemes is offered.

Seating

A lot of work has been carried out to make the interior as comfortable as possible. The seats are built up on spring cases, with soft rubber Vitafoam fillings covered with best quality leather. The front seats are separately adjustable for leg room; the angle of the back rests (which are curved to give lateral support when cornering) is not variable. Central folding arm rests are provided, and there is an arm rest on each front door.

The floor of the rear compartment is flat, and in front there is only a shallow protruberance over the gear box. Close-fitting carpet covers the whole floor, and a rubber mat protects it from concentrated wear by the heels of a driver's shoes. Each front door has a map pocket with a spring-loaded flap; there is an ashtray in the forward part of the garnish rails in addition to one in the back of the left front seat.

One of the striking features of the body interior is the quality of the walnut veneer facia and door rails; these extend round the window frames and windscreen, and the door centre pillars are also in walnut veneer. The work is well carried out, and absence of screw heads is appreciated.

Instruments

In a rectangular central panel of the facia are grouped the switches and the front compartment heater controls with

--- **SPECIFICATION** ---

ENGINE		
No. of cylinders	...	6 in line
Bore and stroke	...	97 x 90mm (3.82 x 3.54in)
Displacement	...	3,990 c.c. (243.49 cu in)
Valve position	...	O.H.V.
Compression ratio	...	7.5 to 1
Max. b.h.p. (gross)	...	165 at 4,250 r.p.m.
Max. b.m.e.p.	...	160 lb sq in at 2,000 r.p.m.
Max. torque (gross)	...	260 lb ft at 2,000 r.p.m.
Carburettor	...	Stromberg DAV42 twin downdraught
Fuel pump	...	AC mechanical
Tank capacity	...	16 Imp. gallons (73 litres) including 2 gallons (9 litres) reserve
Sump capacity	...	14 pints (8 litres)
Oil filter	...	Full flow
Cooling system	...	Pump, fan and thermostat
Battery	...	12 volt, 64 amp hr

TRANSMISSION		
Clutch	...	Fluid torque converter
Gear box	...	Borg-Warner automatic
Gear lever position	...	Steering column lever, intermediate gear hold.
Overall gear ratios	...	Direct top 3.77; intermediate 5.41 to 10.82; low 8.674 to 17,348; reverse 7.574 to 15.148.
Final drive	...	Hypoid bevel, 3.77 to 1.

CHASSIS		
Brakes	...	Hydraulic, vacuum servo assisted; front disc, rear drum
Disc diameter	...	11.82in
Drum diameter and shoe width	...	12 x 2.25in
Suspension: front	...	Independent, coil and wishbone
rear	...	Semi-elliptic leaf springs

Dampers	...	Armstrong telescopic
Wheels	...	Steel disc
Tyre size	...	6.70—16in
Steering	...	Burman integral power
Steering wheel	...	Two-spoke, 17in dia
Turns, lock to lock	...	3¼

DIMENSIONS		
Wheelbase	...	9ft 6in (289.6cm)
Track, F	...	4ft 9.875in (147cm)
R	...	4ft 9.5in (146cm)
Overall length	...	16ft 2in (492.8cm)
Overall width	...	6ft 2in (188cm)
Overall height	...	5ft 2in (157.5cm)
Ground clearance	...	8.5in (21.6cm)
Turning circle	...	38ft (11.58m)
Kerb weight (with 5 gal petrol)	...	3,920 lb

PERFORMANCE DATA		
Top gear m.p.h. at 1,000 r.p.m.	...	21.8
Torque lb/ft per cu in engine capacity	...	0.94
Brake surface area swept by linings	...	Front, 280 sq in; rear, 170 sq in
Weight distribution	...	F, 51 per cent
(dry)	...	R, 49 per cent

PRICES

STAR SAPPHIRE: Saloon, with Borg-Warner automatic transmission, disc front brakes and Burman integral power steering: **Basic £1,763; Purchase Tax £882 17s; Total £2,645 17s.**
SAPPHIRE 346: Limousine with synchromesh gear box: Basic £1,910. Purchase tax £956 7s; **Total £2,866 7s.** Limousine with automatic gear box: Basic £2,099; Purchase tax £1,050 17s; **Total £3,149 17s.**

Star Sapphire

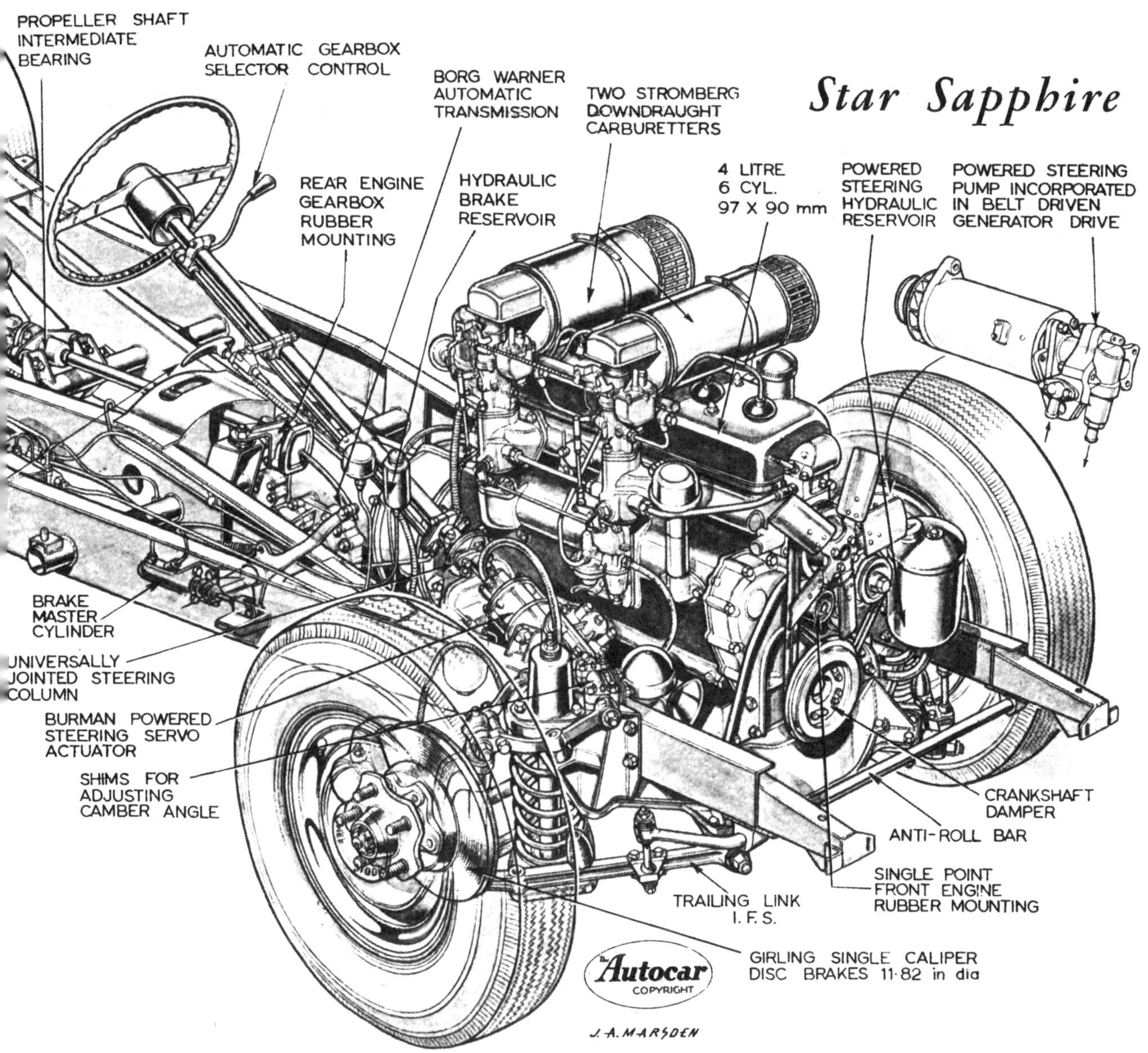

PROPELLER SHAFT INTERMEDIATE BEARING
AUTOMATIC GEARBOX SELECTOR CONTROL
BORG WARNER AUTOMATIC TRANSMISSION
TWO STROMBERG DOWNDRAUGHT CARBURETTERS
REAR ENGINE GEARBOX RUBBER MOUNTING
HYDRAULIC BRAKE RESERVOIR
4 LITRE 6 CYL. 97 X 90 mm
POWERED STEERING HYDRAULIC RESERVOIR
POWERED STEERING PUMP INCORPORATED IN BELT DRIVEN GENERATOR DRIVE
BRAKE MASTER CYLINDER
UNIVERSALLY JOINTED STEERING COLUMN
BURMAN POWERED STEERING SERVO ACTUATOR
SHIMS FOR ADJUSTING CAMBER ANGLE
CRANKSHAFT DAMPER
ANTI-ROLL BAR
SINGLE POINT FRONT ENGINE RUBBER MOUNTING
TRAILING LINK I.F.S.
GIRLING SINGLE CALIPER DISC BRAKES 11·82 in dia
The Autocar COPYRIGHT
J. A. MARSDEN

additional space for a radio; at night, a small concealed light illuminates the switch panel. In front of the driver are a large speedometer, and a matching dial containing fuel, water temperature and oil pressure gauges, and an ammeter; a clock is placed between the two dials. On the right are the usual warning lights, and the control for the screen washer. The direction flasher lever is on the right of the steering column, which has a quick-action adjustment for length.

Heating

The Star Sapphire is one of the few cars to be equipped with a separate heater installation for the rear compartment; it is included in the standard specification, and is under the control of the occupants of the rear seat. The heater unit, housed in a compartment beneath the seat cushion, is of the recirculatory pattern—it draws air from the interior of the car, heats it to the required temperature and recirculates it. Exit vents are placed in the lower edge of the seat cushion and provision is made for rear window demisting by conducting warm air from the heater unit, along ducts placed behind the seat squab, to longitudinal vents which direct the air on to the window.

In the front compartment the heater is of the usual fresh-air type, with a booster fan and windscreen demisting vents.

Preliminary experience of the Star Sapphire on the road confirmed that the car has good acceleration and is capable of a high cruising speed. There is freedom from roll on corners, and immediate response to any movement of the steering wheel. The brakes are impressive, a lightly loaded pedal giving a smooth, powerful response.

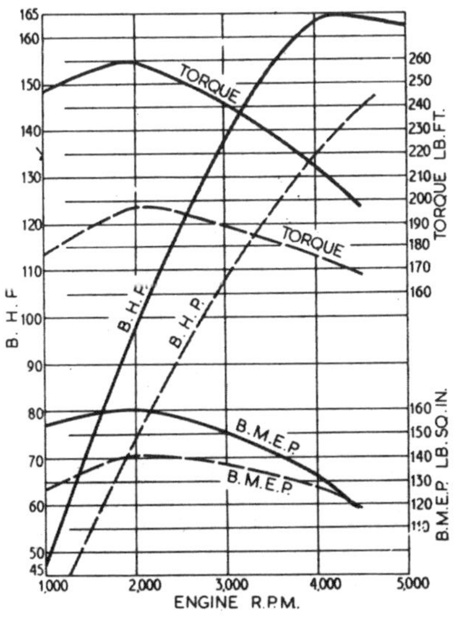

TORQUE
TORQUE
B.H.P.
B.H.P.
B.M.E.P.
B.M.E.P.
B.H.P.
TORQUE LB.FT.
B.M.E.P. LB.SQ.IN.
1,000 2,000 3,000 4,000 5,000
ENGINE R.P.M.

Left: Gross power curves for the Star Sapphire (continuous line) and the Sapphire 346 (dotted). Below: The front wing line sweeps down to merge into the rear wheel spats. Opening quarter panes provide ventilation when the main windows are closed

RW 442

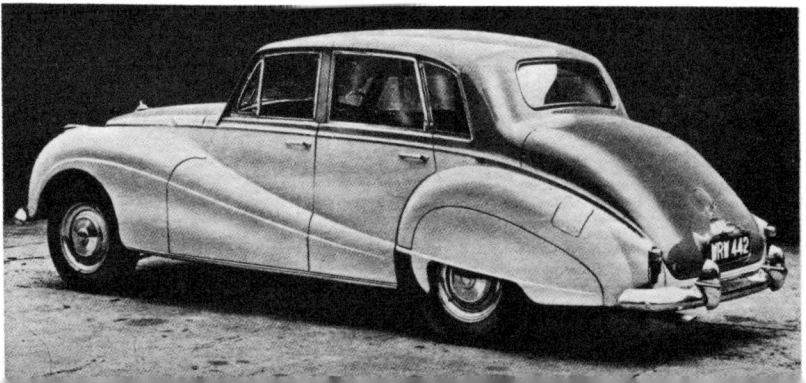

Make: Armstrong Siddeley.   **Type:** Star Sapphire.

Makers: Bristol Siddeley Engines Ltd., Parkside, Coventry.

Test Data

World copyright reserved : no unauthorized reproduction in whole or in part.

CONDITIONS: *Weather : Warm and dry with light wind (Temperature 57-69° F. Barometer 29.4-29.8 in. Hg.) Surface : Dry concrete and tarred macadam. Fuel : Premium-grade pump petrol (approx. 96 Research Method Octane Rating).*

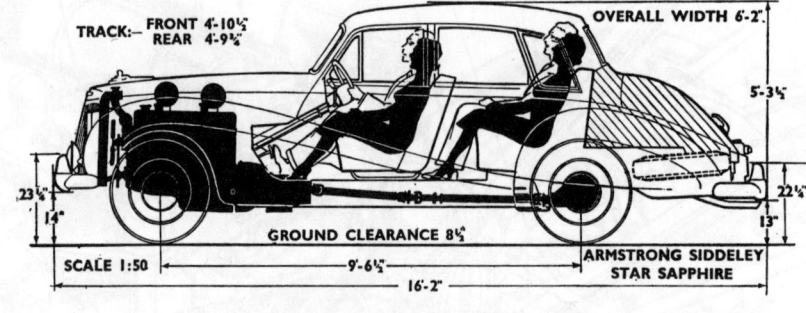

TRACK:— FRONT 4'-10½" REAR 4'-9½"
OVERALL WIDTH 6'-2"
5'-3½"
23¾"
14"
22¼"
13"
GROUND CLEARANCE 8½"
SCALE 1:50
9'-6½"
16'-2"
ARMSTRONG SIDDELEY STAR SAPPHIRE

INSTRUMENTS
Speedometer at 30 m.p.h.	..	..	1% fast
Speedometer at 60 m.p.h.	..	..	3% fast
Speedometer at 90 m.p.h.	..	..	4% fast
Distance recorder	..	..	accurate

WEIGHT
Kerb weight (unladen, but with oil, coolant and fuel for approx. 50 miles) .. 35 cwt.
Front/rear distribution of kerb weight 53/47
Weight laden as tested .. .. .. 38¾ cwt.

MAXIMUM SPEEDS
Flying Half Mile.
Mean of four opposite runs .. 99.6 m.p.h.
Best one-way time equals .. 100.6 m.p.h.

"Maximile" Speed (Timed quarter mile after one mile accelerating from rest).
Mean of four opposite runs .. 96.4 m.p.h.
Best one-way time equals .. 97.8 m.p.h.

Speed in Gears automatic change-up speeds)
Max. speed in 2nd gear .. .. 63 m.p.h.
Max. speed in 1st gear .. .. .. 37 m.p.h.

FUEL CONSUMPTION
21.0 m.p.g. at constant 30 m.p.h. on level.
19.0 m.p.g. at constant 40 m.p.h. on level.
18.0 m.p.g. at constant 50 m.p.h. on level.
16.5 m.p.g. at constant 60 m.p.h. on level.
15.5 m.p.g. at constant 70 m.p.h. on level.
14.0 m.p.g. at constant 80 m.p.h. on level.
12.5 m.p.g. at constant 90 m.p.h. on level.

Overall Fuel Consumption for 3,361 miles, 233½ gallons, equals 14.4 m.p.g. (19.6 litres/100 km.)

Touring Fuel Consumption (m.p.g. at steady speed midway between 30 m.p.h. and maximum, less 5% allowance for acceleration), 15.4 m.p.g.
Fuel tank capacity (maker's figure) including reserve 16 Gallons.

STEERING
Turning Circle between kerbs :
Left .. .. 34½ ft.
Right .. .. 37 ft.
Turns of steering wheel from lock to lock. 4

BRAKES from 30 m.p.h.
0.90 g retardation (equivalent to 33½ ft. stopping distance) with 60 lb. pedal pressure.
0.80 g retardation (equivalent to 37½ ft. stopping distance) with 50 lb. pedal pressure.
0.38 g retardation (equivalent to 79 ft. stopping distance) with 25 lb. pedal pressure.

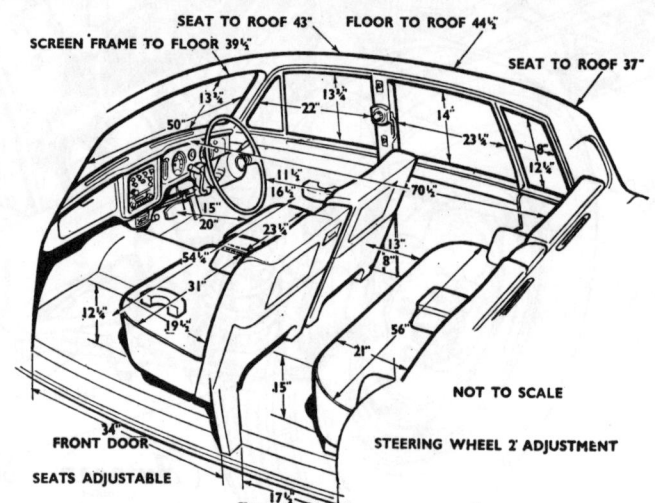

SEAT TO ROOF 43"
FLOOR TO ROOF 44½"
SEAT TO ROOF 37"
SCREEN FRAME TO FLOOR 39½"
13½" 13½" 22" 14" 23¾" 8" 12½"
50" 11½" 70½"
15" 16½" 13"
20" 23½" 8"
54½"
31"
12½" 56"
19½" 21"
15"
NOT TO SCALE
STEERING WHEEL 2" ADJUSTMENT
34"
FRONT DOOR
SEATS ADJUSTABLE
17½"
REAR DOOR

ACCELERATION TIMES from standstill
0-30 m.p.h.	..	..	..	..	5.9 sec.
0-40 m.p.h.	..	..	..	..	8.8 sec.
0-50 m.p.h.	..	..	..	..	11.3 sec.
0-60 m.p.h.	..	..	..	..	14.8 sec.
0-70 m.p.h.	..	..	..	..	19.6 sec.
0-80 m.p.h.	..	..	..	..	27.6 sec.
Standing quarter mile	..	..	..	21.1 sec.

ACCELERATION TIMES on Upper Ratios
		Top gear	"Kick down"
10-30 m.p.h.	..	—	3.7 sec.
20-40 m.p.h.	..	—	5.1 sec.
30-50 m.p.h.	..	—	5.4 sec.
40-60 m.p.h.	..	8.0 sec.	6.0 sec.
50-70 m.p.h.	..	10.3 sec.	8.3 sec.
60-80 m.p.h.	..	13.5 sec.	12.8 sec.

HILL CLIMBING at sustained steady speeds.
Max. gradient on top gear, approx. 1 in 7.3 (Tapley 305 lb./ton)
Max. gradient on 2nd gear, approx. 1 in 5.4 (Tapley 410 lb./ton)

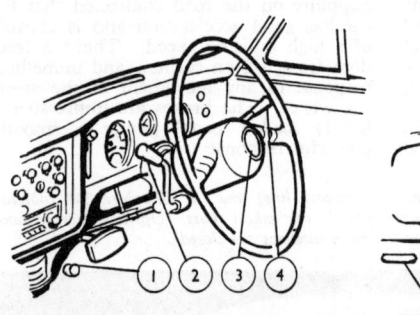

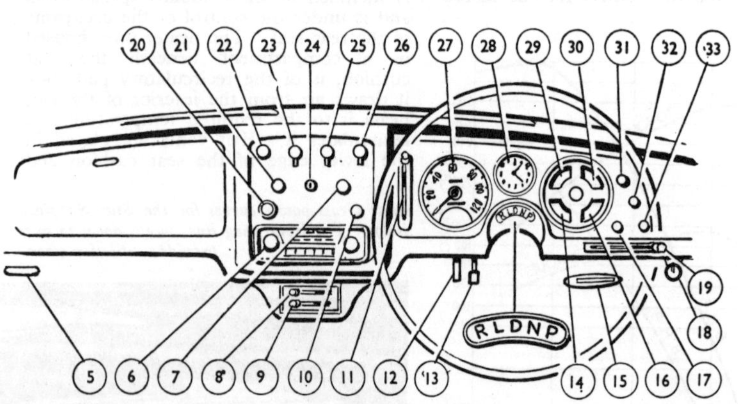

1, Headlamp dipswitch. 2, Gear selector lever. 3, Horn button. 4, Direction indicator switch and warning light. 5, Bonnet release. 6, Radio. 7, Starter switch. 8, Heater temperature control. 9, Heater / de-mister air distribution control. 10, Fog and spot lights switch. 11, "2nd gear hold" control. 12, Scuttle ventilator control. 13, Trip re-set control. 14, Oil pressure gauge. 15, Hand brake. 16, Fuel contents gauge. 17, Choke warning lamp. 18, Radiator blind. 19, Choke. 20, Cigar lighter. 21, Reserve petrol tap. 22, Panel and map reading lights switch. 23, Heater fan two-speed switch. 24, Ignition switch. 25, Windscreen wipers two-speed switch. 26, Side and headlights switch. 27, Speedometer. 28, Clock. 29, Ammeter. 30, Engine thermometer. 31, Headlamp main beam warning lamp. 32, Dynamo charge warning lamp. 33, Windscreen washer control.

The Armstrong Siddeley Star Sapphire

SMOOTHER treatment of a radiator grille which continues to carry the traditional Sphinx emblem identifies the new Star Sapphire, which proved its comfort and stamina on Alpine as well as on British roads.

Highly Civilized Motoring in a 4-litre Saloon with Power Steering, Disc Brakes and a Refined Two-pedal Transmission

GENERAL similarity of shape between the 1959 "Star Sapphire" model and the somewhat smaller-engined Armstrong Siddeleys which have been in production since October, 1952, has led many motorists to regard the latest model as just another "face lifted" old design. Driving and being driven in a Star Sapphire for several weeks, on British roads and also as far afield as southern Italy, we were delighted to find that what was a promising new design 7 years ago has, almost suddenly, now matured into a car offering the highest standards of refined motoring. At a price (inclusive of purchase tax) rather below £2,500, there is now offered a beautifully furnished car complete with almost every possible "extra," which accelerates effortlessly up to a quiet top speed of just about 100 m.p.h. and has finger-light brakes and steering.

Fundamental to the new refinement of this car is the use of an engine which, enlarged by 16%, is only asked to give 10% more power at maximum r.p.m. What is now available is really generous engine torque at moderate engine speeds, so that excellent top gear acceleration and the ability to reach a 3-figure speed are both obtained on an axle ratio which provides effortlessly silent high-speed cruising. Apart from one sparking plug on which Italian fuel formed a "whisker," the engine proved delightfully inconspicuous, starting easily, warming up readily in early summer weather, needing a quart of oil only about once per 1,000 miles and using no water in Alpine pass-storming, and giving an unashamedly heavy car notably good acceleration and hill-climbing performance.

Educated Automaticity

Very happily mated to the 165 b.h.p., 4-litre engine is a Borg-Warner automatic transmission, incorporating a hydraulic torque converter and three epicyclic gear ratios. This works very well indeed either around town or on the open road, a light touch on the throttle easing the car smoothly away from rest and bringing top gear into use at about 20 m.p.h., whereas flooring the accelerator pedal gives a very fast getaway indeed and does not let top gear engage until 60 m.p.h. is exceeded. Whilst "kick-down" changes out of top gear are always possible below 60 m.p.h., only very firm pressure on the accelerator causes a change down at speeds above 40 m.p.h. and normal acceleration is obtained quietly and smoothly in top gear.

Twice crossing the Alps and the mountain backbone of Italy, we much appreciated a unique refinement, in the form of a "2nd gear hold" control on the facia which is fully progressive in its action. Moved the whole way down its calibrated quadrant, this control keeps 2nd gear in use up to 63 m.p.h. regardless of throttle opening, but the control can be set intermediately to let top gear engage at any desired lower speed. Climbing an Alpine pass, it was often convenient to set this control to the 40 m.p.h. mark, so that on short sections of road linking hairpin corners 2nd gear remained in use, but whenever a more open length of road was reached top gear engaged normally. For a critical driver, this progressive control eliminates the main objection to the principle of automatic gearboxes by allowing him to regulate the frequency of upward and downward gear-changes, and it adds the final touch of perfection to a very attractive engine/gearbox combination.

Fully automatic transmissions which engage top gear whenever the throttle is closed can impose severe loads upon brakes, but in all our crossings of mountain passes we never discovered any weakness of this car's disc-type servo brakes; we never used the emergency 1st gear setting of the transmission to provide engine braking, yet there was never any fade, "hot smell" or loss of adjustment when Alpine passes were descended at a pace which required acceleration out of every corner followed by as rapid braking as was acceptable to passengers in a well-laden car. Furthermore, the brakes did not grab, or lose power in rainy weather, our one mildly critical comment being that the slight contact involved in their self-adjusting character occasionally made a faint rubbing noise audible as the car was driven between buildings.

Complementary to the high-torque engine and powerful brakes of this car is a standardized installation of power assisted steering which, without eliminating all "feel" from straight-road driving, makes this car at least as effortless as an 8 h.p. model to drive along winding roads—and much lighter to park. Cornering on wet roads, a driver sometimes had the impression that even greater "feel" would have let him approach the limit of tyre adhesion with more confidence that this limit would

In Brief

Price (including power steering, disc brakes and automatic transmission) £1,763 plus purchase tax £735 14s. 2d. equals £2,498 14s. 2d.

Capacity		3,990 c.c.
Unladen kerb weight ...		35 cwt.
Acceleration:		
20-40 m.p.h. in "kick-down" gear		5.1 sec.
0-50 m.p.h. through gears		11.3 sec.
Maximum direct top gear gradient		Approx. 1 in 7.3
Maximum speed		99.6 m.p.h.
"Maximile" speed		96.4 m.p.h.
Touring fuel consumption ...		15.4 m.p.g.

Gearing: 21.6 m.p.h. in top gear at 1,000 r.p.m.; 36.6 m.p.h. at 1,000 ft./min. piston speed.

The Armstrong Siddeley Star Sapphire

CONCEALED running boards assist entry to the four-door body, but greater angles of door opening would be welcome. Luxurious as well as handsome, the seats can accommodate six people when required.

"bench" is split to the right of the armrest so that individual adjustment of the two halves is possible when a central passenger is not carried. There is good room in the back, but if slight heel-wells could be contrived it would be possible to use the available toe-room even more comfortably. On first stepping into the Star Sapphire, the facia and controls seem rather to crowd upon the driver and front passenger, and limited amounts of door opening were criticized by the elderly, but after covering 1,076 miles within a period of 32 hours it was still possible to say that the seats were as comfortable as they look.

Well Furnished

A fine air of luxury is conveyed by the interior furnishing, the generous glazed areas nowadays expected being combined with polished walnut furnishing, nicely fitting pile carpets and well-applied leather upholstery. Rather small and awkward front ashtrays were criticized (that in the rear compartment is excellent), but in almost every other detail this car is furnished with all that is needed to let an owner "live" happily with it. On the facia the big glove box has a lid which opens to form a flat Formica-surfaced picnic table, and concealed in the doors are pockets which swallow up a veritable library of maps.

Screen washing sprays are standardized, as are two-speed wipers which work quietly and park themselves. Twin fog lamps (one of wide-beam pattern and the other a spotlight) supplement headlamps with commendably long but rather narrow beams which serve best on straight, uncrowded roads; there is also a reversing lamp. The steering column is adjustable for length, and the armrests on the front doors can be set to any desired height. In the tail of the body, the spare wheel and a fitted tool drawer lie below the flat car-

not inadvertently be exceeded, and at times a reduction in the movement needed to attain full lock would have been welcomed, but in the main this is a big car which offers small-car driving ease without making its driver unsure of himself.

So light are all the controls, in fact, that smooth motoring depends very much upon the driver. With the amounts of effort needed by the steering and brakes hardly greater than are applied to the accelerator pedal, the controls are (in aeronautical parlance) "well harmonized"; but, if a driver unaccustomed to such effortless controls is clumsy, it is easier for him to discomfort his passengers with alternate extremes of acceleration and braking than it is on lower-powered, less well-braked models. Driven sympathetically, the Star Sapphire is certainly one of the smoothest cars which money can buy, around town and also on open road.

In harmony with other characteristics of this highly civili ed car is a suspension system which lets it glide over reasonably well surfaced roads such as prevail in Britain and the U.S.A. in beautifully smooth fashion. At speed on the indifferently surfaced highways of some poorer countries, the suspension proves to have less damping than is desirable, the car showing a fair amount of up-and-down movement; but, whilst not at its best on bad roads, the Star Sapphire does not

bottom its springs when covering them or otherwise protest at hard work, its standards merely dropping from "exceptional" to "good average." For the sort of conditions associated with the adjective "colonial," however, a driver needs to bear in mind rather limited ground clearance beneath a central silencer and also beneath the exhaust tail-pipe.

Not in any sense of the word a sports car, this model behaves quite vicelessly when cornered fast, but with the tyre pressure recommended for sedate motoring some body roll is accompanied by easily-provoked tyre squeal. Too much extra air in the tyres provokes some body shake on rough surfaces (rubber insulation between steel body and X-braced chassis contributes to the model's exceptional quietness but not to its rigidity) but a compromise setting can be chosen which retains good comfort yet allows very fast company to be kept on winding roads. Almost entirely shock-free, the power-assisted steering nevertheless has effective self-centring action.

Without being as wide as are today's American cars, this model is quite able to seat three people abreast in either the front or rear compartment, the transmission-cover inconveniencing centrally seated passengers far less than it does in many lower-built cars. Both seats have folding central armrests, and the front

---

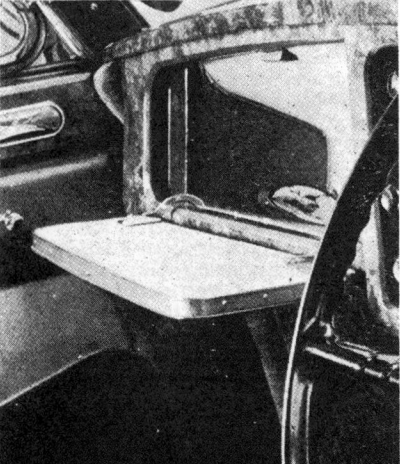

FORMICA lining of the glove-box lid invites its use as a picnic table. Also visible is the cover over a very large door pocket for guide-books.

PROGRESSIVE adjustment of the minimum speed at which top gear engages, by means of this facia-panel control, allows a driver to match the car to his personal tastes.

WARMTH for rear passengers is regulated by the temperature control and fan switch seen here mounted on a door pillar, a separate heater serving the front compartment.

STOWAGE for luggage is provided beneath a counterbalanced lift-up locker lid, on a flat carpeted floor of substantial area. The spare wheel is on a lower shelf, as is the fitted tool drawer.

peted floor of a luggage locker which, less vast than is nowadays fashionable, nevertheless is of very large capacity. Apart from the criticism that the volume of fresh air admitted by a scuttle ventilator began to seem inadequate when the outside temperature rose beyond 80° F., this car has a good heating and screen de-misting installation, supplemented by a virtually inaudible two-speed fan, and with the desirable feature of a separately-controlled heater which can blow out warm air below the rear seat and on to the rear window. The driver has a reserve tap which proved to hold back rather less than the claimed 2 gallons of petrol, and can have either full instrument lighting or an invisible glow which merely keeps the instrument pointers and figures gently fluorescent.

Although it is not likely to be a factor of prime importance to buyers of this car, the matter of fuel economy must be mentioned. In quite severe conditions 15 m.p.g. can be expected, and any British premium-grade fuel gives freedom from pinking, of which the 90-octane fuel of France produced only a faint trace. On the maintenance side, chassis greasing is only suggested at 2,500 mile intervals, the disc brakes are self-adjusting (and eventually very easy to fit with new friction pads), and the power steering requires only occasional checks on fluid level and pump-belt tension (which were still normal after our extended test).

For those who do enough motoring to value a car which is truly untiring to drive or to be driven in, who need effortless high performance rather than sporting verve, and who can afford to buy and run a high-quality car but do not wish to pay an extremely high price, the Star Sapphire must have very strong appeal. At its best on reasonably well surfaced roads, and with effortless performance and controls to make the frustrations of heavy traffic more than usually tolerable, it nevertheless also tackles rough surfaces at least as well as most other cars, and either up or down a mountain pass is apt to surprise the drivers of sporting models by its rapidity.

Specification

Engine

Cylinders 6
Bore ... ... 97 mm.
Stroke ... ... 90 mm.
Cubic capacity ... ... 3,990 c.c.
Piston area ... ... 68.72 sq.in.
Valves ... O.H.V. (2 lines inclined at 70°) operated by pushrods and rockers
Compression ratio 7.5/1
Carburetters ... 2 Stromberg DIV42 downdraught
Fuel pump ... ... AC mechanical
Ignition timing control ... ... Centrifugal and vacuum
Oil filter ... ...Purolator full-flow
Max. power (gross) ... ... 165 b.h.p. (145 b.h.p. net)
at ... ... 4,250 r.p.m.
Piston speed at max. b.h.p. 2,510 ft./min.

Transmission

Clutch ... Hydraulic torque converter
Top gear 3.77
2nd gear 5.41
1st gear 8.674
Reverse 7.574
Propeller shaft Hardy Spicer divided open
Final drive... ... ... Hypoid bevel
Top gear m.p.h. at 1,000 r.p.m. 21.6
Top gear m.p.h. at 1,000 ft./min. piston speed 36.6

Chassis

Brakes: Girling Vac-hydro power-assisted hydraulic (disc front, drum rear).
Brake dimensions:
Front discs ... ... 12 in. dia.
Rear drums ... ... 12 in. x 2¼ in.
Friction lining area ... 30.5 sq. in. front plus 90 sq. in. rear
Suspension:
Front ... Independent by coil springs, trailing wishbones and anti-roll torsion bar
Rear ... ... Semi-elliptic leaf springs and rigid axle
Shock absorbers ... Armstrong telescopic
Steering gear ... ... Burman integral power steering
Tyres ... Dunlop tubeless, 6.70—16

Coachwork and Equipment

Starting handle ... ... No
Battery mounting ... ... On scuttle
Jack ... ... Smith's Bevelift
Jacking points ... 4 external (front bumper brackets and rear springs)
Standard tool kit: Jack, wheelbrace, set of open-jaw and box spanners in fitted tool drawer, adjustable spanner, pliers, distributor key, tyre valve key, carburetter jet key, timing pin, tyre pressure gauge, grease gun.
Exterior lights: 2 headlamps, 2 sidelamps, wide-beam lamp, spotlight, 2 stop/tail lamps, number plate lamp, reversing lamp.
Number of electrical fuses... ... Two
Direction indicators ... Self-cancelling amber flashers
Windscreen wipers ... ... Electrical two-speed two-blade, self parking
Windscreen washers Trico vacuum operated
Sun visors ... ... Two, hinge mounted
Instruments: Speedometer with decimal trip distance recorder, ammeter, fuel contents gauge, oil pressure gauge, coolant thermometer, clock.
Warning lights: Dynamo charge, headlamp main beam, choke, direction indicators.
Locks: With ignition key... Ignition switch and driver's door
With other key ... Luggage locker
Glove lockers ... One on facia, with lid
Map pockets: 2 large compartments in front doors, 2 pockets behind front seats.
Parcel shelves ... ... None
Ashtrays ... ... 2 in front doors, 1 behind front seat
Cigar lighters ... ... 1 on facia panel
Interior lights: 2 on body pillars, with manual switch and courtesy switches on all doors.
Interior heater: Fresh air type (with intake shutter closed, air is re-circulated) with screen de-misters. Separate re-circulating heater in rear compartment de-mists rear window.
Car radio: Optional extra H.M.V. Radiomobile (provision for second speaker in rear compartment).
Extras available ... ... None
Upholstery material ... ... Leather
Floor covering ... ... Pile carpet
Exterior colours standardized: 9 colours (and combinations thereof) and 8 interior trim colours (also combinations thereof).
Alternative body styles ... ... None

Maintenance

Sump ... ... 14 pints S.A.E. 30 summer, S.A.E. 20 winter
Gearbox 15 pints automatic transmission fluid
Rear axle 2½ pints S.A.E. 90 hypoid gear oil
Steering gear lubricant Automatic transmission fluid
Cooling system capacity 26 pints (2 drain taps)
Chassis lubrication: By grease gun every 2,500 miles to 17 points.
Ignition timing 3–5 degrees before T.D.C. static
Contact-breaker gap ... ... 0.015 in.
Sparking plug type... Lodge HLN, 14 mm.
Sparking plug gap ... ... 0.028 in.
Valve timing: Inlet opens 12 degrees before T.D.C. and closes 48 degrees after B.D.C. Exhaust opens 48 degrees before B.D.C. and closes 12 degrees after T.D.C.
Tappet clearances (Cold): Inlet and exhaust 0.008 in.
Front wheel toe-in ... ... 1/8 in. to 3/16 in.
Camber angle ... ¾ degrees to 1¼ degrees
Castor angle ... 1¼ degrees to 1¾ degrees
Steering swivel pin inclination ... 5½ degrees
Tyre pressures:
Front ... ... 22–24 lb.
Rear 22–26 lb., according to speed and load
Brake fluid ... Girling heavy-duty Crimson
Battery type and capacity: Lucas 12-volt, 64 amp. hr.

A CAR of ultra-conservative, almost old-fashioned appearance, the Star Sapphire has sports car performance.

been reached where virtually no high-powered luxury cars are being sold with manual gearboxes, and so it is not necessary to offer alternative transmissions.

Disc brakes are fitted in front, and large drums at the rear. The discs are shielded from water which may be splashed from the road, and the vacuum servo has a large reservoir. A pistol-grip parking brake is hidden under the dashboard.

Of all-steel construction, the body is rust-proofed and sprayed with sound-deadening material. Extremely comfortable seats are fitted, and though the front ones are separate, they may be used as a bench if the central arm rest is folded away. The upholstery and carpets are of the highest quality, as is the walnut veneer which is used extensively on the body interior. A

John Bolster Tests . . .
The Armstrong Siddeley Star Sapphire

IF ever there were a wolf in sheep's clothing, this is it! Imagine a very large car of ultra-conservative, indeed almost old-fashioned appearance, with all the walnut panelling, leather upholstery, and elaborate equipment of the traditional British limousine. That is a fair description of the Armstrong Siddeley Star Sapphire.

Then, imagine a car with kick-in-the-back acceleration, an easy 100 m.p.h. performance, sports car roadholding, and immensely powerful brakes. That, too, is a fair description of the Armstrong Siddeley Star Sapphire!

The heart of the new car is a 4-litre 6-cylinder over-square engine, with pushrod operated inclined valves in hemispherical combustion chambers. The block and head are of cast iron, and the main and big end bearings are

Vandervell lead-indium shells. Two Stromberg downdraught carburetters are fitted with large air silencers which lie across the top of the engine. Compared with previous Armstrong Siddeley power units, a very great increase in torque has been achieved in the valuable middle ranges, and 165 b.h.p. is developed at the quite moderate speed of 4,250 r.p.m.

There is nothing unconventional about the chassis frame, though the details work repays close study. The front wishbones have a considerable angle of trail, and the rubber bump stops, front and rear, come into action easily, becoming graduated auxiliary springs in effect. Power-assisted steering is built into the chassis as standard, and a Borg Warner automatic gearbox is also a part of the specification. A point has now

separate heating system for the rear compartment has a control on the central right door pillar, and efficiently demists the back window—a most valuable safety feature. The steering column has an effective adjuster which is hidden from view.

The Star Sapphire is therefore an exceptionally well appointed 5/6-seater luxury carriage. It has large wheels to permit smooth riding at speed over bad roads, and every modern device has been incorporated to make the driver's work as easy as possible. A large and efficient engine ensures that a useful performance shall be available, and the highest standards of British engineering ensure a long life. Yet, there is much more to it than that.

I found that all the doors were easy to enter, and that they closed with the

THE driving position (left) is excellent, and the car, says Bolster "is just about the most lavishly equipped on the market". INSTRUMENTS, as seen from the back seat, are well placed and easily read.

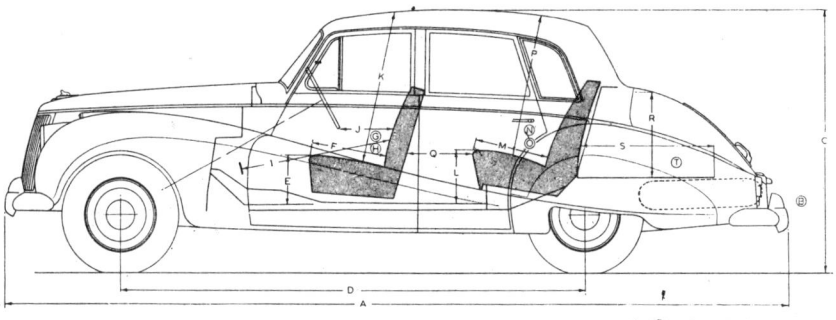

ARMSTRONG SIDDELEY STAR SAPPHIRE

Dimensions and Seating Arrangement Plan

A. Overall length 16ft. 2in.
B. Overall width 6ft. 2in.
C. Overall height 5ft. 2in.
D. Wheelbase 9ft. 6in.
E. Height of front seat cushion 1ft. 0½in.
F. Depth of front seat cushion 1ft. 6in.
G. Width of front seat 4ft. 5¼in.
H. Width between arm rests (front seat 3ft. 11½in.
I. Pedals to seat squab min. 3ft. 10in., max. 3ft. 3in.
J. Steering wheel to seat squab 1ft. 1½in. adjustable.

K. Height from cushion to roof (front) 3ft. 0in.
L. Height of rear seat cushion 1ft. 1in.
M. Depth of rear seat cushion 1ft. 6in.
N. Width of rear seat 4ft. 5½in.
O. Width between arm rests (rear seat) 3ft. 11½in.
P. Height from cushion to roof (rear) 2ft. 10in.
Q. Leg room between front and rear seats min. 10¼in., max. 1ft. 3¼in.
R. Height of Luggage boot 1ft. 8in.
S. Depth of luggage boot 2ft. 4½in.
T. Width of luggage boot 4ft. 6in.

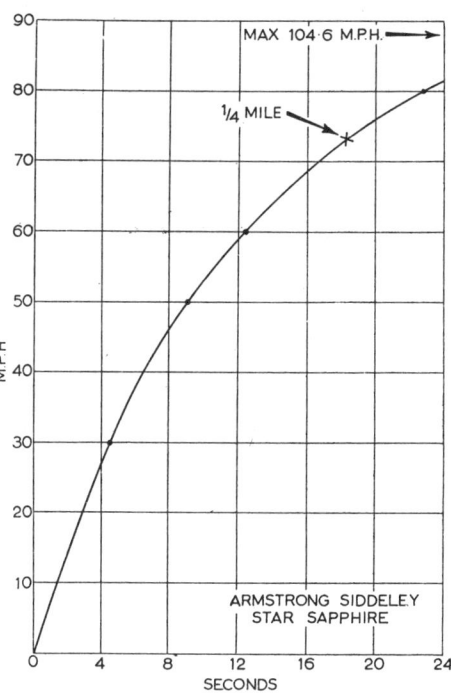

MAX 104·6 M.P.H.

¼ MILE

ARMSTRONG SIDDELEY STAR SAPPHIRE

ACCELERATION GRAPH

gentle click that has for long been the hallmark of quality coachbuilding. The driving position is excellent, and the all-round visibility is quite good, though a wrap-around rear window is not featured, being out of keeping with the severe body lines. The engine starts easily, though one must avoid "over-choking," and the idling speed is slow and regular. This is an important point, for a fast tickover inevitably causes some creeping with an automatic trans-mission. The Star Sapphire is one of the very few "automatics" which never attempts to creep away while the engine is ticking over.

When one drives off, it is at once obvious that the pulling power of the engine is quite out of the ordinary. The engineers of Borg Warner have appre-ciated this, and have married the power unit to a gearbox which permits it to do a lot of its work on top gear. There is, of course, the usual "kick down" if one presses the accelerator to the floor, and there is also a graduated control for "holding" second gear up to various indicated speeds; this is an exclusive feature. However, for most journeys it is particularly pleasant to stay in top gear, which is done simply by using the accelerator pedal with a little restraint at low speeds. The big machine is really lively, and the pick up on top gear is equal to the third gear acceleration of less powerful cars. Yet, that "kick down" is there when it is wanted, and one overtakes slower vehicles with a sudden, silent rush.

The acceleration graph repays close study. A standing quarter mile accom-plished in 18.2 seconds indicates accelera-tion that is right out of the ordniary. There is, too, the impressive way in which the surge continues well past the 80 m.p.h. mark. That hefty six-cylinder engine is more than master of the big body it has to pull, and even at maximum revolutions it remains smooth and quiet. Early in the morning, I covered many miles at a genuine 100 m.p.h., and there was not the slightest impression that the power unit was being pressed. At all times, there is a "soft-

ness" and silence about the car that one associates only with the most costly machines.

This is by no means a low car, but there is surprisingly little roll on sharp corners. The roadholding is very good, and somehow gives a feeling of con-fidence to the driver on quite short acquaintanceship. Although the power-assisted steering is light at all speeds, it does not lack "feel." I found myself tempted to throw the Star Sapphire around like a sports car, and what is the good of temptation if you don't give way to it? The suspension, both front and rear, has considerable travel, and is not damped particularly heavily. Yet, the car always feels steady and under full control.

A big, fast car presents serious problems to the brake manufacturer. I am happy to say that these prob-lems have been completely over-come, and the Girling brakes can stand up easily to the most ruthless driving. The power-assisted steering has per-mitted a reasonably "quick" ratio to be chosen, and in consequence an incipient skid on wet roads may be killed at birth. In general, though, this Armstrong Siddleley is particularly free from skidding even on dangerous surfaces.

The sturdy construction and elaborate equipment of the vehicle inevitably dictate that the weight shall be fairly substantial. To accelerate more than a ton and three quarters up to high speeds must consume a fair amount of petrol, however efficient the engine may be. Under the circumstances, an average of 17 m.p.g. cannot be regarded as excessive, and an extra mile or two per gallon would be the bonus of a more moderate driver. Even when one drives as hard as possible on fast roads, the consumption does not fall below 15 m.p.g.

The Star Sapphire is not the kind of car which attracts a crowd, for it is entirely unobtrusive in appearance, apart from its size. That it does not look anything like as fast as it is may be considered an advantage by some pros-pective buyers. It must be admitted that

many hurrying motorists stared in amazement as the great carriage flashed past them and disappeared irrevocably into the distance.

There are some drivers who have tried an automatic transmission but have returned to a clutch and gear lever without regret. If they were to try this car, I think that they would change their minds. The very high torque of the engine demands the minimum of gear changing, as the machine is never fussy, yet the Borg Warner gearbox can produce performance figures which it would be difficult to equal with a manual box. The graduated "hold" control for second speed may add interest when one feels in the mood for a personal variation of the speed and frequency of upward changes. Person-ally, I confined its use to the ascent of winding or traffic-infested hills.

Much the same sort of comment may be made on the power-assisted steering, for some types have been marketed which were altogether too vague in their response. Nobody could object to the "feel" of this steering, yet it is outstand-ingly light, particularly for parking. The point is that it is an integral part of the design, and not an optional extra hung onto an existing car. As the brakes are also servo-assisted, it can be stated that all the controls are at least as light as those of the smallest cars.

The new Armstrong Siddeley is easily the best car that its makers have ever produced. It is just about the most lavishly equipped car on the market, and it combines exceptionally smooth and silent running with a really brilliant performance. Among luxury vehicles, it cannot be considered to be expensive.

The Autocar
ROAD TESTS
1742

Armstrong
Siddeley
Star Sapphire

The traditional lines of the Star Sapphire belie its very modern performance. Fog and spot lamps are standard

AT the last London Show, the Armstrong Siddeley Star Sapphire made its bow; since then it has earned the reputation of being quite the best model to come from these manufacturers for some years. The full Road Test which it has now been possible to complete confirms this view, for the staid appearance gives no hint of the high performance and many of the road-holding virtues of a good sports car. The power-assisted steering is feather-light, and the disc front, drum rear brakes with vacuum servo assistance are splendid. Yet there is no fuss, and as a docile, luxuriously-appointed town carriage, owner- or chauffeur-driven, the Star Sapphire has few equals even beyond its price range. In town and on the open road the automatic transmission, fitted as standard like the power-assisted steering and disc brakes, proves well suited to the characteristics of the 4-litre six-cylinder engine. It also has the unique feature of a variable speed setting for the intermediate gear hold.

With an average load the all-up weight approaches two tons, which may give some indication of the great strength of the chassis frame and other major components, including the "separate" body. Clearly no structural sacrifice has been made for the sake of weight reduction, and it is to the credit of the over-square, 165 (gross) b.h.p. power unit that the acceleration is so brisk. Upon initial examination of the car the immediate impression is of quality, evident in general and in detail. The carpeting and leather upholstery are of top grade, and rich walnut veneer is used tastefully.

In the extent of its equipment, too, this Star shines. Within reach of driver or rear passenger there are separate controls for regulating the heating of the rear compartment, and the system includes a very useful pair of demisting slots for the back window. Each of four occupants has an individual, hinged ventilator window and can rest both elbows, unless room is made for five or six passengers. In addition to the locker in the facia, there is good space for cameras, maps and other oddments in the front doors, and in the front seat backrests are further compartments for the convenience of rear passengers. The inside of the facia locker lid, covered with Formica, drops down to make a useful table. Strangely, it cannot be locked.

Other equipment, by no means run-of-the-mill, includes a fine set of small tools fitted in a rubber-lined drawer in the luggage locker, the rubber being soft and thick, so that although the tools are held securely they can be removed easily. A vanity mirror is on the back of the passenger's flush fitting sun vizor, and there is a cigarette lighter mounted centrally in the facia. Everyone in the car has an ashtray within reach.

Further attractive items of equipment are apparent when the car is put to work. In many ways this Star Sapphire is a driver's car. For example, the choke control is a manually-operated lever sliding in a horizontal quadrant; it stays put in any position to which it is set, and a red warning light guards against absentmindedness. In the fairly warm weather which prevailed during the test it was never absolutely necessary to use the choke, although a slight application—not enough to make the engine idle too quickly for manœuvring—was useful if the car was to be driven off as soon as the engine fired. The warm-up was quick, and a normal tickover without choke was achieved in a matter of moments.

Before discussing the performance it is worth while to have a closer look at the Borg-Warner transmission, and particularly at the gear hold system. The three-speed box has torque multiplication of the lower ratios in the customary B.-W. fashion. First rises from 17.35 to 8.67, second starts at 10.80 rising to 5.41, and top is direct at 3.77 to 1. With Drive selected and the throttle fully depressed, maxima on first and second are 36 and 65 m.p.h. If Low is engaged, the transmission will not change out of first, in which the maximum goes up to about 44 m.p.h. —with no governor to protect the engine from overspeeding.

The intermediate hold has two functions. Its control lever, working in the vertical plane, may be set to any speed from 20 to the 65 m.p.h. maximum. If maximum is selected, for example, then every time the throttle is opened below that speed intermediate will be engaged. The car free-wheels on over-run, and the box changes into top when 65 is exceeded. On winding, flat or downhill roads the usefulness of the gear hold is reduced by the free-wheeling on over-run, but the mechanism has its uses,

The comprehensive array of instruments includes a clock between the main dials. The choke lever is at the lower edge of the facia on the right, and the intermediate gear hold control is beside the speedometer

Armstrong Siddeley Star Sapphire

While rear seat passengers enjoy a measure of privacy, all-round visibility is not seriously impaired. Wide doors are hinged at their leading edges, and all four windows on each side may be opened

particularly when fast climbing on tortuous roads is required. Whenever the hold is set above 25 m.p.h., first gear does not engage at all. Such are the engine characteristics that, allied with this transmission, intermediate is a good gear for starting from rest. It provides a little extra silkiness in town, coupled with a reduction in fuel consumption. For most purposes, therefore, a setting of about 30 m.p.h. on the gear hold lever is satisfactory, and the lever can be returned to its minimum setting if first gear is required for fast getaways.

As usual, a kick-down switch is provided so that at appropriate speeds, lower ratios may be engaged immediately the throttle pedal is' pressed right down. Alternatively, practically full throttle can be used in top and intermediate without a gear change necessarily taking place; for this the throttle pedal must not be pressed hard enough to operate the switch. Most of the acceleration figures on individual ratios given in the data tables were obtained in this way, and the vigorous acceleration is praiseworthy, considering the size and weight. A standing-start quarter mile in comfortably under 20sec is good, and at the end of this distance the speedometer records a true 70 m.p.h. The more prosaic 30 m.p.h. can be reached in 4.6sec and 80 m.p.h.—a particularly pleasant cruising speed in suitable circumstances—in 26sec exactly.

Normal upward and downward changes, and snap kickdowns alike, are made smoothly; indeed the transmission as a whole suits the car very happily. In addition to the gear selections already mentioned, there are, of course, neutral and reverse, and a park position which locks the transmission completely. The starter can be put in circuit only when the selector is at Neutral or Park.

A cruising speed of 80 m.p.h. has been mentioned; it should be added that the Star Sapphire will top the true 100 m.p.h. with negligible engine fuss. The power is delivered unobtrusively, and with 21.6 m.p.h. per 1,000 r.p.m. available in top gear, even a three-figure speed is provided at no more than about 4,600 r.p.m. which is not excessive for an engine with such a relatively short stroke. Throughout the rev. range the unit remains really smooth, and never is there any suggestion of strain. However, high cruising speeds produce very distinct wind roar around the body; the opening of a ventilator window at speed is enough to rule out comfortable use of the radio.

While running costs may not be a major consideration when set against the price of a car in this class, the fuel consumption of the Star Sapphire is such that even the 16-gallon tank allows a safe range of some 200 miles only. Consumption of the car tested was under 10 m.p.g. in the worst possible rush hour traffic. Driven really hard on the open road, the car covered not more than 14 miles to the gallon, reaching 16.6 m.p.g. only when driven quietly at cruising speeds in the lower fifties. Carburation was not perfect and the slow running was set too fast, causing quite powerful creep from a standstill in Drive unless the car was held by the brake. The model has a reputation of being

free from such troubles, and almost certainly better fuel economy could be achieved with more careful tuning.

Few cars of this size achieve such a high standard of suspension. While it feels firm at all times, there is no harshness, and nothing to mar the impression of an impeccably-mannered town carriage. Yet on open, twisting roads in England one finds the degree of roll finely limited, and the nearly neutral steering characteristics enable fast corners to be taken very quickly indeed. This attribute, perhaps, is not of special interest to many buyers, but it provides a big safety margin.

Standard tyres are Dunlop Gold Seal and these, of 6.70in section on 16in wheels, help to give a smooth ride over indifferent surfaces. This type of tyre is entirely suitable with only the proviso that anyone likely to maintain maximum speed for long periods should substitute Road Speed tyres or their equivalents—Road Speed tyres were used in a prolonged check on the car's maximum performance.

Most of the effort is taken out of steering by the power assistance, it being possible to complete parking manoeuvres easily with one hand. The turning circles between kerbs of 34ft 9in (left) and 37ft are excellent for a car of this size, but the four turns required from lock to lock might perhaps be reduced, thanks to the power assistance available, to give a gain in sensitivity. Occasionally one feels the effect of the power cutting in and out, as for example when a series

The six-cylinder, four-litre engine is fed by two Stromberg carburetters of Zenith manufacture, each having a big air-cleaner-silencer. A special spanner is provided for removing the recessed sparking plugs. The bonnet lid is not self-supporting

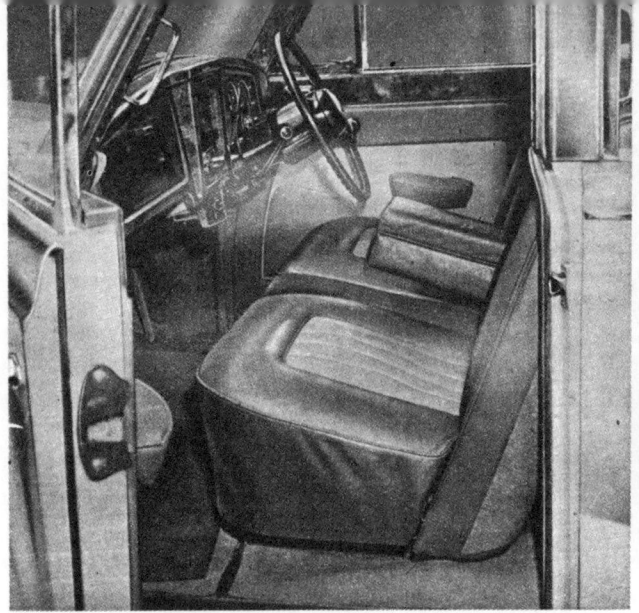

Each passenger has an armrest, a grab handle and provision for stowing oddments. The quality of the finish and appointments is exceptionally high

of small changes in direction are made on a well-cambered road, but generally the mechanism cannot be faulted. There is less feel than with fully manual steering, and this must be taken into account when the roads are slippery. Little tremor passes back from road to wheel, and even this is confined to occasions when the going is rough.

Braking deserves full marks in nearly all respects. Cars with discs at the front and drums at the rear can suffer when operating heat produces differing effects fore and aft, but this problem has been overcome in the Star Sapphire's Girling system. On every occasion the car stopped all square and, measured at 30 m.p.h., efficiency reached the high figure of 93 per cent. The powerful servo, with a big vacuum reservoir, makes pedal pressures as light as anyone could wish, yet there is no lack of sensitivity. The drum brakes are silent, and only occasionally at low speed is there any squeak from the discs. The brake pedal is of the normal size found in three-pedal layouts, presumably because of its proximity to the steering column. A wider pedal which could be used with the left foot during restarts on inclines for example, would be preferred.

The handbrake lever is of the pull-out type under the facia, but that on the car tested was not adequate for holding the vehicle on any appreciable slope. The Park position of the transmission was selected when at rest, to ensure full security.

It was mentioned earlier that the Star Sapphire, in addition to its other accomplishments, is a driver's car. More than the speed and handling prompt this conclusion, for the driving position is exceptionally good—one of the best encountered. The driver sits well up and is semi-independent of his one or two front seat companions. While the seating may be made into a bench by aligning the two sections, the driver has individual control of rather more than a third of the area available. The steering wheel is placed low, where its upper section does not intrude at all into vision above facia level. It is adjustable, with the mechanism concealed; short and tall drivers alike find that they can adopt a good position in relation to wheel and pedals.

Instruments, set in the walnut facia directly in front of the driver, can be read easily through the upper part of the wheel. Included are speedometer with trip and total mileage recorders, clock, ammeter, and gauges for oil pressure, fuel level and coolant temperature. There are indicator lights for choke, ignition, direction indicators and main lamp beam. In addition to a radiator blind, other items not always found as standard equipment include the two speed wipers, windscreen washer, two-speed heater fan, fresh air ventilator on the scuttle, fog and spot lamps and a petrol reserve switch. Several of the switches are mounted centrally, but all are easily reached. The bonnet release is on the passenger's side of the car.

There is an ashtray in each front door, and, when in use, that on the driver's side, in conjunction with the indicator lever and the proximity of the steering wheel, makes operation of the window rather awkward.

A good balance has been struck between the degree of privacy associated with this type of carriage and the demand for all-round visibility. While the rear window is smaller than most in current use, rearward visibility is satisfactory; the side windows, terminating in the rearward ventilator panels, run well back to avoid any serious blind spots. Screen pillars are thick, but do not affect forward vision seriously. In fact, visibility is better than appearances would suggest at first sight.

Because of the amount of glass in the sides, passengers in the rear compartment have an excellent view, improved further by a higher-than-average seating position. Reasonable leg room and particularly well shaped and padded seating help also to make the rear compartment very pleasant for travel.

Horns are penetrating without being offensive, and the lamps give range for fast travel, and suitable cut-off on dip, without annoying other road-users. The luggage locker

A range of hand tools and spares is provided in a tray which fits under the upper floor of the locker, above the jack. The spare wheel is clear of luggage, and the locker itself is carpeted to the same high standard as the passenger compartment

Armstrong Siddeley Star Sapphire . . .

is quite big, though not ideally shaped, and is lined with high grade carpet. The spare wheel is held in a separate compartment under the floor alongside the jack, wheel brace, and the tray of small tools. The self-supporting lid does not necessarily need a key to open it, but its curvature is such that care is advisable when using the boot to avoid knocking the head.

Quite apart from the extremely wide choice of colour combinations available, and the evidence, rather rare these days, of skilled handwork and individual attention to detail of finish, three qualities in particular give the Star Sapphire its appeal: handling and performance close to sports car standards, town carriage behaviour when required, and the luxury of its appointments.

ARMSTRONG SIDDELEY STAR SAPPHIRE

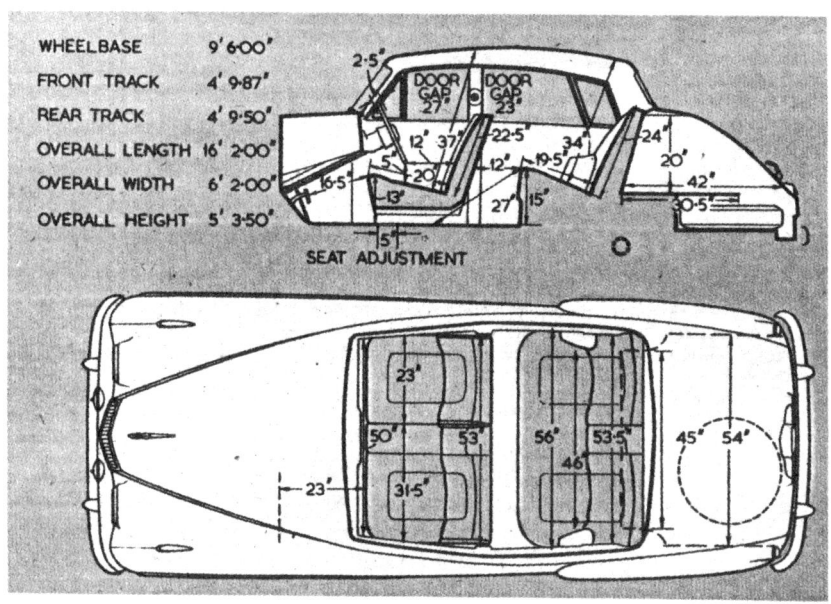

Scale ¼in to 1ft. Driving seat in central position. Cushions uncompressed.

- DATA -

PRICE (basic), with saloon body, £1,763
British purchase tax, £735 14s 2d.
Total (in Great Britain), £2,489 14s 2d.

ENGINE: Capacity, 3,990 c.c. (243.5 cu in)
Number of cylinders: 6.
Bore and stroke: 97 × 90 mm (3,818 × 3,543in)
Valve gear: o.h.v., pushrods.
Compression ratio: 7.5 to 1.
B.H.P.: 165 at 4,250 r.p.m. (B.H.P. per ton laden 86.7).
Torque: 260lb ft at 2,000 r.p.m.
M.P.H. per 1,000 r.p.m. in top gear: 21.8.

WEIGHT (with 5 gal. fuel): 35.06 cwt (3,927 lb).
Weight distribution (per cent): F, 53.1; R, 46.9.
Laden as tested: 38.06 cwt (4,263lb).
Lb per c.c. (laden): 1.3.

BRAKES: Type: Girling.
Method of operation: Vacuum hydraulic with servo and vacuum reservoir.
Drum dimensions: R, 12in diameter; 2¼in wide.
Disc diameter· F, 12in.
Swept area: F, 280 sq in; lining area: R, 90 sq in.

TYRES: 6.70 × 16in.
Pressures (lb sq in): F, 22; R, 22 (normal). F, 24; R, 26 (fast driving).

TANK CAPACITY: 16 Imperial gallons.
Oil sump: 14 pints.
Cooling system: 26 pints.

STEERING: Turning circle:
Between kerbs: R, 37ft. L, 34ft 9in.
Between walls: R, 39ft. L, 36ft. 9in.
Turns of steering wheel from lock to lock: 4.

DIMENSIONS: Wheelbase: 9ft 6in.
Track: F, 4ft 9⅞in; R, 4ft 9½in.
Length (overall): 16ft 2in.
Width: 6ft 2in.
Height: 5ft 3½in.
Ground clearance: 8½in.
Frontal area: 25.3 sq ft (approximately).

ELECTRICAL SYSTEM: 12-volt; 64 ampère-hour battery.
Head lights: Double dip; 48-48 watt bulbs.

SUSPENSION: Front: independent coil springs. Anti-roll bar. Rear: Live axle, semi-elliptic springs.

PERFORMANCE

ACCELERATION (mean):

Speed Range, Gear Ratios and Time in sec.

m.p.h.	3.77 to 1	10.80 to 1 5.41 to 1	17.35 to 1 8.674 to 1
10—30 ..	—	—	3.6
20—40 ..	—	5.3	—
30—50 ..	8.9	6.3	—
40—60 ..	9.8	7.3	—
50—70 ..	10.8	—	—
60—80 ..	13.1	—	—
70—90 ..	—	—	—
80—100 ..	—	—	—

From rest through gears to:

30 m.p.h.	..	4.6 sec.
40 ,,	..	6.9 ,,
50 ,,	..	10.1 ,,
60 ,,	..	14.2 ,,
70 ,,	..	19.6 ,,
80 ,,	..	26.0 ,,

Standing quarter mile 19.2 sec.

MAXIMUM SPEEDS ON GEARS:

Gear		m.p.h.	k.p.h.
Direct	(mean)	99.8	160.7
	(best)	102.2	164.5
Intermediate	..	65	104.6
Low	..	36—44	57.9—70.8

TRACTIVE EFFORT (by Tapley meter):

	Pull (lb per ton)	Equivalent Gradient
Top	315	1 in 7.2
Intermediate ..	450	1 in 4.9

BRAKES: (at 30 m.p.h. in neutral)

Pedal load in lb	Retardation	Equivalent stopping distance in ft
25	0.34g	89
50	0.78g	40
60	0.93g	32

FUEL CONSUMPTION:

Steady speeds in direct top:

30 m.p.h.	21.2	m.p.g.
40 ,,	18.0	,,
50 ,,	16.3	,,
60 ,,	15.6	,,
70 ,,	14.0	,,
80 ,,	13.7	,,
90 ,,	11.4	,,

Overall fuel consumption for 1,235 miles, 14.1 m.p.g. (20.0 litres per 100 km).
Approximate normal range 10-17 m.p.g. (28-16.6 litres per 100 km).
Fuel: Premium grade.

TEST CONDITIONS: Weather: dry, still. Air temperature 72 deg F.
Model described in *The Autocar* of 17 October 1958.

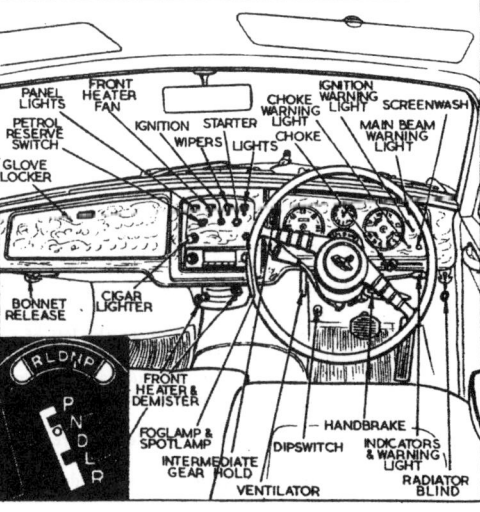

SPEEDOMETER CORRECTION: M.P.H.

Car speedometer:	10	20	30	40	50	60	70	80	90	100
Electric speed:	11	20	29	38	48	57	66	76	85	95

The Armstrong Siddeley Star Sapphire

A Gentleman's Motor Carriage which is Extremely Easy to Drive Yet Exceeds 100 m.p.h., with the Security of Girling Disc Brakes.

BRITAIN still manufactures high-class beautifully-appointed luxury cars which have no equal anywhere in the World. Such a car is the Armstrong Siddeley Star Sapphire which was introduced at the time of the last London Motor Show. This 100 m.p.h. gentleman's carriage has many interesting and commendable features, such as a 4-litre six-cylinder "over-square" engine with inclined o.h. valves operated, not by an overhead camshaft but by different length push-rods and rockers, fully automatic gearbox with an ingenious form of "hold" selector, Girling disc brakes on the front wheels and a separate heating and ventilating system for the rear compartment which includes rear-window de-misting. These aspects of the impressive Star Sapphire are apparent when examining the car but only road experience brings out the ease with which this large, powerful car can be driven. Such ease of handling transcends the control afforded by two-pedal control and disc braking and stems from excellent forward visibility over a low-set steering wheel and the feeling that this isn't such a wide vehicle as some other V.I.P. carriages.

In fact, although there is accommodation for six persons in great comfort in this newest Armstrong Siddeley, the Star Sapphire does not spread itself as do other cars in the same category. The four-door body is relatively close-coupled and there is scarcely any parcels storage between back seat and rear window. Thus there is just a flavour of the sports saloon about this dignified motor car that stems, perhaps, from its great forebear, the Siddeley Special. However, this Star Sapphire makes little concession to modernity, with normal windscreen, long bonnet which masks the near-side wing, thick screen pillars, and a rear window which makes no pretence at wrap-round. Indeed, while slaking our thirst in the bar of a remote country inn at Tangley we were amused to find, on catching sight through the open door of just the vee-radiator grille and bonnet of the modern Armstrong Siddeley in the car park outside, that it reminded us irresistably of the original Thirty of forty years earlier.

It is the slimness of the front of the car and the view from a driving seat set up like a club armchair, rather than a wide field of vision which would necessitate a brief bonnet and thin screen pillars, that makes a driver feel at home in the Star Sapphire even in heavy traffic. He is also greatly reassured by the smooth functioning of the Borg Warner automatic transmission, the finger-light Burman power steering and the Girling disc brake security, the brakes being vacuum-servo assisted.

The deep burr walnut facia contains a huge non-lockable cubby hole, a recessed central switch panel, and three dials before the driver, the last-named consisting of a Smith's 120 m.p.h. speedometer with trip and total mileometers, an extremely accurate clock and a four-in-one dial dealing with oil-pressure, amps, water temperature and fuel contents. A stalk on the right of the steering column controls the flashers, this being the sort with indicator light at its extremity, rather crude for a car of this class. Radio and heater controls for the front compartment are below the central panel. There are nine neat but confusing switches, three of which have pendant finger grips. These latter control the two-speed heater fan, two-speed wipers and lamps, the remainder looking after panel and map-reading lights, petrol reserve, starter and fog and spot lamps. The ignition key is separate from the starter button. A cigar-lighter is provided. Three warning lights to the right of the driver on the facia warn of full lamps beam, no dynamo charge, and choke control in use. These are flanked by the washers button. The choke control is in the form of a lever sliding across a quadrant. A scuttle ventilator is fitted and the control for the notable separate rear-compartment heating, ventilation and de-misting consists of a knob on the r.h. door pillar.

The gear lever is cranked up to the left of the steering column to give the usual R, L, D, N and P control over Mr. Borg Warner's automation. This lettered quadrant is illuminated permanently when the car is in use, which is excellent in daytime but a bit dazzling after dark.

Instead of a flick-switch or selector lever for obtaining a hold over second gear, the Star Sapphire has its own unique system. An upright quadrant to the left of the speedometer has a lever which can be set to 20, 30, 40, 50 or 65 m.p.h., second gear being held until the selected speed is reached. This is a pleasing idea, but in practice it is likely that while auntie will leave the thing at "20" and the press-on driver will have it permanently at "65," intermediate positions will seldom be used. Indeed, the big 165 b.h.p. 4-litre engine of this Armstrong Siddeley does most of its work in the 3.77 to 1 top gear and although accelerator kick-down control of the gearbox is also provided the action is comparatively stiff, encouraging this effortless top gear motoring.

Without interference, upward changes happen at 37 and 63 m.p.h. and thereafter the Star Sapphire will accelerate to fractionally over 100 m.p.h. under ideal conditions. Acceleration is not as brisk as that of some other luxury cars but is adequate.

The Star Sapphire is luxuriously equipped, both front doors having adjustable arm-rests and deep pockets with spring-loaded lids. The front seats are in the form of separate arm-chairs, the passenger's being wider than the driver's so that, with the central arm-rest retracted, three can be carried abreast. The back seat has a very high back and central arm-rest, and the rear quarter-lights open. The doors shut nicely and have effective "keeps," high-quality leather upholstery is used, and there are vestigial running-boards. The back of the front seat squabs contains two spring-loaded pockets and a central ash-tray and the aged are assisted in rising from the back seat by metal grabs on the door pillars. Swivel ashtrays are found in the front-doors and the cubby-hole lid is lined with Formica to provide a small picnic table.

As the car is rather close-coupled the bases of the front seats are cut away to give foot room to back-seat passengers but they are still limited in respect of head space and top hats would have to be removed. There is an interior light operated by opening the doors or using its switch on the off-side pillar. Good carpets enhance the comfort of the occupants. Push-button exterior door handles are used and Triplex toughened glass is fitted to screen and windows. The bonnet naturally terminates in the famous Sphinx mascot. The steering wheel is of small diameter, set low, and in the roof are recessed rigid anti-dazzle vizors, with mirror for the passenger. A good wide rear-view mirror is provided. The front-door window handles take two turns to fully lower the glass, the rear handles likewise. The front quarter-windows are devoid of rain gutters or thief-proof catches.

The test car was in an odd colour combination which drew crude comments from some of our acquaintances. There were Lucas 490 side lamps with tell tales visible to the driver and Lucas spot and fog lamps.

On the road this Armstrong Siddeley Star Sapphire saloon is impressively quiet, its big engine inaudible when idling. The suspension is fairly supple, promoting some up-and-down motion and roll when cornering fast, the latter slightly spoiling the accuracy of the steering. Generally, however, this big car gets round corners satisfactorily but we were disappointed to hear too much protest from the Dunlop Gold Seal tubeless tyres when cornering, even slowly, or braking. This problem was worrying the Armstrong Siddeley directors last October but apparently Dunlop failed to find a solution.

The servo-assisted Girling front disc brakes call for a mere caress to pull the car up from cruising speed, and the action is pleasantly progressive. There is very powerful retardation in reserve should an emergency intrude on the Star Sapphire's silent, purposeful progression, which enhances the driver's peace of mind. And peaceful is the key-note, inspired by the comfort, luxury appointments, automatic gearbox and extremely light steering. The steering wheel needs four turns, lock-to-lock and effortless control is assisted by quick castor-return action. No shocks are transmitted to the wrists, indeed this is faintly vague steering, excused by the light work it makes of parking manoeuvres.

The driving seat is very generously upholstered and supremely comfortable except for an impression that one was sitting facing slightly inwards. There is an appreciable transmission hump in the front compartment.

Driving reasonably hard, fuel consumption is rather heavy at

THIS FULL SIDE VIEW of the Star Sapphire emphasises that, in spite of high performance and modern amenities, this fine car retains traditional Armstrong Siddeley appearance.

THE ARMSTRONG SIDDELEY STAR SAPPHIRE SALOON

Six cylinders, 97 by 90 mm. (3,990 c.c.). Push-rod-operated inclined overhead valves; 7.5 to 1 compression-ratio; 1,656-h.p. (145 net b.h.p.) at 4,250 r.p.m.

Gear ratios : Borg Warner fully automatic transmission with selective override. First, 8.67 to 1; second, 5.41 to 1; top, 3.77 to 1.

Tyres : 6.70 by 16 Dunlop " Gold Seal " tubeless on bolt-on steel disc wheels.

Weight : Not weighed. Maker's figure : 1 ton 15 cwt. (kerb weight).

Steering ratios : Burman power steering; four turns, lock-to-lock.

Fuel capacity : 16 gallons, including approximately a gallon in reserve (range approximately 237 miles).

Wheelbase : 9 ft. 6 in.

Track : Front, 4 ft. 9⅞ in.; rear, 4 ft. 9½ in.

Dimensions : 16 ft. 2 in. by 6 ft. 2 in. by 5 ft. 2 in. (high).

Price : £1,763 (£2,498 14s. 2d. inclusive of p.t.).

Makers : Bristol Siddeley Engines Ltd., Parkside, Coventry, England.

14.7 m.p.g. This represents a range of approximately 237 miles. A reserve supply, said to be two gallons, is brought in by a knob on the facia but we have painful recollections of walking to a garage under a blazing sun because this supply is exhausted after only 15 miles of low-speed driving !

At night the lamps are adequate but facia lighting is rather dull—the knob first gives facia illumination, then pulls out further to bring on a centre flood light—a map lamp before the passenger would be better. After 1,000 miles the dip-stick indicated far above the " full " mark. Thinking there must be a special method of wiping the stick we asked for it to be checked when the car was returned to Armstrong Siddeley's Cricklewood Service Depot. They confirmed our reading. While we do not believe that the car incorporates a hidden oil-well, owners need have little fear of heavy oil consumption !

The bonnet has to be propped open to reveal the impressive engine with its ingenious push-rod operation of o.h. valves inclined at 70 dg., twin Stromberg carburetters beneath transverse drum-type air cleaners and two three-branch exhaust manifolds. Not as attractive as the Jaguar twin-cam power unit, this is an interesting engine, the valve gear of which Humber has been pleased to crib.

The boot lid, which is lockable, rises automatically to reveal a rather shallow luggage space, the cases having to occupy a shelf over the spare wheel. Tools are carried in a drawer within the boot. The small petrol filler cap is secured by a chain and lives under a flap in the near-side back wing.

Not offering as good value for money as the Jaguar Mk. IX, less brisk and more thirsty than the Daimler Majestic, the Armstrong Siddeley Star Sapphire shines as a fine car of the old school, sober in appearance and particularly easy to drive. It is priced at £1,763, which purchase tax inflates to £2,498 14s. 2d.—W. B.

1960 CARS

A Star Sapphire Limousine

New Version of Armstrong Siddeley 4-litre Car

THE modern limousine is no longer merely a town car whose running is restricted almost entirely to city streets; today, it must also be capable of conveying its passengers in great comfort at high cruising speeds along motorways at home and abroad. The new Armstrong Siddeley Star Sapphire limousine has been designed from the start with both these roles very much in mind, and the engineering staff has sought to combine exceptional refinement in operation with such unusual limousine features as a 90-m.p.h. maximum and a disc-braking system.

The Star Sapphire limousine is basically a longer and wider version of the Star Sapphire saloon, with the wheelbase increased from 9 ft. 6 in. to 11 ft. 3 in. and the track increased by 1 in. at the front and by 3½ in. at the rear. The wheelbase, incidentally, is 2 in. longer than that of the 346 limousine which this new model replaces, but the overall length has not been increased. The engine of the limousine is fitted with only a single Zenith 42 WIA downdraught carburetter instead of the two Zenith carburetters of this type with which the saloon is equipped, for even in single-carburetter form the 3,990-c.c. engine produces 140 b.h.p. with a great deal of torque.

In order to obtain smoother idling at low r.p.m., the engine is mounted at four points instead of three, the single front mounting of the saloon being replaced by bobbin mountings on each side of the crankcase inclined at an angle of 45 deg. A four-speed synchromesh gearbox with steering-column control is normally fitted, but the Borg-Warner automatic transmission is available as an optional extra. Both front and rear spring rates have been modified and the rear spring leaves have been increased in width from 2 in. to 2½ in. Metacentric eccentric rubber-bushed mountings are employed at the front of the rear springs and Contrasonic bobbin-type bonded rubber mountings at the rear in place of normal shackles to prevent road noise from being passed on to the chassis and body.

Burman integral power steering is standard equipment, and the Girling servo-assisted braking system consists of disc brakes at the front and drum brakes at the rear, much experimenting with different pedal ratios and cylinder sizes having produced, it is claimed, 87% retardation with a pedal pressure of 80 lb. from 60 m.p.h.

The seven-seater body follows Star Sapphire saloon styling at the front, but the rear treatment is quite different. The interior is beautifully equipped and is exceptionally roomy, the rear seat being 2 in. wider than in the previous limousine model, and there is an additional 2½ in. of knee room. Standard equipment includes an individual rear heater which also de-mists the rear window, a clock, and a nylon floor rug over the usual carpeting. Electrical operation of the division and a positive air-cooling system are among the optional items of equipment available.

Price of the Star Sapphire Limousine is £2,222 10s., plus £927 3s. 4d. purchase tax, making a total of £3,149 13s. 4d. The Borg-Warner automatic transmission is available at an additional cost of £116 10s., plus £48 10s. 10d. purchase tax, giving a total of £165 0s. 10d.

No. 162 1956 ARMSTRONG-SIDDELEY SAPPHIRE 234

PRICE : Secondhand £850 ; New—basic £840, with tax £1,411

Petrol consumption 21-25 m.p.g.	Mileometer reading (see text) 27,361
Oil consumption 800 m.p.g.	Date first registered 18 September 1956

NOW that Armstrong-Siddeley have ceased car production, the preservation of existing examples of the marque is specially rewarding. It is reassuring, therefore, to find that thoroughly well cared-for or renovated 2·3- and 3·4-litre Sapphires are still obtainable, such as the 234 which is the subject of this test.

A complete respray in dark green has been carried out on it and the finish has been renewed to such a high standard that there is little evidence to show that it is not still wearing the manufacturer's original paintwork. Slight scratching on the chromium and traces of rust on the bumper overriders can be found, but these do not spoil the 234's extremely well-kept exterior appearance.

Even higher standards of cleanliness and absence of the usual marks of ownership are apparent inside the car. Small cracks are

present in the varnish of the wooden trim on the doors, but that on the facia panel is unmarked. The green p.v.c. seat upholstery and door lining are practically as new, and the white plastic roof linings come almost into the same category. Possibly the floor carpets—also green—have been replaced, and this is confirmed by the less immaculate appearance of the fixed section covering the propeller shaft tunnel.

In mechanical condition and its behaviour on the road, the 234 comes almost (but not quite) up to the high standards of its interior and exterior appearance. Hamtune Motors declare the true mileage to be approaching 50,000. The worst fault was a severe front-end shake at speeds just over the 60 m.p.h. mark. This was traced to excessive out-of-balance of the front wheels, and the car was re-tried after four new Dunlop Gold Seal tyres had been fitted and balanced. Apart from a scarcely noticeable tremor of vibration at steady 55 m.p.h. the shake has been cured completely and the car is now decidedly more enjoyable to drive.

The four-cylinder 2,290 c.c. engine, of "square" bore-stroke dimensions, has the harshness often associated with "big-four-cylinder" design. Engine noise throughout the rev range is considerable, but is no worse than that remembered on the model when new. In hard driving, 4,000 r.p.m.—the red line on the rev counter occurs at 5,250 r.p.m.—may be used repeatedly without any impression that the power unit is being over-stressed. Starting is immediate and there is no need for use of the choke in mild weather. Carburation is by twin S.U.s which are in good tune, although it was not possible to match the acceleration figures obtained in the Road Test of the model when new (5 October, 1956).

A sharp click is heard as each gear engages, and the central

gear change remains precise, with effective synchromesh on all four ratios. In addition to grab handles on the door pillars and two wing mirrors, Laycock-de Normanville overdrive is the only accessory added to the car, and it is understood that this unit has just been renewed. The change into or out of overdrive occurs smoothly providing that the conveniently placed control (near the driver's right hand on the steering wheel) is used only when the engine is pulling, and overdrive gives an extra range of acceleration in third gear and quieter, more leisurely cruising speed in top gear. Engine revs in top at 80 m.p.h. are reduced by the overdrive from 4,700 r.p.m. to 3,650 r.p.m., and it is at this speed that the car settles down to sustained cruising with reasonably little effort.

A steering fault noticed, for which no explanation was found, was a slight tendency for the car to pull to the left on the straight, and when holding a steady course the cross-bar of the steering wheel is not horizontal, as it should be. Inspection of the underbody did not reveal any evidence of accident damage to explain this. The control itself is light and adequately precise, while fairly low-geared for the sporting character of the 234.

Suspension damping is still adequate, although the car tends to pitch over wavy surfaces, and the ride is smooth over rough roads. On dry roads, which persisted throughout the test, the car corners well, with little tyre squeal; there is commendable absence of roll.

The servo-assisted brakes are powerful in return for light pedal pressures. They halt the car in a straight line and can be used from high speeds with confidence. The hand brake is no more than adequate.

A small exhaust leak from the rear silencer was noticed at the start of the test, and although it did not become worse it requires attention to prevent exhaust fumes from finding their way into the car. A complete set of tools is provided, including even a new foot pump and tyre pressure gauge, and there is a new handbook in one of the front door pockets. A fresh-air heater-demister was standard equipment on the car when new; it is working efficiently and warms the interior quickly.

All of the electrical and mechanical equipment is in perfect working order, with the sole exception of the boot lock, which will not fasten correctly.

It deserves emphasis that the appearance of this 234 is outstandingly good for any four-year-old, and obviously much care has gone into its preparation for sale (no more than the usual few hours' warning was given before taking the car away for test). Only the few small points mentioned, and the heavy oil consumption, prevent the same high praise from being given to the mechanical condition of the car; and in overall assessment the high asking price quoted above seems fully justified.

Windscreen washers, two-speed wipers, electric clock, automatic reversing lamp, and a luggage locker lamp are all part of the standard specification of the Armstrong. The headlamps are in need of adjustment

PERFORMANCE CHECK
(Figures in brackets are those of the model when tested new)

0 to 30 m.p.h. .. **6·6**sec (4·7)	Standing quarter-mile .. **22·1**sec (20·2)	
0 to 50 m.p.h. .. **14·3**sec (10·9)		
0 to 60 m.p.h. .. **20·8**sec (15·5)	20 to 40 m.p.h. (top gear) .. **12·5**sec (9·3)	
0 to 70 m.p.h. .. **30·6**sec (21·8)	30 to 50 m.p.h. (top gear) .. **12·4**sec (9·4)	

Provided for test by Hamtune Motors Ltd., Park Garage, Wellingborough Road, Weston Favell, Northampton, Northamptonshire. Telephone : Northampton 32093-4.

No. 182 1947 ARMSTRONG SIDDELEY TYPHOON

PRICE: £37½; New—basic £975, with tax £1,247

Petrol consumption	19-21 m.p.g.	Date first registered	5 June 1947
Oil consumption	120 m.p.pint	Mileometer reading	51,773

USED CARS
on the Road

WHEN the war ended in 1945, Armstrong Siddeley were just about the first manufacturers to launch a new design—the 2-litre Lancaster and the Hurricane convertible. They were immediately successful, and were supplemented by the two-door sports saloon model called the Typhoon, announced in August of 1946. This newcomer was equally well-liked, and many are still running around today, so when recently one was advertised in The Autocar at only £37 10s, it was decided to assess it in the "used cars" feature.

Asked to provide the car, A. B. Price Ltd. were anxious to make it quite clear that inclusion of anything so old among their stock was exceptional. They had accepted it in part exchange against a Sapphire, and had decided that its condition justified them in offering it for direct sale.

To be acceptable on British roads, such a car must not only be safe, it must also be capable of keeping reasonable station with modern traffic speeds, and the Typhoon fulfilled this requirement perfectly satisfactorily. Acceleration is adequately brisk, and speeds up to 55 m.p.h. may be used without overstressing the machinery. From hot or cold the engine starts well, but at all times there is considerable noise from the little ends, tappets and pistons. Blowby is indicated by the amount of smoke issuing from the engine breather, and a distinct smell of engine fumes is one of the least pleasant features of the car.

In other respects the mechanical condition is reassuringly good. The chassis appears sound, and the extent of free play in the steering is still within tolerable limits. The clutch operates smoothly and the gears are quiet. The floor-mounted gear change is sufficiently precise for use of it to be quite a pleasure, and although the synchromesh has weakened appreciably there is no difficulty in making silent gear changes.

On first acquaintance with the Typhoon it was reassuring to find that the brakes were capable of stopping the car rapidly in response to reasonably light pedal pressures. For the front wheels, hydraulic operation is used, and this is combined with the normal (for those days) Girling mechanical linkages to the rear brakes. New flexible brake hoses have been fitted. Occasionally the offside front brake tended to grab, resulting in a pull to the right. The handbrake is adequately effective.

By today's standards the ride is somewhat bouncy, and a fair amount of pitching, particularly at the front end, is noticed. Weakness in the suspension dampers was suspected, although on the independent torsion bar front suspension of the Typhoon

Visibility is restricted by the positioning of the mirror and by the shallow windscreen—now happily a feature of a bygone age. In most respects the condition is acceptable in relation to the price asked

these are duplicated, and have the second damper working directly on the nose of each torsion bar.

Naturally the bodywork and interior condition show the excessive deterioration which the price asked for the car must lead one to expect. The roof, which is constructed in the once popular combination of metal covered by a waterproof material, has been patched and partly recovered. Considerable rust on the front apron and many of the wing and body joints, com-

bines with a rather battered radiator grille and corroded bumpers to make the car look unnecessarily sorry for itself.

Inside, age has taken its toll of the cloth upholstery and door trim, and of the polished wood facia and window fillets, but the roof linings are unexpectedly sound. The window winding mechanisms still work satisfactorily, while the doors close and lock with a sturdy action and are rattle-free. The seats tilt forward to give access to the rear compartment, and they remain comfortable to sit on, though the driver's seat has sagged. The upholstery gives off a stale, musty odour.

A useful improvement to this Typhoon is the addition of amber flashing indicators at front and rear, but the slots of the original semaphore indicators remain. Adequate illumination for night driving is provided by the headlamps, despite a rather severe cut-off when dipped. Most of the electrical equipment, such as the panel lamps, horn and obligatory lighting, but not the interior lamp, is working efficiently. The windscreen wipers have been fitted with blades which are too long and foul the top of the windscreen.

A rather useless foglamp, a dipping interior mirror and a recirculatory heater are the only accessories the car has gathered in 14 years. An alarming "banshee wail" is emitted by the heater when cold.

Tyres will soon need attention. Except for the spare, which is a well-worn Michelin, all are Homerton remoulds; their treads are no more than half worn, but the tyres on the right wheels show signs of cracking in the sidewalls. Side jacks are built-in; there is no toolkit, but the car now sports two starting handles, although the battery seems to be sound.

There is much that a keen owner may do for such a car to make it more presentable and certainly there seems no reason why it should not give some further service without being a nuisance on the roads.

PERFORMANCE CHECK

(Figures in brackets are those of the original Road Test, 27 February 1948)

0 to 30 m.p.h. 9·4 sec (7·6)	20 to 40 m.p.h. (top gear) 14·1 sec (13·9)
0 to 50 m.p.h. 25·0 sec (19·5)	30 to 50 m.p.h. (top gear) 17·0 sec (15·7)

Standing quarter-mile 26·7 sec

Provided for test by A. B. Price Ltd.,
Hardwick House, Studley, Warwickshire.
Telephone: Studley 521

Fig. 1. Blackened big-end bearings which were otherwise unworn.

Overhauling an
ARMSTRONG
SIDDELEY

by D. G. Sandercock

Fig. 2. Removing the valves, wooden blocks engaged with pins in holes in the cylinder head, hold it conveniently off the bench, leaving room for the valve lifter to work.

Fig. 3. Wooden block in gudgeon pin recess holds piston with head out clear of the bore.

THE principal problem with these cars is that the pistons cannot be removed through the top of the cylinders because the large bearing caps will not pass through the bores, nor can they be removed from the bottom of the engine due to the limited clearance between the crankshaft and the sidewall. In fact, the only way to remove them is by dropping the crankshaft, a major operation in which the entire—and large—engine would normally be taken from the car.

But without resorting to such drastic measures, a satisfactory job of ring fittting can be done on the car. With the pistons pushed up through the bores as far as they will go, there is sufficient clearance to work on the rings.

A further difficulty may be encountered with the suppliers of the rings; they generally prefer to have the pistons sent in and fit the rings themselves. However, in this case, once the difficulty had been explained to them they not only readily supplied the rings but assisted with hints on fitting. And this will probably be found to be the general experience.

The model which was the subject of this overhaul was eating oil —about 70 miles to the pint—although its history gave a mileage of only 30,000, and the negligible wear on other parts of the car supported that figure. The early life of the car had been spent in Malta, where no doubt repeated short steep runs had taken their toll.

It was decided to use Wellworthy Duaflex oil rings since these could be fitted without any alteration to the lands. The two compression rings and the scraper were standard replacements, again requiring no land alteration. The top compression ring was stepped to clear the wear step in the bore.

New Bearings

While the big-ends were being dismantled to free the pistons, it was obviously good practice to renew the shell bearings. In actual fact no wear was found on the big-end shells at all when their thickness was checked with a micrometer against the new set, but the white metal surfaces had become blackened and hardened (Fig. 1). Their replacement will undoubtedly prolong the life of the journals.

There had been some timing chain rattle so it was decided while the engine was stripped to renew the timing chain, and, of course, do a complete decarbonising job as well as renewing the piston rings and big-ends.

The removal of the old rings and the fitting of the new turned out, despite early misgivings, to be quite a simple matter to do *in situ*. Although the rings were badly worn, the lands in the pistons were quite satisfactory and accepted the new rings with no undue play.

Stripping down for the removal of the head was straightforward. Wooden mounting blocks, fitted with studs to engage in the head, make for ease of working when removing and refitting the valves (see Fig. 2). *Note* that the tappet filter on the near side of the block under the crankcase breather must be removed and the aperture left open before the engine is turned over for decarbonising, otherwise the oil pressure is liable to blow out a hydraulic tappet.

Sump

Before removing the sump, undo the four front bolts and the one top bolt on the track rod linkage mounting so that the track rods can be lowered to give the necessary clearance. If this is not done the sump cannot be dropped clear.

Removing the big-ends is straightforward, and the pistons can then be pushed up through the cylinder bores. For simplicity one was done at a time, the rings and new bearings fitted and bolted up again before going on to the next piston. This had the advantages of keeping the journals shielded from dust and also allowing the engine to be turned over without fouling the con-rods.

Take care which way round the con-rod is so that it is not reassembled 180 deg. out. Note also which way round the bearing cap is fitted. Finally, do not over-tighten the bearing cap bolts. The castle nuts are only quarter inch and could easily be stripped; about 20 to 25lb.-ft. is sufficient torque.

Great care must be taken not to introduce any dirt or foreign matter on to the journals when fitting the new big-end shells. It is also advisable to oil the surfaces before clamping up so that there will be an oil film protection to prevent any initial bite when the engine is turned over.

To deal with the pistons, a suitable piece of wood pushed into the gudgeon recess or a cutaway in the piston skirt will hold the piston up in position while working on the rings (Fig. 3). It is advisable to leave the lowest ring in place while cleaning the other lands as a safety check in case the piston slips off the wood. Do that land last, taking extra care, or slip a ring temporarily back on to one of the upper lands.

A file tip ground to suit the lands will make a useful scraper, but be careful not to cut the aluminium alloy. The cleaning can be finished off with a coarse piece of string, dipped in petrol, looped around the land and pulled from side to side.

Fitting the Piston Rings

Before fitting the new compression rings they must be checked for gap. This can be done in the top of the bore, having first cleaned out the carbon deposit (see Fig. 4). Check also that the ring when in its land can go in flush with the piston face.

The type of ring clamp used in this case was designed to slide up from the skirt of the piston, but by wedging it open with a bit of wood it was possible to work the rings carefully into it (Fig. 5). The wedge was then removed, allowing the clamp to tighten on to the rings, and the piston tapped down into the bore with a piece of wood.

On the decarbonising side the only points of note are the polishing of the valves (see Figs. 6 and 7) and the use of new valve springs. Incidently, these are all old valves going back after being machined before grinding in.

New valve springs were used after confirming that the ones in use were more than 10 per cent weaker than when new. This was done by putting the double springs in opposition—new against old—and screwing up to a normal compression stress in the valve lifter, when the collapse of one was measured against that of the other (Fig. 8).

Timing Chain

Replacing the timing chain required the removal of the radiator. A connecting link is provided on the chain for ease of replacement, the clip being on the back of the chain. Ensure that the timing is not disturbed when the chain is off. The teeth of the sprocket wheels are marked for adjacent setting.

While the timing chain cover is off it might be worth carrying out a modification to the vibration damper. It was found on this car that the damper friction ring had been getting insufficient oil owing to the tight fit of the faces and considerable tearing of the metal surfaces had occurred. A radial channel was cut across the faces to provide an oil-way. The vibration damper is shown in its working position in Fig. 9.

Re-setting the tappets requires some patience. The rockers must be prised steadily up until the oil has been forced out of the hydraulic tappet before setting the gap at .075in. Immediately it is released the rocker will spring back on to the valve stem and should be solidly there. If it can be sprung open by finger pressure the oil has not been drawn back into the tappet cylinder. The plunger may have stuck open; in this case when the engine is started there will be a heavy clatter from the tappet in trouble, but usually it will clear itself.

The final result was a change from 70 to the pint to 500 miles to the pint, and an engine which at speed only murmurs like a turbine and is inaudible at tickover!

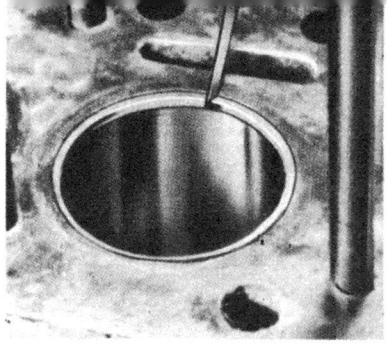

Fig. 4. Checking the ring gap in an unworn part of the cylinder.

Fig. 5. Ring clamp in place. Note the adjacent completed piston has the cylinder covered with rag to keep out dirt.

Fig. 6. Ready for re-assembly with set of valve springs and the original valves cleaned and polished. The vibration damper friction ring is bottom right of the picture.

Fig. 7. Note the polished heads of the original valves.

Fig. 8. The turns of the old spring on the right are collapsing more rapidly than those of the new spring on the left.

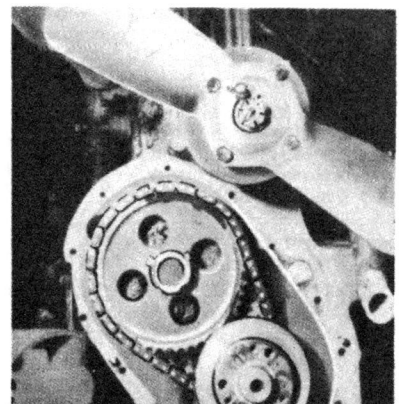

Fig. 9. New timing chain fitted and vibration damper shown in place on end of engine crankshaft.

USED CARS
ON THE ROAD

No. 229 • 1959 ARMSTRONG SIDDELEY STAR SAPPHIRE

PRICE: Secondhand £355 ; New—Basic £1,763; with tax £2,499

Petrol consumption 10-15 m.p.g.	*Date first registered* (see text)
Oil consumption 300 m.p. pint	*Mileometer reading* 40,539

JUST five years ago this week, a Star Sapphire stood proudly on the Armstrong-Siddeley stand at Earls Court, resplendent in all-ivory finish, and boasting many features which for 1959 were quite advanced. It had power steering—still a novelty then—one of the early Borg-Warner automatic transmissions with the rare feature of a variable-speed hold control, and front disc brakes. Within nine months it went out of production, but the makers announced that spares and service would continue for a further 10 years.

For buyers of the limited number of used examples available, a good spell therefore remains before they have to start worrying about a dearth of spare parts. The Star Sapphire itself is typical of some large models whose heavy running costs result in limited secondhand demand and galloping depreciation. With the example chosen at random for test, the price has dropped by more than £2,000 in five years.

The body appears both to have lasted quite well and to have been thoroughly restored to clean condition ready for sale. This has included an almost complete respray of the two-tone grey exterior finish (with the lighter colour below the waistline). Most of the chrome, particularly at the front, shines well, but appears to have been polished rather too enthusiastically at the rear, and is showing the base metal in places. The general exterior impression is of an outstandingly good example of the model.

It is in similar cared-for condition inside, and the cream p.v.c. roof lining, polished walnut facia, and the grey and maroon leatherwork, are all extremely clean and unspoilt. The seats are comfortable, and give a good driving position without any seat-sag and restricted visibility, often serious problems with this sort of used car.

Performance

Similarly kind words cannot be used for the Sapphire's mechanical condition, as the engine is in bad shape. A check has been carried out on the ignition, but the engine is still pulling roughly and delivering nothing like the power of which this 3,990 c.c. six-cylinder unit was capable. The acceleration figures make a poor comparison with the relatively vigorous performance of the original road test car; but it could well be that a top-end overhaul may put matters to rights. Some piston slap is audible, but oil consumption is not excessive, so the wear may not justify reboring.

The transmission works more or less as it should, apart from the facia-controlled variable hold. Low never comes in for starts from rest unless the selector is moved to L, whereas with the system in correct adjustment Low is introduced for starting if the hold is moved to the low-speed end of the scale. At the upper speed setting of 65 m.p.h., intermediate is held to this speed on full throttle.

It was a pleasant surprise to find how good the power steering is on this car, even by modern standards. There is little response to the initial inch or so of movement of the steering wheel rim, making it difficult to steer through narrow gaps in traffic, although at higher speeds the good directional stability makes up for any looseness in the steering. The power assistance is really effective, and helps to make light work of manoeuvring. The steering column is adjustable for length.

Ride comfort is fair; there is excessive body movement occasionally over surface irregularities too small even to be noticeable from the driving seat before the car passes over them. Most of the time, however, the ride is "dead," and there are few rattles. It comes as quite a surprise to refer to the specification and find that front disc brakes by Girling with a powerful vacuum servo are fitted, because—although they stop the car reasonably well—with some tyre squeal—when the pedal is pressed hard, they lack real bite. The handbrake is frail, but there is a parking lock on the transmission.

Severe vibration at 60-70 m.p.h. shows need for wheel balancing; but in fact four new Firestone tyres have been fitted. The spare is a well-worn Dunlop. Jack, wheelbrace and most of the tray of fitted tools remain in the luggage locker.

Such a car recalls pleasant memories of the days when it was truly a star, but now it feels a little dated and cumbersome. Yet it still offers a lot of comfort and luxury, and deserves the engine overhaul which should turn it into one of the better examples of the model. Incidentally, the Sapphire has been involved in an ill-fated hire purchase transaction, as a result of which its registration book has gone astray, and the exact date when it was first licensed is not known.

There is no radio, but standard equipment includes an effective fresh air heater with separate controls and outlets for the rear compartment. Only the clock, windscreen washer and one each of the brake and interior lamps are not working

PERFORMANCE CHECK

(Figures in brackets are those of the original Road Test, 11 September 1959)

0 to 30 m.p.h. 9·3 sec (4·6)	Standing-quarter-mile 23·4 sec (19·2)
0 to 40 m.p.h. 13·2 sec (6·9)	
0 to 50 m.p.h. 17·3 sec (10·1)	
0 to 60 m.p.h. 23·7 sec (14·2)	
0 to 70 m.p.h. 33·5 sec (19·6)	20 to 40 m.p.h. (top gear) 11·2 sec (—)
0 to 80 m.p.h. 49·8 sec (26·0)	30 to 50 m.p.h. (top gear) 11·9 sec (8·9)

Car for Sale at: Jacquier Ltd., 229 Hammersmith Road, London, W.6. Telephone: RIVerside 6677

Last descendants of a proud line

Armstrong Siddeley Sapphires

WHEN Bristol Siddeley Motors Ltd. announced in the summer of 1960 that production of the Armstrong Siddeley Star Sapphire models was "no longer an economic proposition", there was gloom in many places besides Coventry for these cars were the last descendants of a proud line which had its beginnings in 1902.

An undertaking was given that service and the supply of spare parts would be maintained for at least 10 years, and it looks as though this will be exceeded because the call for spares has been less than anticipated and because the Service Department (with its quarters in Quinton Road, Coventry, and The Hyde, Hendon, London) has also undertaken service of certain Continental cars.

The first Sapphire was introduced in October, 1952, for the '53 season and created much interest because it replaced the immediate post-war 2·3-litre design which was more notable for roominess and refinement than sheer performance.

It had an entirely new 3·4-litre six-cylinder, "square" engine with inclined overhead valves and the option of a straightforward clutch and synchromesh gearbox or automatic centrifugal clutch with an electric pre-selector gearbox.

Bodywork

The coachwork was of good quality but the design included one or two rust traps. In both the "346" and "Star" models, the section of the left-hand rear wing, which carries the petrol filler, forms a mud and salt trap which can cause bad internal rusting if neglected. The symptoms are blisters round the trap-door which conceals the filler cap.

Less severe rusting can also occur on the inside of the rear wings and it is wise to remove the spats for a proper inspection. Also examine the under parts of the body sills. On the Star Sapphire there is one further point to watch—the rear end of the front wing, where it meets the leading edge of the door, because the latter closes in such a way that it is almost impossible to dry the surfaces concerned.

The engine

Both the "346" and Star engines have an excellent reputation for long life, and mileages of 100,000 before major overhaul are on record.

A clatter, which is at its worst at about 1,500 r.p.m., is likely to be due to a slack timing chain. This need cause no concern as there is a simple external adjuster on the front of the timing case and the seller can be asked to cure the trouble right away.

A dull tap is likely to be caused by wear in the tappets, which run direct in the cylinder block. This can be confirmed by pouring a little oil down the push-rods temporarily to quieten the noise. The permanent cure is to fit oversize tappets. If wear is not severe, tappets which are 0·001 in. oversize can be used without attention to the housings, and this can be done if the cylinder head is removed. In bad cases a cure can only be effected by honing the tappet bores and fitting new tappets of 0·005 in. or 0·006 in. oversize, but this is a garage job.

Careful tightening-down of the cylinder head is necessary. Carelessness can cause poor gasket sealing and water leaks from the jackets into the cylinders. The ultimate result is bearing trouble, which can be recognized by a heavy rumble.

To check whether water is, in fact, reaching the sump, inspect the dipstick for beads of water and an emulsified appearance of the oil. Normal condensation can sometimes cause a few water beads but, if all is in order, further water should not appear when the sump is re-dipped. If it does, remove the valve cover and look for condensation on the inside: if water is present to an appreciable degree, the car is best left alone.

A reconditioned exchange engine for the "346" currently costs £150 including the clutch but not the auxiliaries, and for the Star Sapphire, £160, fitting extra.

Transmission

Four types of transmission were used during the Sapphire run. The single-dry-plate clutch and synchromesh gearbox call for no comment. With the centrifugal clutch, watch for judder, which is likely to result from wear on the input shaft or centre splines, or to partial seizure of the bob-weight levers; all of these troubles call for complete stripping.

With the Rolls-Royce-built automatic gearbox, an important point to check is that there are no serious oil leaks, because lack of lubricant can cause the rear clutches to burn out and complete replacement is then necessary. Have the filler cap removed: trouble will be revealed by a strong smell of burnt oil and friction material. The cost of a replacement gearbox will be upwards of £100.

With the Borg-Warner automatic transmission fitted to the Star Sapphire, few troubles are likely unless lubrication has been neglected. A gearbox only is available on an exchange basis for £45 and an additional £27 covers the cost of a new torque-converter.

Excessive transmission backlash—denoted by judder at low speeds in top gear—is likely to be caused by worn

Look for tell-tale signs of internal water leaks on the dipstick (see text).

universal joints, but can also be caused by loose rear-axle U-bolts.

Drive the car over a wavy road which, besides showing up suspension faults, can also reveal a further transmission trouble in the shape of a worn centre propeller-shaft bearing; if this trouble is present it will produce an intermittent howl on this sort of surface. The cure is to replace the short propeller shaft and centre bearing—at a cost of £7 18s.

Suspension and steering

The wavy-road test suggested will immediately show up spent shock absorbers. Some " 346 " models were fitted with Girling dampers, and these can be replaced at £2 7s. each, front or rear. Other " 346 " cars had Armstrong units, and these are exchangeable at £4 4s. each, front or rear. Armstrong dampers were also used on the Star Sapphire—exchange price, £2 19s. each.

A car which has a very "down-at-the-front" look is probably in need of spring replacement. Check the clearance between the snub rubbers and their stops, which should be 1 in.: if the gap is down to ½ in. or less, new springs are essential. At the rear, settled springs are indicated when the nave-plate is concealed by the rear-wing spat. It is generally possible for helper leaves to be fitted.

Look for wear and tear of ball-ends and the steerage linkage generally. On some early " 346 " models serious swivel-pin wear occurred, but this was traced to the use of grease (which hardened) instead of oil as a lubricant.

A Burman recirculating ball steering box is used on " 346 " models, and this is provided with an adjustment. Power assistance was available as an optional extra. This was arranged as an addition to the normal steering gear and users who do not wish to go to the expense of reconditioning the power system can remove it and develop their arm muscles!

Star Sapphire models were provided as standard with the later Burman built-in power assistance, which proved extremely reliable.

Brakes

The original " 346 " models had only 11-in. drums and no servo, and were not up to the performance of the model: fade can be sudden and drastic. A few cars were converted to 12-in. drums and a servo, and whether or not this has been done can be checked by looking to see if there is a servo unit below the brake pedal. On later models the brakes gave no trouble.

BRIEF SPECIFICATION:
Engine: Six-cylinder, o.h.v., 3,435 c.c. (Star Sapphire, 3,990 c.c.).
Transmission: 3·4-litre models supplied with conventional clutch and synchromesh gearbox or centrifugal clutch and electrically-operated pre-selector gearbox; automatic gearbox (R·R-built) also available on 1955 models onwards. Star Sapphire fitted with Borg-Warner automatic transmission on saloon and manual gearbox on limousine.
Dimensions: Sapphire—length, 16 ft. 1 in. (limousine, 17 ft. 8 in.); width, 6 ft.; dry weight, 31 cwt. (limousine, 36 cwt.). Star Sapphire—length, 16 ft. 2 in. (limousine, 17 ft. 8 in.); width, 6 ft. 2 in. (limousine, 6 ft. 2½ in.); dry weight, 35½ cwt. (limousine, 37 cwt.).

PERFORMANCE:
Maximum speeds: (1) * 100·1 m.p.h., (2) * 95·9 m.p.h., (3) * 99·6 m.p.h.
Acceleration: 0–50 m.p.h. through gears, (1) 8·9 sec., (2) 11·4 sec., (3) 8·8 sec.
Touring fuel consumption: (1) 18·1 m.p.h., (2) 15·6 m.p.h., (3) 15·4 m.p.h.
Braking from 30 m.p.h.: (1) 37·5 ft., (2) 34½ ft., (3) 33½ ft.
*Footnote: Models tested were (1) 1954, two-carburetter model with manual control, (2) 1955 single-carburetter model with R·R-built automatic transmission and (3) 1959 Star Sapphire (two carburetters and B-W automatic transmission standard).

IDENTITY PARADE:
October 1952: Introduced as four-door, five/six-seater saloon. Single-carburetter, 3,435 c.c., six-cylinder engine developing 120 b.h.p. at 4,200 r.p.m. Transmission option of conventional clutch and synchromesh gearbox or centrifugal clutch and electrically operated, pre-selector gearbox.

September 1953: Two-carburetter engine available as extra. Output, 150 b.h.p. at 4,800 r.p.m.
October 1954: Automatic gearbox (Rolls-Royce-built) introduced as third transmission option. Brake drums increased 1 in. in diameter to 12 in.; Girling Autostatic operation with two self-adjusting, trailing shoes at front; Clayton-Dewandre vacuum-servo operation.
March 1955: Limousine model introduced on long-wheelbase chassis.
August 1955: 3·4-litre model now known as Sapphire 346 (3·4 litres and six cylinders) to distinguish it from new smaller " 234 " (2·3 litre four-cylinder) and " 236 " (2·3 litre, six-cylinder) models. Girling power steering (with adjustable power assistance) introduced as optional extra; Telaflow-Hi-duty rear dampers with adjustable ride control also offered as optional extra.
September 1957: Internal modifications to limousine to give roomier seating without increased overall size.
October 1958: Star Sapphire introduced. Extensive mechanical improvements included larger engine; 7·5 : 1 compression ratio; two carburetters; power output 165 b.h.p. at 4,250 r.p.m.; Borg-Warner fully automatic transmission standardized; Burman power-assisted steering; front track increased to 4 ft. 9⅞ in.; Girling disc brakes at front with suspended vacuum servo. Bodywork more luxurious and fitted with independent front and rear heater units.
October 1959: Limousine version of Star Sapphire introduced. Features generally similar to saloon but single carburetter and 4-speed synchromesh gearbox normally fitted.
July 1960: Production ceased.

ARMSTRONG SIDDELEY MOTORS – A POTTED POST-WAR HISTORY – BY BILL SMITH

Armstrong Siddeley Production Figures 1919 to 1960

Type	Years of manufacture		Total Built	Number Surviving
16/18 hp	1945 - 1953		12639	700
Sapphire 346	1953 - 1959		7697	1000 approx
Sapphire 234	1956 - 1958		796	130
Sapphire 236	1956 - 1957		609	
Star Sapphire	1958 - 1960		902	240
Star Limousine	1960		74	
************************************				
Total Production	1919 - 1960			
Total Survivors	1919 - 1960	=	84024 cars	2564 cars
Total Production	1919 - 1940			
Total Survivors	1919 - 1940	=	55807 cars	494 cars
Total Production	1945 - 1960		22717	
Total Survivors	1945 - 1960	=		2070 cars
**************				

In 1945 the first post war cars rolled off the production line. In fact the first new British design to emerge was the Drophead four seater. The Hurricane, a 16 hp vehicle of 1991 cc a development of the pre-War 16 hp. In early 1946 the Lancaster six light version followed. Again the cars were straight sixes and featured Independant Torsion Bar front suspension and Semi-Elliptic rear suspension.

In Mid 1946 the hard top version of the Hurricane, the Typhoon, was introduced.

The 16 hp was uprated in 1949 to 2309 cc and classified the 18 hp. The Typhoon was phased out and replaced by the four door Whitley Saloon.

There was an option at this time of Syncro of pre-selector gearbox. 1949 also saw the introduction of the Station Coupe and Utility Coupe. The long chassis limousine was introduced in 1950 and between then and 1952 125 cars were built.

The Lancaster ceased production in 1953 but the Whitley and Hurricane persisted until 1954.

A new model the Sapphire 346 was introduced in 1953 again a six cylinder car of 3435 cc and engine of square format 90 mm x 90 mm. The car was capable of high performance with a maximum speed approaching 100 mph available in four or six light styles. The engine design was an innovation with a valve layout which enables the benefits of hemispherical combustion chambers and inclined valves to be obtained with a single side camshaft. This car was the mainstay of the Armstrong Siddeley range from 1953 to 1958. It could be had with Pre-Selector Synchromesh or Automatic Gearbox (1954) Servo Brakes (1954) Twin Carbs (1954). In 1955 a limousine chassis was introduced with wheelbase increased from 9'6'' to 11'1'' seating five in the rear, with pre-selector transmission. Overall length is 17'8'' width 5'11'' and a height of 5'8½''.

A new range of AS cars came in 1955 in the form of 2.3 litre 4 and 6 cylinder cars known as the Sapphire 234 and 236. Both Saloons were of four light form. The prototype 2.4 Jaguar was very similar in line though its refined form was preferred by the buying public. The 234's performance is very superior to the 2.4 Jaguar. Unfortunately only 1,400 of both models were produced.

This model was available with a six cylinder or four cylinder overhead-valve engine. Both had a capacity of 2.3 litres. Both cars were fitted with the same four speed all-synchromesh gearbox. The 234 has a normal centre gear-charge with laycock-de-Normanville overdrive unit and foot-operated clutch. The 236 has the Lockheed Manumatic gear change, with two-pedal control, no clutch, and simple but not automatic gear changes.

The final production car built by Armstrong Siddeley was the Star Sapphire. The 3,990 cc engine was the 90 mm x 90 mm engine bored out to 97 mm with water spaces between the cylinders. The engine was generally uprated to cope with the stresses of higher performance.

This roomy car was capable of over 100 mph and is well capable of keeping up with its more modern contemporaries. This car was available with the Borg Warner Automatic Gearbox. The Star Sapphire was seen as a more powerful and smoother car than the 346. It had more comfort and was roomier and lavishly equipped. The limousine version was built on a longer chassis. The Star was built between 1958 - 1960. Production ceased in 1960 with one solitary Mk II Star built. Projections for a Mk III Star and a 346 replacement were on the way but these were abandoned.

Armstrong Siddeley
Owners Club

For owners of Armstrong-Siddeley and associated marques. Best stocks of warranted spares in the world (24 hr telephone service) Information service second to none. Library of information and literature available to all members. Area meetings regularly all over the United Kingdom, as well as active areas world-wide. National rallies and events. Award winning monthly Newsletter.

In recent years the Armstrong Siddeley Owners Club has reached a level of appreciation commensurate with the marques pre-eminence during its years of production. The complete range of models are now eagerly sought after, and command a good price for vehicles of their quality, but are not as yet overvalued. They represent good value for enthusiasts and investors alike.

MEMBERSHIP SECRETARY
Peter Sheppard, 57 Berberry Close, Birmingham. B30 ITB.

In the 60's some power trucks were built and bodywork for Sunbeam cars. But the main involvement was to concentrate on Aerospace. Aero engines are still being built and tested where they were in 1917 so one tradition continues well into the Nineties. Alas cars are no longer built but every year the Armstrong Siddeley Owners' Club displays a selection of the fine cars at the factory and continue a tradition that goes back over eighty years.

The Armstrong Siddeley Owners Club founded in 1960, refounded in 1964 and incorporated as a limited company in 1974 has for 23 years maintained a lively interest in the Armstrong Siddeley and Pre AS cars, both by rallies, meetings and the purchase and sale of thos spares passed onto Rolls Royce.

Today Spares are remanufactured and cars built from 1919 to 1960 are assured of survival.

Production figures

Post War

16 hp 7,155, 18 hp 7, 347, Long 18 hp 126
Total 16/18 production 14,628 cars,
346 production 7,697, 2.36 =609, 2.34 = 796

Star Sapphire 905, Star Limo 77

TOTAL Post War Production 1946 - 1960

= 24,709 cars

Total Production 1919 - 1960 - 1960 = 85,759 cars

Survival Rates

The 700 club members own 1,200 cars between them. The Registrar system has so far located a total of 2,500 survivors worldwide, about 500 of these were built between 1919 and 1940. The projection is that at least another 1,500 cars are surviving but remain to be located.

Bill Smith
A.S.O.C. Historian

The Sapphire Story

The history and development of the Armstrong Siddeley Sapphire 1952–1960

By Peter Fawcett

OCTOBER 1952 was a notable date in the annals of Armstrong Siddeley history. Earls Court at that time saw the introduction of the new Sapphire which was to dispel forever the traditional Siddeley image of sobriety and lethargy, and yet was to revive standards of refinement and luxury equalling those of Parkside's better pre-war offerings.

By 1950 the limitations of the post-war 16/18hp range of cars were becoming painfully apparent and the Armstrong Siddeley management felt that a replacement was long overdue. Consequently the design team was presented with a brief for a six-seat high-performance saloon of sober appearance and minimum weight, a car which could restore their position in a highly competitive sector of the market. The result, with its technically advanced engine of square dimensions, its elegant coachwork and stiff chassis amply satisfied the brief as witness the eulogies in the motoring press which accompanied the Sapphire's introduction in October 1952.

Quite the most outstanding feature of the new car was its six cylinder motor whose 90mm × 90mm dimensions were a departure from previous Armstrong Siddeley practice, as were the inclined valves and inclined unequal length pushrods operated from a single camshaft. Prototypes had been produced with conventional pushrods and also with twin overhead camshafts but the latter had been rejected on account of excessive timing chain length (ironically reviving a failing of the pre-war range), and its attendant noise problems. The final design with its inclined valves (incorporating a 70 degree angle), hemispherical combustion chambers, and ingenious pushrod arrangement, was to be repeated by both Humber and Fiat in their six-cylinder engines of the late 1950's. A "cross-flow" head design incorporated individual exhaust ports feeding a pair of three branch manifolds, each in turn leading to a small primary silencer and large secondary silencer. Inlet arrangements were a single downdraught Stromberg carburettor feeding a four-branch manifold which in turn was connected to a longitudinal passage in the head. This passage incorporated a baffle at its centre so that the front three cylinders were in effect fed by the front two manifold branches with a similar arrangement for the rear cylinders. Such a head design necessitated water heated induction. The remainder of the engine followed conventional practice, but the square dimensions made for low piston speeds, and a stiff crank and generous big ends and mains of respectively 2¼in and 2¼in diameter ensured robustness and longevity. Even in its mild 120bhp form as introduced, the 3·4 litre six endowed the 31cwt Sapphire with a lively performance, as witness the 0–60mph time of 15·5sec and a maximum speed into the nineties.

Like the 18hp range (which was to continue in production alongside the new model until late 1953) the Sapphire was offered with an option of four speed synchromesh gearbox with column change and conventional clutch, or a fourspeed preselector gearbox with centrifugal clutch. However, the manual selectors which had traditionally appeared on Siddeleys since 1928 were eschewed in favour of a switch moving in a minute gate mounted on a steering column stalk. The switch connected to a series of solenoids mounted on the gearbox casing, which, when energised by pressing the gearchange pedal, operated the appropriate brake band to engage the pre-selected gear. It was a refined and ingenious system which made for easier driving, but the electrics were more prone to failure than was the superseded mechanical linkage.

The completed chassis weighed a mere 621lb

more than that of the 18hp range whilst its torsional rigidity was greatly increased. The basis of such stiffness was a channel section main frame with cruciform brace, a pressed steel section supporting the front engine mounting and front suspension, transverse tubes amidships and a channel rear member to complete the structure. Orthodox front suspension comprised coil springs with concentric dampers and unequal length wishbones, whilst semi-elliptic leaf springs slung beneath the axle served the rear. A Burman recirculating ball steering box was fitted affording three and a half turns for a 42ft 6in turning circle and Girling hydraulic brakes were of 11in diameter. Chassis refinements included a one and a half gallon fuel reserve and a Smiths Bevelift jacking system.

Since their inception in 1919, Armstrong Siddeleys had always looked handsome and dignified and the Sapphire was no exception. The prototype Sapphire had been fitted with a Whitley body and the roofline of the production Sapphire owed everything to the recently introduced six-light 18hp Whitley. The styling epitomised the large luxury car of the period (vide Jaguar Mark VII, Bentley "S" and Daimler Regency) in its adherence to the exaggerated bulbous wing line, sloping tail and "marque" radiator grille, thankfully reintroduced for a very conservative clientele. Internally, the appointments were a vast improvement on the austere 18hp cars but curiously, the steering wheel and instruments were leftovers from the latter range. The doors supported about a central pillar utilised the wing line to provide internal stowage. Initially, an option of four or six light saloon coachwork was available, whilst the bonnet was adorned by a rather uneasy-looking Sphinx which had mysteriously grown jet engines from its flanks! The Sapphire name had, of course been culled from the turbo-jet engine by the same manufacturer. In this guise, the Sapphire represented excellent value at £1574.

It was obvious that such a technically interesting engine was presented in 1952 with a degree of tune well below its potential. There were good reasons for such caution, as Armstrong Siddeley felt that too much emphasis on performance could possibly deter long-standing customers who associated themselves with the staid characteristics of the marque. This attitude was in some measure responsible for the mild 120bhp produced by the first Sapphires. However, the Sapphire was an outstanding success in overseas markets (particularly the USA where Briggs Cunningham was a notable devotee) owing to the very virtues that Armstrong Siddeley had felt expedient to suppress. Such was the demand from overseas by 1953, that Parkside had adopted a three-shift system of working around the clock and 90% of Sapphire production was being exported. A twin carburettor version developing some 150bhp had been developed for export markets and this version became available on the home market in September 1953, one season after the model's introduction. All cars received higher compression ratios for the 1954

The Sapphire Story

season (from 6·8 to 7·0 : 1) and export models were fitted with winking indicators and white-wall tyres.

For the 1955 season the Mark II Sapphire was introduced at the 1954 Earls Court Motor Show. The car had undoubtedly been a greater success than any previous Siddeley and had enhanced Parkside's flagging reputation, but only time would reveal the inherent design weaknesses of the coachwork. Poor detailing produced large mud traps and the bodies were prone to excessive corrosion after a few years of service. The Mark II allowed for yet another transmission option. This was in the form of a four-speed Rolls-Royce automatic gearbox with column-mounted selector quadrant. As early as 1935 Armstrong Siddeley had converted a preselector gearbox to fully automatic actuation with some success, but the Mark II "no-clutch" Sapphire was the first two-pedal control production Siddeley. Parkside catalogued this option as the "No-clutch transmission" in an attempt to invest it with something rather special. In reality it was a normal three train (one for reverse) epicyclic box with a fluid coupling. In like fashion the 1938 season had witnessed the introduction of "Balanced Drive", which in reality was nothing more than an admission that Armstrong Siddeleys at last had gearboxes in unit with the engine. The other major refinement fitted to the 1955 cars was Girling Autostatic power assisted brakes with an increased drum diameter of 12in, self-adjusting at the front, and a Clayton Dewandre vacuum servo. Other mechanical refinements included a simplification of the highly complex throttle linkage on the twin carburettor models, a five blade fan to replace the original two blade affair, and the coil was moved from the scuttle to shorten the excessive length of high tension leads.

The Mark II version could be distinguished externally from its predecessor by various alterations to the coachwork. Winking indicators were now fitted to all cars, the boot lid shed its central chrome strip, and the rear wings gained black moulded rubber stoneguards at their leading edges. Internally, the fascia was slightly revised to include new dials, a clock, and an array of warning lights to replace some of the Mark I's instruments. Separate front seats were now available as an option to the standard bench device with central armrest. Even at this stage, the Sapphire Mark II represented good value at £1722 for the least expensive synchromesh version and £1990 for its automatic stablemate.

For the 1956 season, the Sapphire was offered with a further range of optional equipment. Armstrong Siddeley became the first concern to offer power assisted steering on a British production car, and furthermore, unlike contemporary American systems, the driver was given full control over the degree of power assistance, or indeed whether he wished to avail himself of the facility at all. The system fitted was of Girling origin with a Hoburn Eaton hydraulic pump, belt-driven from the crankshaft. This refinement added £75 to the price of the car and for another £32 the discerning customer could specify adjustable ride control for the rear dampers whilst the self-indulgent could have the doubtful benefit of power operated windows for a further £121.

Unfortunately, the Sapphire chassis did not attract the specialist coachbuilders as some of its competitors had done and there is a dearth of non-standard cars. Harold Radford produced an ingenious "Countryman" version of the Mark II which, according to the brochure, transformed the car into a "combination of town car, shooting brake and continental tourer". It was lavishly equipped with such invaluable items as shooting stick, pigskin cigarette case, pigskin notebook, electric razor and Grundig tape recorder but at a total of £804 over list price, the ensemble must have been unattractive to a prospective buyer with £3000 at his disposal. The factory produced a handful of bizarre-looking pick-up trucks for their own use whilst a massive formal limousine (overall length 17ft 8in) achieved some popularity as a mayoral carriage. An interesting diversion was a Healey-Sports-bodied Sapphire chassis which looked almost identical to the Healey Alvis announced at the 1952 show. It did, however, incorporate a much larger boot to accommodate the extra chassis length of the Sapphire. Unfortunately, this unique vehicle was written off in 1960.

With such a respectable performance, it was inevitable that the Sapphire at some time in its career should be considered eligible as a rally car. Two Sapphires were entered for the 1954 Monte Carlo Rally, one driven by Mike Couper, who had previously had success in the Concours de Confort with a Rolls-Royce Silver Wraith, and Mark VI Bentleys. However, the performances of these cars were inauspicious, Couper finishing 82nd overall and Air Vice-Marshal Bennet achieving 110th position with the other entry. Couper did, however, repeat his former successes with the Concours de Confort. For the 1955 Monte a team of five twin carburettor Sapphires was prepared and marginally better results were achieved, Bennet upon this occasion gaining 33rd place with the experienced Tommy Wisdom at 39th position overall.

During the pre-war years Armstrong Siddeley had offered a wide range of vehicles and an attempt to restore such diversity was made for the 1956 season with the introduction of the 234/236 Sapphire range at the 1955 Motor Show. At 15ft overall length, the cars were smaller than the discontinued 18hp range and were seen as direct competition for the well-established P4 Rovers.

The most controversial feature of the new range was its bizarre styling with vestigial tail fins, a curious rear wing line which flared forwards into the door panels, and lurid two tone colour schemes. The 236 used the old 18hp engine which, with new carburation and bigger valves was persuaded to produce a further 10bhp to achieve 85bhp. The 234, however, used a four-cylinder version of the Sapphire 3·4-litre six (now designated the Sapphire 346) to produce 120bhp at 5000rpm. It was obvious that the cars were to be quite dissimilar and different engine characteristics were accentuated by the provision of AP Manumatic transmission on 236 models only. Unfortunately, the Manumatic system with its vacuum servo operated clutch proved less than reliable and was no match for the traditional Wilson preselector set-up.

Naturally the 234 emerged as much the better car with its lusty 2·3-litre four-cylinder motor giving acceptable performance figures of 15·5sec for 0–60mph and a maximum speed of 97mph. The chassis was orthodox with channel and box sections and the front suspension design was inherited from the larger 346 cars. Burman recirculating ball steering with three and a half turns from lock to lock gave a 39ft turning circle and Girling brakes with vacuum servo assistance were fitted.

The body utilised a composite construction of hiduminium and steel which, whilst contributing to an acceptable overall weight of 26½cwt, nevertheless produced ideal conditions for excessive corrosion by electrolytic action.

Dreadful coachwork and its lack of durability marred what was potentially a fine car (at least in 234 guise) but it was left to external factors to bring about the demise of the small Sapphires after a mere three years of production. Unfortunately for Parkside, William Lyons at Jaguar was light years ahead in design, marketing, and production methods and none but the most blinkered of Siddeley devotees could have passed over the 2·4 Jaguar introduced one season after the 234. It was infinitely better in every respect, as, indeed, were the offerings from Solihull.

Following the limited successes in the Monte Carlo Rallies of 1954 and 1955 with the large Sapphires, Parkside prepared a team of three 234's for the 1957 rally where it was thought that the car's compact overall dimensions and lively performance would stand it in good stead. Unfortunately, the Suez Crisis intervened and Armstrong Siddeley's last attempt at gaining honours in a major rally was thwarted.

With the failure of the small Sapphires to gain a niche in the medium sized car market, Armstrong Siddeley found themselves once more marketing one model, the 346 Sapphire, albeit with a wide range of optional equipment and a limousine variant. In 1958 this one model policy was consolidated by the introduction at Earls Court of the four-litre Star Sapphire, a direct development of the

Above, and example of the smaller 234/236 Sapphire range introduced in 1955 and right, Sapphire in chassis form. Note the power assisted steering, the first to be offered as an option on a British car.

Above and right, a fine example of the model; a 1956 Armstrong Siddeley Sapphire 346 automatic owned by G. A. Horrox of Crowthorne, Berkshire. He has owned it since 1963 and it has covered only 39,000 miles!

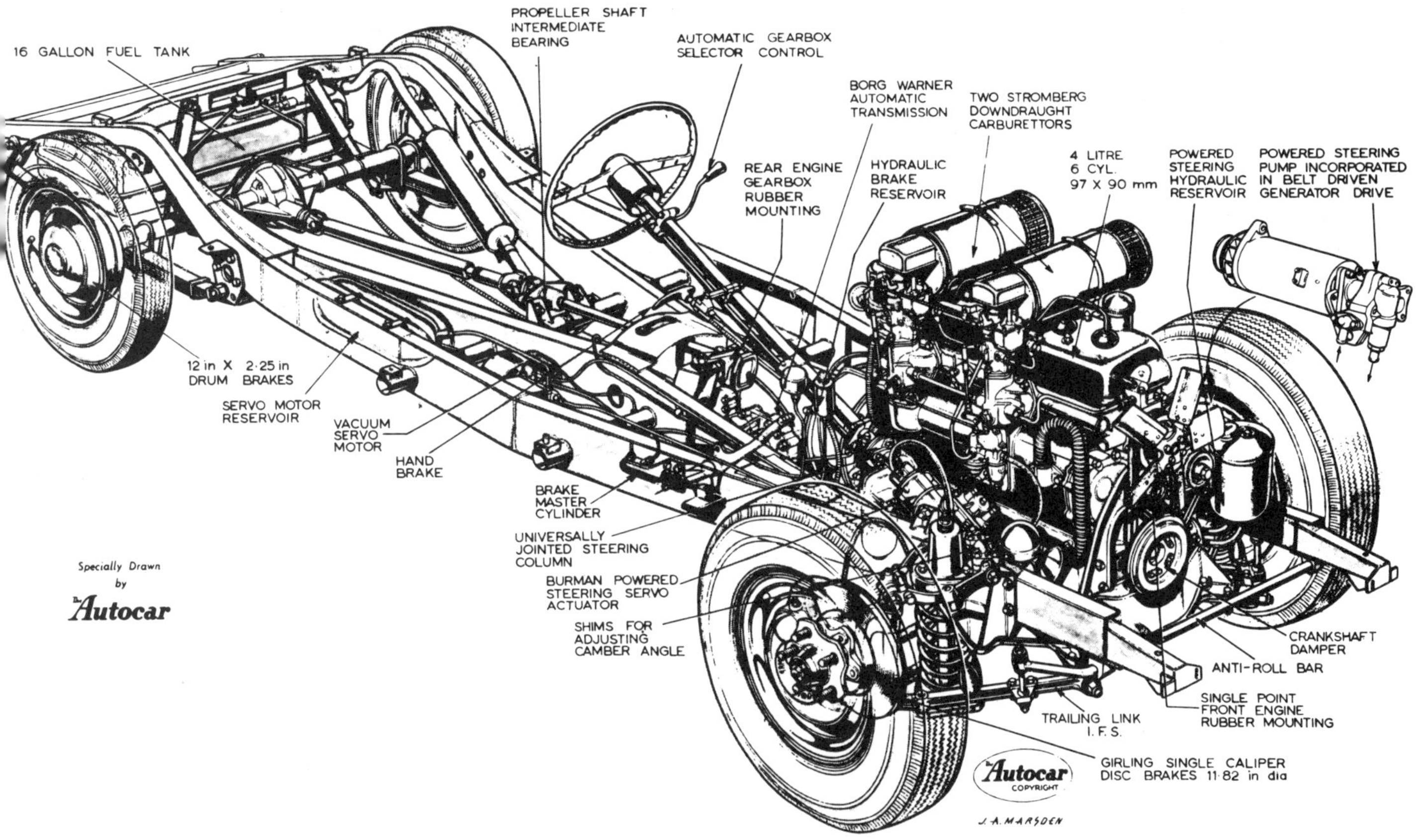

Specially Drawn
by
The Autocar

16 GALLON FUEL TANK

PROPELLER SHAFT
INTERMEDIATE
BEARING

AUTOMATIC GEARBOX
SELECTOR CONTROL

BORG WARNER
AUTOMATIC
TRANSMISSION

TWO STROMBERG
DOWNDRAUGHT
CARBURETTORS

REAR ENGINE
GEARBOX
RUBBER
MOUNTING

HYDRAULIC
BRAKE
RESERVOIR

4 LITRE.
6 CYL.
97 X 90 mm

POWERED
STEERING
HYDRAULIC
RESERVOIR

POWERED STEERING
PUMP INCORPORATED
IN BELT DRIVEN
GENERATOR DRIVE

12 in X 2·25 in
DRUM BRAKES

SERVO MOTOR
RESERVOIR

VACUUM
SERVO
MOTOR

HAND
BRAKE

BRAKE
MASTER
CYLINDER

UNIVERSALLY
JOINTED STEERING
COLUMN

BURMAN POWERED
STEERING SERVO
ACTUATOR

SHIMS FOR
ADJUSTING
CAMBER ANGLE

TRAILING LINK
I.F.S.

CRANKSHAFT
DAMPER

ANTI-ROLL BAR

SINGLE POINT
FRONT ENGINE
RUBBER MOUNTING

GIRLING SINGLE CALIPER
DISC BRAKES 11·82 in dia

Autocar COPYRIGHT

J.A.MARSDEN

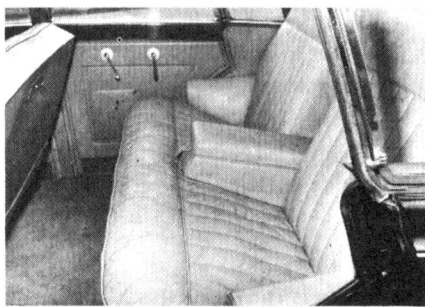

346, but with so many improvements that it was to move into another market sector, that of the exclusive high performance luxury car. The price had escalated to £2646 but the increase in power to 165 bhp, the lavishly trimmed interior, and the fitting of power steering and servo disc brakes as standard offered some justification.

The Sapphire 346 block was bored out to 97mm to produce 3990cc with the same 90mm stroke dimension as before, whilst all cars were fitted with Borg-Warner automatic transmission and torque convertor. An intermediate gear hold control in a sliding quadrant could vary the speed at which top gear was engaged. The departure of the Armstrong Siddeley preselector gearbox after thirty years' production this passed almost unnoticed by the motoring press.

The styling received much detail attention with a handsome new grille, (ironically in this last production Armstrong Siddeley giving more than a hint of the first Armstrong Siddeley Thirty of 1919) revised lamps, bumpers, and wheel spats. The interior was transformed with high quality veneers, individual front and rear heaters, and sumptuous leather trim.

A notably handsome Star Sapphire limousine appeared on the long chassis but, like it predecessor, the Star Sapphire never reached the specialist coach builders although the company produced a gargantuan pick-up truck for its own use on the limousine chassis, and a few prototype Mark II versions with twin head lamps, wrap around rear windows and revised interiors were produced.

The Star Sapphire was the last Armstrong Siddeley to be produced and was undoubtedly the most refined and best developed vehicle to emanate from Parkside, but alas, the company's production potential was to be diverted to more pressing and more profitable pursuits than car manufacture and Star Sapphire production lasted a mere two seasons. Car production ceased late in 1960 but Armstrong Siddeley continued to supply spares and to give their legendary service for a decade more.

Thus, after almost forty-two years of motor car production the name Armstrong Siddeley entered the realms of "Lost Causedom". No doubt that staid and sober clientele who had traditionally patronised the Parkside concern saw this as a mere palastable alternative than the badge enginerring which had consumed some of the competition.●

Looking back to the motoring magazines of the early fifties it is rather a surprise to discover just how many makes have since disappeared without trace – Riley, Alvis, Lanchester, Lea Francis, and of course Armstrong Siddeley, are just some of them. The interesting thing about the makes I have just named is that they were all competing for customers not in the lower nor in the most expensive price ranges and they all had an aura of respectability and quality in a way that would reflect their owners' good taste.

Nearly all of the lost makes had established a sound reputation between the wars and were the sort of cars whose owners often bought (say) a Riley or an Armstrong, "because we have always had one" — those were the days of marque loyalty.

Looking back it is difficult to draw a word picture of the typical Armstrong-Siddeley owner other than to suggest that they were well-off rather than rich and they expected their cars to be well-made, reliable and comfortable. They did not buy an Armstrong to impress the neighbours, nor to enjoy nerve tingling performance and they certainly were not the sort of people to throw their cars around roundabouts in a lurid scream of tyres, or to spend money having spectacular interiors cluttered with gimmics built into their cars — no, to own an Armstrong Siddeley you were likely to be a pillar of discreet society!

As manufacturers, Armstrong Siddeley were very much like their customers and they rarely entertained any notions of building the fastest nor the most technically advanced cars. When, in the late thirties, most British manufacturers were quickly designing new chassis or adapting existing ones to accommodate independent front suspension Armstrong took their time about it and their new ranges were therefore well-thought out and, perhaps by accident, admirably timed for the end of the war.

As we have pointed out on many previous occasions when private car production re-started after the Second World War there

The handsome lines of the Typhoon rely upon the minimum of brightwork and give the impression that the car is even larger than it is.

The Arm Typhoon

strong Siddeley

John Williams drives an elegant carriage for gentlefolk.

were relatively few entirely new designs. The majority of "new" cars produced were in fact the realisation of plans made before the war and featured new chassis incorporating independent front suspension, a development of a pre-war power unit and, in many cases, new bodywork.

This bodywork took either the form of late pre-war styling trends or a tentative guess at future trends finalised in the latter stages of the war as armaments contracts petered out. The stylists were working in the dark with only an inkling of what their rivals were going to do and really very little idea of the market conditions they would face.

The range of cars the British manufacturers offered was therefore as varied as it was interesting but what we have to remember, looking back over a quarter of a century, is that petrol rationing and shortages of materials to build cars played a major part in the way things turned out. Britain's balance of payments was not at all healthy and the government policy was to tell motor manufacturers that they would only be allocated materials if they would direct a large proportion of their production overseas – especially the United States. Such a small proportion of the cars built came onto the British market that there were enormous waiting lists and in many cases potential customers paid a deposit and sat back to wait for their car to be built, even having to sign an undertaking not to sell the car for two years to make sure that the black market trade in new cars was kept within reasonable bounds.

The situation dictated that new car buyers had to settle for what they could get and in at least some cases what they could get was the cars that were not selling very well in overseas markets. The other side of the coin was that the manufacturer who could supply cars was in a strong position almost regardless of whether his product was a new design or merely a pre-war product in new wrapping.

Armstrong Siddeley were possibly the first British manufacturer to put a car on the market after the war, their first post-war offerings being the Hurricane which appeared in November 1945 and the Lancaster which followed in February 1946. The Lancaster was a four-door saloon, the Hurricane a two door drophead coupe. The Typhoon was introduced in August 1946 and this was simply a Hurricane with a very well designed roof section instead of a folding hood, so well designed in fact that it is hard to think of it as a modification which was grafted on as an afterthought. All three models shared a newly designed chassis with torsion bar independent front suspension, and all three were fitted with the six cylinder, two litre overhead valve engine which dated from the 1930s.

Mr Alan Swainson (the Post-war 16 and 18 hp Registrar of the Armstrong Siddeley Owners Club) kindly put his 1947 Typhoon at my disposal and displayed not the least alarm at my tentative driving efforts. Alan's Typhoon is almost entirely original and unrestored. The car was owned by a London company until about 1952 when it was sold to a dental surgeon who ran it until 1965 when it

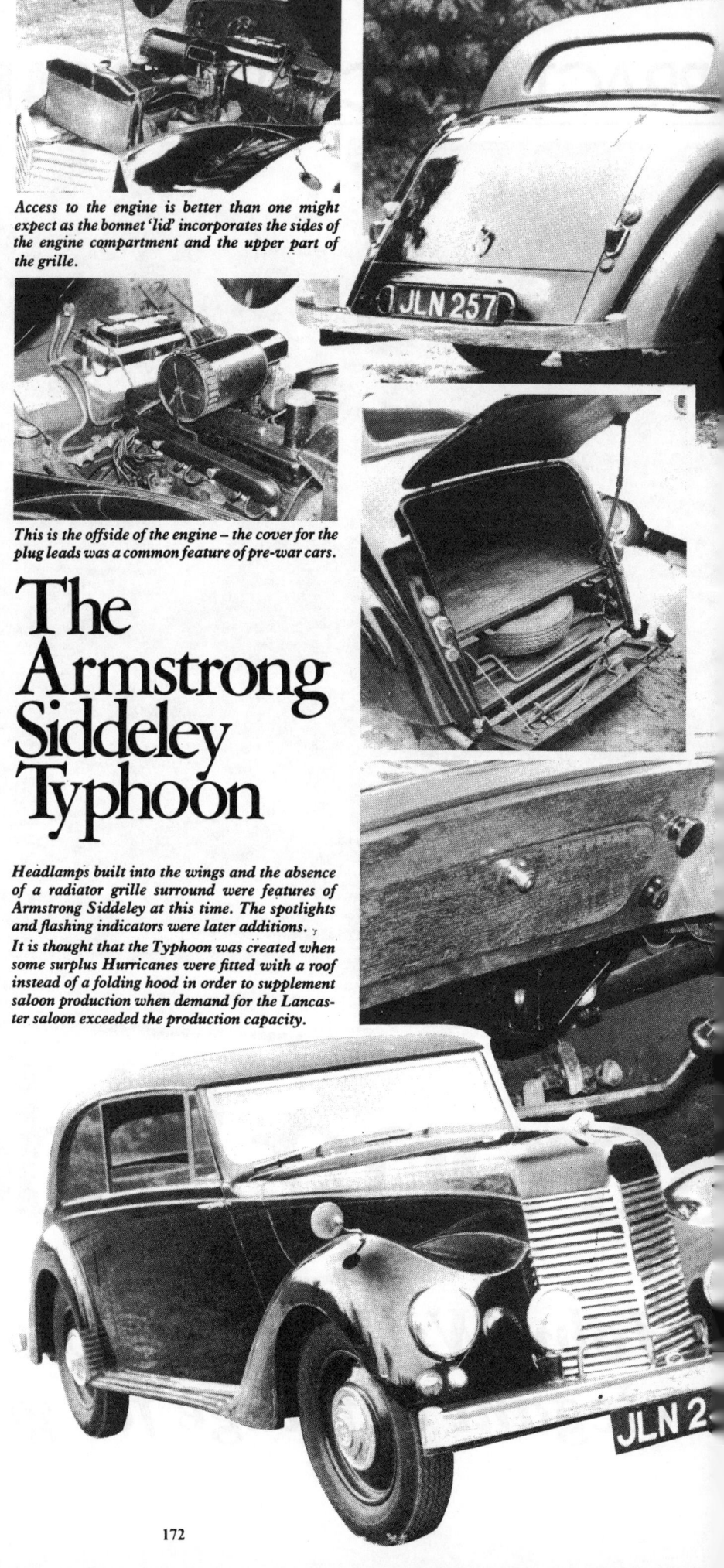

Access to the engine is better than one might expect as the bonnet 'lid' incorporates the sides of the engine compartment and the upper part of the grille.

This is the offside of the engine – the cover for the plug leads was a common feature of pre-war cars.

The Armstrong Siddeley Typhoon

Headlamps built into the wings and the absence of a radiator grille surround were features of Armstrong Siddeley at this time. The spotlights and flashing indicators were later additions.

It is thought that the Typhoon was created when some surplus Hurricanes were fitted with a roof instead of a folding hood in order to supplement saloon production when demand for the Lancaster saloon exceeded the production capacity.

The interior is light and spacious and the seats are very comfortable in their own right. This impression is reinforced by the car's excellent behaviour on the road.

The rear window allows adequate visibility for normal driving but reversing would require practice...

...and the boot capacity is limited. The lid of the spare wheel compartment can be hinged down like this after the rear bumper has been released from the thumb screws on each side and swivelled out of the way. The original rear lights are adjacent to the rear number plate so cannot be seen when the spare wheel compartment is open. In this situation small light (to the right of the spare wheel in this picture) automatically switches on.

There is one jack on each side of the car just forward of the front seats. On lifting a lockable flap in the floor panel the jack is raised into the operating position and a detachable handle is used – the latter has a built-in ratchet or can be used for continuous winding.
A useful kit of hand tools was supplied with every Typhoon and this stows below the lefthand side of the dashboard.

The interior is tasteful rather than eye-catching but all the driving controls are close to hand...

...and most of the switches (including the later additions on this car) are on a panel to the right of the instruments.

was laid up. It was still laid up when Alan bought it in December 1982 and since then it has been used frequently. Apart from bringing the headlights up to modern standards Alan has done no major work on the car and the 46,078 miles which it has recorded is believed to be genuine.

Typhoons were available with either manual or preselector gearboxes, and customers were given some choice as to materials used for the interior trim. The subject of this article is a manual model, with leather upholstery, solid oak door cappings and a veneered dashboard, and, incongruous though it may seem, a plastic headlining. The interior is light thanks to a generous window area, simple in design, spacious and comfortable. Indeed it offers luxury but without frills and certainly without ostentation. The dashboard, for example, is a quietly functional feature rather than strikingly beautiful.

Although the significant seat and seat-to-pedals dimensions are almost the same as in my Sunbeam Rapier I found the driving position in the Typhoon quite odd, at first anyway. With the adjustable steering wheel little more than an inch from the instruments, and the seat well forward I began to suspect that

my 5' 8½" was in fact well below an average drivers height, but I soon overcame the sensation of being trapped between the back of the seat and the steering wheel once on the move. All the controls are close to hand, the ignition, starter, reserve fuel and light switches are on a small panel to the right of the instruments, the heater and windscreen wiper controls to the left, and the original indicator and dipswitch are on the centre of the steering wheel. The umbrella type handbrake is to the right of the steering column and the instruments comprise a speedometer (with mileometer and trip counter), oil pressure and fuel gauges.

There is some engine noise but much of this is "top end clatter" which diminishes noticeably as the engine warms up. The engine revs freely and pulls the car away from a standing start very smoothly indeed, and the performance seems equally effortless on steep uphill gradients – effortless, yes, but by no means startling. The steering is light but there is some 'feel', and gear changing is also easy although there seemed to be a lot of movement in that long lever and the driver needs to be decisive about changes rather than hover about (as I did once or twice) in neutral. The shallow windscreen allows ample forward visibility and the driver's view to each side is excellent thanks to deep side windows which extend back to the rear seats, but reversing would require some practice with well adjusted wing mirrors. Alan's Typhoon accelerates fairly briskly and without fuss and I am assured that it will cruise all day at 50 mph and probably faster if necessary. Contemporary road tests indicate that the maximum speed is about 75 mph. The suspension behaviour is almost impeccable, there is virtually no tendency to lean over on corners and the only fault I detected was an excessive degree of front end bounce when passing over poor road surfaces, not that the wheels lost their grip in this situation but the bonnet did behave like a yo-yo. I am told that this was a weakness in all the Armstrong Siddeleys of the early post-war period and that the company tried all sorts of shock absorbers in an effort to overcome the problem. I did not find this a serious fault, more of an irritation in fact, as in other respects the car was so well behaved.

Between 1946 and 1949, some 1700 Typhoons were made and about half of these were exported, mainly to Australia, New Zealand, Canada and Europe. It is worth noting that Australian conditions, long distances and plenty of rough roads, greatly reduced the useful life of many British cars of this period but the Armstrong Siddeleys coped rather well. In general these cars were not scrapped because of rust but because they became obsolete with all the related problems of spares availability, and their performance also became obsolete in terms of a rather high fuel consumption. All of this happened around a quarter of a century ago and it is a fine tribute to the construction of these cars and to the materials used that thirty-six years on Alan Swainson's Typhoon still survives in remarkably sound original condition. □

THE BABY SAPPHIRES

Why weren't the small Armstrong Siddeleys successful? Roger Bateman examines the cars and drives two examples in an attempt to find out

RACING improves the breed, of that there can be no doubt. After all, it has been proved many times by such firms as Jaguar, Ferrari and . . . Armstrong Siddeley.

Armstrong Siddeley? Strangely enough, yes. Renowned as dignified, refined motor cars, the products of Parkside in Coventry are not remembered for sporting prowess despite their creditable performance in rallies during the Fifties.

But perhaps it is not surprising when one recalls that the Chairman of the company was Sir Thomas Sopwith whose sporting achievements in yachting and aviation are well known. His son, Tommy Sopwith, was involved in research and development at Armstrong Siddeley and built a sports racing car, appropriately called the Sphinx, which was entered by *Equipe Endeavour*. Endeavour was the name of Sir Thomas' racing yachts which challenged the America's Cup in the Thirties, and the car was painted the same shade of dark blue.

This car made its debut at Goodwood on March 27, 1954, and took second place to a Jaguar XK120C. It was built on an Allard JR chassis with an attractive sports racing body with flowing lines typical of the period, and used a highly modified Armstrong Siddeley six-cylinder 3.4-litre engine producing 215bhp at 5,200rpm. And this, of course, is where our story really starts.

A year and a half later, one of the best kept secrets at the 1955 Earls Court Motor Show was the introduction of two new cars from Armstrong Siddeley; the 234 and 236 'Baby' Sapphires. They caused quite a stir in motoring circles, not only because their introduction came as such a surprise, but also because their design was a radical departure from the company's traditional designs. As well as being replacements for the old-fashioned, post-war Hurricane/Whitley models, the new cars were also trend setters which were intended to steer Armstrong Siddeley into the second half of the 20th Century by going after the newly emerging 'middle class executive' market, rather as Jaguar did the same year with the 2.4 saloon. It is therefore ironic that this model probably contributed to the eventual demise of Armstrong Siddeley five years later.

Outwardly identical and using the same chassis, the two models were as different as chalk and cheese. The 234 was nothing less than a luxurious sports saloon, setting its cap squarely at the new Jaguar 2.4. It had a brand new 2.3-litre, 120bhp engine developed directly from the Sphinx, driving a four-speed all-synchromesh gearbox with optional overdrive through a conventional clutch. The maximum speed was 100mph with a creditable 0-60 time of 15.5 seconds (comparable figures for the Jaguar are 100mph maximum, 0-60 in 14.5 seconds). A competition clutch was available for those who wished to take full advantage of this performance.

The 236 on the other hand had a six-cylinder, 85bhp, 2.3-litre engine which was the final guise of the 18hp engine which had been used in earlier Armstrong Siddeley cars. This model was the version intended for the traditional Armstrong Siddeley client. It was refined, smooth and quiet, and was the first car in the world to be fitted with the new Lockheed Manumatic clutch providing two-pedal driving through the same four-speed overdrive gearbox. With 30% less power, the performance of the 236 was nothing like as outstanding as the 234 but it would run up to a maximum speed of 85mph, which was quite fast enough for the sort of person who would have bought this car in 1955.

The extremely stiff cruciform-braced chassis was developed on Armstrong Siddeley's special deflection rig and the body was rubber-mounted to it. The suspension was coil spring independent at the front and semi-elliptic supporting a live axle at the rear, with telescopic dampers all round. The brakes were 11in

servo-assisted drums front and rear, and wire wheels were available as optional extras.

The interiors were a blend of the traditional and contemporary. Deep pile carpets, walnut dashboard and door cappings, and the same white headlining that Armstrong Siddeley had used since 1938, were complemented by leather cloth seats with a new type of ventilated nylon facing, ultra violet illumination for the instruments, and child locks on the rear doors — possibly an Armstrong innovation?

The body engineering was an interesting concept which owed much to the parent company's activities in aircraft design. It consisted of a steel frame with all the panels made from an aircraft specification alloy called Hiduminium 22, with the exception of the steel outer wings. The influence of aircraft design was evident everywhere. For example, there were no stress points where cracks could start, and the bonnet hinges were designed with a weak spot so that if the bonnet should burst open, the hinges would break, the bonnet flying over the roof of the car without causing further damage (or consternation to the driver). One presumes that the only problem would be if the car following ran over it.

The cars were smaller than anything else Armstrong had produced before. The body styling was incredibly *avant garde*, a curious mixture of rounded and angular, and some of the colour schemes were rather brash. The effect was stunning. Nobody really knew what to say.

The sales catalogue gushed that: "Its graceful, sweeping lines set off the modern yet dignified exterior colour schemes to perfection . . ." *The Autocar* commented politely that "Opinions differ as to the appearance . . ." but the *Sunday Express* was more honest and said that the design was "Enterprising . . . whether they have succeeded is a matter of personal taste."

The 234/236 registrar of the Armstrong Siddley Owners Club for many years was Basil Tasker, who has owned his 1956 236 for 20 years. He is fortunate enough to have known the car since new and to have been able to maintain it for the first owner, Mrs Raikes, who was the sister of Sir Thomas Sopwith. Basil's car has now covered 155,000 miles and is still his everyday transport.

The powder blue bodywork is still in

John Banyard with his 1958 234 saloon

Above, the Armstrong Siddeley 234 was pitched fairly and squarely in Jaguar territory but the styling was not universally admired

Below, 120bhp was a healthy output from the 2.3-litre engine and the resultant performance was impressive for the day

good condition, although beginning to show its age with rust spots here and there around the steel wings. The only weakness in the body design shows up with age: water thrown up from the front wheels corrodes the steel A-posts so that the front doors drop alarmingly. On Basil's car this has been forestalled by fitting aluminium wing liners to deflect spray from the vulnerable area. The interior is very tidy for a car which is unrestored and regularly used, although the carpets aren't original and the nylon seat facing shredded after a few years and were recovered with another material. The seat covering is, in fact, the only thing the owners of these cars seem to complain about.

This car has only been repaired in a garage workshop once in its life when the rear jacking point had to be welded two years ago. The only other repairs this 31 year old car has required were a replacement clutch at 85,000 miles (the linings were only renewed as a precaution — it was the release fork which had broken); the engine was decoked at 95,000 and the Manumatic control box replaced at 150,000. Oh yes, and the car is on its third set of brake linings.

Basil is a firm believer in regular maintenance and puts the reliability of this car down to a combination of this and Armstrong Siddeley's excellent engineering. He changes the engine oil every 2,000 miles. and more frequently in

the winter. He has only ever used one make of oil, Filtrate, grade 20 in winter and 30 in summer, never multigrade.

Now in his seventies, Basil will never change this car for another one. "You can't get a car like these days", he says — and means it. He averages 3,000 miles a year and his main concern now is what will happen to his 236 when he can no longer drive it.

John Banyard succeeded Basil Tasker as Registrar of the Armstrong Siddeley Owners Club in 1985. He purchased his 1958-registered 234 from the original owner nine years ago and initially used it as everyday family transport, although it is now only taxed for the six fine months of the year.

THE BABY SAPPHIRES

The car has covered 60,000 miles and its smart appearance is no doubt helped by having had new wings and a respray in the original BRG before John bought it. The interior is also very well cared for, with original green carpets, but the nylon facings on the front seats have long since been covered up, although they are hardly worn at the rear.

John has found the car to be very reliable — like Basil, he proudly says it has never let him down — and the only difficulty he has ever had was finding someone to make a replacement windscreen. In fact, he would be more than happy to use the car every day of the year if he weren't conscious of the detrimental effect that the wear and tear would have.

The heavy doors of the 234 open wide to 90 degrees and you step up, almost, into the large individual front seats which reach high up to the shoulders and far forward under the thighs. Then the doors shut with a solid 'thud' and your awareness is dominated by the large steering wheel, the three 6in instruments arrayed in the centre of the lovely walnut dashboard and, above all, the impression of quality.

The engine starts with an unexpected, lusty roar from the air cleaner intakes and as you glance down the bonnet sloping gracefully away to the sphinx mascot you are reminded forcibly of the Jaguar 2.4 again. The pedals are workmanlike and the clutch squeaks at the end of its travel, but the gearchange is so sweet and the lever snicks into first; a trace of clutch judder and the car moves off.

Change into second gear and the engine pulls strongly and noisily with a pleasant whine from the indirect gears. For most purposes 3,000rpm is a practical limit but the car will pull powerfully up to 4,500, or even 5,000 if required. Change into third, then top by 40mph and the overdrive comes into its own, the engine noise dropping with the revs. Sixty mph comes up with unexpected suddenness, emphasising that this is no ordinary Armstrong Siddeley.

The recirculating ball steering box has a little lost motion which is not helped by the car's tendency to react to road camber and irregularities, but once familiar you can position the car with unerring accuracy, the strong castor action spinning the wheel back after a corner. It only takes 3½ turns lock-to-lock, but the turning circle is 39 feet, making parking in today's traffic conditions a nightmare.

The 234 handles better than one might expect, cornering with a commendable absence of roll and holding the road markedly well. The ride is firmly smooth, and although unexpected irregular bumps catch it out, the car barely notices cattle grids and the like. The brakes are powerful and pull the car up dead straight with a hiss from the servo underneath the back seat.

The noise level inside the car is surprisingly high, even when the engine isn't working particularly hard, but once you settle down to a sensible cruising gait it reduces to an acceptable level. There are no body rattles whatsoever. Visibility is good, even to the rear, and the thoughtful design shows again with the driver's window which lowers completely with a single 90 degree movement of the lever.

It is remarkable that two cars can look so alike but perform so differently; the 236 has none of the power or the feeling of latent urge that its sister has. Driving the 236 is altogether a more stately affair.

When you get into the car the door closes behind you with the same mellow clunk so noticeable on the four-cylinder model and the first difference the driver notices is the absence of the big tachometer. In its place the minor controls have been grouped around the centre of the dashboard. Then the other thing you realise is that there is no clutch pedal, since this car has the Manumatic transmission. In all other respects, seating position, legroom and so on, the two models are identical inside.

Despite having not been used for several days in view of the cold weather, the engine of Basil's 236 started instantly and settled down to a lazy long stroke tick over. Basil explained the rudiments of the transmission system and then it was off down the road for a test run. Select second gear — Basil finds first is too low for anything other than a steep hill start — press the accelerator and the car pulls gently away as the centrifugal clutch bites. Into third by 20mph and top at 30mph, all changes being accomplished smoothly and silently by just pushing the gear lever. The clutch is operated automatically by a vacuum servo activated by a pressure sensitive switch in the gearlever knob. When changing down, a servo operated by manifold depression speeds up the engine for a smooth takeup. There is a faint whine from the indirect gears which is not unpleasant, but Basil points out that the gearbox has become noisier with age.

Above 30mph the overdrive can be flicked in with the switch conveniently mounted to the right of the steering column. The engine is so beautifully flexible that, for all intents and purposes, the car can easily be driven in top and overdrive top without any strain whatsoever. In fact, the engine will pull smoothly and strongly from below 20mph in top gear.

The 236 rides very smoothly, all noise is pleasantly subdued and there are no rattles from its 30-year-old body. The occupants sit comfortably in the large armchair-like seats while the car appears to iron out all imperfections in the road. Since it shares the same chassis with the sporty 234, it is not surprising that the handling, the steering with its characteristic strong castor action, and those powerful servo brakes are more than adequate.

With the benefit of hindsight it can be seen that the 234/6 models prepared the ground so that cars like the Rover 2000 could bear fruit in the same market sector three years later.

Above, Tommy Sopwith, son of Armstrong Siddeley Chairman, Sir Thomas Sopwith, in Equipe Endeavour's Sphinx sports racer at Goodwood in 1954. The Sphinx's much-modified 3.4-litre six-cylinder Armstrong Siddeley engine generated 215bhp making the car a potent performer

Below left and below right, Basil Tasker's 236 is a well-used car that has demonstrated remarkable reliability during its 155,000 miles

Above, an interesting variation on the 234 theme was this nicely proportioned example with special body by Michelotti. Does it still survive?

Exactly why the cars did not sell that well is uncertain, but despite an exhaustive development programme the company had somehow got the formula wrong and the 'baby Sapphires' were quietly dropped before the 1957 Motor Show after a production run of just two years. Undoubtedly there was a market for this type of car, for Jaguar and Rover — to name but two — prospered. Nor could it have been the price, because in 1957 the 234/6 sold for £1,066, whereas the Jaguar 2.4 was £1,495, the Daimler Conquest £1,894 and even the Riley Pathfinder was £1,411.

The most likely reason was the styling, which found few friends. The British motorist, particularly the Armstrong driver, was a very conservative fellow and didn't react favourably to radical ideas. The Italian designer, Michelotti, knew this and seeing the potential of the 234 chassis, produced a beautiful body for it with truly classic lines. The ASOC records indicate one chassis being despatched to him, and the photograph shows what he did with it.

Racing may improve the breed, but for the enthusiast it has also got to look the part. What a tragedy that Armstrong didn't take up the design. If they had, the company's fortunes might have been reversed, preventing the gradual decline after the heavy investment in the unsuccessful new models which led to the end of all car production in 1960.

And who knows, Armstrong Siddeley cars might still have been in the showrooms today.

Above: The Jaguar with its huge four spoke steering wheel. Below: The Sapphire with its bench seat

	Jaguar Mk V11M	Armstrong Siddeley Sapphire 346
Engine	In-line 'six'	In-line 'six'
Bore/Stroke	83mm × 106mm	90mm × 90mm
Capacity	3442cc	3435cc
Valves	Twin overhead cams	Pushrod overhead valves
Compression	8:1	7:1
Power	190bhp at 5500rpm	150bhp at 4800rpm (twin carb model)
Torque	203lb.ft at 3000rpm	176lb.ft at 1000rpm
Transmission	Four-speed manual with overdrive	Four-speed preselector gearbox
Brakes	Drums front and rear, with servo	Drums front and rear, servo from late 1954
Front Sus.	Ind. by wishbones, torsion bars, anti-roll bar	Ind. by wishbones, coils, anti-roll bar
Rear Sus.	Live axle, semi-elliptics	Live axle, semi-elliptics, anti-roll bar
Steering	Recirculating ball	Recirculating ball
Turns (lock to lock)	4¼	3½
DIMENSIONS		
Turning circle	36ft 0in	42ft 6in
Tyres	6.70 × 16	6.70 × 16
Length	16ft 4½in	16ft 1in
Width	6ft 1in	6ft 0in
Height	5ft 3in	5ft 3in
Wheelbase	10ft 0in	9ft 6in
Weight	34½cwt	32¼cwt
PERFORMANCE		
Max speed	105mph	100mph
0-60mph	13.5sec	13sec
Standing ¼ mile	19.3sec	20sec
Overall fuel consumption	20mpg	19mpg
Years built	1954/1957	1953/1955
No. built	9261	7207
Price when new★	£1140 (£1616 total)	£1285 (£1821 total)

★October 1954

It was the dawn of a new era. The year was 1952, all rationing – except for petrol – had just ended and Earls Court played host to the most important motor show for many a year. After the Second World War motor manufacture continued in a time warp – pre-war designs became post-war models and it wasn't until the early 1950s that the car makers picked themselves up and considered something new.

Among the countless exciting new machines on show at Earls Court that year was the Armstrong Siddeley Sapphire.

'An entirely new model from the Armstrong Siddeley factory would command special attention by reason of the company's reputation for quality and finish – a reputation which, not unnaturally perhaps, seems common to car manufacturing concerns with aircraft associations. In the case, however, of the new Armstrong Siddeley Sapphire, there are two other notable reasons for this new model having a special claim to attention.' That was how *The Motor* greeted the arrival of the Sapphire.

It went on: 'One is that, with its unusual 3.4-litre, six-cylinder 'square' engine developing 120bhp and its relatively light dry weight of 31cwt, it marks the entry of Armstrong Siddeley Motors Ltd into the high performance class with a potential maximum speed very well in excess of 90mph.

'The other reason is the keenly-competitive price, bearing in mind the appointments, finish and specification, of £1110. With purchase tax added, the total cost is £1728 3s 4d.'

'The keenly competitive price' . . . although the idea of knocking advertisements which extol the

virtues of one particular car at the expense of others was not playing the game in the early 1950s, it was still very important not to price your product out of the market. And the car that had everyone on their toes had been announced a couple of years earlier.

In 1950 Jaguar showed off their new Mk V11 at the Earls Court show. With independent front suspension and a brand new twin overhead camshaft engine, the Mk V11 lifted the British motor industry out of its post-war depression. It was initially for export only – the United States being the major benefactor. By 1952, however, a few cars were being built for sale – and being road tested by the motoring magazines. As *The Motor* put it: 'In the opinion of the test team the Jaguar, judged upon a basis of value for money and all-round merit, is one of the best cars submitted for road test in the post-war years.'

Startlingly similar

If Armstrong Siddeley were regarded as manufacturers of a rather upper-crust horseless carriage, then Jaguar were surely of the 'young upstart' variety. And yet while the Sapphire and Mk V11 respectively their paths crossed. The Jaguar path was on the up, the Armstrong path if not actually on the down, was meandering along in its own rather gentlemanly fashion.

On paper the specifications of the two cars were startlingly similar. Both were of 3.4-litre capacity. Both hand in-line 'sixes', though the Mk V11 was the first saloon to use the dohc XK engine while the Armstrong had pushrods. Both had twin carbs (the Siddeley's were optional, though), independent front suspension by wishbones and live semi-elliptically sprung rear ends. Steering was by

recirculating ball and both relied on drum brakes to slow down more than 30cwt.

The similarities and coincidences continued. Both models had similar power outputs – though the Jaguar was in front on bhp – and both were of broadly similar size. Both came from Coventry . . . and they even shared a name. When William Lyons, as he was then, decided post war that the company's name of SS should go, he chose Jaguar. And he asked permission to use the name from Armstrong Siddeley who had produced an aero-engine called the Jaguar during the First World War.

But how have they fared over the past three decades? For anyone considering buying one, which should he choose?

Finding one loving owner who is prepared to allow a stranger to drive his pride and joy is difficult

COVENTRY CLASSICS

Armstrong Siddeley Sapphire or Jaguar Mk VII – which is the better buy? Matthew Carter and Peter Nunn report

enough. To find two is . . . 'Our' Sapphire 346 twin carb model is owned by John Martin who uses the car during the summer and only sparingly when our roads are covered in snow, slush, salt and water.

It is stored at the back of a giant aircraft hanger in deepest Bedfordshire and despite a very flat battery, started with the aid of jump leads soon enough. The Armstrong is in Corinthian Green, a slightly lighter shade than the Jaguar's BRG and, inderlining the upper crust appeal, was once owned by the Rothschild family. Despite being first registered in 1953, the recorded 27,000 miles are believed to be somewhere near the truth.

Coincidences seem to be the name of the game as far as these two cars are concerned. The Jaguar, which is currently for sale at Graig Hinton's Jaguar emporium in Hinckley, also has a believed genuine 27,000 recorded miles. This car – a Mk VIIIM, the M standing for overdrive – is a 1955 model and belonged to a Newcastle-on-Tyne based Scandinavian consul . . . the only other name in the log book. Before Hinton bought it, the Jaguar had been off the road for 21 years.

Exceptional shape

Jaguars of that vintage have a propensity for rust . . . a badly rusted example isn't worth saving in this day and age, but BEC 555 was in such exceptional shape that once it had been through Hinton's capable hands, its value increased accordingly. It is currently for sale at £5750. The Sapphire, too, is on offer, though £3500 is demanded in this instance.

Two cars, both from the same era, both appealing to largely that same sort of buyer and both imposing and desirable cars of their time. But – and with the

benefit of hindsight – it was always going to be the Jaguar that had the better chance of survival. The Armstrong Siddeley, even then, harked back to a bygone era when quality was of the utmost importance. Like a modern Mercedes, the Sapphire feels as if it has been carved out of a solid lump of metal, hewn and fashioned into shape by loving hands. Never mind the cost, feel the quality.

But then look at its old-fashioned, awkward rear-hinged front doors – not only dangerous, but difficult to seal against wind and rain – its bench front seat and its continued use of semaphore trafficators, and you begin to feel that maybe its manufacturers were not quite as forward looking as they might have been . . . about the only period pieces the Jaguar has are the split 'screen, and that huge four-spoke steering wheel.

Both companies carried on, of course. The MkV11 became the Mk V111 with duo-tone paintwork and a single piece front 'screen, which in turn became the Mk IX with the 3.8-litre XK engine, disc brakes and power steering. Armstrong Siddeley broadened their horizons with the 2.3-litre Sapphire 234 and 236 – and then wished they hadn't. In 1958 they dropped the 346 which by this time had become the first British car with power steering as an option, replacing it in late 1958 with the 4.0-litre Star Sapphire. This looked externally similar to the 346 but had front hinged doors and a modern image.

The last Star Sapphire was sold in 1960. Armstrong Siddeley Motors had merged with Bristol Aero Engines to form Bristol Siddeley Engines in 1959 (nearly a decade later Hawker Siddeley sold their share in Bristol Siddeley to Rolls-Royce), and the Sapphire was no more.

It is easy to say that the death of the Armstrong Siddeley came about thanks to the Jaguar car with its reputation for Grace, Pace, Space and cheapness . . . but this is strongly denied by the faithful Siddeley Owners Club members. The company, say the ASOC, had full order books at the time of their demise. The fact remains, however, that what Armstrong Siddeley were offering, was also available from others at a lower price. And of course the company had other interests to occupy them, too.

The announcement came in the summer of 1960. Bristol Siddeley Motors stated simply that the production of the Star Sapphire was "no longer an economic proposition" but that spares would continue in supply for some years yet. Jaguar, well they're still here . . . and so's that XK engine. Maybe they *had* done their sums correctly.

Feel the quality . . .

At first sight, a back-to-back comparison between a Jaguar Mk V11M and an Armstrong Siddeley Sapphire Mk 1 might seem slightly incongruous. After all, the Mk V11 is fast, sleek and desirable, isn't it? It still has the traditional Jaguar attributes of grace, space and pace in generous quantities, and an impressive competition history, to boot. The Siddeley, on the other hand, is a nice car in many ways but it's sort of, well . . .

That, it's probably true to say, is most enthusiasts' overall view of both marques, never mind the cars. The Jaguar is already revered as an acknowledged 'classic' whereas the Siddeley – despite its fiercely loyal owners club following – tends to be underrated by the Great British Public far too often. It just doesn't possess the Jaguar's widespread appeal even though (as a close study of the technical specification chart on the opposite page will reveal) the two cars are very similar in quite a few ways.

Despite the intriguing similarities above and below the skin – both cars have 3½-litre straight six engines, and bodies of approximately the same size and weight, to name but two – we suspect that the two cars were bought by different classes of customer when new. Granted the Jaguar had beauty and performance in abundance, but might it not have been a little too flashy for the Siddeley driver who perhaps wanted a little more dignity, comfort, exclusivity and refinement with his straight-line 'go'?

By all accounts, the position hasn't changed that over the last 30 odd years; if you are thinking of buying one of Britain's mid 1950s upper crust limousines today, you could take your pick of the Jaguar or Armstrong reviewed here, or perhaps choose an Alvis TC 21/100. Then there's the Daimler Regency or if money's no problem – what about a Rolls Silver Wraith or Bentley Standard Steel? In

Open wide . . . Sapphire and Mk VIII at rest

terms of performance and excitement per £ though, both in the 1950s and present day, the Mk V11 and the Sapphire would arguably be the pick of this group.

Sit behind the large steering wheel of either car and you are immediately confronted by a nostalgic wooden facia and dashboard. The trafficator control lever (operating semaphore arms on the Sapphire) is fitted to the steering wheel on both cars. To start either engine, you must turn a key and press a starter.

Perhaps the biggest difference between the Mk V11 and John Martin's Sapphire concerns the transmission. The 'M' designation in the Jaguar's full title means it has a four-speed manual gearbox with overdrive whereas the Sapphire has an ingenious pre-selector arrangement. Following ERA practice, you engage your required gear on the Siddeley using a small, spring-loaded lever but it's only when you depress and release the clutch pedal that the gear is fully engaged. It sounds and looks complicated to begin with, but with a little practice, the set-up works very smoothly. The Moss 'box in the Jaguar, on the other hand, should be more familiar to readers of this magazine; there's no synchromesh on first and the gear lever movement between first and second on 'our' Mk V11 was amazingly long. The overdrive switch is ideally-placed, though, and the 'box is a delight to use.

If the Mk V11's gearbox is celebrated (or should that be notorious?) then the 3.4-litre XK engine under the bonnet is near immortal. Suffice it to say that this superb six-cylinder unit fully justifies the 'classic' tag but as its many commendable characteristics are so well known, perhaps a few words on the Siddeley's remarkable engine might be

The makings of a classic. The Mk VIII was the first Jaguar saloon to carry the famous XK engine

Hidden under the twin air filters is the Armstrong Siddeley's lusty – and torquey – pushrod straight six

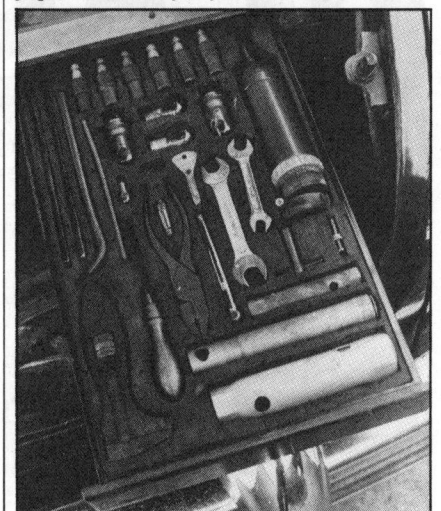

Details from the Sapphire: Left: the neat boot mounted tool rack, still complete after all these years. Above: the pre-selector gear change. It works well once you've got the hang of it, offering smooth and quick changes

of interest before we go any further. Briefly, it's a very smooth and torquey 'six' with push-rod-operated overhead valves as opposed to the Mk V11's renowned twin overhead camshafts. Nevertheless, the Sapphire's engine is beautifully-made, incredibly tractable, and perfectly capable of pulling from well below 1000rpm in top gear without a trace of hesitation. It really is an impressive piece of work.

From a body styling point of view, the Sapphire's somewhat angular shape is pleasing, not to say imposing, whereas that of the Mk V11 is simply beautiful. The upright radiator, swept back wings and rear-hinged front doors of the Sapphire is so evocative of the 1950s but the more bulbous Mk V11 styling could almost be '60s vintage.

Deceptively quick

Out on the open road, there's no doubt the Sapphire can be made to travel very quickly indeed. John Martin's car has twin Zenith carburettors, thus enabling the silky smooth engine to produce a respectable 150bhp, but even the single carb Sapphire Mk 1 will be no slouch. Make no mistake, once wound up the Siddeley is a deceptively quick car, so don't be fooled by the beast's outwardly stodgy nature.

Driving a well-sorted Jaguar is always a pleasurable experience as a spell behind the wheel of Graig Hinton's Mk V11 proved admirably. Naturally some acclimatisation was needed before moving off in the Siddeley (the epicyclic gearbox proved rather daunting at first!) but one can slide behind the Jaguar's steering wheel and immediately drive away in complete confidence. It's as simple as that. This Mk V11 behaves like the thoroughbred it is at all

times, but then it has been professionally restored.

That's the real problem with this particular test – it would have been fairer to have driven two cars in similar condition. As it was, we couldn't help but approve of the Mk V11, in contrast to the Sapphire which, it must be said, kept on breaking down on us. The Siddeley – poor old thing – suffered from overheating problems and an undercharged battery while in our tenure but in its defence we should state that the car *had* been standing unused for nearly four months prior to our test so it would be a little churlish to criticise the Siddeley for a little temperament in this instance . . .

A fully restored Sapphire would presumably be Some Motor Car Indeed and a repeat test at some later date should provide a more realistic day's motoring. In the meantime John Martin's Sapphire would not need a great deal of work to bring it up to scratch and our thanks go to him and to Graig Hinton for the generous loan of the cars.

To sum up then, the Siddeley is a desirable, exclusive 'aircraft quality' car with great period charm and character. The mere fact that it *is* an Armstrong Siddeley is one of its biggest assets in my view. There's a discerning owners club for enthusiasts of the marque and nearly every spare part for the car is available via the ASOC whose secretary, Denis Robinson, can be reached at 15 Plantation Drive, West End, South Cave, North Humberside. As for the Mk V11, it's still a 'classic' after all these years – and it's continuing to do well in Classic Saloon racing. Plus there's the JDC at Jaguar House, 18 Stuart Street, Luton, Beds, a never-ending series of books on the marque and a host of Jaguar specialists to help keep the Jaguar enthusiast happy. ⌐⌐